Alchemical Psychology

Alchemical

THOM F. CAVALLI, PH.D.

Foreword by Robert A. Johnson

JEREMY P. TARCHER / PUTNAM
a member of Penguin Putnam Inc.
New York

Psychology

Old Recipes for Living

in a New World

Most Tarcher/Putnam books are available at special quantity discounts for bulk purchase for sales promotions, premiums, fund-raising, and educational needs. Special books or book excerpts also can be created to fit specific needs. For details, write Putnam Special Markets, 375 Hudson Street, New York, NY 10014.

Jeremy P. Tarcher/Putnam
a member of
Penguin Putnam Inc.
375 Hudson Street
New York, NY 10014
www.penguinputnam.com

Library of Congress Cataloging-in-Publication Data

Cavalli, Thom Frank, date.
    Alchemical psychology : old recipes for living in a new world ; a book of contemporary alchemical psychology / by Thom Frank Cavalli ; with a foreword by Robert A. Johnson.
        p.   cm.
    Includes bibliographical references and index.
    ISBN 1-58542-140-5
    1. Jungian psychology.   2. Alchemy—Psychological aspects.   3. Jung, C. G. (Carl Gustav), 1875–1961.   I. Title.
    BF172.C432   2002   2001054199
    150.19'54—dc21

Printed in the United States of America
10   9   8   7   6   5   4   3   2

This book is printed on acid-free paper. ♾

BOOK DESIGN BY LEE FUKUI

I dedicate this book to my mother,
my daughter, Ananda, and
my soror mystica, Suvasini.

Contents

List of Tables

List of Figures

Note on Capitalization

Special use of capitalization is made to denote differences between words having similar meaning. For example, god, nature and mercury are sometimes capitalized in order to distinguish different ways in which each word is used. Generally, a capitalized word indicates that it is being used in a personified rather than literal way. Mercury, using the capitalized form, refers to one of the Greek gods as opposed to mercury, the metal. The capitalized God additionally refers to one deity that is central to monotheistic religions. Capitals are used to discern these differences, not to indicate value of any kind.

Life is a spell so exquisite that everything conspires to break it.
EMILY DICKINSON

Alchemical Psychology

Foreword

ROBERT A. JOHNSON

I have spent many years telling stories that teach people, young and old, important lessons about how we mature into complete individuals. These stories are taken from mythology, a subject hardly taught in schools anymore but one that is a treasure-house of wisdom. Myths need retelling especially now that it has become so easy to be distracted from them by computer games, special-effects movies and the tabloid media. These do more to titillate our senses than challenge us in any meaningful way. They stimulate us to excess and rob us of the need to wonder, dwell and actively use our imagination. The old myths are changed every time they are told. One of the oldest myths I know is alchemy; it is a wild adventure story of intrigue and mystery.

Alchemy is a combination of magic, science, religion, mythology and psychology. No one knows its origin and no one can predict its future. Just when you think alchemy has ended it reappears. This has happened at least twice in modern times. In the scientific area, alchemy transformed into chemistry. Much of alchemy's lore was discarded with this change. Chemistry is an objective science. Perhaps the magic and mystery of alchemy found its way into psychology. This marked alchemy's second reintroduction into modern times. Toward the end of his career, C. G. Jung devoted three major volumes of research to an intensive exploration of the unconscious using alchemy as his model. In these complex works we discover riddles and recipes, signs and symbols,

1

incredible images. Jung's works are no less easy to understand than the formulas found in an advanced biochemistry textbook.

When we try to follow the convoluted logic of alchemy we typically end up in knots. Even in its modern versions, the subject becomes abstract. It is easy to lose sight of the real gold, what alchemy has to do with our everyday experiences. It seems that the student of this ancient practice is either a fool or a very wise person. The author of this book is a bit of a royal fool and a wise alchemist. Above all he is a psychologist, and in a daring attempt to keep our heads from getting lost in the clouds and our feet agile he gives us an accessible guidebook on the royal art. I expect his book will frustrate the rational scientist and annoy some artists. This is how it is whenever we try to capture the awesome beauty of Nature. This book hits us right between the eyes, that place where everything comes together. It is intended for all of us who, wanting it or not, are on a path to wholeness.

Nature pulls us in many directions, causing confusion and contradiction when we try to define her absolute laws. We would like to think that splitting alchemy between chemistry and psychology is the solution. It's not. Each has a hand on the same elephant, describing only a small part of this magnificent beast. The more science delves into the mysteries of nature the more it realizes how much psychology plays a critical role. Of course the converse is equally true: the more psychology peers into matter the more it must rely on objective science to get the whole story. Like the yin-yang symbol, each of the two halves contains a bit of the other. This is the way of alchemy! It returns us back to wholeness.

Today the practice of alchemy seldom involves laboratory work. The wholeness we seek more commonly comes out of psychological labor. The alchemist's flask is the vessel of soul, its contents filled with the dualities of conscious and unconscious ingredients. The alchemist is both artist and scientist, using the imaginative mind and the objective psyche. There is no one recipe for the endless mixing, separating, blending and uniting that can guarantee success. Most work is trial and error. Teachers who possess knowledge can help us save time and keep us on track.

In *Alchemical Psychology,* you will find one such teacher. A wise teacher knows how to present difficult material in an entertaining way. Alchemy can be a confounding subject. It takes effort to grasp its most basic theory and its insightful views of inner life. I thoroughly enjoyed

the economical way alchemy is introduced in this book. The major concepts are summarized without doing injustice to alchemical tradition,
no small feat. What's more, the author engages us in a way that gets us
thinking differently about alchemy and psychological work.

In reading this book, I found myself entranced by its magic and
scholarship. Dr. Cavalli adds the ingredients not found in most books on
alchemy. He gives us just enough historical information to excite our
imagination without becoming lost in unnecessary detail. He makes
alchemy readable, simple and, most important, usable. The book blends
the imaginal world with the facts of ancient history and modern science.
I am happy that Thom has brought back the royal opus into our lives. He
supplies us with an introduction and an approach that enlightens us to
the psychological meaning of alchemy. The philosopher's stone is not
gold, diamond or white light. It is fulfillment. This book is a recipe for
finding it.

Discovery

I first truly discovered the presence of fire when flames leapt dangerously close to our home in Staten Island, New York. Although I was only sixteen years old at the time, the fire department was taking on all volunteers regardless of age to fight the blaze. There was a mixture of fear and excitement as they strapped an Indian pump onto my back. I rushed into the forest and squirted water on burning trees and bushes. It wasn't long before I had nearly emptied the small tank on my back and found myself alone, cut off from the others. The flames nearly surrounded me, leaving only a small path for my escape. There was a moment before the panic set in when I felt something I can only describe as awe. At sixteen that word wasn't in my vocabulary and even now it's hard to describe the feeling I experienced. All I know is that my head told me to run and some other part of me stopped dead in my tracks and felt awed by the beauty of this fiery hell.

Many years passed before I experienced the power of wind and air. I was living in upstate New York, working as a counselor in a residential treatment center. It was the first time I had lived outside urban New York and the first time I truly fell in love with nature's beauty. The wildflowers, the rolling hills and a beautiful lake took my breath away. This beauty I learned has two faces: one quiet and serene, the other thunderous. It was mid-afternoon and I was alone in my apartment when the sky turned ashen black in a matter of seconds. The wind roared and the scene outside my living-room window looked like something out of *The Wizard of Oz*. The tornado was twisting trees up out of the ground as if they were twigs. It was like a film in fast motion; my eyes could not keep up with everything moving so fast; it was a blur. Time crashed into the immediacy of a single moment. I hid in the closet as the wind's fury smashed in every window. There's no telling how long this went on but it seemed that the tornado moved quickly from its origin—not 500 yards from my apartment—to its destination several miles away. I remember taking walks in the days following the storm on the winding path cut by the tornado through my beautiful forests.

My experience of the power of water took place when I nearly drowned on two separate occasions. The first occurred as a child when I fell off a water slide into a lake. I vividly recall going underwater twice, thinking with alarm that my third submersion would be my last. That thought shot through my head like a rocket, launching me right out of the water. Fortunately I caught hold of the slide and a girl helped me get back to shore. There my father greeted me with unexpected disdain. With the shock still not having yet subsided in me, my dad threw me back into the lake, thinking this would erase all future fear of water.

His reaction was strange, especially given the fact that I was born with a powerful talisman that sailors traditionally believe protects people from drowning. I was delivered with my face covered by a thin membrane known as a caul. (I was pleased on learning many years later that Sigmund Freud was also born with one.)

My second encounter with water took place just a few years before writing this book while I was swimming off the coast of Newport Beach. It was the last swim of the season and although the surf wasn't particularly rough, the unseen currents silently drew me out to sea. I kept my cool and swam parallel to the shore hoping to find calmer waters. There was absolutely no one on the beach and no swimmers in the water. As exhaustion set in and my feet still could not touch bottom a strange inner calm overcame me. Suddenly, out of nowhere, I sighted a lone surfer on a boogie board. I managed to clutch that board the same way I had grabbed the slide many years before. The caul had worked its magic a second time.

California is a land that regularly reminds you not to trust the earth beneath your feet. While I have lived through several major earthquakes, the most profound lesson involving the earth element came with a close call that left a good deal of anxiety in its wake. In 1998 I was invited by a good friend to join her in Oahu, Hawaii. This was a work trip for her and a sudden getaway for me. We only had one full day together to explore the island. We'd debated on what to include and what to leave out of our itinerary. Although both of us had been to the island before, we'd never visited the Sacred Falls on the north shore. We tried to assess how long the trek would take and whether we could afford the time, but every person we asked gave us a different answer. In the end we decided to go for it.

The path wound its way through banana fields and lush, tropical forests. My friend, following the example set by others before us, piled rocks up along the side of streams to honor the gods and ask for their protection. Inwardly I felt this was silly and just wanted to get on with our trek to conserve time. But I stayed the few minutes it took and half-heartedly honored the impromptu ceremony. We reached the falls, plunged into its black pool and were thrilled as the waters from a 100-foot cascade poured down on our heads. We felt renewed by the waters of these sacred falls. The next day, Mother's Day, we left for home and on our return were shocked to learn the news that merely hours after our visit, huge boulders had collapsed at Sacred Falls, killing eighteen people and injuring many more. Needless to say, I was then very glad we stopped to pay homage to the water spirits!

We can read about creation in the book of Genesis but it doesn't have much meaning until experience brings the words to life. My encounters with Nature brought the elements of creation into full relief. When I hold a rock I now know the enormous power packed into it. I still enjoy the ocean but having nearly been swallowed by her, respect the forces that dwell in her depths. In each of these experiences, I have, at risk to leg and limb, learned to bow before the elements of Nature's awesome beauty. In being confronted by her powerful forces, I have learned a great deal about myself and am humbled by her majesty. I know fire, air, water and earth in a different way now. They have been impressed in my memory and I can no longer see them superficially. Nature brought me closer than any other experience in my life to see, feel, touch, hear and smell God.

I discovered the elements through crisis. Sometimes that is the only way we will stop and look deeper at the world around us. Here's an example of what I mean. In graduate school, I was in a terrible head-on collision. A sailor had fallen asleep at the wheel and crashed into my car at 55 mph. My old clunker, which I'd bought from a Hari Krishna ashram, had no seat belts. To this day I believe Krishna sat in that car with me and decided it wasn't my time to die. This crisis slowed me down; in fact, it brought me to a complete stop for several months. It made me look even deeper into my fast-paced life.

When I resumed my studies I knew there was much more going on than the statistical world being taught in school. I became more interested in the actual experience behind the data, what depressed people really felt and not how a diagnosis of depression might define them. I was studying to become a therapist and I needed to know what made people sick and how they change for the better. How does nature move through people? What do the inner storms and conflagrations look like?

I was having my own psychological crisis and needed help. As chance would have it, my path crossed with Robert Johnson, a Jungian analyst, at St. Paul's Episcopal Church in San Diego. I saw Robert for a little over two years and I think I matured ten in that same time period. We could not have been any more different in terms of our personality. He called me his dark brother. And yet, despite our differences, we shared at least one passion: India. We both had been to the subcontinent and were smitten with its love of ritual, passion for life and the world behind the illusion of Maya. In that place, there were no differences, Robert and I were one.

More than any special technique, Robert's true healing powers rest in his gentle presence. Since I had no money, we would meet very early in the morning and he hardly charged me anything. Even when I would be annoyed with his occasional yawns (we met at seven in the morning) I knew, without a doubt, that he was fully present for me.

The world was fast gaining another dimension—depth. Life was teaching me another lesson about the elements. They don't just exist in the material world. My inner storms were teaching me as much about the winds of change as the tornado. With Robert's guidance I learned about the elements of my own personality. This was a great awakening for me. Somehow we exclude ourselves from the world out there, as if we were alien to nature and not composed of the very same stuff as trees, clouds and even the stars. I realized that the clay of my being is made of the same earth that lay beneath my feet. The only element that was not easily discerned was fire. Where might I find fire in myself? I could easily locate earth, water and air in my body but not fire.

To find fire I had to go into the interior of my body and imagination. Fever is the result of high body temperature. It reflects heat that must come from some internal furnace. I also realized that burning feeling you sometimes get in your stomach. Too much acid, I thought, must also relate to some kind of chemical fire. But fire wasn't just physical; it has a psychological dimension. It is found in the heat of sexual passion, the heat of the moment, hot flashes and hot heads. I have had a burning desire for some things and at times felt burnt by others. I was learning that the fire element is very much a vital part of what I am physically, emotionally and even astrologically. In fact, I discovered that each of the elements has a psychological counterpart. Water relates to my feelings, air to my thoughts and earth to my senses. The world was really coming alive for me. I was learning how I am put together, and that is not so different from the world around me.

As I searched further I found that fire had even more dimensions than I initially expected. Fire is a very energetic element. It, like water, is ever moving and causing other things to change. But, unlike water, it comes and goes. Like passion, fire heats up the moment and things are quickly reduced to ash. Fire, I learned, relates to consciousness. It is a symbol of our awareness and our capacity to change all that we see and touch. It transforms everything in its path.

By this time I was busy writing my doctoral dissertation and had no idea that these thoughts would find their way into my study. I was investigating chemical dependency and how it changes consciousness. What were the hidden dynamics behind chemical addiction? We know so much about the chemistry but what could be said about the mind of the abuser? These questions led me deeper into the psychology of people than their illnesses. I wanted to understand the dynamics of change. Just as I had learned that there was much more to nature than what meets the eye, I wanted a peek at the realm of consciousness lying beneath the surface of personality and behavior. What is it in nature that compels addicts to play with fire and allows their lives to go up in smoke?

This was not something new to psychology. There were already great studies on perception, motivation and cognition. I wanted to go deeper, to consciousness itself. In short, what I needed was a psychology that dared to venture into the deepest levels of unconsciousness, the place where everyone is indistinguishable from everyone else. At first I thought Freud's theory of psychoanalysis would take me to this place. It was a great point of departure. Unfortunately, it seemed to speak of the unconscious as if it were the exclusive province of the body and had limited power to make vital connections needed to be drawn between physical and psychological reality. Then I discovered Jung's depth psychology and found in it a method, language and practice for answering many of my questions. Actually, it did much more than that. Jung put me in touch with my soul.

Jung spent sixty years researching the psychology of the unconscious. His collected works stand proudly on my library shelves, each representing a journey of mind, body and soul. Jung's major work culminates in three large volumes on the study of alchemy. Of all the wild adventures of my life this one took the cake. Just prior to entering graduate school I took my last fling before settling down. I knew I would not be able to travel much once I began school so I spent three months in India, traveling as far north as Nepal and south to Madras. I thought nothing could compare to the surrealism of this journey. Indeed I have yet to experience any country like it. But just as I had come to appreciate the connection between the elements and myself, I came to find that Jung's adventure into the psyche was just as personal and wilder than even the subcontinent.

The year was 1975 and I began studying the psychology of medieval alchemists in order to understand the nature of human change. Alchemy, I thought, is about changing lead into gold. What on earth could that have to do with human psychology? The answer to this question took another twenty-five years. While I didn't know it, I had been thinking and working very much in the same tradition as alchemists for most of that time. Until I met Robert Johnson and began therapy with him I was virtually asleep. With his help I learned that the crisis I was having was nature's way of waking me up. Alchemy, as I was to learn, begins in chaos and darkness.

I resisted the study of alchemy for years. Not unlike most people, I thought alchemy was nothing more than the crazy misadventures of quacks and charlatans. I went about my work becoming a therapist, applying one theory after another to help people with every imaginable problem. I worked in hospitals, jails and university clinics treating hundreds of people. Talk about chaos! When we see what disease can do to the human body we shudder in sympathy and disgust. While psychological disease isn't always visible it is no less gruesome in ravaging mind and soul. Working as a clinical psychologist, I used Jung's theory where it might help my suffering patients. I shoved alchemy to the back of my mind. What I now understand is that the same resistance I had to the seemingly bizarre notions of alchemy was the same I had for the bizarre behaviors of the patients I was treating. We cringe in the face of chaos. Psychosis, addiction and especially the inhumanity of daily life disturb us. We shudder and turn away. Chaos threatens our peace, stability and sense of order. It throws us back to a time before consciousness came along and transformed chaos into cosmos. In the face of such daunting awareness, resistance might well be the smart thing to do. Deny, rather than embrace the madness of life. Turn away, accommodate, adjust and settle for what you can get. Don't ask the deeper questions.

In my case, I had no choice but to go further. Mere survival was not a compromise I could make. I wanted more, even if it meant taking greater risks with others and myself. Life is an experiment where you try different things and see what happens. Hopefully, the thousands of trials will pay off and you become healthy, wealthy and wise. Perhaps you are already seeing how this approach is no different from alchemy. I had to know how to change the miserable lead of unconscious existence into a refined, golden opportunity of a creative, fulfilling life. This connection with alchemy became an inescapable conclusion to years of study and many close encounters with death. I could no longer resist nor dismiss alchemy as so much nonsense. Jung found as much meaning in the babbling of psychotic patients as he did in occult systems like alchemy, astrology and the Kabbala, not to mention the sophisticated theories of psychoanalysis. But first, he had to fight the urge to flee from the strange words and images bubbling up from the unconscious.

Alchemy begins its work with first matter, *prima materia,* which, like psychotic behavior, is similar to the tornadoes and earth slides I mentioned earlier. These raw materials are brute reminders of the tremendous forces compacted into every particle of matter, be it human or inanimate. When Nature bellows out in volcanoes and tsunamis, we take notice. They are exaggerations of the relatively tiny crises that we face throughout the day. Having acquired a view of dark, hidden layers of the unconscious psyche, I appreciate the place from which psychological disturbances stem and treat those who suffer these psychic faults and fissures. Rage is an eruption of murderous anger. Mood swings blow us around like the winds. Thought disorder is a collapse in the bedrock of reason.

People intuitively know that symptomatic cracks originate from some place deeper down in their unconscious mind. With the slightest reflection they know that their complaints go far deeper than what they were initially willing to admit. And despite what insurance companies pay for, patients want more than simple comfort and advice. They know there is no magic bullet that can immediately make them completely well. That requires hard work, endless experimentation and a deep appreciation of the unconscious world from which both problems and solutions arise.

Why, then, should we care about an old occult system like alchemy? The answer is this: alchemy offers recipes of change that are enduring prescriptions for improved health, increased wealth and wisdom. These rewards are not delivered on a silver platter. They require hard work. This book may make the job a bit easier. Let me describe it in some detail so you can decide whether you are willing to risk the comfort of the scientific world for possibly more revealing truths of an ancient wisdom tradition.

We begin by observing a few of the most important events that make up alchemy's ten-thousand-year history. Owing to its oral and mystical tradition, there can never be a full and comprehensive history of the art and science of alchemy. There are so many definitions that have been crafted out of cultural, religious and political influences that alchemy is better understood as a mythology than as either art or science. Even a cursory study of its history shows alchemy to be an odd mix of facts and fictions, combined equally to reflect the many vicissitudes of human experience.

The first seven chapters introduce the newcomer to a fuller and deeper meaning of alchemy. The discovery of what alchemy meant to the ancient Egyptians, Greeks, Chinese and Arabians offers a convincing argument that alchemy was much more than a greedy pursuit of riches. As we shall see, instead of changing physical substances, alchemy is about transforming consciousness. These chapters describe the fundamental ideas that grew out of the minds of wise people working in darkened laboratories and hallowed cells where experiment and experience were regarded as being equally important. Alchemy, more than any other philosophy, has constructed the world's most profound thinkers and it's most common workers and craftsmen. These chapters set a foundation for anyone wanting to begin the psychological work of personal alchemy.

I have relied heavily on the work of Carl Jung to help translate the archaic and symbolic language of alchemy into a modern idiom we can more readily understand and put to use in our lives. While Jung was not a practicing alchemist, his work on the subject made a profound contribution to modern psychology. He makes it clear that the gold sought by alchemists was in fact a search for an authentic, fulfilling and meaningful life. Thus, I equate the philosopher's stone with the archetype of the Self, the "real gold" of both the alchemist's labors and what Jung calls the individuation process. Taking care to honor alchemy and its traditions, I define in concrete behavioral terms what this philosophical stone means behaviorally so that we have an opportunity to experience this golden state of consciousness. Not wanting to lose sight of the mystery that pervaded this occult art, I go further than most behavioral scientists, including Jung, by describing a Self that is as divine as it is human. Here, I step lightly into the occult, treading carefully with evidence drawn from modern theoretical physics to keep my feet on the ground.

Alchemy is always about making something less into something great, so I invite experimentation to verify whether any of the recipes show the alchemists to be the wise men I hold them out to be. In my own experience, alchemy has proven itself as a wisdom tradition that satisfies the criteria expected of any true royal art: timeless beauty and exquisite effectiveness. The final chapters bring this bounty into our lives. By applying old alchemical recipes to the imponderable questions that challenge us in daily life, we discover the Royal Art of Living.

This book then is an in-depth introduction to the great opus of alchemy. It is neither a step-by-step manual nor a complete description of the work. Instead, I've attempted to simplify and personalize this very arcane subject by offering samples of alchemical theory, images and recipes. While there are some exercises, the real alchemical experiment is left to you. Alchemy is personal and experience brings it to life. It is best left to each individual to cook up their own special recipe for success. The proof of alchemy's worth is in the eating of the pudding.

Bon appétit!

Chapter 1

Directions

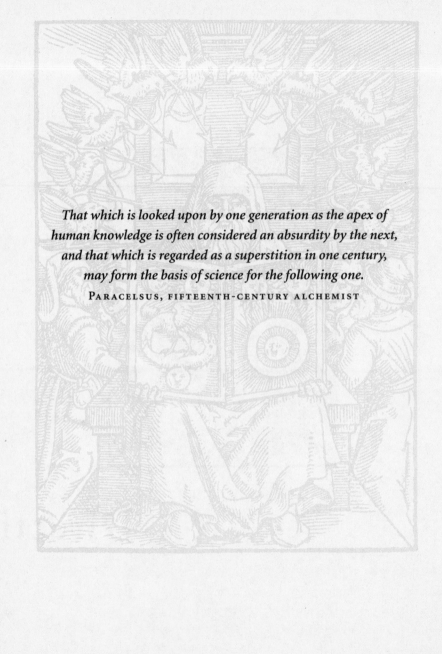

That which is looked upon by one generation as the apex of human knowledge is often considered an absurdity by the next, and that which is regarded as a superstition in one century, may form the basis of science for the following one.

PARACELSUS, FIFTEENTH-CENTURY ALCHEMIST

Alchemy is the process of changing lead into gold; at least this is its most popular definition. It was practiced in many countries throughout the world for hundreds, maybe even thousands, of years. As a result, alchemy has many definitions. It meant one thing to an Egyptian high priest and quite another to a fifteenth-century apothecary. Still there are common elements that bind alchemy together into a coherent subject having well articulated principles for theory and practice. Alchemy, as we will see, set the stage of modern civilization, and its wisdom continues to inspire us in many ways. In light of enormous advancements being made today in the physical and psychological fields, this is a particularly good time to review alchemy.

What does alchemy mean to us today? What possible use can we make of it? How can we apply old methods to the problems we encounter in today's world?

To begin answering these questions, I need to make it clear that I do not believe alchemy is dead. We will therefore not be examining alchemy as if it were extinct or some sort of magical artifact of history. With over twenty years of research, I am convinced that alchemy represents a wisdom tradition that is generally neglected and misunderstood. In writing this book it is my intention to tell alchemy's story. I will primarily tell it from a psychological point of view because that is what I am most familiar with. While I respect the approach taken by others, for me the real gold in alchemy can be found in its magnificent psychology.

Though alchemy goes by many names, the essence of its long tradition continues to inspire the thoughts and ideas of contemporary artists, scientists and theologians. Increasingly, I hear the word used, and misused, in the media and even literature. We have some very old, superstitious ideas of what alchemy used to be. My aim is to correct some of these mistaken beliefs by adding factual data and, more importantly, having us discover what alchemy means in the course of our own personal development. When we deeply understand the efforts made by men and women who practiced alchemy in one way or another over thousands of years we immediately realize that alchemy left the laboratory long ago and has taken its place in the hearts and minds of people everywhere.

Discovering alchemy beneath the surface of the fast-moving, expedient pace of modern life requires us to pause and think in imaginative ways. We must check our impulse to put the past behind us, so that we might rush to put in something—anything—to fill the vacuum. Rather than "out with the old, in with the new," why not take the best each has to offer. In this way we create a New World.

> Where then might we find today's alchemy? It's all in your head! Alchemy is "the greatest of all arts for it [concerns] an ideal entity which exists only in the mind."[1]

Just as we might consider ourselves psychologists, why not imagine that we are also alchemists? For any time we interact with others or the material world we are attempting to change the lead of common experience into something more than it was before.

In this chapter, I begin by sampling historical data drawn from different parts of the world where alchemy was widely practiced. Then, in a second section, I will identify some of the underlying psychological principles that contribute to alchemical psychology. This overall history will give us a foundation on which we can then derive a working definition of alchemy that will be used throughout this book. By the time we arrive at the ten recipes in chapter 8 we will be well prepared to put alchemy to work in our lives.

What Is Alchemy?

Defining alchemy is no easy task. Its history spans a good portion of human civilization and its variations are many. Most people will quickly tell you that alchemy is an old system of changing lead into gold. There were, of course, alchemists who experimented with artificial ways of making gold, but there were many others with very different aspirations. Fiction oftentimes twists the facts. In early history, it was iron, not gold, that primitive people wanted. They were not nearly as interested in getting rich as they were in simply staying alive. Iron was the magical substance they used to make weapons and the tools needed for tilling the soil. The discovery of iron alone could not make these things possible. For that they had first to master the use of fire.

Masters of Fire

Fire enabled our ancestors to cook food and find warmth on cold wintry nights. It lit the night sky, sealed wounds and burned down enemy camps. It is not surprising then that fire is the central metaphor in every aspect of alchemy. It represents life and death, consciousness, "glowing imagination" and transformation.

No one knows for sure when fire was discovered, but archeological evidence indicates that humans first used fire 1.4 million years ago. A species of humans known as *Homo erectus,* who lived between 1.8 million and about 30,000 years ago, used fire on a consistent basis. They were probably the first to use fire to cook food. When these people left Africa, they took with them the secrets of fire.

Alongside these people, Neanderthals (*Homo neanderthalensis*) and *Homo sapiens* evolved. There is evidence of organized Neanderthal settlements in Israel some sixty thousand years ago where hearths were found. Thirty-five thousand years later early people were using flint and iron to ignite their campfires. Soon after, there were a number of fire setting techniques used throughout Iraq and Asia. By 6500 B.C., potters in Mesopotamia were using fire to harden clay into pots and cooking vessels. Three thousand years later, Egyptian potters had earthen kilns in which they made bricks composed of mud and straw.

The use of fire in metalworking began about 4000 B.C. Initially, Sumerian artisans used primitive earthen hearths to melt copper ores to make tools and weapons. In time, the hearth was lined with stone, transforming the earthen vessel into a genuine furnace. Using bellows to pump air into the furnace dramatically increased the temperature. This blast furnace provided the means for hardening metals. For example, steel was one of the early products developed by Indian alchemists. By 1200 to 1000 B.C., metallurgy was being practiced on a wide-scale industrial basis and had spread from the mountains of Armenia throughout the Middle East.

While archeological evidence reveals objects produced throughout the Metal Age, it is more difficult to describe the images that gave rise to mastery over fire. This point is made clear in a brilliant historical analysis of alchemy, *The Forge and the Crucible.* "As is often the case," writes historian Mircea Eliade, "the image, the symbol and the rite anticipate—sometimes even make possible—the practical applications of a discovery."[2] A mythology, psychology, as well as a primitive technology of fire formed around the importance this element had for survival. In this sense the Iron Age in particular represents the triumph of humans over plant, animal and mineral kingdoms, and at the same time was a period in which the means to make war became available.

The discovery of fire simultaneously originates in nature and in the human mind. As an element of transformation, fire is central to all work in alchemy. It can symbolize consciousness just as well as it does the chemical reaction that causes combustion to happen. Whether describing physical alchemy or psychological alchemy, fire represents a ubiquitous power that has the ability to change matter and mind. In this sense, fire, heat and the secrets of combustion did as much to draw people together as set them apart. As we will see later on, one of the oldest alchemical recipes, *Solve et Coagular* (separate and unite), stems from this dual aspect of fire.

It is important to retrace these early steps so that we can understand how gold came to be the alchemist's main concern, not only as a metal but also as a symbol of physical and even spiritual immortality. In the next chapter we will discover more clearly how alchemy became more of a psychological means to extrude gold from the depths of our psyche than a physical attempt to make gold out of base metals.

It took thousands of years for primitive peoples to shift their attention from basic survival toward more sophisticated uses for fire. In this time, a mythology grew up around shamans, blacksmiths and medicine men. Heroes were made of anyone who knew how to use fire to transform metals into weapons and tools for farming. Every aspect of the metallurgical process—the smith, the ores, the furnace and, of course, the magical products—became part of this mythology. Humans had discovered the power to transform their world, and in the process they were also being transformed. The alchemists, who guarded this sacred knowledge, came to be known as the masters of fire.

Just as dating the discovery of fire is difficult, so too is it virtually impossible to date with any real accuracy the origins of alchemy. Some crude forms of alchemy may have existed as long as ten thousand years ago. Part of the problem in dating alchemy stems from the fact that the psychology of early humans is vastly different from that of the modern psyche. No one can accurately date the moment when a shaman, magician or high priest distinguished the difference between fire seen strictly as a physical manifestation to one that served symbolic, psychological and mystical uses. The vast literature on the subject, from the ancient

Egyptians to the Renaissance alchemists, is muddled. Yet, in striving to define alchemy we cannot exclude any of the contributions that led to the establishment of alchemy as a formal system of science.

In the following, I offer a brief survey of various cultures that were particularly important in the development of alchemy. It is very likely that alchemy has three main birthplaces: Egypt, China and India. In its family tree, Greece and Arabia were also particularly important. Although each culture provides a slightly different view of alchemy and its goals, I will show in the conclusion of this chapter that there are a number of elements common to every form of alchemy. I will present some of the more remarkable features that made alchemy special in various regions of the globe.

One of the most sacred of all alchemical documents is the *Emerald Tablet,* dated by some to be ten thousand years old.[3] It describes thirteen recipes for creating the famed philosopher's stone. In much the same way as Genesis describes God creating the heavens and the earth, the *Emerald Tablet* describes in symbolic language methods alchemists could use to transmute metals and in the process acquire the wisdom of the Philosopher's Stone.

This stone is variously described as a means for transmuting metals, a panacea for healing disease and even extending life indefinitely. For our purposes, the Philosopher's Stone is a concept that describes the most sophisticated psychology a person could ever hope to achieve. Accordingly, changing lead into gold psychologically means transforming our base, unconscious nature (symbolized by lead and called the *prima materia*) into the philosopher's stone. We will have the opportunity in later chapters to describe the various characteristics of this development, recipes and even techniques for creating this golden consciousness. Throughout this book, I will refer to this superior state of mind as the Individuated Self.

Legend tells of Hermes Trismegistus, a mystical figure who authored the *Emerald Tablet*. The image at the beginning of this chapter is a portrait of Hermes. In concluding this chapter I've provided some interpretation of the mystical symbols in this woodcut. Using the picture as a touchstone, we will have Hermes' spirit to guide us through the twists and turns of alchemy's long history.

Egyptian Alchemy

Egyptian alchemy was borne out of the black soils of Africa. Its accomplishments can be seen in its profound knowledge of astronomy, mathematics and architecture. The great pyramids could not have been built without the many skills of the alchemists. They used the stars to align the channel through which the entombed pharaoh would travel on his journey to heaven. Engineering devices were developed to lift massive blocks of stone and put them precisely into place. The deceased were embalmed using special techniques that mummified flesh and bones for thousands of years. Finally, high priests recited magical incantations and performed sacred rituals to insure the safe passage of their king from this world to the next.

The Step Pyramid was the first large pyramid. It was built by the high priest–magician and alchemist Imhotep over 5,500 years ago. Many of these pyramids still stand today. Even now, scientists are not clear how the ancient Egyptians were able to execute these incredible engineering feats. Where could this knowledge have come from? Archeologists are now asking whether it was magic alone that enabled the Egyptians to transform tons of rock into these mighty structures. One theory that is not unique to Egypt has it that such knowledge came from a mysterious civilization that existed at the beginning of time.[4]

Whatever the source, we are left with a very different impression of magic than the one we have today. More than superstition, magic was the principal form of science practiced for thousands of years. In my view, alchemy was the seed buried within this magical system that would come to bear fruit in the first laboratory experiments. The movement from magic to alchemy to modern science meant that each link in this chain had to be radically changed in order to strengthen its overall constitution. So it was that Egypt fell to Alexander the Great in 332 B.C. because of "the excessive use of magic."[5]

> By magic I mean a practice in which a person commands that nature be changed by directing the powers of spiritual entities. Alchemy, by contrast, involves the participation and interaction between the operator and nature.

Greek Influences

The Greeks were lovers of wisdom. Their philosophies embraced alchemical psychology. The writings of Plato, Aristotle, Plotinus and Heraclitus espoused a Hermetic philosophy that has become the cornerstone of modern civilization. Democracy has its roots in the Hermetic

Ideal of "all for one, one for all." The practice of one person, one vote originated in ancient Greece. Psychology too borrowed a great deal from the Greeks. The Swiss psychiatrist Jung's concept of archetypes was modeled after Plato's alchemical notion of eternal forms. The four elements—fire, water, earth and air—were initially described by Democritus and later systematized by Aristotle. Centuries later Jung would extend these four elements to include psychological functions that describe how the personality operates.

The Greeks also believed that everything in nature is a living part of the whole cosmos. Every part of this vast system is interrelated; change any one part and the overall pattern is changed. In Heraclitus's philosophy we find a dynamic model in which opposites are in constant flux, moving from one extreme to the other. According to Aristotle, change was not haphazard. It followed a specific pattern that included four things: a base material, a tendency for things to individuate (gain a unique identity), a recipe or formula and some end product. As we shall see, these are the key components of alchemical psychology.

Chinese Alchemy

Although there was no word for gold in the Chinese language until the fifth century B.C., the art of transformation was an implicit part of Chinese culture dating back a thousand years before, when animism was the common belief. By the third century B.C., alchemists in China and India were using gold to concoct elixirs, potions and juices for healing purposes. The first actual Chinese alchemical texts did not appear until the second century B.C. The Chinese words for alchemy were *lien tan,* meaning "pill of transformation." Chinese alchemists sought to radically transform the mind through practices that disciplined bodily functions, meditation and the ingestion of specially prepared elixirs. Their aims were less centered on metallic transmutation than on bodily transformation. The goal of these alchemists was to extend life indefinitely.

They were interested in discovering the secrets of immortality. Eternal life on earth was their definition of the philosopher's stone. Chinese alchemists, especially the Taoists, envisioned themselves becoming *hsien,* immortal beings who would live forever and even fly to heaven at will. The literature on this subject includes the three great Chinese sages—Lao-Tzu, Chuang Tzu and Lieh Tzu.

Taoism is China's oldest philosophy. It is based on three principles: *chi* (the essence of all energy), *yin* and *yang* (the female and male principle) and five elements. The Taoists' five elements (fire, earth, wind, wood, ether) differ slightly from the basic four elements of fire, earth, air and water introduced much later by the Greeks. As we'll discuss in the next chapter, a fifth element, known as the quintessence, shares some similarity with the Taoist concept of ether. Each of these Taoist principles contributes to the alchemical opus in special ways but the overarching emphasis is more on transforming mind and body than on making gold.

Taoists were fiercely opposed to having their philosophy follow any particular canon because they believed this would detract from the transcendent, unutterable essence of their message. It is said that Lao-Tzu, advancing in age, left his province to retire to the mountains of Tibet. He was denied entry until he agreed to put in words the whole of his wisdom. This is how the *Tao Te Chi* is said to have originated. But, true to his inner belief that the truth of alchemy is inexpressible, Lao-Tzu said,

> The Tao that can be written is not the true Tao.

Alchemy, so beautifully expressed in Taoism, is best achieved according to Lao-Tzu in every single moment of our lives. While books can be helpful, there is no substitute for experience. We will want to keep this guiding principle in mind as we go on to explore other elements that help us gain a comprehensive definition of alchemy.

Indian Alchemy

Rasa or *rasayana,* "the way of mercury," is the Indian word for alchemy. The father of Indian alchemy was Nagarjuna. He wrote the first Indian classic on alchemical practice, the *Rasarathnakara,* dated around the year 800. Like many great alchemical texts, the *Rasarathnakara* became the source for many later writings on the subject. To give some sense of the vast scope of the alchemist's vision, I quote from another very old tract, the *Rasarnavakalpa,* or *The Manifold Powers of the Ocean of Mercury.* In it are described not only

> the powers of different substances to transmute base metals like lead and copper into silver and gold but also [recipes for] curing diseases,

preventing decay, rejuvenation, perennial youth and beauty, immense strength, sexual power, grace, supernatural vision, invisibility, material immortality, levitation, and the ability to fly in the air and to observe at will the 'three worlds.'[6]

Indian alchemists used many of the yogic techniques developed by Patanjali in the third century B.C. Prior to Patanjali, yoga had been a mystical tradition for at least a thousand years. Although Patanjali did not invent yoga, his *Yoga-sutras* significantly changed its mystical tradition into a living, practical doctrine of philosophy.

Claiming to be India's oldest religion, the followers of Tantra yoga combined these mystical and practical aspects into a unique practice of refining physical and psychic consciousness. It is difficult to date the origin of Tantra since Hindu zealots destroyed many of its texts. Whereas yoga strives to unite "the inner and the outer, the microcosm and the macrocosm—Tantra is the practice of weaving such a union, of expanding the self to embrace the Universal Self."[7]

By joining the forces of Shiva and Shakti, the initiate achieves this divine state of consciousness. The practice is an alchemical opus taking place completely within the human body. Tantric texts, dating to the tenth century A.D., describe esoteric passages very similar to alchemists working in physical laboratories. "Though ostensibly concerned with the transmutation of baser metals into gold," writes Benjamin Walker, ". . . this alchemy [Tantra] actually takes place within the body itself. It is a hermetic distillation, as it were from the bodily fluids, with the aid of instruments and utensils provided by the body itself, of the gross substance within oneself, into the subtle quintessence that can reinvigorate the physical frame, make the body grow, activate one's supernatural faculties and put one in communication with any entity in the universe."[8]

Another major contribution of Indian alchemy was the development of Ayurveda. This is perhaps one of the first organized systems of holistic medicine. Again we see how the basic elements are used to construct an intricate system of healing. In Ayurveda, each of the five elements gives birth to the manifest world. Space gives birth to air, air to fire, fire to water, and water to solid form. Out of solid form comes earth, which then leads to the growth of plants; from plants we get the seeds and food out of which comes living being. Later on in this book we will use this cosmology as a basis for understanding how psychology also developed out of the elements.

Arabian Alchemy   The tradition of alchemy that is most familiar to Westerners came by way of the Islamic world and Judaic influences. Alchemy was practiced throughout Syria, Persia and Iraq beginning in the mid-eighth century. From this time and up until the late fifteenth century, Islamic Moors occupied Spain, bringing with them the works of Jābir ibn Hayyan, one of the world's greatest alchemists.

Jābir is known in the West as Geber, the greatest Arabian alchemist and father of European as well as Islamic alchemy. Great mystery surrounds his name, and as with many alchemists before him, his writings are difficult to authenticate and his language a challenge to interpret. So many translations of his work circulated around Europe during this time that both the author's name and his texts deteriorated into our word for nonsense—gibberish.

Jābir's works, however, are anything but gibberish. His name derives from the Arabic *gharbala,* meaning "to sift the fine from the coarse,"[9] an apt phrase for describing the very heart of the alchemical work. His writings represent the very best of the alchemical tradition, a vibrant mix of chemistry and religious philosophy. He was especially known for his medical elixirs, many of which recall the ancient alchemical healing practices of the Chinese.

Jābir was also interested in numerology, a subject that reflects his Sufi background and draws an important parallel to the ancient Pythagorean school. Numerology was one of the very few occult sciences to survive the transition from magic to science occurring over these five centuries.

Numbers, in Jābir's alchemy, are holy expressions of universal truths. Like many other alchemists who would follow him, Jābir practiced a mystical form of Judaism known as Kabbala. The concept of unity achieves one of its greatest expressions in Kabbala. Numerology, or gemateria, is an important key to unlocking the mysteries of Kabbala's cosmology. According to Rabbi David Cooper, Kabbala "includes every possible dimension of creation, angels, demons, thoughts, feelings, past, future, this incarnation, and all others."[10]

Gematria was a tool used by Kabbalists to discover the latent meaning in each letter of the Hebrew alphabet. Using numbers to represent each letter, words expressed deeper, more complex meanings. The number ten, for example, represented *yod*, the tenth letter of their alphabet and *hey* the fifth. These are the first two letters that make up their name for God, *yod-hey-vav-hey*, or as expressed in the language of gematria *tetragrammoton*. We are not accustomed to seeing the deeper spiritual and mystical meaning in letters and numbers, but for alchemists and Kabbalists, these represented a rich vocabulary of symbolism. Quoting Rabbi Eliezer, Cooper conveys the power invested in sacred words like *tetragrammoton*. "God says, 'If you follow my ways, my name will be with you; but if you do not, I will take away my name and you will become fire.'"[11] In knowing god, fire can be used creatively to make gold—the living essence of fire—but in the absence of god, fire, like the flames of hell, is dangerous and potentially very destructive.

Using gematria and other alchemical methods, Jābir sought to achieve a perfect balance and unity among all things. He summed up his work in a single recipe:

One is the stone, one the medicine, and therein lies the whole magistry.[12]

Jābir also practiced a mystical form of Islam known as Sufism. Through dance, meditation and prayer, Sufis sought ecstatic union with God. Like practitioners of Islam, they too strove to "free the mind from dependence on physical appearance and to prepare it for its voyage to the intelligible realm and for a vision and experience of Unity."[13] The symbol used by Sufis to signify this ecstatic union was the winged heart. It is this impulse that gives rise to a state of golden consciousness that transcends normal psychological experience. In this book, this exalted state will be known as the Divine Self.

The philosopher's stone can be visualized in many ways. For the Sufis, it manifested in the dance of the whirling dervishes. To behold this dance is truly to see poetry in motion. As the dancers whirl in a clockwise direction, their full attention is focused on the central axis of their being, which connects earth and heaven. The thirteenth-century Sufi mystic Rumi founded the order that created this ecstatic dance. Along with the *Thousand and One Nights*, which was read to me as a child, I have a tender place in my (alchemical) heart for Rumi. His words give alchemy a voice that resonates with magnificent beauty.

Arabian, Islamic and Judaic traditions provided alchemy with a conduit to cross from the Old World into Europe. Not only did it bring with it a host of new theories and practices on how to transmute metals, but it also added poetry and dance to our expanding definition of alchemy.

European Alchemy

Alchemy flourished throughout Europe from the eighth to the sixteenth century. Many books have been written about famous alchemists who developed alchemy and made enormous contributions to science and medicine during these eight centuries. I will only mention some of their names at this point and will throughout this book make reference to some of their insights. Most of the recipes we will be studying in depth in chapter 8 are credited to European alchemists like Robert Flood, Michael Maier, Heinrich Khunrath, Thomas Norton, Albertus Magus and Basil Valentine. At the end of this book I have added a list of sources for the recipes we will be studying. I would also recommend the interested reader to Arthur Waite's excellent book *Alchemists through the Ages* for splendid biographies of some of the world's leading practitioners of the Art. (In keeping with tradition, I shall at various times refer to alchemy as the Work or the Art.)

The Middle Ages represents an explosive period as human consciousness transitioned out of the Dark Ages and began building the foundations for modern life. As modern science emerged out of old magical traditions, a whole new age of invention and innovation captured the minds of the world's leading scientists. For some, advances in chemistry and physics provided the physical means of fulfilling some of the alchemists' oldest theories. For others, modern science sounded the death knell for alchemy. As science moved its methodological base from argument to observation and finally to experiment, it lost touch with the sacred world that was so critically important to alchemy. There is no better example of this transition, for better or worse, than can be found in the life of Isaac Newton.

By any measure, Newton was a tortured soul, genius, alchemist and "last of the sorcerers." His life represents a microcosm of the alchemical soul and a macrocosm of the scientific mind. Even a cursory review of his work reveals the fact that every one of his revolutionary discoveries came from his endless alchemical experiments. His work in optics, gravitation and celestial movement was fueled by his deep spiritual convictions and alchemical beliefs. Newton's ability to translate the dark secrets of alchemy into repeatable, verifiable experiments marked the beginning of a whole New World paradigm of consciousness. According to one of his biographers, "if the arrival of the modern scientific age could be pinpointed to a particular moment and a particular place . . . it would be 27 April 1676 at the Royal Society" when Newton transformed "a hypothesis into a demonstratable theory."[14] That date will go down in history as the moment separating two great worlds.

Had there been psychologists in the late seventeenth-century, they would have had no difficulty pronouncing Newton profoundly neurotic and at times completely out of touch with reality. But given his amazing accomplishments, there was clearly a method to his madness. In addition to his breakthrough discoveries, he possessed an insatiable curiosity and wonder about the world, traits common to many alchemists.

In his paper "Newton, the Man," mathematician John Maynard Keynes describes the source of Newton's insatiable curiosity, a quality we would certainly do well to emulate:

> [Newton] looked on the whole universe and all that is in it as a riddle, as a secret which could be read by applying pure thought to certain evidence, certain mystic clues which God had laid about the world to allow a sort of philosopher's treasure hunt to the esoteric brotherhood.[15]

We see a similar passion and love of paradox in the later work of Einstein, who wanted "to know the mind of God," the developer of quantum physics Niels Bohr, and the theoretical physicist who currently holds the Newton Chair at Cambridge, Stephen Hawking. Along with these modern-day alchemists are the pioneering psychological works of Sigmund Freud and Carl Jung. These adventurers of matter and mind keep the magic of alchemy alive. It seems that more than discovering new worlds, they invent them.

American Alchemy   While you will not find many active alchemical laboratories in operation today, you will find alchemy's legacy in the world's great institutions. Perhaps more than most countries, the United States exemplifies the struggle to bring some of the most important alchemical principles into the lives of its people.

The founders of this great nation brought with them an alchemical tradition steeped in centuries of European history. Their individualism and pioneering character has become part of the American psyche. Some of the most enlightened of the founders reached for a vision that would insure the survival and spiritual prosperity of the new nation. We do not have to look far to find evidence of alchemy in their work.

The central idea of a country that guarantees individual human rights and freedoms, where one is all, and all is one, is written into the U.S. Constitution. The flag and the great seal of the United States are emblazoned with many of the old alchemical symbols. Diversity, tolerance for differences and respect for individualism within collective society are some of the ingredients that have gone into this melting pot. Still, even after two hundreds years, it remains to be seen whether this great alchemical experiment will succeed.

There is another place where alchemy continues to thrive even today. If Jung is correct and the human psyche contains the whole history of human civilization then what I have described in this chapter continues to live on in the minds and hearts of every person in the world. There is, in other words, some piece of the alchemical gold residing in everyone. One need not look far to see alchemy at work in their personal experience. The psyche consists of the great mythologies of Egypt and Greece, the philosophy of China and mystical insights of the Arabian nations, not to mention the contributions made by European alchemists and physicists.

I believe that the alchemical opus bequeathed to us represents a

Examine the reverse side of a one-dollar bill. Notice the pyramid adorned by a single, open eye, surrounded by the Latin words *Annuit Coeptis* ("He [God] has formed our understanding"). Below the pyramid is the inscription *Novos Ordo Seclorum* ("new order of the ages"). According to historian Manly P. Hall, this pyramid represents the building of human society, which is still in the process of completion. It is the pyramid of Gizah, believed by many Egyptians to be the tomb of Hermes Trismegistus. Using gematria, Hall interpreted the seventy-two stones making up the pyramid to be another Hebrew name for God. The all-seeing eye further emphasizes the universal wisdom needed for an enlightened society.

perennial philosophy, one we continue to develop and learn from. Alchemy is a wisdom tradition known in past times as the Hermetic Science and today is best appreciated as the Science of Mind.

From our brief review of world alchemy, I think it becomes evident that alchemy is much more than simply changing lead into gold. Although we will limit our focus to the study of psychological alchemy, we should bear in mind that every contribution made by alchemists throughout the world adds something special to the spirit of the work. In her book *Alchemy,* historian Cherry Gilchrist makes this important point:

TOWARD A DEFINITION

> Mainstream alchemy is a discipline involving physical, psychological and spiritual work, and if any one of these elements is taken out of context and said to represent the alchemical tradition, then the wholeness and true quality of alchemy is lost.[16]

Alchemy is the only one of the three basic occult sciences (the others being astrology and the Kabbala) that deals directly with the transmutation of matter. As we have seen, alchemy is to some a craft and to others a sacred science. Still others consider it a black magic, superstition and a curious oddity of science. Having provided this short survey of alchemy's rich historical background we can see that alchemy involves elaborate physical, psychological and spiritual disciplines. For us, alchemy will take a decidedly psychological course that emphasizes psychological change through the use of some very old alchemical recipes.

> Alchemy is the archetype of change, whose energies perpetuate all that is conscious and unconscious, miniature and macroscopic, spiritual and physical, to evolve along an accelerated course of evolution by synthetic means, into superior and whole form.

The personal practice of alchemy does not require allegiance to any one tradition, but it does demand an acceptance that nature can be synthetically (as in synthesis) altered using physical and mental means. Alchemy is about making things happen using the powers of mind to change matter and the very fabric of reality.

THE ESSENTIAL
CHARACTERISTICS
OF ALCHEMY

1. Animism

Central to all of alchemy is the concept that everything in life is alive. There are many terms that could be used to represent this founding stone of the alchemical arts. I use the word "animism" because it suggests the presence of "a single consciousness [that] permeates all being and things, known as God, *Anima Mundi,* Universal Mind, Great Spirit, world soul."[17] *Anima Mundi* means world soul. She animates all matter and brings the world to life.

This archetypal energy infuses all matter, from the smallest pebble to the most complex creature, with some amount of consciousness. It is axiomatic that all life is therefore sacred. How can it not be? If we value everything then all we have is treasured. No one thing is any more important than another, only forms differ. Mother Nature, like Lady Justice, is blind to differences, and in fact, welcomes diversity. There is no prejudice or any judgment that makes one flower prettier than another, no animal more deserving than another. All life is equally precious.

Contemporary science is bent on *proving* what the alchemists intuited about the unity of cosmos. With modern methods of imaging the operations of the living brain, scientists are finding evidence to show how the experience of god can be physically verified. At the same time, major changes are happening on the collective level where a vision of an all-encompassing concept of earth is gaining attention at the global level. In my view, these developments prove that the alchemist's intuitions and observations of nature were extremely accurate. Whether through the lens of science or the alchemical imagination, *Anima Mundi* teaches us that the world is a sacred place for every living creature.

> Imagine that everything has a soul or is part of one big giant soul. This attitude inspires a reverence for life and expands the Golden Rule to include respect for all people, plants, animals and even minerals.

2. Oneness

The second common element in alchemy is the emphasis put upon oneness. While there exist many different approaches to alchemical work, and there are even many disagreements on its methods, the bottom line requires that all disparate parts be brought into one harmonious union. The premise underlying this requirement is that all life is interconnected; it is a system in which each part, to some extent, depends on all the other parts. We are beginning to learn this in science. Chaos theory states, for example, that even the flutter of a butterfly's wings contributes, in some infinitesimally small way, to the creation of a hurricane. This may sound impossible and perhaps short of being a physicist, it is difficult to understand how such a thing could

> Look for the pattern that connects you to everything in your life, in the world, in the galaxy. Start by meditating on the stars some warm and dark summer night. Simply ponder the vast universal network of which you are a vital element.

be so. But then, who hasn't had an unusual experience where the most unlikely circumstances coalesce, defying all rational explanation but bringing unrelated bits of life into order?

Since alchemists did not divide the worlds of matter neatly into scientific categories like time and space, transpersonal phenomena often occur in the alchemical experience.

3. Transcending Time and Space and Reason

Jung studied the occurrence of events having no identifiable cause yet having the curious effect of connecting circumstances in meaningful ways. He called this strange phenomenon synchronicity.

Synchronicity is an acausal connecting principle that describes the "coincidence in time of two or more causally unrelated events which have the same or similar meaning."[18] "Their 'inexplicability' is not due to the fact that the cause is unknown, but to the fact that a cause is not even thinkable in intellectual terms."[19] There are many examples of synchronicity in Jung's life, in physics and in my own life. Jung observed that parapsychological events like synchronicity are not uncommon in psychotherapy. Even he was taken aback when a beetle came crashing into his office window right at the point when he was interpreting the significance of such a creature in a patient's dream. Her resistance to his interpretation dissolved instantly when the beetle made its entrance. Added to the oddity of the situation was the fact that beetles of this kind are not natural inhabitants of Zurich. The beetle's body structure reminded Jung of the Egyptian scarab beetle whose death and rebirth myth he was well acquainted with. The synchronicity between his patient's dream and the arrival of the beetle could not be explained intellectually, but in the context of the unconscious work, it helped enormously.

In my life, I have found that synchronistic events often occur when I am in the grip of some unresolved, highly emotional situation. For example, at nineteen years old I had my first real relationship with a woman. Being young and inexperienced I fell quickly and deeply for this young lady. Unfortunately it ended abruptly and I was left broken-hearted. Although I deliberately moved on in my life, my unconscious must have remained brooding for a long time. I had moved from New York to California, had a number of relationships with other women, but this first wound still apparently needed healing.

It was seven years later when I next returned to New York City for a weeklong visit. I'll never forget the day when I was leaving an art gallery on West Fifty-seventh Street. As the elevator doors opened I stood face-to-face with my old flame. She was as shocked as I. We exchanged a few nervous words but quickly each of us sensed that this was a meaningful coincidence. As we talked further it became obvious that we had both matured and were now able to put things into a better perspective. The night ended with an invitation to the opera, for which she had tickets but no one to escort her. I accepted her invitation, realizing that this synchronistic meeting would bring our past relationship to a peaceful close. Since then we have become good friends and continue to enjoy each other's company.

> Consider the synchronistic events that have occurred in your own life. Don't dismiss them as mere accidents. Now imagine that you can make them happen at will. Such occurrences are not uncommon in the practice of psychological alchemy.

4. Transformation

The fourth common element is the progressive nature of changing seemingly worthless materials into precious ones. The work of alchemy always begins by finding the *prima materia*. This is the material chosen by alchemists as the initial, base matter, which began their experiment. Exactly what the *prima materia* consists of is one of the greatest mysteries in alchemy. It is variously called the rejected stone, vulgar gold or something horrid that can only be found in the dung heap.

The *prima materia* is not necessarily something physical. Consequently, your garden, laboratory, church or temple is not the place to find the *prima materia* used in personal alchemy. Rather, a good place to begin the search is in our mess, our crisis, our broken dreams, our worst

> The Chinese word for "crisis" contains a root term meaning "opportunity." The *prima materia* often appears black and repulsive, but working with it using the operations described throughout this book will reveal the gold hidden in it.

nightmare, disasters—all those horrible experiences that are associated with the shadow aspects of life. That is where we are most vulnerable and most apt to summon up the courage to make dramatic changes.

Throughout the history of alchemy we find many visionary individuals who espoused unorthodox theories often at the risk of losing their lives. Such boldness, reflected in their writings, encouraged practitioners to use the Art to transcend the ordinary limits imposed by nature. Two of alchemy's greatest documents, The *Emerald Tablet*[20] and the third century *Corpus Hermeticum*,[21] state that mere mortals can do the work of the creation by "adaptation." The *Emerald Tablet,* credited to the mythical Hermes Trismegistus, describes "marvelous adaptations" that result from applying its recipes to mind and matter. Adaptation means that the alchemist must suspend the normal objective view of reality and change his mind to accord with the powers of heaven and earth. The role of the adept executing these operations is to join nature in order *to facilitate the course of evolution*.

5. Facilitation

We are then imitating the creator, acting as co-creator, to quicken the pace at which all things evolve. Words from the *Corpus Hermeticum* encourage us to be daring in our work, that we use extraordinary (supernatural) imagination and most importantly, work from the heart.

> If you don't make yourself equal to God, you can't perceive God; for like is known by like. Leap free of everything that is physical, and grow as vast as that immeasurable vastness; step beyond all time and become eternal.[22]

The alchemists often talked of both being guided by Nature and at the same time helping her. If we hold to the alchemist's belief that all matter (including human being) is materialized consciousness, then we will see the absurdity in thinking we might somehow be outside, above or in control of nature. Unlike the magician, the alchemist worked with nature by adapting his or her mind to join the elements with focused intent and deliberate purpose. We mimic her ways but also make our own individual contribution. In doing so, the normal pace by which things change is accelerated.

> Alchemy is riddled with paradox. Rather than try to resolve the confusion through rational means, hold the paradox in your mind and apply the powers of your imagination.

6. Creating New Life

The sixth common feature in alchemy is the belief that new forms of creation can be borne by human intervention. This goes one step further than adaptation. Having learned something of nature's secrets, it becomes possible to create new life-forms. To prevent wholesale arrogance that could easily accompany such lofty ambitions, we must constantly bear in mind that we are part of Nature and, short of becoming neurotic, can never be separate from Nature. However much power we might acquire, Nature will always in the end have the upper hand. As the Persian alchemist Ostanes put it: "Nature rejoices in nature, nature triumphs over nature, nature dominates nature."[23]

Perhaps the most common example of biological alchemy is seen in the birth of a child. Out of the physical and emotional interaction between two people, a child is born. It will have some of its mother's features and some of its father's. Provided both parents are healthy, the infant is born with relative ease. With today's medical science even if physical problems are present, much can be done to artificially assist the reproductive process. But the arm of medicine reaches far beyond simple repair; it aims at nothing short of creating a child from the DNA of a single person.

It appears that our alchemical impulses are pushing us further into uncharted territory. While we have already seen cloned animals born out of laboratory experiments, it is nearly all but certain that human cloning will take place within our lifetimes. Alchemy, I pray, will make its own invaluable contribution by developing methods for instilling a loving soul into this first humanoid, the new Adam.[24]

> What kind of life could you imagine you might create if you applied these characteristics to yourself? I suggest it would be one in which all life is respected, necessary, dynamic and mysterious. Ask yourself whether you subscribe to this alchemical way of viewing life:
>
> - Do I believe that everything in life is an essential part of the overall creation?
> - Do I believe that everything, no matter how chaotic, simple or complex, is part of the "stuff" I need to bring harmony into my life?
> - Do I believe that everything changes, regardless of temporary setbacks, into ever-more refined expressions of nature?
> - Do I believe that everything holds a mystery that I desire to know? And the most important question of all:
> - Do I believe that I can adapt my life to these beliefs and expect living, tangible results?

These are the principles that underlie alchemy. Your affirmations are the active ingredients that give recipes the power to change lead into gold.

Chapter 2

The Royal Art of
Living Consciously

Imagination is more important than knowledge.
Knowledge is limited.
Imagination encircles the world.
ALBERT EINSTEIN

Alchemy was brought into the modern world by the Swiss psychiatrist Carl Gustav Jung. As with many things in his life, alchemy came to him by way of a dream. Although Jung had already established his reputation as a scholar long before delving into his alchemical studies, he still searched for a theory to encompass the entire scope of his vision. Alchemy would become his *magnum opus*. Jung's initial interest in alchemy sprang from one special image that came from a dream he had in 1926. In this dream, he saw a closed-off section of his home within which were stacks of medieval books, all written in an obscure language.[1]

Jung took his dreams to heart. He wrote them down and spent many hours interpreting their meaning. Jung came to realize that these books represented the works of medieval alchemists, written in a mysterious, symbolic language. "Finally," he writes in his memoirs, "I realized that the alchemists were talking in symbols."[2] As a result of Jung's "momentous discovery,"[3] he spent nearly sixty years translating alchemical texts and building a theory based on alchemical principles. Those books, first seen in his dream, eventually filled the shelves of his bookcases in his home in Zurich.

In a letter Jung wrote in 1946, he describes another auspicious dream that underscores the real goal/gold of personal alchemy. He wrote:

> Yesterday I had a marvelous dream: one bluish diamond, like a star high
> in heaven reflected in a round quiet pool—heaven above, heaven below.
> The *imago Dei* in the darkness of the earth, this is myself.[4]

This dream not only expresses the extraordinary state of mind Jung achieved during his life but it articulates his thoughts about alchemy as a psychological model of mind. Just as alchemists believed all metals mature over the course of time to become gold, Jung felt that people developed from a relatively unconscious state to a fine, perfected one. He called this alchemical development of consciousness the individuation process. Jung believed that there is in each of us the potential to use this process to realize our true inner nature and in doing so, develop extraordinary psychological powers.

Individuation is the process that gives us the opportunity to separate from collective groups (family, state, country) in order to develop our personal, individual identity. Involved in this process are a number of critical tasks, some of which we discuss from a psychological point of view in this chapter and others that will be viewed from an alchemical perspective in later chapters.

In an unusual dream I had during the writing of this book, I experienced no visual images, but only heard a voice. It said very clearly, "For heaven to be on earth you shall walk as gods." On awakening I immediately associated the message of the dream with the words from the Lord's Prayer, where it reads: "Thy will be done, on earth as it is in heaven." In my imagination I assumed that my dream voice was God giving me an instruction on how to achieve heaven on earth. How then do I walk as a god and see, as Jung did, the image of god in "the darkness of earth" and myself?

My early upbringing answered the question with the immediate invective to "be good." This Christian belief was put to the test when I embraced the challenges posed by my individuation process. Added to this was the experience of world travel and learning very different ways of seeing life. I especially learned, from Eastern spiritual teachings, to see through the veil of illusion, Maya, and seek to experience the oneness of all being. The notion of good and evil seems to have less significance from this broader perspective. As I inspected my beliefs, some fit well together and others were in conflict. What I knew most certainly, however, was that a process had begun and there was no turning back.

In my immediate, everyday world I faced the trials and tribulations of life just like everyone else. Walking like a god must therefore mean that I should carry myself with integrity and conduct my affairs in the same way. I must strive to be conscious of all that I am and all that I do, and to the best of my ability form a relationship with my unconscious to understand its mysterious language. This process of self-examination became a terrific and worthwhile challenge. In retrospect, I came to realize that the work of individuation requires me to examine, refine and integrate all my various parts, not just the good ones, into one harmonious whole.

Jung's model of individuation has given me a method of revealing the golden consciousness that lies deep in my leaden, unaware consciousness. My effort to transform this unconscious lead into gold gives my life purpose and direction. I consider this process a sacred gift. My dream describes how I shall walk the golden path.

Individuation is not a choice but something that happens whether we're ready for it or not. For those who welcome psyche's urge toward further development, the road may not be easy but it is certainly more rewarding than if we continue down an unconscious path. I have many patients whose material wealth is valued in millions of dollars, but whose souls are impoverished. Psychic bankruptcy is disconcerting and takes an enormous effort to mend. An example of this awful situation comes to mind.

> "Individuation means becoming an 'in-dividual,' and in so far as 'individuality' embraces our innermost, last, and incomparable uniqueness, it also implies becoming one's own self. We could therefore translate individuation as 'coming to selfhood' or 'self-realization.'"[5]

Some years ago I treated a psychologist who was having difficulties in his marriage. Despite the fact that he came to me for help with his failing marriage, all I remember was his obsession with money. Everything, including his marriage, revolved around finances. I found this a bit disturbing since he was in the practice of helping others and should therefore place a greater value on matters of the heart. But of course no one is exempt from the temptations placed in our way on the road to individuation.

In therapy he complained about the money problems he was having with his business and only secondarily raised the problems in his marriage. He mostly wanted to focus on the money issues and could not see how these were really the barrier keeping him from finding happiness with his wife. Finally one day I had had it—off came the gloves. I emphatically said to him, "It's only money!" My words shot through him like a lightning bolt. This was about the craziest thing he had ever heard. But it rang through his head over and over again. In due course we were able to deal with the real source of his pain and bring some healing to what was really wrong in his life.

I fondly refer to this man as my Midas patient. Recall that Midas was the king whose touch turned everything to gold. This was his reward for having helped Dionysis. But, was this really a gift? When the bread he ate and the water he drank turned to gold, he quickly realized that he had been cursed. Greed, not service, appeared to have been the impulse behind Midas's wish for gold. Gods see through us and reward us in kind.

Eventually, the king was released from the spell and he even rejected all wealth and splendor. But, unfortunately, Midas never acquired the real gold—giving is its own reward. In the end, Midas fled his kingdom and took residence in the forest.

Midas, like my patient, was being sent a challenge in the form of a gift. Although my patient had acquired a great deal of money, it seemed more of a curse than a blessing. Money could not buy him everything; neither could it bring him to a level of consciousness where he would appreciate the deeper values of life. Whatever healing he obtained from therapy it clearly didn't go far enough. In fact, he ended the therapy, grateful but acknowledging the limit of his capacity for growth. He said simply, "I'm not that deep." He, like Midas, turned away from material gold, but did not discover the real gold. Until we go deeper, we will never marry the contradictions residing in ourselves. At best, we may safeguard ourselves from glittery entrapments, but unless we go into our depths, we will never become fully alive.

The fifteenth-century alchemist Gerhard Dorn instructed his students to "transform yourselves from dead stones into living philosophical ones."[6] To this Jung would add, "The most important alchemists were not concerned with the manufacture of common gold, of *aurum vulgi,* but with the *aurum nostrum,* the symbol of an illumined soul."[7] There is no escaping this psychic imperative. Evolution flows through nature and psyche with unstoppable force. When impeded, painful alarm bells go off and stop only when healing begins. Medicines for the body and therapy for the soul are then required to restore good health.

HEALING AND IMAGINATION

Healing requires great imagination. No medicine will ever work if a patient doesn't have faith in the doctor who prescribes it. The imagination must embrace the powers contained in the healer, the medicine, the therapy, nature and prayer; they all play a critical part in the healing process.

Time also must be treated imaginatively. It is a great healer of physical injuries, but with psychic wounds, it often works in reverse. In cases of trauma, these types of wounds exist outside of time: the rape, divorce, accident that happened twenty years ago are experienced as if they occurred only yesterday. Illness must be pictured this way because time in the unconscious is not the same as the ordinary time of clocks and calendars.

Not long ago I treated a newly married woman in her mid-forties. She and her husband wanted to have a child, but every physician she consulted told her she was too old. They prescribed fertility treatments, but even she was not convinced they would work because of her age. In her first visit to my office I asked her what she dreamt the night before coming for her appointment. Some of the dream images involved her trying on one pair of clothes after another then looking in the mirror to catch other people's reactions. In discussing the meaning of her dream it became clear to both of us that she had persona problems; having a baby would give her "what everybody else has," a status she needed to gain approval.

Persona is that part of personality that we use much as an actor uses a mask. It is the face we show the world. Depending on the situation, we automatically change the persona usually to put us in the best light. Persona is accompanied by the actor's script. In other words, donning our masks defines the role we play in a particular circumstance. If conscious of our persona we can use these masks and roles to our advantage. Once we examined this woman's persona and saw how out of touch she was with it, I realized the problem. It wasn't that she was too old; quite the opposite, psychically she was too young to have a child!

She was stunned, broke down in tears and told me that I had verbalized what she knew in her heart was true. It was not that the doctors' opinions were incorrect, but they unfortunately suffered from too narrow a view. A person is not simply a statistical reality, nor is she or he restricted to the confines of physical laws. The soul must be taken into account and if necessary, ministered to with the same level of care extended to the body. Brain and mind are not interchangeable concepts. This woman's needs were as much about how she thought about herself as they were about her reproductive organs.

Jung often referred to alchemy as an *opus contra naturum,* meaning that its operations work to accelerate the natural healing process in unnatural or synthetic ways.[8] At first this seems paradoxical. In working with this woman, I used some paradox to shake her out of the distorted image she had of herself. She never really accepted the doctors' judgments because the messages from her psyche were in contradiction to them. The real work of psychotherapy was to reconcile the opposing information between her body and her mind. This is a real alchemical problem. While her body refused to produce a child, her mind was alive with all sorts of creative possibilities. But before she could explore these options she had first to eliminate from her mind the idea that success could only be achieved by physically producing a child. We were dealing with her physical and social instincts on the one hand and her psychic desire on the other.

The work of alchemy aims to resolve opposites, and in this case there was a real conflict between body and soul. This woman was trying to meet conflicting needs, one having a physical component, the other psychological. The only way to resolve the problem without doing harm to the body or mind was to create a third option, one that transcended the opposites and offered a satisfying solution. Had she not come for psychological treatment, time alone would have solved her problem. She would have lost all chance of physically having a child, but like my Midas patient, she would have missed the opportunity of resolving the real source of her dilemma. As long as there was any chance of having a child, her problem was a real one and offered real possibilities for growth. Psychotherapy, just like alchemy, was a method for facilitating the healing process by capitalizing on what nature has to offer and appending it with creative methods of intervention.

Alchemists, facing similar problems, used psychological methods as much as physical methods in their laboratories. Psychology, of course, did not exist as a formal discipline during most of alchemy's history. But we find it embedded in philosophy and theology, both in theory and practice. In his book *Mysterium Conunctionus,* Jung sheds light on a medieval practice that sounds more psychological than religious. He quotes Ruland's definition of meditation as "the name of an Internal Talk of one person with another who is invisible, as in the invocation of the Deity, or communion with one's self, or with one's good angel."[9]

Jung adapted this method to facilitate the individuation process. He called it active imagination. In Jung's words, here is how active imagination works:

> Take the unconscious in one of its irrational moods, an affect, or something of the kind, and operate with it. Give it your special attention, concentrate on it, and observe its alterations objectively. Spare no effort to devote yourself to this task, follow the subsequent transformations of the spontaneous fantasy attentively and carefully. Above all, don't let anything

from outside, that does not belong, get into it, for the fantasy-image has "everything it needs." In this way one is certain of not interfering by conscious caprice and of giving the unconscious a free hand.[10]

In other passages Jung gives practical advice in getting the most from this method. These include:

- don't get caught up in the intrigue or fascination of your "inner drama"

- write down everything

- be an unbiased recorder but an active participant

- keep a running commentary

In the case of the woman having the persona problem, we used dreams and active imagination to get at the source of her difficulty. After several sessions of actively dialoguing with her unconscious, she saw an image of herself in a large ship. Asking further what her position was on the ship, the unconscious responded decisively. She giggled in telling me that she had to be the captain of her own ship. As she continued working with dreams and doing active imagination, she eventually came to realize that her real desire was to return to school and become a counselor.

In doing active imagination it helps to:

- suspend reality—it doesn't have to make logical sense

- let some time elapse before going back and making sense of what took place

- ask yourself how you might put into behavior what you've learned from your active imagination

- be patient—this technique is like everything else, "practice makes perfect"

- consult trusted friends and colleagues or your therapist to help you when you are stuck, confused or missing something important

> "Every active imagination . . . is a direct experience of the spiritual powers of the psyche."[11]
> "Active imagination . . . relates one to the world beyond the psyche, to the spiritual domain and reality in which the divine resides."[12]

COMING TO TERMS   While Jung stopped short of saying that alchemists actually transmuted metal through the powers of their mind, his whole psychology suggests that he did believe in the enormous potential of mind over matter. Rather than find any value in the alchemist's alleged metallic transmutations, he found greater significance in their psychology. He felt that the alchemists were projecting unconscious images onto the substances in their vessels. Projection is an unconscious process where we send out subjective images onto an object. The object, in this process, gains attributes that it may not physically possess. An alchemist, for example, might see colors whirling around on the oily fluids in a flask and give the name "peacock" to the change he believed was happening. For him, the rainbow of colors represents the whole spectrum of white light and must, he concludes, signify the immanence of wholeness.

Some have argued that Jung did not go far enough in giving the alchemists credit. Morris Berman, in *The Reenchantment of the World,* remarks how modern human beings like Jung "cannot fathom the relationship between becoming golden and making gold. The medieval alchemist, on the other hand, was completed by the process; the synthesis of the gold was his synthesis as well."[13] Jung used alchemy as a model for his theory of individuation but that is as far as it went—so the criticism goes. Repeatedly Jung says that the alchemists "did not know what they were doing," a sentiment held by many and one I hope to change. Jung drew a clear line between actual transmutation and projection. The philosopher's stone, he said, was the "projection of the unified self."[14] Obviously Jung valued alchemy more for the wealth of unconscious data it provided him in corroborating his theories than any possible means of transmuting physical substances.[15]

This unconscious process of projection taught Jung more about the psychology of alchemists than the actual results of their physical experiments. Tracing the projected images back to their source, Jung discovered a great deal about the adept's personality and the psychology of the unconscious. His ideas about the development of personality from an undifferentiated mass to various levels of refinement accord precisely with the alchemist's symbolism of transmuting the gross *prima materia* into the philosopher's stone.

In order to see the world through the eyes of an alchemist we must suspend rational judgment and ordinary conceptions of reality. These often interfere with actual proof of alchemy's effectiveness. "Our ancestors," Morris Berman writes, "constructed reality in a way that typically produced verifiable results, and this is why Jung's theory of projection is off the mark."[16] To be sure, Jung needed a receptive audience in the academic community. To the extent that every scientist, including the alchemist, must necessarily be somewhat political, Jung was not off the mark. He repeatedly refers to himself as an empirical scientist and decried criticisms aimed at dismissing his theories as magical, mystical or even religious. Fortunately, we are not held back by such constraints, and with the advancement of science, we can more daringly take alchemy further.

Jung made a great contribution to our modern understanding of alchemy with his scholarly interpretation of alchemical terms into psychological language. His penetrating analysis of the collective unconscious provided him with rich images to translate the mysterious words and symbols of alchemical texts.

Alchemical recipes and images that emerge from our dreams and fantasies can be used to describe the psychological operations that accelerate the development of personality. Some of these images correlate directly with specific states and conditions of our progress along the way. Here are some examples: The *massa confusa* describes the chaotic, unconscious state of the child and regressions suffered by adults during times of crisis. The sun (*sol*) represents the eternal archetype of the Self, gold the perfection of the ego personality and its integration with the Self, or the Individuated Self, which I will be discussing shortly.

The image of the queen represents soul (*L. anima*) or the feminine aspects of personality, and the image of the king, its masculine-spirit (*L. animus*) aspects. The movement of images from hermaphrodite to androgyne describes the integration of these opposing aspects of personality from a grotesque creature to one harmonious being. Each of the four elements—fire, water, air and earth—corresponds to specific aspects of temperament and psychological function. What Jung achieves in this alchemical psychology is a composite picture of mind-body consciousness that has the potential to unify the psyche and bring about meaningful accommodation with the environment. Individuation then is an alchemical experiment that takes place inside the laboratory of one's psyche.

The following table summarizes some of the basic alchemical terms and their Jungian equivalents:

TABLE 1: ALCHEMICAL AND JUNGIAN TERMS

Alchemical terms	Jungian terms
Massa confusa	unrealized unconscious, natural chaos
Prima materia	first order of consciousness in personality
Philosopher's stone	conscious realization of the Self
Sol (sun)	masculine consciousness, *animus*
King	spirit
Luna (moon)	feminine consciousness, *anima*
Queen	soul
Salt	grounding energy of soul
Sulfur	explosive energy of spirit
Mercury	trickster archetype as integrating agent
Rebis (double thing)	undifferentiated opposites
Hermaphrodite	initial joining of opposites
Androgyne	integration of opposites
Nigredo, albedo, rubedo	stages of the individuation process
Four elements	four psychological functions
Transmutation	transformation
Operator	individual, therapist
Operations	differentiation and integration
Meditation	Active imagination

Imagination, as the alchemist used the term (*imaginatio*), is a means of translating objective phenomena into the language of psyche. As such it is the chief method of conscious individuation and ultimate achievement of the Individuated Self. Roberts Avens, poet and philosopher, gives us an understanding of imagination as both alchemists and Jungians use the term:

> The Jungian attitude is . . . similar to that of medieval alchemists who repeatedly warned against confusion between daydreams . . . and creative imagination. In alchemy *imaginationes* are not immaterial phantoms or nonsense but a sort of "subtle body" of psychoid nature, forming an intermediary realm between mind and matter and blending both in an indissoluble unity.[17]

IMAGINATIO

For Jung, images are "the only reality we apprehend directly." At first this way of relating to the world appears archaic, but a revolution in thinking, beginning with the discovery of quantum physics, requires exactly this sort of imagination for a true understanding of the physical universe.

Jung viewed alchemy as a model that describes the path of individuating consciousness, transforming the personality into a refined Self that gives tangible meaning to the philosopher's stone. Alchemists, of course, had a broader understanding of their precious *lapis,* their word for the philosopher's stone. Some alchemists thought of the *lapis* as an actual stone or powder that could transmute inferior substances into gold. Others thought of it as a powerful elixir that could rid the body of disease, raise the dead, give life to artificial creatures and even immortality to living ones. In my studies of alchemy I have settled on an understanding of this mysterious stone as a concept from which we can derive practical psychological methods for individuating consciousness.

The stone, in my view, is a catalyst for transformation. It not only transforms a person but simultaneously everyone who comes in contact with that individual. Unlike Midas, such a gift is earned through the consciousness-raising work of personal alchemy. In my experience, there is some evidence that this is true. I have felt the strong positive effects on my conscious states when I've had the good fortune to be in the company of individuals who had obviously attained a very high level of individuation. Being in the presence of people like the Dalai Lama or

Mother Teresa most certainly has a consciousness-lifting effect even without as much as a word being exchanged.

But, closer to home we might ask what behaviors describe these individuated states of consciousness? What does individuation "look like" in terms of specific behaviors? How, in other words, can we bring this lofty concept of a philosopher's stone down to earth so that we may know what personal alchemical work can do for us?

In describing the "Real Self,"[18] James Masterson, a Freudian analyst, summarizes ten characteristics that give the philosopher's stone a substantial basis of meaning in everyday behavior:

1. The capacity to experience a wide range of feelings deeply with liveliness, joy, vigor, excitement and spontaneity

2. The capacity to expect *appropriate* entitlements (things like food, clothing and shelter that we naturally expect to be given as conditions of early life)

3. The capacity for self-activation and assertion

4. Acknowledgment of self-esteem

5. The ability to soothe painful feelings

6. The ability to make and stick to commitments

7. Creativity

8. Intimacy

9. The ability to be alone

10. Continuity of self (knowing and maintaining who we really are regardless of who we are with or what circumstances we happen to be in)

Rest assured that alchemists would look at this list with contempt. To reduce their precious philosopher's stone to a list of behaviors would most certainly rob it of its mysterious and supernatural power. I only provide it to indicate the very lowest level order that is represented by the extraordinary consciousness associated with the *lapis philosophorum*. I provide this list, not so much to demystify or degrade the stone, but to describe the powerful changes that can take place as we begin working with the psychology of the alchemists.

In this example I want to emphasize the exponential effect that distinguished one of the main properties of the philosopher's stone, and that is its ability to multiply (*multipliatio*). It was sufficient to have a stone that could change one piece of lead into gold, but the true stone, the *lapis,* was believed to be capable of transmuting and multiplying base metals indefinitely!

AN EXAMPLE OF THE REAL SELF

Alchemy is not about addition; its effect on our lives is measured exponentially. The outcome is determined by what we are willing to put into our healing. The investment might be as simple as setting time aside each day to care for our soul, nature or relationship to god. In other cases it may require sacrificing an old way of doing things, or humbling oneself, admitting faults and surrendering to a higher power. For one of my patients, the investment required revealing a terrible secret that she had carried around for many years.

Even though she didn't use the word, this patient put alchemy to work in her life. The principles used, and certainly the outcome, bespoke an effort worth its weight in gold. The return on her investment was greater than she could ever have imagined. She was raised by an abusive, alcoholic father in a small rural town in Canada. When she was old enough, she ran away from home and ended up living in California. Though she had come to find physical safety she could not leave the awful memories behind. They came knocking on her door in the form of terrible symptoms. She had flashbacks, panic attacks and a fierce depression that at times immobilized her. By the time she arrived at my office she was suicidal and in desperate need of help. She was in severe pain and didn't know why. She had lost her job because of her many absences, and in truth, she wasn't productive or very pleasant to be around.

My work in alchemy and psychotherapy has taught me to see the gold hidden in the lead, no matter how obscure it may be. I saw this woman's gold, the purity of her self that even she could not appreciate. I listened to her complaints and began to rearrange her jumbled history of physical and sexual abuse into something that made sense; something that, in the end, would explain her pain and unburden her of the guilt and shame she'd carried around for years. Eventually, she too was able to see past the pain and the terrible memories. She began reassembling the broken pieces of her early life as if it were a giant jigsaw puzzle. In these struggles she caught sight of her innocent self. It was pure and virgin in the original meaning: "being one's own." Within a matter of months she was able to embrace this new sense of self and learned that no man could ever assault her again. With this insight she had found her gold.

The more she concentrated on this image of self, the more it seemed to multiply. The more it multiplied, the better she felt about herself. She could then see how badly damaged she was as a result of the physical abuse and the self-abuse that followed. The lead was turning into gold and it began to shine in her life.

With courage and persistence she forged ahead in therapy, confronting memories, hidden feelings and a variety of distorted self-images. Eventually, her shame dissolved and other painful symptoms evaporated. She began working at a new job she enjoyed. Even so, it took many months of therapy before she was able to accept the praise she now received from her supervisor and coworkers.

The part of this story I most appreciate came when she told me that one of her cousins called from Canada. What I next learned was shocking. This cousin, and virtually every woman in the extended family, had been sexually abused. Apparently, there was a long history of abuse going back for generations. With the help of my patient, her cousin summoned the courage to bring criminal charges against an abusive uncle. This was the very first time any woman in this tiny remote town had refused to conceal the dark secrets that plagued her family for generations.

My patient's therapy set in motion a change that would redirect the course of a crippled evolution that until now left so many precious souls devastated in its wake. The gold my patient discovered hidden in her higher Self multiplied beyond her own life and brought riches to a town that was spiritually and morally bankrupt. Her alchemical process changed the history of this family.

Perhaps the exponential reward that came with this young woman's courage in therapy extends even beyond her family. In a sense, the world is changed whenever any one of us has moved consciousness to a higher level. As for my part, it is satisfying to see that that alchemy had worked its magic.

In Jungian psychology healing is not limited to simply treating mental disorders. Individuation is a process that goes on in everyone's life and can be of great benefit as a means of enriching the personality. Jung's work is particularly helpful to ordinary people who take an extraordinary interest in caring for their psychological well-being. I frequently utilize Jungian techniques in therapy because they emphasize using healthy attributes of the personality to engender healing and promote growth. One favorite method is found in Jung's theory of personality types. As we will see, this theory stems from a very old system of temperament described by Hippocrates.

In their work on psychological types, Kiersey and Bates describe temperament as a "moderation or unification of otherwise disparate forces . . . a kind of thematization of the whole, a uniformity of the diverse."[19] There have been many systems that attempt to describe temperament, including Jung's typology. Jung saw at once the relationship between temperament and alchemy's goal of coalescing the various parts of personality into a meaningful whole. "One's temperament," Kiersey and Bates go on to explain, "is that which places a signature or thumbprint on each of one's actions, making it recognizably one's own."[20]

> Take a look at how the areas described in Figure 1 relate to alchemy and which are most common to your experience. Which ones come easiest? Which ones require a lot of effort?

In the following diagram I describe four areas of human activity that reflect some aspect of alchemy. Whether we use the words "temperament" or "type," our interest lies in how we might use these attributes in the alchemical work of individuation.

In Jung's theory of types, he described four basic ways people orient themselves to life. He called these personality types functions, a somewhat awkward word that suggests the various ways reality is handled by one or any combination of types. The four types and functions are:

THE INTELLECTUAL TYPE. This includes people who are usually described as thinkers. Their approach to life is typically rational, cognitive and analytical. In Figure 1 they gravitate toward knowledge.

In the extreme, an intellectual type can be very impersonal. This can serve them well when all that is needed is a dispassionate argument. It

THE FOUR CORNERS OF PERSONALITY

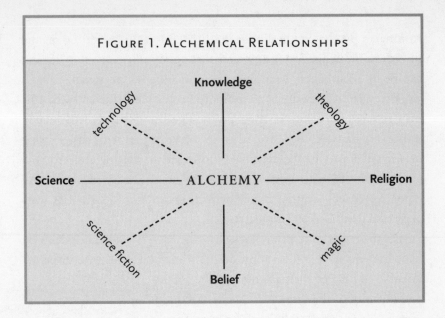

FIGURE 1. ALCHEMICAL RELATIONSHIPS

can also, of course, be the source of many difficulties where the need calls for empathy and caring.

THE FEELING TYPE. Feeling and thinking are the rational functions. Jung believed that "thinking marshals the conscious contents under concepts, feeling arranges them according to their value."[21] Feelings, in this case, are not just passing moods. Like attitudes, feelings give order to the way we feel about things. The feeling function can help organize moods, attitudes and dispositions. I associate this function with the area marked "belief" because our belief system has a powerful influence on how we feel and express emotion.

THE INTUITIVE TYPE. Intuition is a noncognitive way of thinking. It doesn't follow a linear, sequential process of thought. Rather, intuitions more often come out of the blue like hunches, guesses and sometimes powerful insights. I relate this function with religion because of the intuition involved in apprehending the invisible world.

THE SENSATE TYPE. The knowledge that comes directly and immediately through our five senses forms the basis of the sensate type. A scientist who loves getting her hands in the dirt in order to discover its texture, its weight and its composition describes this type well. Where

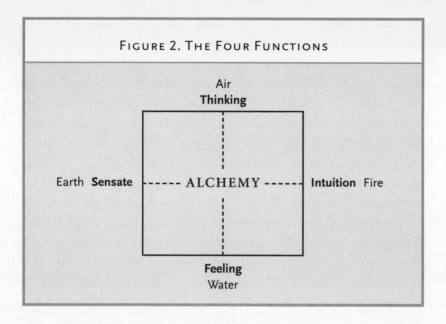

FIGURE 2. THE FOUR FUNCTIONS

Air
Thinking

Earth **Sensate** ----- ALCHEMY ----- **Intuition** Fire

Feeling
Water

the intuitive type tends to be innovative, the sensate is down-to-earth and practical.

Just as the senses are constantly busy picking up new sensory stimuli, the sensate type enjoys all forms of activity. They are most at home with the buzz of the city, crashing waves, cheering crowds and noisy parades.

While there has been much innovative work done to expand Jung's basic model, much can still be gained by simply focusing on his core ideas. As I have noted, Jung's concept of types stems from the early ideas of alchemists. Since, in their view, the four elements compose the entire makeup of the world, so too did they form the physical and psychological dimensions of being human. For this reason, each function is associated with one of the four elements.

Later we will explore the nature of elements and how by "circulating" through them we further the individuation process. But, for now, we can immediately put this scheme to work by using two very powerful methods.

METHOD 1. By identifying your personality type and the way you primarily function in life you will gain a great deal of knowledge about yourself. This position is called your "superior function." Seldom is it the case that a person is a pure type. More often our type includes some characteristics of other types.

Start by identifying your type by choosing one of the cardinal points in figure 2. Then, ask yourself whether you have any of the neighboring traces, either to the right or left, of the type you first identified. There are a number of psychological inventories that can more "scientifically" identify your typology.[22]

Once you've located your superior type, mark it with an "S". Then look to the opposite quadrant to find your inferior type. It should be exactly opposite. Mark it with an "I." Inferior doesn't mean bad. That's the beauty of this model: there is no moral weighting or pathological label. Inferior simply means functions that are least common to your experience. The work of individuation then asks that you strive to develop your inferior functions by becoming more conscious of them and putting them to work in your life.

In addition to the four functions, Jung described a fifth function known as the transcendent function. As we saw in Chinese and Indian alchemy, there were five elements. Some alchemists referred to this fifth element as the ether and others saw it in more idealized forms (a star, the cross, a sacred circle). If everything that is emerges and returns to the ether then is it not possible that the secret of the philosopher's stone can be found in this fifth element?

The quintessence is the alchemical name given to this function. When we are conscious of each element and how it functions in our personality, we have the opportunity to use the transcendent function to meet the specific requirement of any situation. Transcending the elements in this way psychologically means that we've transmuted lead into gold. We have, in other words, fused the four elements, or states of consciousness, and transformed them into a superior state of golden consciousness. This is the reason I put alchemy directly at the intersections in both figures 1 and 2. The quintessence is the perfect alchemy that harmonizes all human activity and every combination of functions necessary for each particular enterprise.

There is no one easy method for describing the discovery and use of the transcendent function. Certainly the use of active imagination can help us tap into it.

METHOD 2. A very special use of active imagination, one used by Jung and many alchemists, was aimed at discovering one's *daimon,* a god or spirit that accompanies you throughout your life. Because the world consists of many spiritual entities, there is no shortage of *daimons* or invisible assistants to aid in one's personal alchemy. Referring to these gods as *theos,* Plato gives us an important description of *daimons* and why we will want to enlist their help.

> The *daimon* is a spiritual agent that mediates between earth and heaven. It is a guardian angel, a constant, inner companion who will, when asked, make important connections between the conscious and unconscious worlds.

> They are the envoys and interpreters that ply between heaven and earth, flying upward with our worship and our prayers, and descending with the heavenly answers and commandments, and since they are between the two estates they weld both sides together and merge them into great whole. They form the medium of the prophetic arts, of the priestly rites of sacrifice, initiation, and incantation, of divination and of sorcery, for the divine will not mingle directly with the human, and it is only through the mediation of the spirit world that man can have any intercourse, whether waking or sleeping, with the gods. There are many spirits, and many kinds of spirits, and Love is one of them.[23]

Our *daimons* are the catalysts we can use to get us in touch with our inner genius. They act as a bridge between the four functions and the transcendent function. In this way we are able to elevate the conscious mind beyond the boundaries of ego. The Real Self is achieved by paying special attention to refinements we can make at the ego level; certainly these psychological functions help in that process. But it is only through the agency of a *daimon* that we can acquire the insights necessary to create even higher forms of the self.

> Reverse the ordinary way you approach things. Instead of working outward from the center, you might work inward to discover ways to bring all the functions of your personality into one integrated whole. Finding your conscious center leads ultimately to discovering your real, authentic self.

One of the main tasks of personal alchemy is to become fully aware of the power of each function and of our ability to use it in the right combination with the others. Becoming aware of our inferior function is a good place to begin. But the real goal of personal alchemy aims at operating on the level of the transcendent function. This insures that no one function will dominate and that all are equally important in the individuation process.

BECOMING WHOLE

Wholeness is not just a cherished goal in alchemy; religions equate wholeness with holiness. In much of the popular literature, wholeness seems to have become the mantra of modern life. Since we will be talking about wholeness over and over again, it is important for us to understand what we mean by it.

If we are striving to become whole, then we must be fairly unwhole to begin with. Our language bespeaks our deep need to feel whole, especially when, in the midst of turmoil, we say we are having a breakdown, or we are going to pieces. Of course we all like to think that the glue that holds body and mind together won't snap under stress, but sometimes this is unavoidable.

In severe cases of mental illness, people really do break down; pieces of their minds become so fractured that they very nearly lose all semblance of an individual identity. In rare instances the psyche is completely splintered into many subpersonalities, a disorder known as multiple personality disorder. Psychosis and multiple personality disorder represent the antithesis of wholeness. The alchemical principle that "as above, so below" can be applied in this situation. Just as an individual might suffer from various degrees of psychic disorder, the same is true of marriages, family and even nations. Individuation is therefore not restricted to individuals. This aspect of alchemical psychology can just as well be applied at a global level.

> The unconscious mind cannot see the unity behind appearances. The individuation of consciousness provides a methodology and a state of mind for discovering that the world is whole. Unity is symbolized in alchemy as gold and the philosopher's stone. In alchemical psychology it represents the Self.

Alchemy holds to the notion that wholeness forms a prototype for all living things. Whether we are conscious of this fact or not, all things evolve in accordance with this grand design. As we have seen, alchemy proposes that we can accelerate this development by applying its principles. "The individuation process," writes Jungian scholar Marie-Louise von Franz, "is more than a coming to terms between the inborn germ of wholeness and the outer acts of fate. Its subjective experience conveys the feeling that some supra-personal force is actively interfering in a creative way."[24]

When we accept that wholeness is stamped on our being at the moment of birth, our entire psychology transforms radically. This first recognition is the threshold of using alchemical psychology to make gold. Instantly our frame of mind enlarges to include nonhuman and even nonearthly powers. Our entire disposition toward life's difficulties changes dramatically and we become creative problem solvers. An attitude that seeks wholeness "does not get annoyed when its growth is obstructed by a stone, nor does it make plans about how to overcome the obstacles. It merely tries to feel whether it should grow more toward the left or the right . . . Like the tree, we should give in to this almost imperceptible, yet powerfully dominating, impulse—an impulse that comes from the urge toward unique, creative self-realization."[25]

We meet our *daimon* when we adopt this perspective. The degree to which this inner voice offers assistance depends on how well we can graciously receive its counsel and discern the origin of its message. Our inner voice, in other words, puts us in direct contact with nature, God and the universe. Without actively listening we are virtually deaf to the cosmic melodies that can change all things.

Wholeness is crucially significant to relationships existing between many subsystems that operate within us physically, psychologically and spiritually. Wholeness is the pattern that holds these systems together. Without tending to wholeness through the work of individuation we leave raw nature to decide our actions through blind impulses and habits. We are then vulnerable to demons of every imaginable kind. On the other hand, having a relationship with our inner voice awakens us to all available energies, their nature and how to work with them.

Wholeness begins when we let go of the illusion that we somehow really have our act together. Such is rarely the case. More often we are at odds with our loved ones and even ourselves. In reality, we are often a mass of conflicting thoughts and feelings, allegiances and disloyalties, good intentions and contradictory behavior. To slap a moral label of badness on ourselves only serves to further fragment our psyche and keep us from wholeness.

> I cannot love you until I first love myself. I cannot wholly accept you until I first wholly accept myself. I must therefore transform my selfishness into empathy, my fears into trust, my doubts into revelations.

Not long ago I saw a play about Jung's life. In it one of Jung's lines struck a powerful chord. Amidst his own marital turmoil, he declares, "I'd rather be whole than good." Alchemy, like nature, persistently strives toward wholeness, meaning that we must at times take the bad with the good in order to achieve the psychological gold, the Individuated Self.

We begin the work of organizing our psyche by forming an inner relationship that heals the many divisions of our mind. In this way we discover increasingly the powers of self that are *already* present. Psychological alchemy is therefore the healing process we use to unify our minds and transform unconscious energies into ones that are conscious and under our control. With such self-knowledge we gain control of our actions. In turn we can then act responsibly with others.

While relationship begins in us, it doesn't end there. Wholeness connects us to people, to nature, to God and country, the world and ultimately the entire universe. It is a good exercise to begin studying the various parts of your inner world, and expanding outward from there.

In India, people greet one another by saying, *"Namaste."* There is a whole philosophy wrapped up in this single word. It roughly means, "the god within me bows to the god within you." This is a lovely way of extending your true Self to others. The greeting simultaneously serves as a reminder that there is only one true Self that exists in all of us. This is a good start, but the alchemist would have us go further.

As we discussed in the first chapter, alchemists believed that the entire world is to some degree conscious. Accordingly, the practice of divine greeting requires you to expand your concept of self to include everything animate and inanimate. While it is surely difficult at

> Start first by considering that consciousness exists in your pets. Children have no problem with this exercise. Even young adults from time to time find themselves staring at their dog or cat, trying as it were to find some signs of sentience in their eyes. To be sure, consciousness is there, but how about your plants? Do they possess any awareness? Research shows that plants and vegetable life do indeed have some amount of awareness. They cringe when threatened and thrive when classical music is played. Now for the big leap: the inanimate world of rocks and minerals.
>
> To proceed further with this exercise it helps to know that at the subatomic level, our physical bodies are composed of the same stuff that comes from the stars. In fact, we are made of the star dust that resulted from a supernova explosion billions of years ago. Basque shamans, known for their deep insight into the nature of the universe, arrived at this startling conclusion long before telescopes were around. They refer to human beings as "walking stars." So when we look up at the stars and see a design that uncannily resembles the human form, you might ask whether this is projection or if it is actually a memory.

times to see past the divisions that separate people, now you are being asked to include objects that do not appear to have any consciousness at all.

The application of alchemy is what brings this Royal Art into our individuation process. In this way, alchemy's old myths and recipes are not just part of history, they are brought to life in the process of our becoming whole. We know the worth of any book on alchemy when we put it to use in our lives and see the results. "The true history of the spirit," said Jung, "is not preserved in learned volumes but in the living psychic organism of every individual."[26]

THE ROYAL ART

Alchemy was known as the Royal Art and its practitioners were referred to as artists. By far the most ambitious goal of their work was to make themselves the object of their own artistic efforts, thereby transforming their untrained minds into ones capable of accomplishing extraordinary feats. In a fourteenth-century manuscript, *Summa Perfectionis*, Geber gives counsel on this important point to the initiate:

> Know, dearest son, that whoever does not know the natural principles in himself, is already far removed from our art, since he does not have the true root upon which he should found his goal.[27]

Modern art has moved away from the traditional fixed mediums of clay and canvas toward the person of the artist. In this new aesthetic form, the artist is the art and the beauty of the art rests not so much in his or her products as it does in the aesthetics of their psychology. How the artist lives life is as much the artistic medium as the work itself. In this view, every act becomes a brush stroke, every word a line of poetry. The artist shapes the nuances of life into an aesthetic that takes art and history to new heights and new depths.

> Alchemy is the Royal Art of living life consciously. The greatest masterpiece produced by this art is the extraordinary individual who has attained wholeness.

With this definition, every person has the capacity to be an artist—an alchemist. The world then becomes a living gallery in which we not only observe but also fully participate.

Jung made his great contributions with the help of his *daimon,* a spiritual being named Philemon. With the assistance of my own *daimon,* Trickster, I wrote this book. It is often the poet who captures the voice of our collective *daimon* and shares it with the rest of the world. In his poem *Alchemy of Love,*[28] Rumi has his *daimon* speak to us:

> *You are the master alchemist.*
> *Through your loving,*
> *Existence and nonexistence merge.*
> *All opposites unite.*
> *All that is profane*
> *Becomes sacred again.*

Chapter 3

At the Threshold

We have not even to risk the adventure alone, for the heroes of all time have gone before us. The labyrinth is thoroughly known, we have only to follow the thread of the hero path. And where we had thought to find an abomination we shall find a god. And where we had thought to slay another we shall slay ourselves. And where we had thought to travel outward we shall come to the center of our own existence and where we had thought to be alone we shall be with all the world.

JOSEPH CAMPBELL

Like everyone else, I celebrated the new millennium as the clock struck twelve on the eve of December 31, 1999. Yet, most of us secretly know that the beginning of the millennium was with the year 2001. Time is ruled more by psychology than reason. We somehow feel more comfortable with whole numbers like 2000, and uncomfortable with endings. The psyche has us skip over the last year of the last thousand years, making 2000 instead of 2001 the starting point for the new millennium; without good reason, we jump right into the next thousand.

We started our journey into alchemy by surveying world history in an effort to appreciate the timelessness and many different facets of this alchemy. In the last chapter we turned our attention to Jung's development of psychological alchemy and learned some methods for changing mental states. Before further exploring some of the basic operations of alchemy, we will look at one final perspective that helps correct the false impression that alchemy ceased to exist toward the end of the sixteenth century. We will be looking at significant events that took place during this period, not so much for the history they provide, but more to understand how the collective psyche changed from the old world of magic into a new age of science and technology.

We will then have three perspectives to understand alchemy and how it continues to be an integral part of the modern world. The material we will cover in the beginning of this chapter can best be thought of as a mythology rather than either a historical or psychological account. Our aim to learn what alchemy can teach us about living life to its fullest remains the same.

One of the most repeated quotes from Jung was his advice to "dream the myth onward." From this view, life can be seen as a mythology and we as actors in a collective drama that reaches from the ancient past and extends far into the future. Alchemy is a vital part of this mythology, one that teaches us how to transform the unconscious through the process of individuation. This mythology encompasses individual as well as collective individuation. Because each of us is part of the collective mythology, we each have the opportunity to contribute to its overall evolution. As we enter the third millennium, I believe we are in a time of great transition that offers enormous opportunity for individual and collective individuation.

Jung was a pioneer in the exploration of consciousness. He salvaged the best of alchemical theory and translated it into a useful, modern language. He was not alone in this effort. There were many others who worked at translating alchemy into a modern science of mind.

One of these great teachers was Manly P. Hall. Although his father was a dentist and his mother a chiropractor, Manly wasn't destined to pursue any sort of medical career. Instead, his passion led him to extensively research the occult and mystical arts. For over sixty years, Manly Hall wrote and lectured on every occult subject from alchemy to ancient Christian mysticism. He wrote his masterpiece, *The Secret Teachings of All Ages,* when he was only twenty-seven years old. While some doubt the veracity of Manly Hall's work, I along with many scholars have found his voluminous writings to be a treasure-house of ancient wisdom. In chapter 5, his alchemical work will help us understand the imaginary beings that inhabit each of the four elements. For now I would like to convey his vision of the great transition of consciousness taking place at the turn of the centuries.

In his book *The Secret Destiny of America,* Manly Hall called for a new psychology that would meet the growing need for integrating objective science with the science of mind. In 1946 he wrote,

> Today we are again seeking for a new world. No longer do there remain undiscovered continents to serve us as laboratories for social experiments, so we are turning our attention to other kinds of worlds—worlds of thought, inner spheres which must yet be explored by daring navigators. Science in the last fifty years has discovered a new universe—the universe of the mind. The infant psychology has but to come of age for us to fully discover a new sphere for new exploration in the science of living.[1]

Among his many books and lectures on the occult sciences, alchemy stands out as having particular relevance to contemporary scientific research. This is especially true as we observe the gradual integration of psychology with various schools of physics and biology. For this reason, I think the infant psychology to which Hall refers is alchemical psychology. Now, fifty years after Hall wrote these words, it is time to start, even in the small-est way, to grow this infant psychology into a practice of daily living. Para-doxically, the place to start is where alchemy was supposed to have ended.

THE MYTH OF ALCHEMY'S DECLINE

In 1572, a tailless star appeared in the constellation of Cassiopea and dis-appeared from the night sky two years later. This celestial event was spied with suspicion by the leading astrologers of the time. Some interpreted it as a sign of great heavenly power being bestowed on the incarnation of King Rudolf II of Hungary as Roman emperor of the entire Christian world. Accordingly, Rudolf was given the title *Dominus Mundi,* Ruler of the World, at the ripe old age of twenty-four.

Rudolf's rise to power reflects the religious conflicts facing Europe at that time. In the early 1500s, Europe was generally divided between the Protestant north and Catholic south. Politically, Charles I, king of Spain, and Rudolf's uncle, the Austrian archduke Ferdinand, controlled most of Europe. Having been raised in Catholic Spain, Rudolf was ex-pected to consolidate the Holy Roman Empire. Instead, Rudolf tried steering a middle course between the extremes of Protestant and Catholic doctrines by engendering a spiritual renaissance that was "uni-versal, tolerant, meditative, as well as scientific." This was no easy task, and despite great strides, Rudolf was not completely successful in the end. In his vision, Prague was to become a universal city that embraced the spiritual dimensions of many faiths and scientific viewpoints.

For all the enthusiasm Rudolf brought to establishing his new king-dom, others had trepidation. The astronomer Tycho Brahe was suspi-cious of the new emperor. He interpreted the appearance and the sudden, mysterious disappearance of a new star that had streaked across the night sky as a very ominous sign. Being the most famous astronomer and alchemist at the time, his interpretation carried a lot of weight. As we shall see, Brahe's prediction was borne out when, in the years 1618–1648, many of the utopian ideals that Prague was to represent went up in flames with the Thirty Years' War.

It is instructive to look more closely at the basis of Brahe's interpre-tation since it offers a glimpse into the scientific thinking at the time. Brahe believed that the disappearance of this star would mean the eventual destruction of the world by fire. He based his reasoning on the current alchemical belief that the celestial world was a place where gods and spirits dwelled in an unchanging, eternal ether. But, this nova[2] seemed to come out of nowhere, signifying that change was as much a part of the heavens as it is here on earth. Something new had not only entered the universe, it came crashing into a consciousness that previously felt safe and secure. A new age of anxiety and uncertainty set in that both explains Brahe's pessimism and upset the canons of science and religion. As developments unfolded, the new star proved to herald an end of a magical era and set the stage for a new world of empirical philosophy.

This period of history is critical to our understanding of alchemy's relevance to contemporary life. It provides a story that explains the confusion surrounding alchemy: how it is different from modern science and what it can offer us today. This is not just a history lesson of some faraway place; it is the story of how modern people came to think and feel about themselves and their relationship with the world.

Rudolf chose Prague as the seat of his royal residence. There were many political reasons for his choice, but perhaps the most convincing one had to do with another cosmological event that occurred millions of years ago. The basin of Bohemia in which Prague is located was created by the impact of a gigantic meteorite. This is the stuff of which myths and legends are made, but there is, in this case, real scientific evidence to prove that this really happened. As a result of the impact, the geology of the Bohemian basin became rich in gold, silver and pitchblende, the natural source of uranium.

In addition to emulating his father's love of freedom, Rudolf also inherited a passion for the occult. Although raised in a Catholic country, Rudolf received much of his early formal education from Philip II, an uncle and Charles I's successor to the throne of Spain, who taught him the secrets of the occult and mystical sciences. For this reason, Rudolf was probably well informed about the lore surrounding Prague and its magical significance. Guided by his uncle, Rudolf learned about alchemy, and as emperor held court to hundreds of practicing alchemists. Rudolf, who had his own alchemical laboratory, came to be known as "the alchemical king."

Under Rudolf's leadership, Prague replaced other seats of power, including Paris and even Rome. Prague would emerge for a time as the heart of Europe. From a psychological perspective, Prague represented a vessel in which were being transformed the old world of myth and magic to a new world that would shift the focus to empirical science. This period represents a major transition in collective consciousness. I believe this period in history describes the birth of modern consciousness. In this sense, even the name Prague, drawn from the word *prah* or threshold, marks the place where the visible and the invisible worlds converge.

Rudolf transformed Prague into a great city. It became the meeting place of such great minds as Kepler, Jakob Boehme, Giordano Bruno, John Dee, and René Descartes, some of the leading scientists and philosophers at that time. But, for as much as their contributions brought Prague to prominence, their personalities and ideologies cast a long shadow. This is as true for countries as it is for individuals: darkness always accompanies greatness.

While a new consciousness of thought struggled to be born, the old world, with its reliance on magic, would not go away easily. Some alchemists held on to their beliefs while others tried to integrate magic with the demands of modern scientific methods. Observation alone would not do in this new age of reason; repeatable, proven experiment was replacing the old methods of argument and observation. The struggle for dominance affected some of the most learned and powerful people of that period. Rudolf himself came under suspicion as being too eccentric, occult and self-possessed. Then there was the whole misadventure of Dee and the infamous Edward Kelly.

John Dee, adviser to the king, was suspected to be surreptitiously acting as a secret agent in the service of Queen Elizabeth. Most certain was the fact that this brilliant mathematician had fallen under the spell of a maverick named Edward Kelly. Apart from his preoccupation with seances and necromancy, Kelly was a known forger with a dubious reputation for secrecy and pretension. Nonetheless, what knowledge he had of alchemy and his special gift for contacting spirits convinced Dee, and even Rudolf, of his powers to transmute metals. With Edward Kelly by his side, Dee conjured up spirits and communicated with angels. Together they commanded respect in the emperor's court, that is, until a spirit named Madimi appeared in one of their many seances. Her suggestion that Dee and Kelly swap wives raised many an eyebrow. This put an abrupt end to their magical studies. Eventually, Dee returned to England after nearly abandoning his serious scientific work entirely.

Kelly stayed on in Prague and was asked by Rudolf to supervise a great alchemical work taking place in the Powder Tower in Prague Castle. Rudolf was so impressed that he made Kelly a "Golden Knight."[3] But, in the end, excessive secrecy and pretensions led to his falling out of favor with the emperor. After killing a servant of the Imperial Court, Rudolf had him imprisoned. Although pardoned, Kelly was jailed a second time. He died trying to escape from prison.

To the extent that Dee epitomized scholarship, Kelly represented the dark world of magic and superstition. Dee turned to Kelly for the imaginative powers he lacked. Without Kelly's reputed angelic communications, Dee's scholarship rang hollow. In this curious pair we find an alchemical mix of science and magic dramatically juxtaposed. One, a well-respected scientist, the other a conjurer, recall the alchemical image of the *rebis,* or double thing. The *rebis* represents a hermaphroditic creature that either joins contrary elements in a metal, thereby transforming it, or worse, a monster at odds with itself. In the case of this illustrious pair, science and magic were competing with each other for dominance. The mixture not only characterizes this curious pair but also the zeitgeist that was giving shape to the new world.

During this period, Prague was both a black, charred, magical cauldron and a bright chemical vessel from which a new alchemy was emerging. To this day, one can feel this strange brew.

Immediately on my arrival in Prague I was struck with two unavoidable impressions: everything is made of stone and there is music everywhere. The cobblestone streets, the bridges and statues, the cathedrals, castles and squares, all made of iron-gray stone. No more were the words "philosopher's stone" merely intellectual or symbolic; in Prague you can't help but feel the permanence of memory etched into these massive stones. There is even a palpable feeling that Prague remains a place in transition, where an old world is still in the process of giving way to a new one.

At the time of Rudolf's reign, the old guard representing the last bastions of magic, religion and the Hermetic Sciences demanded radical change. No longer would magic suffice. Science now had to serve the public's need, not just that of the privileged few. These ideas swirled around in the minds of thoughtful people from all factions of society. The religious mystic Jakob Boehme tried to invigorate Lutheran piety with the mystical alchemy of the fourteenth-century work of Paracelsus. While he espoused the glory of inner, transcendent experience, the great philosopher of reason, René Descartes, condemned alchemy as nothing more than a throwback to animistic magic. His famous maxim, "I think therefore I am," declared supremacy of the intellect and separation between body and mind. Many sincere, scholarly people joined the battle marking this intellectual and spiritual revolution. Unfortunately, it would take blood and guts to usher in the Age of Reason.

Even Descartes was not spared from participating in actual warfare. He served in the Imperial army and took part in the famous Battle of White Mountain. As historian Robert Vurm points out in his book *Rudolf II and his Prague,* Brahe correctly predicted that "all the hopes of the religious world of Europe, as represented by Rosicrucian ideals, were to perish in the fires of the Thirty Years' War."[4] The war between Lutherans and Catholics raged on from 1618 to 1648, gutting central Europe and claiming the lives of nearly a third of the peoples living in Bohemia.

The seeds of the Thirty Years' War began at the end of Rudolf's reign and indeed his life. Caught between various religious factions and political intrigues, Rudolf's attempts to chart a course between the bastions of social classes and religious strongholds ultimately failed. In 1609, he was "compelled to sign the so-called Charter of Toleration, the Letter of Majesty, guaranteeing spiritual freedom,"[5] a document that went further than Rudolf was prepared to go. Accused by his brother Mattias, who had always coveted the throne, for neglecting the affairs of state in favor of lofty alchemical experimentation, Rudolf was ultimately deposed in 1611. Thus ended Rudolf's dream of the Prague he once envisioned as a universal city. Bitterly alone and exiled, Rudolf cursed the great city he had built:

> Prague, ungrateful Prague, I have made you famous but now you are driving me, your benefactor, out. Let revenge come upon you and damnation befall you and the whole Czech nation![6]

With this crushing defeat, the formal practice of alchemy came to an end. Without government sponsorship, alchemy lost its credibility and leading scientists would henceforth conduct their alchemical experiments in private. Nonetheless, even as war erupted out of the Rudolfine period, Europe would never again be the same. Out of the ashes of the thirty-year war, a new world that embraced religious diversity and a new scientific paradigm was born. I see Rudolf as the person who symbolizes a confluence of opposites—magical and scientific, religious and spiritual—that would come to represent an alchemy that would ultimately contribute to the establishment of a new world.

Prague was a daring political and religious experiment in government. In this period we witnessed a struggle for new religious freedoms and spiritual expression that became the foundation of our modern era. Science had come to a crossroads where an old tradition of magic was being left behind and a new empirical science took center stage. Alchemy, being a mixture of magic and science, had to radically change. While its open, formal practice was forced underground in the sixteenth century, its main goal of uniting the opposites remains a challenge still to be met three centuries later.

> • Alchemy is an inextricable part of the history of science without which we would lose the important contributions made by the occult sciences.
> • Alchemy is the cornerstone of a contemporary psychology of the unconsciousness. Jung's psychology of individuation is a modern example par excellence of alchemical psychology.
> • Alchemy is a piece of world mythology that describes the collective individuation of consciousness.

This brief summary of Rudolf and his attempts to join the disparate needs of faith, government, and science represents a piece of world mythology that helped set the foundation for the modern age. Contemporary science and religion have come to represent a pair of opposites in the modern psyche that need to be united if ever we are to learn how to live as whole and fully conscious human beings.

A NEW WORLD   In chapter 8 I will present ten recipes drawn from very old alchemical manuscripts. By putting them into historical context, we discover the depth of their meaning and use them in more powerful ways. We carry history around in our mind and body. The brain is a structure in which the whole of evolution is etched: the reptilian brain continues to carry out orders of an ancient time while the cerebrum cortex functions in more complex, creative ways. Psyche, the brain's counterpart, is an immense storehouse of images, archaic memories and ancient knowledge. From this perspective, the essence of alchemical wisdom is already present and operating in the minds and hearts of everyday people. Our job is to bring this wisdom to the forefront of consciousness and fulfill the alchemists' dreams of peace and harmony.

Even as I write these words, it seems astounding that we are really capable of accomplishing the alchemists' goals. However, being a psychotherapist, I spend a good amount of my time working to help individuals make the unconscious conscious. These experiences answer my doubts with convincing evidence that our goal is well within reach. Daily I find myself amazed by the alchemical processes going on in peoples' lives. The evidence comes from the young woman who walked out of the hospital on her own feet after suffering psychological paralysis that had immobilized her legs for years. It comes from the young couple I successfully treated for the compulsive sadistic behaviors that they thought were necessary before having sexual relations. It's the woman who came to me for help days after she'd fallen into a drunken stupor and parked her car in the fast lane of a major highway.

Seldom do I mention the word alchemy to my patients, but to my mind these examples come straight out of alchemy's textbook. There is the king and queen and their association with our inner sexual beings; lead as it relates to depression, death and unconscious; Mercurius, the trickster god who goads us onward in the individuation process. In our continued adventure into alchemy we will unveil these images and see directly the psychological aspects they represent. Once you know a bit about the Royal Art, you can see lead being turned into gold right in front of your eyes. For as foreign as alchemy is to most people's everyday experience, we need not look far before it emerges in some of the most ordinary places.

In my experience, patients want healing recipes to take home with them. These may be sayings, proverbs and alchemical phrases that represent wisdom handed down to us from past generations. We will have the opportunity of recalling some wonderful alchemical recipes in chapter 8. Remembering them and applying recipes to the right situation at the right time brings old wisdom to life.

All too often, some of our modern biases blind us to the benefits recipes have had for millions of people who came before us. I suggest that we need to recall this special kind of common sense that went into crafting old recipes and meld it with the fantastic developments happening in virtually every area of modern science and technology. The science of mind is a conscious endeavor to use the recipes of common sense—and some that are not so common—to bring peace, harmony and wholeness into our lives and the world.

America is still the New World, where this kind of alchemy is happening at every level of society. Alchemists are not limited to healers or patients. Alchemy is woven into the character of all Americans by dint of their cultural diversity, pioneering inventiveness and sense of limitless adventure.

We are young in spirit, old in soul; the two make a splendid recipe for making us whole. How then do we proceed?

DIRECTIONS FOR PERSONAL USE

Alchemy is as much about *doing* as it is about *understanding* human psychology. Having explored some of its history, myths and lore, we will want more practical knowledge about how to do the work of psychological alchemy. Here are some guidelines in preparation for making good use of alchemy and its recipes.

WHERE DO I START? You have already started. Alchemy is an ongoing process, whether it operates at a conscious or unconscious level. The body, for example, is an exquisite alchemical machine. The information contained in this book will assist you in making your alchemy a conscious process and an important part of your individuation. When we consider the first recipe, this question will be answered in a more precise way. Specifically, the recipe helps us identify the *prima materia,* or first matter of transformation.

HOW DO I APPROACH THE WORK OF PERSONAL ALCHEMY? With an open mind. This is not as easy as it sounds. Most of us born and raised in the United States are materialists. When Americans approach the unconscious psyche in a materialistic way, it reacts in kind. As one Jungian analyst put it, "the unconscious takes the same attitude toward the ego as the ego takes toward it."[7] It is best to adopt an attitude that leaves open all possibilities, not just the ones dictated by the rules of a materialistic culture. Gold is not the goal of alchemy; it is a reflection of its success.

In psychological alchemy, imagination is just as important as cognition. It relies more on an intuitive approach to the work. So even when things do not appear rational, do not dismiss them. Dreams, fantasies and hunches are ingredients that go into the psychic vessel of transformation. Especially be alert to odd happenings, chance encounters and unexpected events. Synchronistic events are good signs that transformation is occurring.

WILL PSYCHOLOGICAL ALCHEMY ENABLE ME TO CHANGE PHYSICAL MATTER? Yes. Without a doubt the mind has mastery over the body. Healing is not limited to psychological change but includes resolving physical illness as well. In fact, there is ample research to show that many psychological practices, including meditation and prayer, not only help cure disease but can prevent it. Alchemical psychology joins with other disciplines in the growing armamentarium of healing practices designed to mobilize the powerful resources of nature contained within the body.

DOES THIS BOOK ADDRESS PSYCHOLOGICAL OR SPIRITUAL ISSUES? I am a psychologist and my purpose in writing this book is to make alchemy a useful psychological technique. However, in order to put alchemy into context, it is necessary to show where psychology ends and spirituality begins. I believe the philosopher's stone represents a set of well-developed behaviors, but it extends well beyond psychology. It is my fervent hope that people will be excited by this prospect and take alchemy to its furthest extent. This book offers a place to begin that journey.

DO I NEED TO SET UP A LABORATORY? No, not literally. The real laboratory is *you* . . . it's your life. We are mostly concerned with esoteric, psychological alchemy. It is actually the highest order of alchemy and therefore the most difficult. Instead of changing physical substances, we are attempting to transform consciousness. This is not to say that working with physical materials is unimportant. On the contrary: alchemy is chiefly about manifestation. With psychological alchemy, the manifestation occurs in having a real-life experience with concomitant behavioral change. The proof of your work is always in the eating of the pudding.

A psychological laboratory is one that seals off your alchemical work from distractions, unhelpful criticisms and unwanted influences. Alchemical work has two faces, one private, the other public. We do our inner work in private while the changes are fortified and tested in the public sphere. Our laboratory is filled with books, journals, music and any objects that stir the imagination.

DO I NEED A TEACHER? Although it is not necessary, it helps. Going it alone requires courage and an incredible capacity to detach your awareness and see yourself objectively. While this sounds impossible, it is not. Actually, we remove our consciousness all the time. We faint, deny and distract ourselves from pain. But, in this case, the object of our detachment is not something external, it is our very own real self. To gain an objective understanding of who we really are we must unpeel the many layers of "false selves" that invariably result from parental, societal, religious and political influences. More often than not we think we know who we really are and then only learn from conflicts in our lives how sadly mistaken we are.

You can see how difficult this process can be without the help of someone else. A trusted teacher helps by reflecting back to us what we need to change.

The greater part of alchemy's history took place during times before the invention of the printing press. Thus, knowledge was transmitted along the lines of an oral tradition. This created a special teacher-student relationship that kept sacred knowledge safe. Alchemical knowledge alone is never enough to complete the work. This is because consciousness is transmitted from teacher to student in nonverbal ways. No book can convey the power derived from a relationship with a gifted teacher.

HOW THEN DO I FIND A TEACHER? There is an old saying in India that directs a person to a teacher. "When the student is ready, a master will come." When you meditate on this desire in a sincere and persistent way, a teacher will come, but if your eyes are closed you will not see him or her. Teachers come in many different ways. They can be tricksters, adversaries, mentors or spiritual masters.

My teachers have come by way of healing. I have had three analysts, Drs. Robert Johnson, Jack Laney and Pan Coukoulis, all very wise and special men who have taught me invaluable lessons. They did not give me lessons in alchemy per se, but rather, helped me plumb the depths of my own unconscious psyche, where I have found my *prima materia*. Alchemy is never about making miracles but, through a teacher, learning how to nurture the riches buried in the soil of your own psyche. Then, sometimes, miracles happen.

SHOULD I KEEP MY WORK SECRET? Not necessarily. Private is a better word for insulating the matter being worked on. Otherwise, it is open to all sorts of contamination: distracting noise, uninvited criticism and competing demands. As with any scientific experiment or physical operation, it is best to create a stable, quiet place so that the changes that occur come from you alone. This sacred space is referred to in the Greek language as a *teminous*. It is a secret, sacred place where you feel safe enough to do most anything necessary to further the work.

ARE THERE DANGERS ASSOCIATED WITH DOING PERSONAL ALCHEMY? Yes there are. Since we are not discussing physical alchemy, I think we can safely rule out the dangers of poison and explosion, which led to the unfortunate end of many an alchemist. The dangers of psychological alchemy are particular to the individual, their temperament and psychological constitution. A solitary individual may become overly detached from reality, a dangerous situation that can lead to depression and even psychotic conditions. Particularly during certain early stages of the work, depression is not uncommon.

Each of the types described in the last chapter can, in the extreme, throw the psyche out of balance. Too much thinking, feeling, sensing or intuition can cause problems. For example, when we overthink a situation, we are subject to "analysis paralysis," where we lose the ability to put our thoughts into action.

There are other dangers that have less to do with the individual's type than their innate constitution. An unbridled imagination can give way to delusions and hallucinations for the person who is not well grounded in reality. Similarly, the use of mind-altering drugs has no place in alchemy. Although it has been argued that some alchemists used psychoactive substances, it is my opinion that such practice is dangerous and misguided.[8]

While I appreciate the desire to immediately gain access to ecstatic experience, it is foolhardy to get there without the "eyes to see it clearly." So to the list of psychological dangers I must add undo haste, desire and addiction. Be forewarned: all haste impedes the process. The goal of alchemy is to raise the level of consciousness, not reduce it to unreal states of mind. Preserving and disciplining ego consciousness is as important in this work as achieving the refined levels of superconsciousness associated with the Individuated Self.

The scope of alchemy is enormous. In doing this work we are changing the structure of matter and the substance of soul. Arrogance is perhaps the greatest danger in pursuing these lofty goals and is why humility must accompany the alchemist every step of the way. Jung speaks of the dangers and rewards of personal alchemy in his commentary to *The Secret of the Golden Flower*. This book on Taoist alchemy was given to Jung by the sinologist Richard Wilhelm. Its ancient text confirmed Jung's early theories that alchemists were searching for ways to transform their minds as well as transmute metals. In his commentary, Jung cautioned:

> The way is not without danger. Everything good is costly, and the development of personality is one of the most costly of all things. It is a matter of saying yea to oneself, of taking oneself as the most serious of tasks, of being conscious of everything one does, and keeping it constantly before one's eyes in all its dubious aspects—truly a task that taxes us to the utmost.[9]

HOW DO THE RECIPES IN THIS BOOK WORK? This book is a collection of very old recipes. These are not cooking recipes. They are, in the true definition of their meaning, prescriptions. Unlike medical prescriptions that too often simply require passively swallowing a pill, these recipes require the participation of soul and spirit as well as body. Swallow and digest these "pills" with great imagination. Define the recipes in behavioral terms that can be applied on every level of experience: mind, body and soul. Practice diligently, faithfully and creatively those experiments you set up for yourself.

As we continue our investigation into the psychology of alchemy we will find many more nuggets of gold in stories, myths and legends of the past. By bringing the gold of the Old World into the light of current reality, we cross an important threshold that promises to restore a sacred view of the world.

Chapter 4

Preparing the Cook

May nature, reason, experiment and reading be the guide, staff,
spectacles and lamp for him who participates in chemistry.

MICHAEL MAIER,
CAPTION FROM *ATALANTA FUGIENS*

Physician, heal thyself.

LUKE 4:23

We have found a strange footprint on the shores of the unknown.
We have devised profound theories, one after another, to account for its origin.
At last, we have succeeded in reconstructing the creature that
made the footprint. And lo! It is our own.

EDDINGTON,
PHILOSOPHY OF PHYSICAL SCIENCE

The secrets of alchemy's origins lie hidden in its own name. The word alchemy has a dual meaning, each meaning pointing in a different direction: one down, the other up. The word alchemy comes from the Arabic *al kimia*. The first word simply means "the," but the second word has a host of meanings. Most often it relates to Egypt as "The Land of the Black Soil," a reference to the "fertile Nile mud [which] was the analogue of the Marsh of Creation in which Hathor moves."[1] In Egyptian mythology, Hathor was known as Mother of the World, endowed with tremendous healing and creative powers. For these reasons, alchemy was sometimes referred to as the "Egyptian Art" or the "Black Art."

Egypt was then the Black Land, and its sacred river, the Nile, the major life force that flows through it. For any desert land, water is the source of life. The waters of the Nile were believed to flow out of the heavens by virtue of the powers of Aten, the Egyptian god of the sun. The riverbed cradling this sacred river was therefore the source of all creation; exposure of its mud as the water receded exposed some part of the deep primordial mystery of all creation. Psychologically, we equate this black mud with the unconscious and its dark, shadowy contents. We are drawn down into this primordial ooze and the depths of the unconscious with this definition.

In perhaps a more familiar way, we find similar associations between this theme of light and dark in the Christian mythology. Lucifer, we recall, was cast out of heaven along with legions of other fallen angels. Alchemists believed that these angels first encountered women, who seeing the heavenly powers they possessed, traded sexual favors in exchange for the secrets of transformation. Intercourse between humans and divine beings is a crude, mythic way of describing the integration between earth and heaven. In this image, we find a connection between the white, pure light of heaven and the dark powers of earth.

Too much has been made of equating darkness with evil. According to Islam, the darkness here relates to Lucifer's refusal to bow down before humans because of his love for the one God. Sexual intercourse then became the agent for transforming his disobedience into love. It is an act of redemption and yet another way of showing how the symbolism of lead is transmuted into gold. To most people, Lucifer is a black angel, but the secret of his alliance with the occult arts is revealed in the meaning of his name, "bearer of light."

Unsurprisingly, alchemy is one of the three basic occult (or black) arts and its craft probably began with the work of blacksmiths and shamans. The black period of our lives calls up times when we were unconscious, either because we had not yet achieved awareness or because we behaved in ways to deny consciousness. When overcome with grief or drugs we black out because our ego cannot sustain the demands put on it. We are in darkness at birth and when we sleep. It therefore makes sense that alchemy is a black art devoted to the craft of bringing light to the dark experiences of the human life.

This craft is included in another, less-known derivation of the name alchemy. It comes from the Greek *chymia,* meaning "to cast," as in casting a metal. Digging deeper into the etymology, we find even more revealing origins. *Chymia* may have been derived from the Egyptian verb *km,* meaning "to complete, bring to a close, execute (the preparation of ointments), finish off (metalwork)."[2] The historian Jack Lindsay explains how these various derivations connect to explain more fully the occult meaning of the word alchemy:

> The work gave the advice needed for completing or fulfilling what the gods had already made inherent or potential in human actions and material objects in the process of creating them. *Km* would thus in one sense mean the repetition of the original creation of the world— expressing human creativity as derived from and imitation of the divine activity.[3]

Casting a metal requires the use of fire. It is this element that bridges the two basic meanings of alchemy. Fire is central to alchemy, making it the art that enables us to take dark, undeveloped substances and cast them into refined, useful and even beautiful objects. Whether that substance is lead or the dark ignorance of the human mind, the alchemist's goal was the bringing of light to darkness. By borrowing from the lessons provided by nature, the alchemist worked to complete what God left undone. With this definition of the word, we are drawn upward. It is a spiritual ascent, with fire being the medium of transformation.

Another surprising discovery we find in exploring the roots of alchemy is that iron, not gold, was the metal regarded by early alchemists as having supreme value. It was neither stone nor gold that symbolized the goal of the work to our earliest ancestors. It was the discovery of iron that uplifted humans out of dark Stone Age consciousness and began a new age of humanity known as *homo faber* (man as maker).

In his brilliant analysis *The Forge and the Crucible*, mythologist Mircea Eliade traces the roots of alchemy's origins to the Iron Age. While stone, as Eliade points out, "is an archetypal image expressing absolute reality,"[4] it was the discovery of iron that precipitated the making of tools and weapons. Many years would pass before humans would discover the iron deposits hidden deep under the earth's surface and invent ways to craft the iron into implements needed to create a civilized world. Before then, humans treated iron as they did stone, but regarded it as a precious substance delivered to them from the gods.

Iron was initially discovered in the remains of fallen stars—meteorites. As a result, primitive peoples believed that iron possessed magical qualities, ones even more precious than gold. It is interesting in light of this evidence that the alchemists eventually drew upon the image of stone to signify the absolute reality that forms the foundation of their metal-making practices.

The great discovery of iron deposits within the earth's crust allowed mining to begin. Eliade describes this transition from meteoric to telleric (mined ore) as a giant leap in the evolution of consciousness. Without it there would have been no Industrial Revolution, much less consciousness of the complexity we find in modern human beings. Iron ore extracted from deep mine shafts was cast by forge and anvil into the materials used to build the modern world. Mining is no easy task. It requires engineering, architecture and a thorough knowledge of materials. These challenges brought an interaction between mind and matter that laid the foundation of alchemical psychology.

How strange it is when I hear worrisome people talk of the possibility of earth being struck by a meteor. What, we might ask, would life be like if by chance no meteor ever struck the earth?

Along with the gift of iron sent down in meteor showers, so too did we receive fire in the form of lightning. Without fire, the blast furnaces

IRON

that melt metals would not have been lit and the whole post–Stone Age history would have been radically different. These are the ingredients critical to discovering our capacity to make things. The nature of consciousness became active, and in concert with nature, we acquired the ability to transform trees into houses, iron into bridges and stone into great cathedrals. We became able, in other words, to invent the world of our dreams.

Creating is a feminine activity in which we allow the unconscious to come through us. Our hands give shape to its message in the form of pictures and poems. Inventing, on the other hand, is more masculine. Now I do not mean the terms "feminine" and "masculine" to be taken literally; they describe two aspects of consciousness—the art of creation and the science of invention.

The great mathematician and physicist Isaac Newton was an inventor; he also practiced alchemy. Gregory Bateson once remarked that "Newton did not discover gravity; he invented it." In Michael White's biography, *Newton the Last Sorcerer,* the renowned physicist's life is seen as the story of a man struggling to integrate the magic of the Old World with the science of a new age.[5] White describes him as a driven, obsessed man who is at times a tyrant at odds with his colleagues and his own soul.

Newton seems to typify many of the great alchemists. A keen intellect, a sharp tongue and laserlike ambition enabled them all to cut through the bedrock of ignorance and mystical intolerance. But these alone were not enough. The gentler qualities that accompany the act of creating require an appreciation for unconscious forces and a deep, abiding respect for nature. These qualities go into preparing the alchemist for the work.

Alchemy has come a long way since these primitive origins, but the archetypal significance of the post-Industrial Age is not unlike the evolutionary transition that took early humans from the passive age of stone to the inventive activities of the Iron Age and beyond. The same fire that was sent down from above dwells within us. It is the spark of inspiration, the seed of invention, that enables us to finish the divine labor of the gods.

Alchemy, the black art, has always been shrouded in mystery. Its art and manuscripts contain images that are dark, paradoxical and surrealistic. To the uninitiated, this visual vocabulary makes no sense. Like a dream, these strange images appear without rhyme or reason. They somehow offend our sensibility and we turn away from them. The psyche, no less than everything else in nature, hangs on a delicate balance between chaos and order. The sparks that fly from this fire ignite our understanding and passion for life. "The most beautiful thing we can experience," wrote Einstein, "is the mysterious. It is the source of all true art and science. He to whom this emotion is a stranger, who can no longer pause to wonder and stand rapt in awe, is as good as dead: his eyes are closed."[6]

Mystery holds the secrets of nature. It keeps the balance that allows the worlds of earth and mind to continue on an orderly course through space. Mystery holds the dark and light aspects of nature in a perfect blend. In Jung's final book on alchemy, *Mysterium Coniunctionus,* we find a wealth of information on how the alchemists attempted to maintain this balance and how to restore it when disturbed.

Native American Indians were well aware of the dangers posed by too much law and order, or too little of it. Many tribes had clowns, fools and tricksters to counteract the ill effects of too much reason, and a chief to maintain the balance. Even great chiefs, like Black Elk, were known as *heyokas,* "contraries" who performed tricks and often acted out the opposite to what most people expected. Joseph Epes Brown, an authority on the Plains Indian cultures, tells one of the many shocking stories of Black Elk's antics:

> How in your own life do you maintain psychic equilibrium? Do you know your mystery? Do others? Is there enough mystery in your life to offset the facts and figures that weigh heavily on your brain? What do you do if there is too much craziness, or not enough of it?

It was in Denver—which was not a very pleasant city in the early 1940s; there was a great deal of prejudice and racism, and we had a hard time finding a hotel room. When we did find one it was a very dingy, horrible room and Black Elk felt bad about Denver and the hotel; he felt unclean and he wanted a sweat bath to cleanse himself of the impurities of that city. I didn't know how this could be done in a hotel room; but the room was heated by a coal fire, and the fireplace was brick and so old the bricks were falling out of it. He said, "Here, let's take these loose bricks, and we'll pull some more out of the chimney and heat them in the coal fire," which we did. Then we took the chairs in the room and put them in a circle, and took all the bedding off the beds and put them over the chairs to make a kind of lodge right there in the middle of the room. We found an old coal scuttle and when the bricks were red hot we put them in the coal scuttle, put that in the little lodge, and stripped down and crawled in; and it was good and hot in there and we sang and prayed and smoked and sweated and it was real good, you know? I think that was the first time a sweat bath has ever been taken in a Denver hotel room; but that is typical of the kind of things that happen with these people—the unexpected, breaking with habitual patterns, adds a dimension to life that I think is terribly important.[7]

Don't try this at home! Nevertheless an ounce of humor is good for the soul. A well-crafted joke often cracks open a truth we've all known but were unwilling to openly admit. This element of humor is a function of the trickster. His role is so important to alchemy that I will have much more to say about him and his cadres of imps, spirits and gods in the next chapter.

The conceptual artist Christo made a profound social statement in his work that is important to personal alchemy. He went around wrapping things up with rope and canvas. If it weren't for the size of the things he wrapped, we probably would never have taken notice of him or his art.

He wrapped up bridges and buildings, leaving them for as long as it took for people to begin wondering what lay hidden beneath the cloth. Christo injected mystery back into the ordinary objects of modern life. The mystery of magic, and alchemy along with it, was all but wiped out with the advent of modern science. People like Newton and Einstein managed to hold on to that mystery, but there have been many more who have lost all sight of it.

> Take a look at your own life and ask if there is any place in it that holds mystery. It seems that one of the most attractive features that women have is their mystery, a feature I find too often lacking in men.

In virtually every book on alchemy, you find writing and artwork produced principally by men. It certainly leads one to conclude that alchemy is a very structured set of techniques. This is one of the most deceptive aspects of alchemy. While it is mostly men who have authored the history of alchemy, its substance is decidedly feminine. A book on alchemy, written from the feminine perspective, is sorely needed. The involvement of the feminine in this book comes from five places: the *Anima Mundi* (world soul), the contrasexual aspect in a man's personality (*anima*), soul (*luna*) as the unconscious aspect in all people, the mystical role of women in the work (*sora mystica*) and women as practicing alchemists.[8] While much more work is needed in this area of research, rest assured of the critical importance the feminine plays at every level of the work.

KEEPING A SECRET

Alchemists went to great lengths to keep their secret recipes out of the wrong hands. However, even if their knowledge happened to fall into unscrupulous hands, the secrets would be useless. Without a mind that had gained insight into itself and the ways of Nature through arduous labor, the true power hidden in cryptic spells, incantations and specific operations of the work would be of no use. The opus then is protected by what Kerenyi called the *arreton,* or the unutterable, and what the poet Goethe referred to as a sacred open secret. It is like something that stands right in front of your face, but you have not the eyes to see it.

Mystery is what happens when vital information is withheld for the purpose of creating a numinous condition. We relish mystery for the sacredness of its experience and the secrets it can reveal to us.

We must of course use discretion to hold back knowledge that might either be misused or impede sacred experience. The physicist Wittgenstein gives good counsel on this matter. "Whereof one cannot speak, thereof one must remain silent."[9] The use of silence is powerful. It allows the soul to well up and find its own beautiful voice among the endless chatter of the mind. When we can silence our minds, the true gold shines through the darkness of the unconscious.

The real secret of alchemy is that it had more to do with transforming one's mind than with changing metals. "To the true alchemist," writes Morris Berman, "gold was the end, not the means. The manufacture of gold was the culmination of his own long spiritual evolution, and this was the reason for his silence."[10] Not only did the gold then reflect endless labors in the physical laboratory, but psychologically, it represented years spent in developing spiritual and psychological character.

> Keeping a secret requires
>
> • silence, which is not to be confused with avoidance
> • discretion in how we speak and what we say
> • reverence for sacred and numinous experience
> • spiritual and psychological practice
> • excellent character

The alchemist worked hard to develop an invincible character in order to maintain the silence necessary for inner transformation. Not only must the vessel holding acids and boiling liquids be strong enough to endure the heat, the alchemist's personality had to hold the secrets, passions and illuminations issuing forth from his experiments. Albertus Magus, a magician who taught Thomas Aquinus the ways of the mystical arts, described some of the necessary traits of character needed to make a successful alchemist. In *De Alchemia,* he suggests that the initiate possess traits of character that include being discrete, reserved, patient, persistent, diligent and unwearying.

To this list he adds another that rings especially true today in the politics of funding research. Magus says that, "Above all [the initiate] should avoid involvement with princes and lords. To begin with, they will urge him to accelerate the Work unduly, and in case of non-success he will be subjected to the worst torments; while if he does succeed, prison will be his reward."[11] Clearly, discrimination and tact are as important to the work as discretion.

Added to this growing list of traits necessary for success in alchemy is another, and perhaps the most important: a single-mindedness to unveiling Nature's secrets as they exist in us and in every particle of life. "Perhaps," explains Jungian analyst Esther Harding, "the most essential requisite for participating in the 'great work' is an attitude of devotion, a seriousness of purpose in seeking to understand the full meaning of life, an utmost striving that the supreme value called the Self may be rescued from the darkness of the unconscious."[12]

The purpose of alchemy is to accelerate the evolution of mind and matter. In this regard, Magus wisely reminds us that we can err by either going too fast or hastening the work for the wrong reason. We cannot, in other words, act out of greed, pride or obligation. Failing to avoid these pitfalls, we run the risk of working counter to alchemy's purpose; that is, we regress into unhealthy states of unconsciousness. Roger Walsh, a well-respected psychiatrist and author of *Essential Spirituality,* tells us that addiction is the extreme and exaggerated end result of attachment.[13] Addictions are, of course, unconsciously motivated, meaning that they work counter to the conscious efforts needed to individuate, spiritually realize ourselves and produce the true gold.

Many an alchemist became obsessed in the course of their work. But there is a clear difference between these dedicated adepts and others whose only ambition was to capitalize on what they perceived to be a scheme to get rich quick. This type merely sought to produce an easy fortune, or swindle others out of theirs. These false alchemists are found throughout alchemy's long history. Known as charlatans, conjurers and puffers, they were despised by true students of the Art. Puffers earned their name by frantically overusing the bellows to fire up a quick fortune. They did not know, or did not adhere to, the alchemist's understanding of the three grades of fire, each used at different stages of the work to carry out different operations. Instead, in their haste to produce material gold quickly, they blew out a lot of hot air that didn't amount to anything. These puffers were themselves filled with a lot of hot air. They were buffoons, from the Latin *follis,* meaning filled up with air. The true adept instead went about the work in much the same way an Indian yogi would use air to control his breath and the flame of consciousness.

There is always a threat posed by insincere or ill-trained practitioners. This is as true today—perhaps more so—as it was centuries ago. Sherwood Taylor, an Oxford museum curator, explains:

> The material aim of the alchemists, the transmutation of metals, has now been realized by science, and the alchemical vessel is the uranium pile. Its success has had precisely the result that the alchemist feared and guarded against, the placing of gigantic power in the hands of those who have not been fitted by spiritual power to receive it. If science, philosophy, and religion had remained associated as they were in alchemy, we might not today be confronted with this fearful problem.[14]

While many scholars agree that "alchemy" comes from the two derivations we've discussed, Jack Lindsay, an authority on Greek, Egyptian and Roman classics, suggests the possibility that *chymos,* not *chymia,* was the root word from which alchemy was derived. There is actually a link between these two Greek word stems, but *chymos* extends the meaning to "include animal juices or humors."[15] This is important because we then find a direct etymological connection between alchemy and healing. Aristotle, for example, extended Empedocles' concept of the four elements to include four humors used in healing diseases of mind and

BEING OF SOUND MIND

body. Humor here does not have anything to do with laughter or comedy. Rather, it refers to an old system that helps us understand how the four elements manifest in human beings.

Richard Grossinger, author of many books on healing, describes the traditional view of humors. In *Planet Medicine,* he writes,

> The elements express themselves in human beings through the humors, which are the complex elements of life. The humors respond to environment, diet, habits, and emotional states. They transmit the temperaments and psychic "meaning" of the elements. Man observes the elements, as lightning in the stormy sky followed by mushrooms on dam logs after the rain, but he also feels them circulating within him, passing from one state to another. When they get out of balance, he experiences distortion, though he may not know exactly what it is. . . . In a sense, the humors are like spirits, phenomenological insights into the condition of being alive.[16]

While the Greek philosopher Hippocrates expounded a working theory of humors, it can also be found in the ancient Chinese texts and the Indian system of Ayurvedic medicine.

A working knowledge of the humors is excellent preparation for doing personal alchemy since it gives us a tool for manipulating the elements of our personality.

In this system, each of the four elements was assigned two qualities such that:

TABLE 2: ELEMENTS AND HUMORS	
Element	**Humor**
Fire	dry and hot*
Air	hot and moist*
Water	moist and cold*
Earth	cold and dry*

It is important to note that one quality takes dominance in elements, indicated by the asterisk in the above chart. All elements are changeable; they pass through the medium each shares in common with another. Fire then becomes air through the medium of heat (hot); air to water through the moist element; water to earth through cold; earth to fire through dry. Since each element corresponds to one of the four psychological functions, we begin to see how transformation of consciousness becomes possible using this system.

When we put the elements, the humors and the functions together, this is what it looks like:

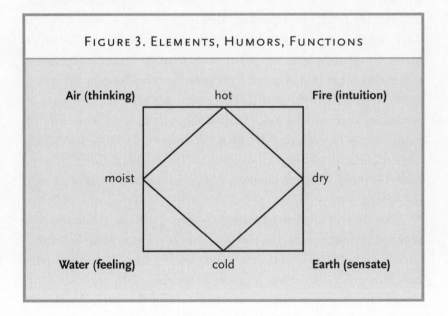

FIGURE 3. ELEMENTS, HUMORS, FUNCTIONS

Air (thinking)   hot   Fire (intuition)

moist   dry

Water (feeling)   cold   Earth (sensate)

Two elements (functions) change when each partner loses the humors they share in common with a third element. For example, when fire and water part with dry and cold, they become earth. Similarly, if earth and air combine, giving up cold and moist, they become water. The only limitation is that identical or contrary qualities cannot be left as a result of the combination.

Jung described the four functions as consisting of two rational (thinking and feeling) and two nonrational (sensate and intuition) operations. Each of us has a dominance in one, and sometimes two of these functions. A pure thinking type is a strict rationalist who relies on cognitive means of understanding the world. Combined with the sensate function, this thinking-sensate type would make an excellent scientist. These functions would equip the person with the cognitive skills necessary to think through scientific problems and the physical abilities needed to do the hands-on work of laboratory experiments. Now, if a pure thinking type would want to develop his feeling function because he is having problems at home, humoral theory indicates he would have to give up the qualities of moist and cold. What does this mean?

Relationships, particularly marriage, involve expressions of feeling, empathy and good communication. These are warm qualities. The modern-day scientist strives to conduct laboratory work in clinical conditions that exclude subjective influences. One might feel passionate about the work, but the rule is to not allow subjectivity to enter the physical experiment. This might bias the effects with what he wishes will happen, rather than what should occur if his hypothesis holds up in the experiment. Feelings, in other words, can contaminate and even invalidate the results. So, after working many years at this, we can begin to see how the requirements of work can take their toll on the scientist's personal life. The recipe for correcting this condition, using humoral theory, is to remove the moist, cold, calculating qualities that get in the way of expressing feeling.

Disease is thought to be a disequilibrium in the elements and their humors. Healing is aimed at restoring proper balance. Ayurvedic medicine uses a similar system to correct physical disorders. If, for example, a condition exists where there is an overabundance of moisture, say problems with congestion and mucus, then ridding the body of water encourages the body to produce more of the dry quality associated with the qualities of earth and fire. If there is too much of a hot quality, like fever, then we would want to increase the moist and cold qualities of water. Ayurvedic medicine is more complex than I am describing it here. I merely want to make the point that systems, based on humoral theory, exist for the purpose of treating physical illness.

While it is debatable whether the manipulation of humors can really heal physical problems, I am convinced, based on my own work as a psychotherapist, that the model is effective in treating psychological disorders.

One of my patients suffers from obsessive anxiety. She has a highly developed feeling function, so much so that she cannot contain the feelings aroused in her by three adult daughters. She is also at odds with herself because she tends to make snap judgments rather than relying on more thoughtful consideration of problem situations. As a result, she became very anxious, and even a bit neurotic, and she felt overwhelmed by her feelings, becoming unable to formulate judgments about the actions of her daughters.

Therapy worked to mend this disbalance by having her strengthen her thinking function. To accomplish this she had to extinguish the hot and moist qualities impeding the thinking function. Her hunches were typically wrong and her moist feelings were drowning out sound judgment. When she became able to think through, rather than emotionally react to her daughters' actions, she came up with judgments that helped her daughters and relieved her own unnecessary worry and rumination.

The first step in correcting disorder begins by giving it a name. The mere naming of a problem offers immediate relief. In medicine, diagnosis is the act of naming the disease and it is actually part of the treatment. We all take comfort in knowing the name of what it is that causes us to fall ill. When a doctor assigns a diagnosis to our infirmity we expect a defined treatment to follow. Lacking a name for what ails us is disconcerting to the doctor and patient alike.

Naming a problem gives us hope. Where we no longer have gods to call upon to "explain" our sickness, we invent meaningless terms like ideopathic and nonspecific. If we look to the origin of the word "diagnosis," we find that it has history and depth. The prefix "dia" means "going in two directions" and "gnosis" means "knowing," not in the sense of applying a label to our disorder, but a deep experience into the cause of our malady. It is a knowledge that is arrived at by way of a two-way conversation, or dialogue, one has with oneself and with his or her doctor.

THE POWER OF WORDS TO HEAL

Do words have the power to cure illness?

Careful research shows that psychotherapy has proven very effective in the curing of psychological and even some physical disorders.[17] The power of words to heal is amply demonstrated when a hysterically blind person regains sight, or a patient suffering debilitating panic attacks finds relief using nothing more than verbal medicine. Less we forget, psychology is the study of soul. It is soul that gives words their depth, animating them with the healing powers of the archetypal realm. Diagnoses, like magical spells and even alchemical recipes, derive their power by making vital connections between (conscious) spoken language and the (unconscious) soul.

It is not the words alone from which healing power is derived. Words are the catalysts through which the energies of healing are carried. When an Indian yogi, for example, chants the sacred sound "Om" or an Eskimo shaman utters the words of an ancient healing spell, they are forming a bridge between inner and outer realities. Through this sound bridge they bring the healing powers of the universe to bear on the source of the illness. Sound becomes the connecting medium that ties together spiritual powers from above with disturbances in the patient.

Illness, in this view, is a dissonant chord in need of tuning. Effective treatment is achieved only when medical "attention" is totally focused on the corrective sound, the mantra, and excludes what distracts the mind. Much like individualized mantras given by gurus to their students, alchemical recipes serve a similar purpose. It is not just following instructions that gives the recipes their power. The sound of the recipe itself serves to change the mind in such a way that the necessary inner transformation occurs. When we use alchemical recipes it is just as important to sound the words out as it is to try to understand what they mean.

Alchemical healing requires knowledge of mind, body and soul. This knowledge is as much to be learned from the psychology and mythology of the human experience as it is from the study of human anatomy and biochemistry. At the same time, it would be absurd to think that a patient might derive relief strictly from the words written on a prescription pad. We need to draw a connection between sound, word and image in doing this kind of alchemical healing. We tend to forget that every drug produced by humans came from intense study of natural processes and that doctors and medicines have a history, all of which are crucial factors in the healing process.

Recognizing that the RX sign is an ancient symbol derived from an old "invocation to Jupiter, a prayer for his aid to make the treatment effective,"[18] assists in the channeling of spiritual power into the patient. Similarly, we do well to remember that the caduceus, still the insignia of the medical profession, was the magic wand used by the Greek god Hermes in reconciling opposites. Beyond these obvious examples are the myths of Asklepios and Chiron, the wounded healer, gods who continue to be the source of great healing power. Connecting words of healing with the images that stand behind them is essential in medical practice. Yogis, shamans and alchemists were well aware of the power of words to heal when used in this way.

Words and sound played an important role in an alchemist's laboratory. In a well-known series of pictures by the nineteenth-century alchemist Heinrich Khunrath called *The Amphitheatre of Eternal Wisdom,* we see a beautiful etching of an alchemist's workshop divided by a laboratory on the right and an oratory on the left. There, kneeling before an altar, is an alchemist deep in prayer surrounded by a number of holy texts. In the foreground is a table on which we see a variety of musical instruments. Clearly, Khunrath is showing us the importance of prayer and music as well as the mixing and combining of chemical substances.

Michael Maier, physician and master adept to King Rudolf II, provides another fine example of the importance of words and sound. Maier produced a body of work known as *Atalanta Fugiens,* which combined music, text and pictures showing the procedure for making the philosopher's stone. Finally, I offer the example of Marcilio Ficino, a Renaissance alchemist-philosopher, who was known to play his lute in healing patients. He believed "musical sound by the movement of the air moves the body: by purified air it excites the aerial *spiritus* which is the bond of body and soul: by emotion it affects the senses and at the same time the soul."[19]

Ficino went on to describe different types of music and their functions. In his scheme, there are three categories: *musica mundana, musica humana* and *musica instrumentalis.* The last of these is the common music we listen to on the radio or at a concert hall. The first is best understood as the music of the spheres: ambient sound created by the slow, organic movements of planets, stars and seasons. The second, *musica humana,* was imagined as the reflection of these cosmic vibrations in the human soul. Whatever the type, Ficino believed music was "another art of memory or imagination, a way of getting the soul in touch with various kinds of spirits . . . a quality of soul itself, an elemental factor in its constitution, parallel to the air element in nature."[20]

How true! Most of us can recall times when a tune gets stuck in our head, or we hear an old song that brings us back to a distant memory.

When I was visiting Prague I felt an overpowering presence of two things: stone and music. Everything in this beautiful city seemed to be made of stone: St. Charles Bridge, Tyn Church, Old Town Square, the cobblestone streets, alchemist's alley, Prague castle. But, against the old solid memories etched in these stone monuments, music wafted through the air. There I witnessed an alchemical principle, known as the fixed-volatile, in real life: stones fixed eternally in their place with music blowing through the air like a soft summer melody.

> Music carries memory through the air, of which the soul breathes.

The impression was redoubled when I made a short trip to Kutná Hora, a mining town not far from the capital. This small, medieval city was once the place where the silver used for coins had been quarried. I was amazed on discovering that miners were entertained by a mechanical music box that stood five feet tall. The image of miners axing away at rock in rhythm to the figures of the music box was a splendid piece of acoustic alchemy.

Frater Albertus, a contemporary alchemist, defines alchemy as "the raising of vibrations." The concept of sound, sacred words, spells and vibration is as old as it is new. Sound, according to the ancient Hindu school of Samkhya, is "not merely one of the five senses—the one caused by air—vibrations—but rather is the parent of all senses."[21] Perhaps only now is theoretical physics taking seriously the possibility that vibrations play a critical role in the very creation of the universe.

GOOD VIBRATIONS

One of the most exciting projects undertaken by theoretical physics in recent times is the search for a formula (recipe) that will explain everything. In fact, it is called the Theory of Everything. This theory aims to complete the work begun by Einstein and in the process solve the greatest mystery of alchemy: how to integrate the macrocosm (above) and the microcosm (the below) for the "making of the One Thing." The problem faced in this daunting endeavor is the fact that matter behaves differently on earth than it does in outer space. The rules that apply to one usually do not apply to the other. A Theory of Everything strives to define a universal law that applies to all realms of matter.

The leading theory that may well solve this problem is called superstring theory. It is based on the idea that there exist many more than our four dimensions and that these dimensions are created by unimaginably small vibrating strings throughout the universe. With the superstring theory, we find a *mysterium coincidentia,* a strange coincidence between past and present that could usher in a Golden Age for all humanity.

Like the elements, matter and mind are in a constant state of movement. Chaos, lacking vibrational organization, is a din of confusion. With sound, vibration achieves its first level of organization. "Sound and aether are," according to musicologist Jocelyn Godwin, "the very first manifestations of objective consciousness."[22] Thought expressed in song and verse are vibrations that have attained literal meaning. Music and the arts in general give expression to consciousness, and are critically important for keeping body, mind and soul in harmony. Eliade's research on alchemy shows historical connections between human life and the natural world. He writes:

> There would appear to have existed therefore, at several different cultural levels (which is a mark of very great antiquity), a close connection between the art of the smith, the occult sciences (shamanism, magic, healing, etc.) and the art of song, dance and poetry.[23]

The importance of sound in alchemy and healing cannot be underestimated. Lacking the means to mass produce and distribute books (the printing press was not in mass operation until the 1500s), alchemy was, for some 1800 years, mostly an oral tradition. While parchments and even stone tablets existed, information was extremely limited and often imbedded in complex symbols. There remains a virtual library of hieroglyphs still needing translation. The transmission of alchemical knowledge was primarily by word of mouth.

As "verbal medicine," psychotherapy is well suited to the practice of alchemical healing; it addresses both the literal and metaphorical functions of the mind. Seasoned therapists know how to use their verbal tools by skillful modulation and timing of their voices as well as by crafting sentences that redirect misguided thoughts.

For centuries magic spells worked in a similar way. Alchemists also made use of prayer and incantations to invite gods to bring the necessary energies from above. Prayer, as the alchemists use it, is little different from chants used by Native American Indian shamans or Jewish cantors.

"The word prayer," writes one contemporary alchemist, "is to be understood not so much an individual petition, but rather the inward—and sometimes also outward—pronouncing of a formula or name directed to God and evoking God (an ejaculatory prayer)."[24] Again I stress the importance of sound, word and image. The act of saying the words is just as important as their meaning. Even when we may not understand their literal meaning, the sounds themselves hold curative power.

I love the sound of alchemy. Words like elixir, spagyric, *rebis* and *coniunctio* require an effort my tongue is not used to, and yet, in some odd way, they breathe familiarity and result in a delightful feeling. Save for those whose churches retain the singing of hymns, there doesn't seem to be much room in our modern world for chanting in a foreign tongue. Good vibrations, as the song title goes, touch us at a very deep, visceral level. The manipulation of sound is a tool of transformation capable of uniting the spiritual world with the earthly realm. While we surely haven't discovered a theory of everything, we still have the ability to experience the unity of the whole universe by hearing and singing the music of the spheres.

"And if spells and other forms of magic are efficient," wrote the Greek philosopher Plotinus, "even at a distance, to attract us into sympathetic relations, the agency can be no other than the one Soul."[25] The phrase "even at a distance" equates directly with the contemporary language of modern-day physics. The term "nonlocal event" is used by physicists to describe an acausal connection, not unlike Jung's concept of synchronicity, that describes one particle copying another regardless of the distances between them. We've passed the threshold between the old world and the new when ancient philosophy finds a direct correspondence with contemporary physical experiment. But, the connection, though to varying degrees unconscious, has been there all along. Plotinus tells us that the above and the below exist in the human soul. And it is in sound and prayer where these two great realms meet and marry. In Plotinus's words, "A quiet word induces changes in a remote object, and makes itself heard at vast distances—proof of the oneness of all things within the one Soul."[26]

Alchemy recognized two great spheres of human consciousness— the material and the psychic—and personified psyche's duality in word and image. Its recipes express the abstract integration of spirit and matter. In this way they work at many different levels simultaneously. If we approach them with an attitude that seeks explanation alone, we rob them of their power to activate the deeper resources of the unconscious. Healing is as much an imaginative process as it is one that relies on material manipulation of the body. Imagination, Einstein said, is as important as knowledge in understanding the universe. Unlike medical prescriptions, alchemical recipes require full engagement of the mind, body and soul, as well as active participation of the imaginative faculty to make them work.

Now it is time to practice some of what we have been discussing so that we begin to do alchemy and not just talk about it. I have selected some of the most powerful alchemical texts to get us started. At this point it is less important to understand the texts than it is to simply allow whatever images that come to mind to be fully present in your awareness.

PRESCRIPTIONS

1. Recite this third century invocation from the *Corpus Hermeticum*. It strengthens the imaginative mind:

   Rise up above every height: descend deeper than any depth;
   Concentrate into thyself all the sensations of created things
   Of water, fire, dry and wet.

   Think of finding yourself simultaneously everywhere in the
   Earth, sea or sky;
   Think of having never been born,
   Of still being an embryo;
   Young and old, dead and beyond death.
   Embrace everything at the same time;
   All times, places, things, qualities and quantities.[27]

2. Follow these instructions. They are from a collection of Hermetic essays written in the third century by Egyptian philosophers. The words provide a powerful example of active imagination.

   Leap free of everything that is physical, and grow as vast as that
   immeasurable vastness; step beyond all time and become eternal;
   then you will perceive God.

Realize that nothing is impossible for you;

recognize that you too are immortal and that you can embrace all things in your mind;

find your home in the heart of every living creature; make yourself higher than all heights and lower than all depths;

bring all opposites inside yourself and reconcile them;

understand that you are everywhere, on the land, in the sea, in the sky;

realize that you haven't yet been begotten, that you are still in the womb, that you are young, that you are old, that you are dead, that you are in the world beyond the grave;

hold all this in your mind, all times and places, all substances and qualities and magnitudes;

then you can perceive God.[28]

3. Memorize this recipe. This is the text of the *Emerald Tablet* purportedly written by the greatest of all alchemists, Hermes Trismegistus. Herein is described the entire alchemical opus. Do not concern yourself with fully understanding its symbolic meaning. Rather the goal is to impress on your memory its words. In this way you might expect even older memories, not of your own experience, to awaken :

   • Truly, without deception, certain and most true.

   • What is below is like that which is above, and what is above is like that which is below, to accomplish the miracles of the one thing.

   • And as all things proceeded from one, through mediation of the one, so all things came from this one thing through adaptation.

   • Its father is the sun; its mother the moon; the wind has carried it in its belly; its nurse is the earth.

   • This is the father of all, the completion of the whole world.

   • Its strength is complete if it be turned into (or toward) earth.

   • Separate the earth from the fire, the subtle from the dense, gently and with great ingenuity.

- It ascends from the earth to the heaven, and descends again to the earth, and receives the power of the above and the below. Thus you will have the glory of the whole world. Therefore all darkness will flee from you.

- Here is the strong power of the whole strength; for it overcomes every subtle thing and penetrates every solid.

- Thus the world has been created.

- From here will come the marvelous adaptations, whose manner this is.

- So I am called _____ (your name), having the three parts of the philosophy of the whole world.

- What I have said about the operation of the sun is finished.

4. Solve this riddle and you will have the *prima materia*. So it was believed that riddles whet the curiosity and, in this case, take rational intelligence to a higher plane. Reason alone will not solve the mystery:

> *A riddle to you I will propose,*
> *Of a common thing which most men know,*
> *Which now in the earth every rife doth grow,*
> *But is of small price as all men know;*
> *And that without root, stalk, or seed,*
> *Wherewith of his kind another to breed:*
> *Yet of that nature that is cannot cease,*
> *If you plant it by pieces itself to increase,*
> *Right heavy by kind, yet forced to fly,*
> *Stark naught in the purse, yet good in the eye,*
> *This something is nothing which seemeth full strange,*
> *Having tasted the fire which maketh it change:*
> *And hath many colors yet showeth but one,*
> *This is the material of our Stone.*[29]

These exercises prepare us for the next step in our journey: the gods and spirits that connect the heaven above with the spirits of earth.

Chapter 5

Gods above,
Spirits Below

On each of these levels, species, exist analogous to those in our world,
but they are infinite. Some are peopled by Angels and the human Elect.
Others are peopled by Angels and genii, others by demons.
God alone knows the number of these levels and what they contain.
The pilgrim rising from one degree to another discovers on each
higher level a subtler state, a more entrancing beauty,
a more intense spirituality, a more overflowing delight.
The highest of these degrees borders on that of the intelligible
pure entities of light and very closely resemble it.

Qu'buddin Shirazi

Alchemy has always been one part art, one part science. These proportions have changed dramatically over the course of thousands of years. The story of this transition describes how chemistry grew out of alchemy, and more importantly, how an old way of thinking gave way to a new world. At the dawn of time, consciousness was nearly composed of totally subjective experiences. This was an era of magic, myth and mystery. In such a mixed-up state of affairs there are few if any distinctions between things. Rocks, sky, animals, lakes and people compose one giant reality. From this oceanic consciousness alchemy and other occult arts find their origin. Shamanism is probably the first of these magical traditions to arise out of the haze of early history.

In all the occult arts we find remnants of animism. As we may recall, animism is one of the essential characteristics of every form of alchemy. In addition to understanding animism as the belief that some amount of consciousness exists in all matter we must also recognize that, according to the definition given in the *Oxford English Dictionary,* the source of this life is the *Anima Mundi,* or world soul. The advent of science makes it tempting to dismiss this kind of magical thinking as primitive and irrelevant. But the structure of the modern human brain reveals vestiges of our history, dating back to this magical era. Not only do our brains bear traces of primitive anatomy, but our thinking as well continues in some of the same ways as our earliest ancestors.

The structure of our brains is layered from bottom to top, the oldest anatomical vestiges of neuroanatomy to the most advanced forms found in the frontal cortex. Similarly, we find two networks operating in our nervous system. The central nervous system consists of the brain and the spinal cord. These are responsible for the carrying out the most sophisticated operations of mind and body. With the ability to think abstractly and carry out the instructions of the brain in an efficient, literally upstanding way, humans ascended to the top of the great chain of being. The second nervous system, called the autonomic nervous system, carries out the vegetative functions of the body, things like respiration, blood pressure and digestion. Its "psychology" is more like that of an animal. Flight and fight operations are an example of autonomic reactions. Unlike the central nervous system, responses in this neural system do not require conscious mediation.

To keep things simple I refer to the central nervous system as the conscious system and the autonomic nervous system as the unconscious one. This information will become important when we discuss ways of modifying autonomic activity through deliberate conscious efforts.

In psychological terms, animistic and primitive thought patterns exist in the various realms of the unconscious. Both brain and mind describe these realms. As a culture, they can also be found in the collective unconscious. In line with alchemy, Jung believed that there is collective as well as individual unconsciousness, that the two mirror each other and to some extent interact with one another. The collective unconscious is a great source of creativity. Artists are accomplished in tapping into the collective unconscious through the use of imagination. But, one need not be an artist to discover the reality of this imaginal realm. Myths, legends, fables and story reveal contents of the collective unconscious. It can be found in individual dreams, fantasies and imagination. This primitive realm of consciousness may also find itself automatically projected in paranormal events, superstition and pathological behavior. Less profound reminders of this very old way of being come to us in the form of symptoms.

We need to distinguish between idle fantasy and what the French savant Henry Corbin called the Imaginal World. "The distinction," wrote philosopher and musicologist Jocelyn Godwin, "is between fantasy or reverie that one invents for oneself, and the objective but nonmaterial world that is presented as images to the inner organ of imaginative perception."[1] Jung and others saw this imaginal world as a vast repository of mythological data that defines the whole of human civilization.

Although developed to quite a sophisticated extent, modern consciousness has not shrugged off this imaginal world. And yet, it remains rooted in our neural makeup, representing a different time and place, connecting us to our origins and perhaps even our collective soul. As much as we avoid, deny or act to destroy this imaginal realm, it remains fixed in our unconscious memory. We can go to great lengths to exclude it from the objective world, but, in the end, we are forced to admit the sheer folly of this kind of misguided limitation.

With alchemy, we cast a wide net over nature, making sure to capture as much of the past as the future. It honors the fool with more than a nod. Ignoring him only incites him to play nasty tricks on us. In my office, on the highest bookshelf, I've placed a little fool doll I've taken to calling Grumio. He sits there all day long, reminding me to keep quiet when I don't know what I'm talking about. He humbles me.

I invite you to explore with me the strange world of magic that exists just beneath the realm of science. Here we meet gods and spirits that energize old alchemical recipes and modern-day scientific formulas. The old saying, "Yesterday's magic is tomorrow's science," provides a continuity that is especially obvious with the technological magic we've experienced in recent years. I ask that you extend the same suspension of disbelief to invisible "presences" that you ordinarily give to computers and cell phones. Honor, in other words, beings that reside in the unconscious and learn what they have to offer.

No alchemical recipe is complete without acknowledging contributions made by the magical beings that inhabit our unconscious world. Even our mathematics ring hollow without the supernatural forces that first gave rise to the archetypal creation of numbers and their calculation. If even for a moment we allow the rational mind to relax, gods and spirits help us resurface long forgotten memories and the archetypal images that inspire science, art and religion. Our memory allows us to recall the infinite source of all creativity. As the poet Rumi said so beautifully, "Although the water and earth of our bodies have caused a doubt to fall upon us, something of those melodies comes back to our memory."[2]

Poets were not alone in knowing the Art of Memory and other techniques used to access this magical realm. Sculptors and architects worked with magical proportions and golden means to defy the laws of gravity. Great composers opened their "inner ears" to hear the muses, God and the Music of the Spheres. In describing his art, Edvard Grieg said, "we composers are projectors of the infinite into the finite."[3]

ELEMENTS AND ELEMENTALS

Armed with spectacular technology, today's science peers into the deepest recesses of matter. Powerful microscopes allow scientists to describe the topology of our interior subatomic world with great precision, but alas, there is no soul, no spirit, no god to be seen. We cannot see what is invisible to the naked eye. We rely on mathematics to envision the unseen physical world, and the imagination to visualize the imaginal realm. There are times when these two ways of seeing merge.

In naming the very smallest subatomic particles (quarks[4]), scientists chose names that sound more like archetypes than scientific descriptions of physical elements. Beauty, charm, upward, downward, sideways and color are the official names bestowed on the gods and spirits of the subatomic world. Most scientists would scoff at any suggestion that magic has any place in the laboratory, but even this prejudice is slowly eroding in the face of new scientific discoveries.

Lyall Watson, anthropologist and ethologist, makes a number of fascinating references to alchemy, or what he terms metal magic, in his book *The Nature of Things: The Secret Life of Inanimate Objects*. He describes an intermediate realm where mind and matter seem almost indistinguishable. Best of all, he draws from the everyday world of myth and reality to reflect what most of us suspect, but lack the courage to say out loud. While empirical scientists busy themselves with proofs and explanations, Watson reminds us of an Old World view in which everything is alive. His survey is extensive. It includes everything from bells, bridges, atoms, gravestones, diamonds, figurines, computers, clocks, chairs, and mountains. Each of these items is a vital thread in the fabric of reality, that place where mind and matter meld into one.

Watson's brilliance lies in unmasking the psychic life of these and many other ordinary things that make up our world. As a contemporary man of letters, he fortifies with objective evidence what Jung long ago called the psychoid realm of consciousness. If we keep an open mind as we go through Watson's descriptions of the inner life of inanimate objects, we can't help finding ourselves agreeing with what he says: "There are biological ghosts lurking in every part of life's wonderful machinery." And further, we come to suspect, as he does, that "one of the most potent of these [ghosts] is the capacity we have to influence the world around us *directly*" [italics mine].[5]

This certainly sounds more like magic than science. Not content to leave it there, Watson goes on to suggest that he is "beginning to believe that it may be possible for an idea, particularly one that is strongly held or generously housed at an unconscious level, to manifest its own independent sort of physical reality."[6] Is Watson suggesting that pure, concentrated thought is capable of bringing life to inanimate objects? Such an idea is not new; it is central to the work of alchemists. Jewish alchemists, for example, were rumored to have produced the *golem,* an artificial man borne out of the unconscious and having "its own independent sort of physical reality." With the word *emeth* (truth) inscribed across its forehead, the clay figure was believed to come to life. And when the *golem* grew to a menacing height, the word *meth* (he is dead) would instantly return it to clay. In alchemy, this little creature was known as the *homunculus,* and in modern-day language, we might call it a clone.

The concept of making *homunculli* dates far back to the early Hebrews and Greeks. The Hebrew word *golem* appears once in the New Testament and several times in the Talmud. It meant matter without form. Now, what's interesting is the Jewish Kabbalists use of divine names, words and numbers to bring the *golem* to consciousness. We see in these myths the seeds of a Freudian psychology that has humans playing the role of the creator using black clay (matter) and magical words.[7]

Aristotle believed that the world is borne out of one archetypal form from which all things enter into palpable manifestation when they have multiplied four times. One is the absolute reality represented by stone, two is the level of opposites, three brings us outside the parameters of ordinary time, and four returns us, renewed and aware, to the realm of reality. The whole process gets its start out of a mysterious ether, a void of pure nothingness that is somehow alive. It is to this same ether that consciousness returns, fully integrated, enlightened and filled with light.

The impulse of evolution and individuation requires us to take this journey from nothingness to complete wholeness. The elements of this human drama unfold in thoughts, intuitions, feelings and sensations. Theoretical physicist Fred Alan Wolf relates each of these to time, motion, energy and space, respectively. These elements enter the material universe through the agency of gods and spirits. In other words, these entities act like catalysts in the service of giving form to matter.

In his book *The Alchemy of Healing,* Jungian analyst and homeopath Edward Whitmont emphasizes the important connection made here between how we are created and how we are made whole. He writes:

Our conscious awareness is privy only to a limited and partial scope of the overall information dynamics available and operative in different dimensions of psyche, soma as well as nonhuman and even "non-live" activities.

Transducive metamorphosis occurs throughout our bodies and minds, catalyzing a constant interchange and communication with the earth and cosmos of which we are integral parts.[8]

As we acquire knowledge of this mysterious intermediate realm, we are empowered in the ways of healing and bringing new life to an old world. "This knowledge," writes another Jungian, "helps maintain psychological consciousness, a middle arena, a hollow space for reflection and incubation, a chamber of resonance and, like the alchemist's retort, a theater of images."[9]

To our list of elements we must therefore add the contributions made by imaginal, elemental beings. This information will assist us in the next chapter, when we study how the elementals participate in major operations of the alchemical work:

TABLE 3. THE ELEMENTS AND THEIR ASSOCIATIONS

Element	Chemical	Physical	Humors	Psychological	Imaginary
Air	gas	space-time	hot-moist	thinking	sylphs
Water	liquid	energy-motion	cold-moist	feeling	mermaids
Earth	matter	energy- space	cold-dry	sensate	gnomes
Fire	combustion	time-motion	hot-dry	intuition	salamanders

While individuation is a process that at first appears linear, leading us from unconsciousness to consciousness, in reality, it is much like the earth and the universe: spherical. We move through the days of our lives like a slow march through the boxes on the calendar, but we are forever looping through experiences that are bounded on one end by memory and the other by dreams of the future. T. S. Eliot described the nature of this movement in "Little Gidding":

> *We shall not cease from exploration*
> *And the end of all our exploring*

Will be to arrive where we started
And know the place for the first time.

Without understanding the structure of reality, the old recipes won't be of much use to our personal alchemy. So let's press on and become acquainted with the elemental beings that populate the world of mind and matter. Be warned that stranger entities await you later on in this chapter.

The mermaid is the most familiar of the undines, those creatures that live   ***Undines***
in oceans, seas, lakes and ponds. Perhaps because we associate the water element with the feminine, almost nothing is known of male undines. Of particular interest in alchemical symbolism are the images of dew, mist, waterfalls and fountains. Each of these images suggests a way that showering, purifying and cleansing are part of psyche's daily chores. Manly P. Hall summarizes this aquatic nature of the undines in these words:

> Their temperament is said to be vital, and to them has been given as their throne the western corner of creation. They are rather emotional beings, friendly to human life and fond of serving mankind. They are sometimes pictured riding on dolphins or other great fish and seem to have a special love for flowers and plants, which they serve almost as devotedly and intelligently as the gnomes.[10]

In Jung's psychology, the undine personifies the feeling function. In its inferior form, feelings are not well defined. A mood can reduce the rock of reason to a useless puddle. Yet, when brought under the sway of consciousness, the feeling function operates as a powerful resource in tempering judgments with empathy to induce a more positive attitude. There are innumerable references that can further illustrate this element of water. I especially recommend Edward Edinger's *The Anatomy of the Psyche,* a book in which he supplies many wonderful examples of all the elements as they specifically relate to the alchemical opus.

Gnomes   The gnomes Hall speaks of occupy the element of earth. These creatures continue to live on in fairy tales. A beautifully illustrated book called *Gnomes* by Huygen is a virtual phenomenology of their world; it is complete with hundreds of drawings that describe their culture. These dwarflike creatures have a very special affinity to the work of alchemy, as you might imagine. They are hands-on scientists and depend on their senses to acquire immediate knowledge. Inhabiting forests, caves and mines, gnomes have great knowledge (*gnosis*) of the earth's minerals, gemstones and metals. In his *Secret Teachings of All Ages,* Hall describes them as having "insatiable appetites [and] a miserly temperament,"[11] but to their credit are extremely conscientious workers. They possess, in miniature, many of the same qualities as those characters that associate with the trickster archetype. Moreover, these same characteristics describe Mercurius, alchemy's most revered god.

Salamander   The salamander lives in the realm of fire. In the image that begins this chapter is a very familiar alchemical plate showing this elemental lying on a pyre untouched by the flames. This immutability to fire symbolizes its transformative ability. The salamander represents the essence of fire and its power to break down the dense matter in the original *prima materia*. Just as fire transforms solid matter into ash, these fiery creatures are useful in reducing obstacles that stand in the way of individuation.

These elemental beings also contribute to other vital functions that are necessary to sustain human life physically and psychologically. They give the body the inner heat necessary to transform food into energy and thoughts into emotions. They can be excellent servants when we need to get "fired up and get going." But, they can also defy us in the heat of the moment with mindless passion and a hot temper.

Salamanders are necessary to our existence but, unlike the gnomes and undines, they are not very friendly to us. They can be dangerous and must be approached carefully. Understanding the salamander's nature gives us insight into ways to safely use this elemental creature in doing transformative work.

Sparks fly when we try to approach the salamander directly. Rather, Hall suggests indirect measures be taken.

Man is unable to communicate successfully with the salamanders, owing to the fiery element in which they dwell, for everything is resolved to ashes that comes into their presence. By specially prepared compounds of herbs and perfumes the philosophers of the ancient world manufactured many kinds of incense. When incense was burned, the vapors which arose were especially suitable as a medium for the expression of these elementals, who, by borrowing the ethereal effluvium from the incense smoke, were able to make their presence felt.[12]

In recent years aromatherapy has made a comeback and many people use it as an aid in healing and issuing an invitation to the salamander. The burning incense is used as a means of connecting patients with these helpful elementals. Smoke is the essence of this connection; white ash symbolizes the purified results of it. "The burning candle," writes Edinger, "generates not only light but also molten matter, as though the living process of the psyche generates a substance—a *coagulatio* of spirit."[13]

Sylphs

Finally, we have the sylphs, who dwell in the element of air. We know them best as figures appearing as angels and spirit fairies. Hall describes their nature as:

> mirthful, changeable, and eccentric. The peculiar qualities common to men of genius are supposedly the result of the cooperation of sylphs, whose aid also brings with it the sulphic inconsistency. The sylphs labor with the ages of the human body and indirectly with the nervous system, where their inconstancy is again apparent. They have no fixed domicile, but wander about from place to place—elemental nomads, invisible but ever-present powers in the intelligent activity of the universe.[14]

These then are the four elementals that make up the imaginary counterpart to the visible world of matter. Where we associate the elements outwardly with the physical universe, these elementals describe an intermediary region between mind and matter. They are expressions of the human psyche that help bring matter into manifested form. This manifested form may take the appearance of a physical object or a behavior, but in either case, some combination of elementals accompany the process whether we know it or not. It is only through the power of imagination that we visualize these amazing characters that inhabit the innermost regions of the mind.

THE SECRETS OF METALS

Alchemists spent as much time cultivating the imaginative faculty as they did working with material substances. The physical product of these labors offered tangible proof of changes they witnessed first and foremost within the realm of their own subjective experience. "The production of metallic gold," writes a contemporary alchemist, "was to alchemy a proof of transfiguration given by a power: the testimony of having realized Gold O, in oneself."[15] When the mind is in perfect harmony with the experimental work, it has the physical effect of rearranging metallic molecules in accord with the form created in thought.

We find this same law repeated by quantum physicists, homeopaths and Jungian psychologists. Again I refer to a great recipe from the *Emerald Tablet:* "In truth certainly and without doubt, whatever is below is like that which is above, and whatever is above is like that which is below, to accomplish the miracles of one thing." There is, in other words, a reciprocal relationship between thought and matter, each impinging on the other, bringing about changes both within and outside the range of human awareness. We can use this knowledge by bringing into consciousness changes that serve to transform the lead of misery into the gold of opportunity.

The alchemists made little distinction between the celestial rocks—of stars and planets—and those that are found beneath the surface of the earth. They believed that metals, minerals and gemstones were grown by the influence of these celestial bodies. It follows that celestial bodies influence us, as much as they exert mysterious power over all of planet earth. With the alchemists, we must agree that the moon's influence acts as much on our bodily fluids as on sea water. We are after all primarily composed of water. Menstrual cycles and the currents of our moods behave much in the same way as the tides of the ocean. Astrology attempts to explain these cosmic effects, taking as its starting point the heavenly bodies. Alchemy does likewise, but it uses earth as its starting point. Astrology and alchemy then both attempt to explain the powers of gods above, spirits below, giving psyche a means to stabilize its reality with the awesome powers of nature.

Changing lead into gold then involves changes in mental as well metal states of consciousness, all of which are influenced by transpersonal and subterranean powers. In human psychology, this simply means that the mind exists in a field of consciousness that is kept in check by a spiritual firmament overhead and a soul that "under-stands" it. Just as our sun is held in its orbit by forces that attract and repel, the human psyche is kept in its place by active and passive forces. In astrology, planets represent the active forces, while in alchemy, metals are considered passive. The planets, having spiritual power, cause metals to change. In Jungian terms, the planets are conditions whereas functions are abilities used to shape and give form to the influences of planets.

In many esoteric systems, there are various levels, degrees or stages that define states of consciousness that we must undergo to integrate the best of both worlds to unify all dimensions of reality. Usually, these states add up to seven. In Yoga there are seven *chakras* and in Christianity there are seven sacraments. Likewise, there are seven metals in alchemy, each influenced by a corresponding astrological god. These are:

TABLE 4: METALS AND PLANETS	
Alchemical Metal	**Astrological god (planet)**
Lead	Saturn
Tin	Jupiter
Iron	Mars
Gold	*Sun*
Copper	Venus
Quicksilver (mercury)	Mercury
Silver	Moon

Several points need to be made to help understand this table. Gold is placed precisely in the middle, not at the end where you might expect it to be. We need to resort to astrology to understand why this is so. You will notice that the seven visible planets are mentioned, but earth is conspicuously absent. Astrology took its point of reference from a geocentric perspective. Earth is where it all begins and ends. It's the alpha and the omega, the lead and the gold. We then must imagine this table as if it were a cloth placed on a kitchen table, with gold being at its center. The flat surface is solid earth, and from it we must draw up the energies of each planet to make gold.

Now lets take a look at each of the astrological gods and how they assert a cosmic influence on minds and metals.

Saturn In the old cosmological maps, Saturn's orbit was the widest and the moon's the shortest as viewed from planet earth. Saturn therefore represents the outer limit of human intelligence. He is lead in the sense that he is most removed, dark and therefore most receptive to a human infusion of life. Saturn is typically portrayed as an old man holding a scythe in one hand and a baby in the other. He stands at the outer limits of time and is therefore understood to cut short our time on earth.

The Greeks knew Saturn as *Cronos* and we are reminded of this old timekeeper in words like chronology and chronometer. Saturn's day is Saturday, known to many as the Sabbath. Just as time keeps us on schedule, Saturn adds structure to our days and limits to our thoughts. His limits are sharply defined, no one is spared the swift cut of his scythe. Like most gods, Cronos jealously guards his power. In one myth he devours his children and heirs in a vain attempt to preserve his dominance over time.

When we try to ignore the savagery of time we fall victim to a leaden condition. Morbid depression, melancholia and lethargy overcome us. We are held captive in the unconscious by Saturn, the Grim Reaper, and suffer rather than learn the importance of death and dying. "In alchemy," writes the Jungian analyst Thomas Moore, "Saturn was identified with the process of putrefaction and as the Black Sun, *sol Niger,* of the *nigredo,* the phase of blackening, psychologically that phase of the soul's work when the mess that has been made is allowed to settle, rot, and putrefy."[16]

As dark a figure as Saturn certainly is, he is not without his merits. Always there is some iota of gold to be found in each metal, including lead. Saturn as *senex* is the wise old man who teaches us to slow down, reflect and have patience. Depression in this sense is Saturn's way of checking our flight from soul. In another part of the myth, we learn that Saturn devours the secret stone of the alchemists. The story has it that a special stone was then substituted in an attempt to save the children from being eaten; thus it came to be that this magic stone represents eternal youth.

> Each of the metals and their gods has a positive and negative "charge." They can therefore mislead us or move us forward. Our job is to locate the "center" or noblest part of each metal, "generate" its knowledge at the ego level and acknowledge its presence in the Self. You might ask yourself where Saturn appears in your life and how open you are to learning from him.

Moon (Luna)

The moon works as the cosmic agent holding body and soul together. This "other sun" is often pictured as a beautiful woman holding a lamp in one hand and a spear in the other; a crescent moon crown adorns her head. The moon is the very opposite of the sun in that she represents the recessive, withdrawing powers of the unconscious. As Saturn is the death aspect of time, the moon is growth. "Eternity," wrote Blake, "is in love with the production of time." The moon takes from eternity and rules growth and generation. Her productions are not like those of the sun because she does not generate any of her own creative power. The moon's secret lies in her ability to reflect any power that shines off her clear white surface.

Luna consciousness can be positive or negative. "A positive Moon," writes Charles Walker, author of *The Encyclopedia of Secret Knowledge*, "gives sensitivity, impressionality, changeability, and (sometimes) a retentive shrewdness and practicality. A negative, or 'baleful' Moon, which is under pressure, intensifies imagination to a point where it tends to lose contact with reality."[17] Moon madness or mania exemplifies this latter morbid condition. A man in touch with his "inner moon," the *anima*, and a woman living in harmony with her *animus* benefit from the positive, life-giving attributes of the moon.

For many years it was believed that the moon emptied itself as it approached the sun. Psychologically, this emptiness, or *kenosis*, is akin to purging. It rids body and soul of its impurities and at the same time, gently allows new growth to take place.

Jupiter   Although the expression "By Jove!" has fallen out of fashion, it once indicated a flash of insight or some fortuitous discovery. Jove, or Jupiter, is the god of spiritual expansion. We find Jupiter in the company of good friends when the air might be described as light and jovial. Flashes of insight are signified in Jupiter's insignias—lightning bolts and arrows. He is also shown as an eagle, able to draw circles around the sun and moon. In alchemy, Jupiter is thought to mix a great deal of sun (fire) with a little moon (water). This fire draws us upward and can lead to negative as well as positive outcomes. A positive Jupiter disposition in a person can inculcate good morals, loyalty and generosity; while a negative disposition produces self-indulgence and prodigality.

Most importantly, Jupiter serves to bring moderation between spirit and body. He does this by infusing a spiritual sensibility to each, and further by bringing heart and soul to community. Jupiter is like the Tin Man in *The Wizard of Oz*. While his ax is ready in hand to cut down a tree, his heart shudders at the thought. By reconciling these forces, a house built with Jupiter's moderating energy becomes a spiritual home.

> All things in moderation. These words might well have come straight out of Jupiter's mouth. I share with you advice once given me by my poetry teacher: "When you fly, soar like an eagle, when you walk, don't stumble."

Mercury   Mercury is a complex entity that must be understood as existing simultaneously in three dimensions. These are:

1. as a planet, or archetypal god (Mercurius)

2. as one of the three basic alchemical principles (the other two are sulfur and salt)

3. as a metal, or host for transmutation (quicksilver)

Mercury's triple nature is critically important to a full understanding of alchemy.[18] Just as a sentence organizes thought and allows us to communicate what we are thinking, mercury is the subject, verb and object of alchemy. Here's a sentence that formulates these various roles: Mercury causes things to join. He is in this sentence, the doer, the action and the object. In the list above this equates with mercury as doer (1), principle of action (2) and object of transmutation (3).

This god holds such a reverential place in alchemy that I have set aside a separate section later in this chapter where we will discuss in further detail his many powerful attributes as an archetypal god. There will be more discussion of the three basic principles of salt, sulfur and mercury in the next chapter.

In the context of astrology and alchemy, mercury is the "womb of all metals," meaning that it serves as both an entry point of spiritual influences and a receptive metal (quicksilver) for transformation. As a god, Mercury makes vitally important connections between worlds and does so on all levels of reality. On the human plane, he works his magic through the skillful use of words. This is not ordinary word play, but eloquence that reveals the deepest meaning of thought. Mercury enjoys that intermediary space between image and symbol, the place where words have not yet been connected to internal thoughts and external senses. The point of this interaction is the ongoing creation, where unconsciousness is made conscious. This flow of creation erupts into spoken language, and Mercury is there, alongside King Neptune, to make sure that the spirit has found its way into the world.

Hermeneutics, the art of translation, takes its name from one of Mercury's many images, Hermes. All astute interpreters are well advised to pay homage to Mercury. He is god of language and the one who mediates the transactions between foolishness and wisdom. Winged Mercury hovers about the borderlands of reality. Wherever opposite sides are taken, he is there to mediate the transaction. Should he spy a pocket of inactivity, he can be counted on to stir things up by creating the necessary tension needed to bring conflict as well as resolution. Thus we find Mercury mixing it up with chemicals, between people at the bargaining table, and flying between planets and metals. He is a shape-shifter, a divine thief and above all else, a spirit of the highest order.

People having a strong mercurial disposition are quick minded, talkative, eloquent and highly expressive. They grasp what other people

> Mercury delights us with surprise and upsets us with shocking news. If we do not understand his divine function, we will be the butt of his jokes. Understanding that he serves to awaken us to connections we would never have otherwise made is the secret to using his gifts well.

mean to say even before the words are spoken. Mercury types can therefore adopt the masculine and feminine aspects of either sexed person, blending these differences into perfect harmony. This potential to fuse, blend and harmonize opposites is so prevalent in Mercury that he was believed to be the personification of the philosopher's stone.

Mars   This god is typically clad in a suit of armor, wielding a sword and shield. He is a born soldier, warrior, a killer. He opposes all emphasis placed on the importance of integration and wholeness. His stark realism aims at destruction in the way fire cauterizes a wound or a sword lops off the head of a brute. Iron and fire are his emblems. With Mars the soul is soft and unable to combat the forces that seek to annihilate it—demanding addicts, con artists, psychic vampires.

But, like other gods, Mars has his redeeming features. Where "Mercury defines, Saturn resolves, . . . Mars divides."[19] In the Tarot cards, intellect is associated with swords.[20] In the same way, Mars cuts through the irrelevant to bring about reason. His indomitable will gives us strength, fortitude and courage. He is a no-nonsense doer, a fixer, enterprising, confident and proud. With enlightened Martian consciousness we have a thoughtful warrior to call on when necessary. Undoubtedly, we have to put up with his lack of patience, his propensity toward boasting and even quarreling, but we can always rely on his loyalty.

> You will find Mars in rage, combat and battles at the office. Rather than condemn him, you might consider marrying him to the Venus in you. In myth, this is exactly what happened, and out of the union between the two, a new child was born, named Harmony.

Mars's influence is an index of a person's indomitable will, aggressiveness and sex drive. So, once again, we see the dichotomy of this image. He may be positive (Mars of Aries) in his forward thinking, or negative (Mars of Scorpio) in his domineering need for control.

Venus   To the extent that Mars seems to typify the masculine character, Venus is just the opposite: warm, cooperative, loving. She is beauty and has a passion for the finer things of life. She is seen holding a heart because she endows the spiritual essence of love to the physical body. She does this through charm, grace and beauty. But, Venus has her earthly side as well. Courtesans, geishas and practitioners of the *Kama Sutra* all ultimately pay homage to Venus. She is queen of heaven and earth, as she "guides and watches over that realm of life which includes both full sensuous enjoyment and understanding. She takes care of the two affections of soul, for body and spirit."[21]

Venus's strength appears when pleasure is under one's control, not the other way round. Prostitution is the alchemical equivalent of schemes aimed at profit and usury. It misses the target—the true gold. Those who use passion to manipulate, or who become emotionally confused, thinking with their heart rather than their head, personify Venus's weakness. They sometimes exaggerate beauty or put on a false front to beguile and take advantage of others. Love is not exempt from having its own dark side.

This dark side of Venus has a double nature: one whose goal is limited to nothing more than pleasure for its own sake, and another which finds pleasure as a channel through which spiritual connection is made. The passionate love Mary Magdalene had for Christ reveals these dark energies of Venus and how they celebrate spirit through the body.

> Venus is not the exclusive province of the female gender. She can be found in a man's soul as well. An old Arab proverb shed light on gender beauty in this way: "The beauty of man is in his intelligence, and the intelligence of woman is in her beauty." The celebration of both, in and between people, is the beauty of love.

Sun (Sol)

Even the skeptic is forced to admit to celestial influences when considering the solar effects on earth. In alchemy and astrology, *sol* is believed to infuse solar energy into every particle of earthly matter. Whereas every planet has two sides (houses) to their personality, only the sun and moon are either wholly masculine or feminine. Where the moon's feminine power lies in her close proximity to earth, her changing form and reflective nature, sun is constant, hot and self-generating. *Sol* is the archetypal male force seen as gold, king and the source for life. Just as the fool moves through the houses (planets) of the Tarot deck, the sun moves through seven levels of consciousness. The fool begins the journey as a naive innocent and by degree learns the lesson (arcana) each house has to teach; if successful, the fool emerges as a full-fledged magus (magician) with extraordinary powers. Similarly, the sun traverses the whole zodiac and evolves into the Red Lion, the name given by alchemists to describe the all-transmuting elixir.

A favorable sun in one's horoscope promotes strong tendencies toward authority, generosity, self-reliance, dignity and an affectionate nature. In the negative, we find dark qualities of vanity, overconfidence, exhibitionism and arrogance. The journey taken by the fool must inevitably pass through the "dark night of the soul," represented in alchemy by the terrifying image of the *Sol Niger*, the Black Sun. This is the relative absence of solar energy and consciousness. In this dangerous state, we feel as if we are dead, emptied of reason and even lacking any purpose to go on living.

Fire, the central motif in alchemy, and the sun, represent the celestial energy below and the terrestrial energy above. Controlling the earthly flame helps burn away negative emotions, impure thoughts and the body's unbridled impulses. Alchemy is an instruction book on how we become masters of fire. A beautiful poem points the way: "By hidden means, remote from our senses, the sun in heaven has many ways in the heart of the mountain of making the ruby red."

When we master this "agent of transformation" we quell the sparks separating things, causing them to turn against one another. Paracelsus observed that humans share an affinity with fire: both of us must feed upon other lives in order to keep alive. Master this secret and all opposites are brought into harmony with the royal qualities of King Gold. As the myth tells us, this king "must be killed and buried, in order that he may awake again to life, and [then], ascending through seven regimes, attain his full glory."[22]

> The Greek philosopher Heraclitus said, "The sun is new each day." This simple but profound statement reminds us that however unconscious we may be, however bereft our circumstance, or however low our spirit, each day brings a new sun to restore life. In fact, the sun shines day and night. Look through the clouds, see through the darkness, and you will always draw strength from the sun.

COURSING THROUGH THE UNIVERSE

The transmutation of lead to gold is a process with a corresponding course through the stars and the developmental steps needed to become fully realized human beings. Thus the alchemical opus is as much about describing the cardinal points of the individuation process as it is about the maturation of metals. Like the shaman who keenly understands the nature of each animal's spirit, the alchemist knew the behavior of metals and their sympathetic alignment with his own soul. "The journey through the planetary houses," observed Jung, "signifies the overcoming of a psychic complex, suitably represented by a planetary god or demon."[23]

In the Hermetic book *Poimandres, the Shepherd of Men,* Hermes is told that these complexes or planetary gods give up their hold on the soul after death. So that,

> At the sphere of the Moon [the soul] leaves behind the power of growth and waning; at Mercury, the power of devising evils; at Venus, the illusion of desire; at the Sun, the arrogance of domination; at Mars, impious boldness and rashness; at Jupiter, striving for wealth by evil means; at Saturn, falsehood.[24]

As a result of this spiritual individuation process, "anyone who has passed through all the spheres is free from compulsion: he has won the crown of victory and becomes like a god."[25]

This apotheosis is the reward for those who succeed in their personal alchemy. Envisioning the individuation process as a horoscope, through which we successively extract and add qualities of consciousness, gives body and spiritual substance to the work. Macrobius describes the virtues of each of these gods with these words:

> In the sphere of Saturn it [the nascent soul] obtains **reason and understanding,** called *logistikon* and *theoretickon;* in Jupiter's sphere, **the power to act**, called *prakitikon;* in Mars's sphere, **a bold spirit** or *thymikon;* in the sun's sphere, **sense-perception and imagination,** *aisthetikon* and *phantastikon;* in Venus's sphere, **the impulse of passion,** *epithymetikon;* in Mercury's sphere, **the ability to speak and interpret,** *hermeneutikon;* and in the lunar sphere, the function of **molding and increasing bodies,** *phytikon.* This last function being the farthest removed from the gods, is the first in us and all the earthly creation.[26]

I highlighted the virtues associated with each god. These really are a recipe for achieving the gold of the Individuated Self. Be not fooled, the course of this psychic chemistry is perilous and fraught with danger.

Thus, I am compelled to consider one last class of spirits that must be understood in order to keep us safely on track.

TRICKSTERS BETWIXT 'N' BETWEEN

Mercurius is the Latin name for the god Mercury, his metal quicksilver and his principle of action. Before describing this quixotic god in more detail, it's helpful to see the context in which he belongs, the archetype of the trickster. Thus far we have examined the elemental beings of earth and the gods in the heavens; in between, there is a whole host of tricksters who serve to connect these two great orders of existence.

Thoth, Maui, Anasi, Coyote and Hermes are other gods belonging to the same archetype as Mercurius. Each represents special characteristics of the trickster archetype. More than elementals and astrological gods, the trickster is more accessible to human perception. We see him in clowns, off-color jokes, pranks and political cartoons. We are, of course, always suspicious of this character and his antics. As a precautionary measure, we in America give him one day a year, April Fool's Day, when we willingly allow ourselves to participate in his tomfoolery. But, if we can drop our guard and open up to his gifts as well as his boon, we see the gold hidden in the jest. We discover then how barren our lives might be, if we were to exist at all, without this cunning aspect of the human mind.

No matter where or when in history you look for him, a trickster is sure to be there, at times appearing as the fool, the holy clown, or the king's jester. Trickster speaks the language of the land, dressed in colorful garb, and juggling morals, opinions and eternal truths.

Thoth, a cosmic trickster god, was one of the most venerated deities of ancient Egypt. He is also credited with having invented language and writing; as such, he was the court scribe who recorded the pronouncements of the final judgment. In later times, we find all types of tricksters throughout Africa, many appearing in animal form. Anasi, for example, was a clever trickster who sometimes appeared as a spider, an image alchemists used in their woodcuts. This spider traveled to the Americas with the West African slaves and settled in the Caribbean, where he shape-shifted into a variety of strange images. Another African trickster, known as Legba, also made the journey to this region, where he became one of the powerful *loa* (god) in Voodoo practice.

The hare and the tortoise run races not only in American folk tales; they each had their own separate mythologies in Africa. Hare, it is believed, made the Atlantic crossing with the slaves, appearing in the well-known stories of Uncle Remus as Brer Rabbit. Tortoise, or turtle, is beloved by Native Americans, where he is the oldest symbol for Earth. They believe he represents grounding, the cycles of life and protection. The Chinese took the first forms of their alphabet from the markings on the back of a tortoise, connecting him again with trickster's affinity with language.

Traveling east from Africa we discover Ganesha, the revered elephant trickster of India. Throughout Asia the elephant is considered a wise creature; Buddhists sometimes represented Gautama Buddha in this noble guise. In my travels around India I saw statues of Ganesha everywhere, used as much by ordinary people as good luck charms as by Hindu priests in sacred ceremonies. In one story, Ganesha is said to have broken off one of his tusks and used it to write the Mahabaratha, a sacred Hindu text.

It seems that Buddha had less tolerance for trickster. According to Buddhist lore, trickster appears as a monkey who, using magic and trickery, forces respect from the high gods by subduing demons and monsters. Buddha puts an end to these shenanigans by imprisoning him, but in the end, it is to no avail. On his release, Monkey remains as deviant as ever. Such is the power of this divine archetype!

In Greek mythology we find a number of tricksters. There's Prometheus, who stole fire from the gods for the benefit of all humans. Alchemists, of course, are much indebted to this god not only for providing them with their basic element, but also for the powers of healing and regeneration that come with mastery over fire. As great a god as Prometheus surely is, his prominence is eclipsed by another famous trickster of Greek myth, Hermes.

In Norman O. Brown's wonderful book on Hermes we learn that "behind Hermes the Thief is Hermes the Trickster, and behind Hermes the Trickster is Hermes the Magician."[27] In retelling the Homeric myth, Brown describes the incredible first days of Hermes—his theft of his brother Apollo's cattle, the invention of the lyre and how he received his magic wand. His stealth and shape-shifting abilities are delightfully described in this incredible tale. We find ourselves liking him despite his unruly ways. Apparently, Hermes had the same effect on his country-men. To this day, you will find "hermstones" placed at crossroads of country lanes, to honor this Lord of the Road.

Another Greek trickster, the goat-footed god Pan, takes a decidedly different turn. Christians adopted the image of Pan as the personifica-tion of evil. Pan, the wily god of shepherds and animals, is alien to the civilized world. His is the realm of nature with all its mystery and sur-prise. Although Pan can instantly transform experience into sudden shock, his prominence as a god of transformation is mostly lost in the modern world.

Pan was unfortunately reduced in the Christian world to the goat-footed Satan who'll tempt at every turn. Lost is his connection to his pa-tron (and perhaps father), Hermes. Lost is his connection to Dionysus, who loved him dearly. Lost is his connection to Echo, the reflective side of his nature. No, in this modern era, Pan is looked at with suspicion as the source of panic attacks and nightmares.

In the northern climes, this evil image of trickster appears in the Scandinavian god Loki. Only in this case killer instincts are very appar-ent. It was Loki who, by killing Balder, father of the Fenris wolf and the Midard serpent, destroys Ragnarok's world. It is oftentimes difficult to accept this dark side of the psyche, but to condemn trickster is to deprive us of the need to destroy whatever gets in the way of developing an Indi-viduated Self. In the act of temptation we have the opportunity to deny what would have us miss the mark. Trickster tests our mettle. He quick-ens our resolve to stay the course. It is certainly better to enlist trickster into our service than make an enemy of him.

One of the best examples of how to befriend trickster is found in Native American culture. In the Winnebago tribe, a whole epic has evolved that delightfully portrays the individuation process through the bewildering exploits of Kunu, the Foolish One. This trickster is so like us that we cannot, even as we are laughing at his crazy self-defeating antics, help feeling sympathy for him. He mirrors our own foolishness, and at the same time, redeems himself. Along with my own personal fool, I cherish Kunu for teaching me how to laugh at myself.

Coyote is another favorite of mine. He shows up in the Navajo na-tion, where wily coyote is not at all as funny as the cartoon. He teaches by way of what we are not supposed to do. His treachery, cowardice and iconoclastic behavior reveal the secrets we all keep hidden from parents and priests. He breaks down traditions when they no longer serve to advance the community.

Tricksters always carry out their mission by using a fool's show to pit contrary opinion and emotions against one another. We can't seem to help simultaneously laughing and crying as trickster carries on in his crazy way. We feel sorry for him one minute and applaud his misguided heroism the next. He has us criticizing him and thanking him. Trickster mixes it up and puts the oddest things together. He juggles our thoughts and feelings in a chaotic whirl that sometimes gets out of control, and at other times, is a brilliant balancing act. If anything, trickster, the antihero, is a shadowy character who puts us laughingly, haltingly and inevitably in touch with the Self.

> Now take a look at your own inner trickster, the one that is contrary, who blurts out embarrassing truths, cracks jokes in churches, belches in restaurants and libraries . . . of all things! If you think you can keep the trickster restricted to one day a year, not only are you kidding yourself, but you are depriving yourself of a very sacred dimension of life. Don't let yourself be fooled! Laugh till it hurts!

Trickster especially likes to prey on those who enjoy taking big risks. In my practice I see how often the biggest risk takers are those who gamble with their own lives seeking cheap thrills. Addiction has been described as a spiritual hunger and the addict is someone who wants to get high (spiritual) without the hard work of conscious development. When the addict then lowers his or her consciousness through drugs or alcohol, he or she opens the door for all kinds of tricks.

I recall an adolescent boy who was clever and very industrious. He constantly busied himself with one project after another, never, of course, finishing one before starting the next. Everything about him appeared to have these tricksterlike characteristics. Although quite smart, he seemed content just getting by. He was always scheming, conning and pushing people to their limit. When he was arrested for drug possession you would think that would have slowed him down, but it didn't. His parents put him on a behavior contract that included random urine testing for drugs. This boy was out of control and needed to be stopped. But, can anyone really stop the trickster when he's got you by the tail?

Well, this young fellow thought of a way to outsmart his parents, or so he thought. When he knew he was "clean" for a long enough period of time to produce a drug-free urine sample, he peed in a vial and stowed it away for the inevitable day when his parents would demand a drug test. He was shocked when the appointed hour arrived and to his utter bewilderment discovered that he had sealed the vial with a cork—glued for safekeeping! Unable to uncork the clean specimen, he was left to give what he knew would be a sample showing he'd used drugs.

I especially like this example for its alchemical humor. The alchemists stressed the importance of hermetically sealing their vessel, but only after many years of hard work and purifying the soul. I guess the moral to my patient's story is that you may be able to fool others but you can't outfox the trickster.

The trickster is a mirror. He holds up a mirror to our devious ways, to society, to conscience and even to God. His effect on us is as quick as the speed of light. Silver, it seems, is the closest we can come to giving him a color. But, as with all mirrors, every color of the rainbow is reflected off his shiny surface. The colors of the motley fool's costume reflect society's foibles. They appear when we con a business associate, share a confidence with the wrong person, or beat someone up with honesty. What goes around comes around.

Although I haven't come across any reference that explains how trickster's attributes coincide with those of his metal, quicksilver, I think the connection has relevance. Prior to Newton, science was principally based on observation. When you observe the physical properties of quicksilver you find a direct relationship between mind (trickster) and matter (quicksilver). For example:

TABLE 5: THE ATTRIBUTES OF QUICKSILVER

Quicksilver	Attribute
Silver	white and luminescent
Shiny surface	slippery
Elusive	difficult to grasp
Fusibility	connects with everything

More than any other trickster, these attributes are most apparent in the god Mercurius. Everything about Mercurius illustrates the noble qualities of nature's calculus, the way it antagonizes and weaves together chaos and order. Pictured with wings adorning his head and feet, Mercurius is a spirit god who takes flight quickly into any and all domains of existence. Better yet, he has flight insurance. Among all the gods, only tricksters can maintain their integrity regardless of what environment they happen to be in. As such, Mercurius represents critical aspects of the elixir, the chemical version of the philosopher's stone. Like a dye, Mercurius penetrates all matter without forfeiting any of his own potency; thus, mercury does not yield its own properties no matter how it is alloyed with another metal. His impermeability is especially necessary in "marrying" metals whose constitutions are antagonistic to each other. The trickster is an excellent negotiator and a master at drawing up alliances between the most unlikely partners, be they chemicals or competitors.

To understand the full meaning Mercurius had for alchemists, we need to place him in an archetypal context. From this perspective, Mercurius is not limited to rational categories. He may be a force, entity or energy, depending on the circumstance of the situation. As an archetype, his transpersonal influence affects all orders of reality, human and otherwise. Because these same characteristics abound in nature, it becomes clear that Mercurius is the catalyst required for any kind of transformation. For this reason, alchemists referred to their precious philosopher's stone as the Mercury-Lapis.[28]

Whether it comes to us as a gift from God, an accident of nature or some combination of the two, there is no greater power we possess than the fact that we are conscious beings. We can pretty much doubt everything else—intelligence, conscience, emotions—but the one enduring principle that sets us aside and yes, above, everything else is the unparalleled depth of our self-consciousness. To the best of our knowledge, this power is not something one either has or doesn't. There is clearly a range of consciousness that we are endowed with from nature through our biological lineage and that is shaped by parents and many environmental factors.

THE WHY FILE: THE TRUTH IS IN HERE

Just as our perceptions reveal a range of sound and color, there is a range of consciousness that seems to begin with plants and vegetation and proceeds up through the many phylum of animate beings, continuing into the human dimension and extending to . . . well, who knows where. Although a number of features distinguish the degree of consciousness marking each creature's place along this spectrum, one hallmark feature that puts humans above the rest is their tremendous capacity to know themselves. However, we came to have this power and to whatever extent we exercise it, our ability, if not our mandate, requires us to make meaning of life using this special power.

Like other attributes of consciousness, awareness is subject to change, for better or worse. There are things we do that work to elevate or diminish it. Jung's theory of individuation would have no meaning without a capacity for consciousness that not only changes over an individual's life span, but also over the life of a whole culture. Alchemy, in this regard, is no different. It would have no purpose if consciousness were fixed to a certain set of immutable laws. But Nature shows us quite differently: it loves change. Mutation is the basis of evolution. To the extent that we embrace this special attribute and nurture it, we can educate our minds to be more intelligent; thus, we open our eyes to more of who we are and where we live. In this sense, Mercurius serves to jolt us out of our resistance to change.

Without trickster we might well stagnate or become fixed, devoid of magic. Sadly, it seems that our spirit has been thwarted by the advent of our modern age of science. While science has created a technology that has produced a world of convenience, longer life and better economic conditions, there has, by way of compensation perhaps, been a dear price paid. It is somewhat ironic, if not paradoxical, that technology enables us to see and move about in unprecedented ways, and yet, at the same time, our degree of awareness has shrunk rather than expanded. The ability to see galaxies that were previously invisible to the naked eye is indeed marvelous, but its beauty is diminished by the scientific impulse to control and dominate the celestial objects of our newfound perceptions. This is not inherently bad, or wrong, just shortsighted.

Long before sailors had the ships, the money and the courage to venture out across the mighty oceans of the world, they must have intuitively known the world to be round. After all, you only need to go as little as twenty miles out to sea before an observer standing on the shore would see your sails slowly sink below the horizon. The ship did not fall off the edge of the horizon and its safe return certainly provided empirical evidence that the world was not flat. It then took science to prove that indeed the world is round. The point I am making is that intuitive knowledge almost always precedes scientific experiment. Observation is an essential ingredient of awareness, and intuitions are observations made from the place where consciousness seems to be more intimately tied to nature.

If observation was restricted to the perceptible world we would not have discovered the existence of the many forms of light that make up the nonvisible spectrum (gamma, X rays, etc.). The dispersion of white light, as seen in a rainbow, must have led scientists like Newton to wonder if light also existed beyond the visible range. In fact, Newton, an ardent alchemist, did some of his most important work with light. When science and imagination work in tandem, startling results often follow. But, when some part of consciousness supersedes, ignores or even denies the intuitive powers of the imagination, then scientific research becomes lopsided and sterile.

Fortunately, there appears to be some sort of regulator that keeps such stagnation from existing too long. Perhaps the mercury in our psychic thermometer tells us when to shut down and when to turn up the blowers. Whether change comes by way of a single person or a whole society, some force or set of circumstances occurs to bring about the needed correction. We have been witnessing this correction in action with the advent of theoretical physics in general and quantum physics more specifically.

This correction, whether it is in the form of a force or a set of fortuitous events, is Trickster carrying out his world-making duties. In fact, creativity and the process of invention are intimately linked to his marvelous ability to see the world in unusual and extraordinary ways. In the context of this chapter, where we have described elemental beings, astrological gods and various imaginary beings, science is purposely being subjugated to the primacy of intuitive, imaginative play. In other words, we are prying open "the doors of perception" and seeing, as ancient mariners did before they set sail, the distance beyond the horizon.

Even without taking such bold steps, the correction of which I speak is already happening. While modern physics appears to be making a deliberate attempt to embrace the imaginal realm, fantastic images are popping up in movies, comics and arcade and video games. To whatever extent an empirically driven science excludes the populace from such imaginings, we find gods appearing not only in our entertainment, but more significantly, in the form of psychological symptoms and nightly dreams. Undoubtedly the correction is forcing us, despite all resistance to the contrary, to include, rather than exclude, the imaginal world.

The imaginal presences that I have described are real, whether or not the modern scientist in you can see or hear them. Just as alchemists described grades of metals in terms of purity, conscious awareness has its degrees of refinement. Alchemists therefore worked as much to increase their power of awareness as they did to purify their metals. Unlike us, however, they did not give a merely perfunctory nod to the imaginal world; instead, they embraced it wholeheartedly. For them, writes Godwin, "belief in the elementals is a way of saying everything is alive—that there is a spark of divine consciousness in every particle of matter."[29]

These divine scientists, he goes on to say, held to a vision of life where the very

> origin of matter . . . and all natural processes of growth [are] the action
> of elementals working on the subtle planes: not anthropomorphic little folk,
> of course, but beings of many different classes, powers, and degrees of con-
> sciousness intermediate between ourselves and the Angelic Hierarchy.[30]

This is not some sort of parallel world but one that, whether we have the subtlety to recognize it or not, is an intricate part of the world *as we know it*. I emphasize this last point because it is critical to all understanding of nature that psyche is an inextricable part of all creation. It is how the world is created; it is how we create the world. To exclude the vicissitudes of psyche or even diminish them would indeed be foolhardy. That part of psyche we call Trickster will not be relegated to one day a year when we allow ourselves to be a little crazy. Reading the daily horoscope or amusing ourselves with a dream that we just happen to recall will not do. Alchemy requires us to accept the existence of the imaginary world not only as real, but, consciously or not, as one in which we are already living.

Chapter 6

Sacred Operations

We are explorers and the most compelling frontier
of our time is human consciousness.
Our quest is the integration of science and spirituality,
a vision which reminds us of our connectedness to the inner self,
to each other, and to the earth.
EDGAR MITCHELL, ASTRONAUT

In this chapter, we leave the world of sprites, fairies and tricksters in order to learn about the actual hands-on work of personal alchemy. As a therapist and lecturer, I am inevitably asked the "How?" question. How questions run the gamut: How do I communicate better with my spouse? How do I overcome my alcohol problem? How do I deal with my anger? Paradoxically, our emphasis on knowing how to solve a problem often gets in the way of its solution. In our approach to alchemy, we have emphasized theory and now we need to take up the difficult task of deciphering its operations. This will require us to separate occult "chemistry" from psychological methods that answer the how questions. In this shift to practice, we should not lose sight of alchemy's overarching philosophy, for that it where its real gold can always be found.

Other cautions: 1) fixing a problem may not bring healing to the overall person (what's right for the moment is not necessarily the best solution in the big picture); 2) alchemical operations are not exclusively the property of any particular psychology (they preceded all formal schools of psychology). While psychology played a crucial role in the alchemists' work, there was never any specific psychology that could make sense of their work until modern times. Despite the exhaustive work applied to this project by Herbert Silberer, Carl Jung, Marie-Louise von Franz and others, there remains more lead to be mined. Perhaps alchemy will always be a work in progress requiring each individual to take up the gauntlet. Remember Rumi's words: "You are the master alchemist."

In turning our attention to practice, the opportunity for personal experiment begins. Our job requires us to go beyond laboratory procedures by drawing out the unconscious purpose behind each method. More than simply telling us what to do, this approach will stimulate the imaginative mind and help us put the principles of alchemy into practice. Then, the work of individuation and healing really begins to happen.

In twenty years of clinical experience, I have found that the greatest healing comes when people work through the problems of daily living. Seen in the context of individuation, we could say that problems are challenges required to spur on development when it falls idle, becomes fixated by trauma, or stunted by addiction and emotional disorder. Problems are necessary to sharpen our wits, test our courage and teach us new ways of dealing with difficult situations. As part of our developmental process, problems often mirror the issues facing us from one age to the next. Adolescents have their difficulties with identity, adults experience age-related issues concerning marriage, business, health and the specter of death. Alchemy deals with the special problems accompanying these developmental stages first by understanding the nature of each period and second by using appropriate operations to deal with particular challenges faced at every critical juncture along the way.

Since we are dealing with a psychological alchemy, I won't be discussing how alchemists went about separating and combining various substances. Instead, our interest lies in learning how they skillfully changed their states of mind. Since matter follows consciousness, changing the mind rectifies the disorder ailing us. Rather than identifying specific changes in physical matter, our interest lies in seeing changes take place in behavior. In either case, however, healing begins by learning how to alter the mind at will. The formula we will then be using goes like this:

> Change your mind and you create change in behavior. Change your behavior and you precipitate changes in matter.

In order to apply this formula we need a manual that delineates operations used for transforming (rather than destroying) obstacles that stand in the way of accessing the powers of the Self. This manual begins by describing three basic stages of the work, three forces, and seven operations.

From this brief introduction, I hope I leave you with the importance of adopting the right attitude necessary to bring about complete healing. Remember:

> Alchemy is about taking steps to help us not only solve our problems, but further bring about an overall transformation of consciousness.

STAGES   The theme of darkness is central to alchemy. We associate it with the realm of the unconscious, the Underworld, ignorance and evil forces. In nature, darkness is neither good nor bad but simply a neutral condition in which things rest, take root and grow. With this logic in mind, the alchemists called the first stage of the work the *nigredo,* which literally means blackening. Like the rich black soil that provides a tiny seed with a matrix in which gestation begins, the *nigredo* is a physical and psychological stage where consciousness first begins to take shape and gain some semblance of order.

The seed, in this case, is the *prima materia* and the *nigredo* marks the movement of this prime matter from a confused state to the first level of organization. Lead describes this inferior (wholly unconscious) material or condition; it is the starting point in the long journey consciousness undergoes in changing from lead to gold.

Nigredo

Where might the lead be in your life? Do you find yourself disorganized and lacking any real vision? Are you lethargic and running short of a real zest for life? Do you suffer from a condition known as anhedonia, which is a severe lack of pleasure? Do you sleep too much or lack the energy necessary to get things done? Or, does your lead come in the form of low self-esteem, passivity and self-doubt? Like lead, is your life gray, indistinct and pliable?

An answer of "Yes" to any of these questions could mean that you are depressed, the psychological equivalent to the *nigredo* condition. Just as depression describes the condition of consciousness just after birth, it is also the first emotional state alchemists dealt with as they began their work. The *nigredo* was sometimes referred to as the *melanosis,* suggesting the meloncholy and depression alchemists oftentimes felt when they themselves retreated from ordinary life to undertake their work.

Depression becomes pathological only when we've achieved consciousness and then try to deny it. We may be fighting back anger, a feeling of inadequacy, lack of courage, etc. In these cases, it is as if our feet were made of lead and we're unable to move forward. With chaos at our heels we do not have much choice but to forge on by bringing order into our lives. This urge to individuate begins naturally enough as a defense against chaos and dissolution, but continues more proactively once a person stops running from fear and begins to embrace clarity of mind and the vitality of being real.

Depression returns psyche to its depths. While depressive episodes are painful, they force us to confront the shadowy figures of our unconscious fears. They are part of the *nigredo* experience and as such, all alchemy begins only by accepting depression as a necessary part of life. Remember this when depression strikes. Ironically, memory becomes a deadweight during these periods, imbued with black recollections of bad times. The process of re-membering transforms this miserable lead into something new and more meaningful.

These terrible times put us in touch with the unconscious. Short of being irreversibly fixated in this dark state of mind, depression can actually be very useful. My greatest insights have come from periods in my life when I've suffered intense depression. I recall for instance having lost the "girl of my dreams" for reasons I knew were beyond my control. Nevertheless, I mourned the loss for years. My attention could hardly deviate from thinking about her. I was locked in an obsessive depression. In time, I had to learn how to burn away the illusion and unhealthy passions that held me prisoner of my darkness. Eventually, I came to realize that my attachment was not so much to the person, but to the intense *anima* image I had projected onto her. The *anima* is the soul image men naturally have in their unconscious to represent the feminine in all her ubiquitous forms.

Years passed before I was able to burn away the "goddess" image I'd projected onto her and see her as a real person. Only then could I begin a mourning process that eventually allowed me to discover the source of my projection, the *anima*. This discovery required a depression in which my psyche could set my mind aside and separate my mixed-up images. It was a real resurrection having that *anima* image move to where it belongs: as a goddess, in some spiritual realm, and as an animating force, within my soul. I believe all men must go through this kind of crisis in order to discover the divine feminine. Certainly a similar process occurs for every woman in meeting her masculine spirit.

Albedo   Darkness alone cannot bring things into life. The light that shines on the *prima materia* causes it to develop and mature. In psychological terms, light symbolizes conscious awareness. Once we bring consciousness to our depressed state, it changes our entire disposition. We lighten up and may even be able to extract some insight from our misery. This is the lightbulb that goes on in newspaper cartoons. As insight matures it is internalized and eventually expressed outwardly in our behavior.

Where black is the color used to describe the first stage of alchemy, this second movement, known as the *albedo,* uses white to represent the illuminating power of light on the *prima materia*. In this condition we experience an uplifting sensation. It's as if we have been released from the gravity of our problems and hope shines on us like a bright star in the sky. This first movement from the *nigredo* to the *albedo* completes the initial stage of the work. It is called the Ascent of the Soul because of the belief that everything originates out of the dark soul and only by moving upward toward the light of spirit is there any possibility of having them join in a royal marriage.

Bringing light to darkness is a recurrent theme in alchemy. Psychologically, this means that consciousness and unconsciousness are fused into one completely new form. The sum of these opposites is the creation of the white stone of the *albedo*. As we will see shortly, this development from *nigredo* (unconsciousness) to *albedo* (consciousness) is not easy to do.

In the beautiful Greek myth *Amor and Psyche* we discover how the soul, personified as a young woman, is released from earth, and after many trials and tribulations, is transformed into a heavenly goddess.[1] When Psyche discovers that her husband, Amor, is a god, she is overwhelmed. Thinking she has lost him forever, she consults Aphrodite, who assigns her tasks that will prepare her to receive love.

The light of consciousness, as it shows up in relationship, can sometimes be too much for us, especially if we are not prepared for it. Again, alchemy is a slow process of preparation to receive this light. Its tasks, or operations, strengthen both inner masculinity and femininity so that we are not dizzied by the heights to which we ascend.

These first two stages describe the multiple dimensions of our world. Soul defines the world below while spirit takes us up. Without these dimensions, psychological life would not be possible. The third dimension is depth. Now here we do not mean depth in the ordinary sense of the word. Depth, in this context, means to bring soul into the picture. With depth, the unconscious gets involved, often compensating ego and its many soldiers (defenses). Depth draws us down into soul. When we operate with depth, we speak with heart, conviction, *gnosis*. Jungian psychology is known as depth psychology because it aims to understand psyche from this third viewpoint.

Rubedo   While I have mentioned three dimensions and their psychological significance, we must now consider time in order to understand the final stage of the work. The *rubedo* is the third stage and its color is red. Blood, being red, was thought by alchemists to contain the essence of life. Medieval people believed that the soul resided in the blood and the heart was therefore the spiritual and physical center of a person's life. We know today that the heart beats 100,000 times per day, and roughly 2.5 billion times in an average life. The heart measures out time. Thus, if we can manipulate the pulse, slow it down, we take stress off this muscle and may well be able to extend our days.

Today we have medicine that can slow the heart down. These are given to hypertensive patients to help control high blood pressure. Complaints of chest pains are more often than not stress pains. In my practice, I often teach stress reduction techniques that help achieve the same effects as these medicines, without the side effects. Yoga especially has been proven to relax the body as well as the mind. There is an abundance of evidence to show that stress is a killer. In alchemical language, stress pain may well be caused by a runaway spirit. I think of the pulse as the physical reflection of one's spirit. If it's too fast, it must be brought back into harmony with its host, the body. Deep relaxation allows consciousness to settle down and rediscover the natural rhythm of life. Failing this, we run the risk of being overwhelmed by unprocessed emotions and feelings. In short, we have a heart attack. The body is the vessel in which spirit and soul find balance. Hopefully, we need not suffer symptoms to force us into taking responsibility for our mind, body and soul.

In this last stage, we move from an emphasis on soul to the movement caused by spirit. This is known as the Descent of Spirit. In the first two stages, our weak ego consciousness struggles to extricate itself from the regressive pull of nature. Now the movement is from above, that is the spiritual energy that comes from the Self. Human efforts alone cannot accomplish the difficult work of individuation.

In the interaction between soul and spirit, transformation takes place. In other words, through our efforts and those of some transpersonal power, the metals, representing degrees of consciousness, are transmuted from their lowly state into pure, refined gold. Lead, then, is transmuted into the white silver of the *albedo,* and gold in the *rubedo.* Such transformation can just as well take place in a day as in a lifetime. Time is determined as much by what we do as by what we witness in nature.

If alchemy is about doing, then what is the work of this last stage? The alchemist Gerhard Dorn gives us specific instructions:

> First, transmute the earth of your body into water. This means that your heart, which is as hard as stone, material, and lazy must become supple and vigilant. . . . Then spiritual images and visions impress themselves on your heart as a seal is impressed on wax. But now this liquefaction must transform itself into air. That is to say, the heart must become contrite and humble, rising toward its Creator as air rises toward heaven. . . . Then, for this air to become fire, desire, now sublimated, must be converted into love—love of God and neighbor—and this flame must never be extinguished. At this point, to receive the power of things above and things below, you must begin the descent.[2]

ON THREE CONDITIONS: THE FORCES OF NATURE

The alchemists believed in an energetic universe where forces keep the solar and lunar world from collapsing. Because sun and moon correspond to spirit and soul, this same alchemical equilibrium is needed to keep human consciousness intact. In the fifteenth century, an Arbian alchemist introduced the three basic specific forces—salt, sulfur and mercury. To these three the innovative Paracelsus added another force to which he gave the peculiar word "azoth."[3] This term, derived from a corruption of the Arabic word "al-zauq," has magical significance because its letters are formed from the first and last letters of the Arabic, Roman, Greek and Hebrew alphabets.

Azoth is another synonym for mercury, but one that literally expresses the A (alpha) and Z (omega) of the whole alchemical process. Like the elements, azoth should not be considered a physical substance. Azoth is commonly defined as "our second water and living water," and used to describe the mercurial fountain in which soul and spirit dissolve in order to be united. While many compounds and substances in the alchemy laboratory have their counterparts in the physical world, their real value is found in their symbolism.

Salt   Salt is not strictly understood as common sodium chloride. It has a much greater significance. The alchemical salt is the ground upon which all creation rests. In human experience, it represents the principle that allows us to apprehend all natural phenomena. It is life's flow experienced through the feeling function. Refined salt then allows us to penetrate our own depths, and there discover wisdom. This is what is meant by the expression "salt of the earth."

James Hillman suggests that salt "gives what one has in one's head a worth among people: tangible value on earth." More particularly, he describes this value as "the ground of subjectivity, its nature is to fixate, correct, crystallize and purify."[4] Salt is a crystal and it represents the principle of energy that is associated with soul.[5] So important is its place in alchemy that the great Geber took as his motto, "Everything in nature is in Sun and Salt." By including salt alongside the symbolism of the Sun, which is the essential fire, this master alchemist shows us the importance he placed on salt.

We cannot live without salt and we are reminded of its essential presence in our blood, sweat and tears. "You must," writes Dennis Hauck in his book *The Emerald Tablet,* "make yourself cry for Dissolution to occur, so do not be afraid to feel the pain again."[6] Tears, he reminds us, were believed by medieval alchemists to be the "remnant of crystallized thoughts." When we cry in this way, we dissolve sad thoughts by allowing them to become felt experiences. Salt dries out the sentiment and allows thoughts to refresh the soul.

Sulfur   Sulfur is that energy that gives inert material the power to burst forth into creation. A belly laugh, flashes of insight, a spontaneous kiss—all exemplify the action of sulfuric energy in human life. On the world's stage we witness spring bursting forth each year, the sun breaking dawn's horizon and volcanoes erupting. Sulfur contains immense and densely packed energy awaiting the moment when the full force of nature can burst forth. The old term for sulfur was brimstone, which conjures up the fiery energies of hell. Sulfur is explosive and it smells bad, but without it we would have neither a campfire nor the Big Bang that put us here in the first place.

Sulfur is the masculine complement to the feminine salt. It forces things into form. For this reason, Chinese and Arabian alchemists combined sulfur with mercury to produce mercuric sulfide, or what they called cinnebar. This "dragon's blood" was used as the *prima materia* for successive work. In the same way, sulfur is the energy that gives form to the creative impulse, the sullen emotion and the latent insight. Without sulfur a good idea stays on the drawing board, but with it, things start to take shape.

Mercury

Mercury is the most ubiquitous energy. It is restless, furtive and highly mutable. As one of the three primal energies, Mercury represents those substances and qualities that act as catalytic agents. They instigate dramatic change in the quality and form of a material. Everything about mercury relates to the quixotic energy of light. Quicksilver represents the essential qualities of this mercuric energy. It is virtually impossible to catch or hold, and its silvery color reminds us of both water and sky.

Mercury possesses the feminine characteristics of water, and the male virtues of sky. It is considered androgynous. Thus it has an amazing ability to bind with most metals, including silver and gold. With mercuric sulfide, craftsmen are able to gild metal objects. Quicksilver is also used to reduce silver and gold to a liquid. The amalgam is applied to a mineral, drawing out the gold. Fire is then added to eliminate the quicksilver, leaving only the precious metal. Another technique for leeching out gold involves washing minerals in a mercuric bath. All these techniques give meaning to a recipe that is basic to all alchemy: *solve et coagula* (separate and unite).

Psychologically, mercury is a method used to extract the best of what life has to offer.

THE OPERATIONS

Alchemists used many methods and procedures in their work. These operations were encoded in obscure words and symbolic images; their order of use varied from one alchemist to the next. We are fortunate to have the work of Jung and other analysts to help us understand how these operations can be applied to the individuation process. I will rely on Edward Edinger's book *Anatomy of the Psyche* to identify and arrange seven of the most important operations. While his work is a marvelous exploration of the operations from a mythological, religious and therapeutic point of view, our present interest is more broadly defined. Alchemy need not be limited to that rare breed of people who dedicate their lives to the pursuit of the philosopher's stone, or therapists who apply the art in the consulting room.

The First Operation:
Calcinatio

Fire is essential to our lives. Our body temperature is 98 degrees, and hotter when we need a fever to fight off infection. When we are intensely angry our "blood boils." Like animals, we go into "heat" when sexually aroused. Fire heals, destroys, creates and most of all, transforms.

Calcinatio sets the initial embers burning. It dwells in the sulfuric energies of passion, crisis and utter despair. This burning passion ignites the soul. In the Christian mythology, passion appears in a variety of images. The burning bush, tongues of fire, flaming sword, purgatory and, of course, hell are images that depict various aspects of fire as a transformative process. In Genesis this is evidenced by a God who "is the gate through which the thinker comes forth from the invisible to the visible, and it is through this gate that he must go to get into the presence of Spirit."[7]

The fire operation also acts to separate the gross from the subtle by purifying and reducing dense matter to fine, white ash. In human terms, this means that we must take command of our instincts to avoid being a slave to their impulsive energy. We need, in other words, to burn away need-driven desires and uncontrollable urges. The alchemists envisioned this operation by depicting a green lion devouring the sun. This is the situation that exists when consciousness descends into the instinctual world. It takes a healing lion to both tame the overwhelming energies of spirit and simultaneously prevent instinct from dominating our will. We do this with the ferocity of a lion: we walk on burning coals, "eat fire," or do a wild, sacred dance.

Zorba the Greek, the protagonist in Nikos Kazantzakis's book of the same name, dances with wild passion when his heart is heavy and otherwise feels like he cannot move. The whirling dervishes of Persia put Rumi's poems into motion as a means of centering themselves in the midst of chaos. Shiva, the Hindu god of creation, gives similar meaning to this fire dance. The best-known image of Shiva shows him dancing within a Ring of Fire. In that same ancient religion we also find Agni, god of fire, who through his triple eyes—sun, moon and lighted lamps—is bound by a vow of truth. This is the trial by fire, the immolation of all-consuming passions that purge the soul and through initiation, liberate the adept from false desire.

People born in the constellations of Leo, Sagittarius and Aries have a special kinship with this operation. Since fire lights the way, these individuals are likely to have well-developed intuitive powers. Astrologically, the sun and Mars govern the fire type. Since I am a Leo, a sun sign, I am well aware of its virtues and pitfalls. I am among those who are driven, ambitious and go out of their way to invite attention and admiration. On the brighter side, *calcinatio* also brings transformation. Out of the fire, the phoenix re-emerges, purified of his old life, and is born anew. *Calcinatio* is the operation we use to bring light to the darkness of unconsciousness, purge it of its inferior qualities and transform it into gold.

Dance like you mean it!

We are born in water and sustained by it. Water is life. Its ubiquity is perfectly demonstrated by water existing in three states simultaneously, as seen in an icy pond where it is a liquid, a solid and a gas. Similarly, a lotus blossom floating on the surface of the water is simultaneously below the surface of the water, sits on its surface and extends above it, giving us insight into the triple meaning of water. First, we dwell in its depths, then we float along its currents, and finally, we break through into full awareness. These images both contain the essence of the water operation, *solutio,* and the matrix in which self-consciousness is born.

With *calcinatio* we learned to deal with fiery passion. *Solutio* teaches us how to contend with moods. I learned from Robert Johnson that there is no such thing as a good mood. Be it a bad mood or a good one, both wash away sound judgment. We are set adrift by tides beyond our control and lest we know how to negotiate these currents we may well drown.

Baptism is the Christian equivalent of *solutio.* It symbolically removes

The Second Operation:
Solutio

the "original sin" that simply comes along with being born into this world. With water we are absolved, renewed and purified. For thousands of years, Hindus regularly bathed themselves in the sacred Ganges River. This ritual reminds them—or more specifically reminds their bodies— of their natural home. Water dissolves the dirt of sin; our psychological blind spots that keep us from hitting the mark.

The water personality is someone who is best described as innocent, straightforward, persistent, shy and sensitive. They are closest to their feelings and just as water is sensitive to the slightest disturbance, this type can pick up on changes in moods quickly. The water personality is under the influence of the moon. Alchemists believed that the source of water comes from the moon, and it controls the tides of oceans as well as our moods. Astrologically, the moon rules Cancer and Neptune, king of the seas. Franz Kafka, a writer who lived and worked in Prague, was a Cancer. He expressed in verse the essence of *solutio*:

> *You need not leave your room.*
> *Remain sitting at your table and listen.*
> *You need not even listen, simply wait.*
> *You need not even wait, just learn to become quiet,*
> *and still, and solitary.*
> *The world will freely offer itself to you*
> *to be unmasked.*
> *It has no choice; it will roll in ecstasy*
> *at your feet.*[8]

The Third Operation:
Coagulatio

Up to this point, the *prima materia* is little more than a speck flying around like a seed on the Wind (air), having been fathered by the Sun (fire) and mothered by the Moon (water). Now it must take root. "Its nurse is the Earth." These movements are more than descriptions; they comprise the third recipe from the *Emerald Tablet*. In other words, Hermes is telling the alchemist how to proceed in realizing the *prima materia* of his own unconscious mind. The earth operation is the first step in transforming the stuff of nature that is to become psyche. "Soul begins," writes Thomas Moore, "in the moist, solid earth, the realm of ordinary experience. Without this embodied world there could be no soul."[9]

This is accomplished through a process called fixation. This term is still used by psychologists but it refers to something that has gone awry in a person's life. We say a traumatic event fixates a person's psychological growth. Some part of their psyche has become stuck in the past. Fixation, as alchemists used the term, refers to any process that "turns something into earth." Where Edinger uses the word "earth" he means reality. *Coagulatio* is therefore the process that uses fixation as a method for transforming unconscious nature into a solid, earthly reality. The *prima materia* at this stage in its development is called ego.

Just as a seed attaches itself to the earth, ego lays down its roots. This process is accomplished through the agency of mercury. Remember, mercury is the catalyst that bonds things together. The ego at this point is frail, but its host (matrix) is Mother Earth. One alchemical woodcut shows *coagulatio* as a woman with the earth superimposed on her midsection. The *prima materia* (ego) is seen suckling at her breast. Edinger interprets the picture to mean "nothing less than the connecting of the ego with the Self, the fulfillment of individuation."[10] This is a vivid picture of how spirit first comes to aid soul (psyche) in manifesting a down-to-earth Real Self.

The earth personality comes under the influences of Venus and Saturn, which in turn are ruled by Taurus and Capricorn, respectively. Taurus governs all things physical, beautiful, and sensual, while Capricorn is responsible for bones, stones and other solid structures. People of this type can be melancholic, real downers. Too much earth in their sign weighs heavy on them, and they can be secretive. This is unfortunate since their close affinity with earth means they have special knowledge of the planet. On the more positive side, these individuals are well grounded, hard working, driven, and most importantly, passionate about nature.

Balzac, a Taurus, exemplified what happens when *coagulatio* goes to extreme. After writing ninety-five novels that comprised his magnum opus, *The Human Comedy,* he said, "My brain succumbed, like a run-down horse."

The best of these qualities are needed to make one a fit alchemist. He or she must have a passion for work, trust their instincts and, above all, love nature.

The Fourth Operation: Sublimatio

Air is the element of spirit and *sublimatio* its operation. It is the medium that carries oxygen, sunlight and language. Without air our soul and body would suffocate. Too much air and we become light-headed. Symbolically, this means our bodies become dizzy and our minds disoriented. We get the bends if we ascend too quickly to the surface. Psychologically, too much air chokes out depth. Fools of this ilk are buffoons, a word derived from the Latin *follis,* to mean "windbag." The Greeks called such folly *hubris,* and in their religion such inflation was regarded as a sin. Such fools were the puffers who exaggerated their claims and overworked the bellows.

The alchemist must find a middle road between too much and too little air. This task is beautifully told in the Greek tale of Icarus. He is the young man who, along with his father, Daedalus, was imprisoned on an island for having offended Minos. Daedalus, a master craftsman, fashioned wings out of wax and the two flew off to Sicily. But Icarus, being young, disregarded his father's instructions. He flew too high and the heat of the sun melted his wings. Icarus plummeted into the sea and drowned.

Sublimatio is the operation that teaches us how to control the spirit of air. Invisible though it appears, air is a palpable medium. A dramatic pause, holding the breath or simply not "coming up for air" gives this element substantiality. The air operation teaches us ways to avoid Icarus's mistake and better, how to infuse mind, body and soul with the living sustenance of spirit.

"In the beginning was the Word, and the Word was made flesh." In this way, the Christian bible describes how the Christ came into existence. *Sublimatio* is the process of transforming sounds into words, and words into action. It does this by elevating "a low substance . . . into a higher form by an ascending movement."[11] Where *coagulatio* grounded ego, *sublimatio* infuses it with spirit. Thus, the alchemists said, "Sublimate the body and coagulate the spirit."

When anything goes from the invisible realm to the visible we expect to find Trickster, the Lord of Boundaries. Creation myths are filled with tricksters negotiating transactions between different realms, and often they're looking out for ways to get the best deal for human beings. What he steals from the gods, he gives to us for the price of revealing our inner shadow. We'll also recall that Trickster, in many of his guises, is lord of language and communication. Thus, spells and incantations, hymns and chants, are the means used in *sublimatio* for connecting us to spirit and transforming the words into deeds.

Mercury, governed by Gemini and Uranus, rules the air personality. Paying homage to Mercury helps ensure eloquence in speech and writing. The great German author Goethe was a Gemini. Jung often referred to Goethe and his great work, *Faust*. This epic poem is very alchemical in its language and imagery. In Part I, Scene I, Faust says to Wagner,

> *If feeling fails,*
> *You never shall succeed;*
> *If it comes not from your spirit,*
> *With elemental speed,*
> *To win the hearts of all who hear.*[12]

The first four operations are derived directly from the four elements. Consciousness is ignited with fire, animated with water, fixated with earth and made spiritual by air. This opening stage of the work is called the Lesser Work, or the Ascent of the Soul. As we consider the closing stage, called the Greater Work or the Descent of the Spirit, we seem to begin all over again. But this is not the case. Both movements are happening simultaneously, soul moving up, spirit moving down, in the work of transforming the leaden, unconscious ego into the full consciousness of the Individuated Self.

The final three operations are devoted to sacrifice, surrender and communion. These are conscious acts that fulfill the highest purpose in life: to serve selflessly. Up to this point, our *prima materia* was acted on by the operations of nature, but now it chooses to act on its own accord. With consciousness comes choice, so now we must choose to give up the pleasures of earthly delights for more lasting ones. This does not come easily. In fact, it requires us to die a psychological death. Only by dying do we free ourselves from the war and play of opposites.

The Fifth Operation: Mortificatio

This is the death operation. Unlike physical death, *mortificatio* does not mean an end to bodily existence. As in a dream, death often foreshadows necessary change, presaging transformation. In the *mortificatio* operation, ego rids itself of false illusions, needy attachments and unwanted contamination. This is not accomplished without pain, suffering and sacrifice. After all, the ego is being made to surrender well-proven faculties in exchange for a whole, different way of being in the world.

This pain, however, is by choice and is therefore made more tolerable. It brings meaning. Individuation is a choice we make to become whole. The sacrifice involved means giving up something less, in exchange for something greater. As Jung put it so well, "The experience of self is always a defeat for the ego."[13] The conscious realization of Self is the prize for going through this dreadful ordeal.

Even when the choice is willingly made, ego feels like it is physically dying. It has a nervous breakdown. Images associated with the *mortificatio* operation are death, black ravens, skeletons and graveyards. The initiate, at this stage, feels as if he or she is physically and psychically being dismembered.

The alchemists had deep insights into the nature of psyche. They knew that the full consciousness of their gold required acceptance of death. In other words, there can be no spiritual enlightenment without first plumbing the depths of life. When we are ready and willing to die for something, not only is our reality completely changed, but so too is the world.

The Sixth Operation: Separatio

To understand this operation we must look at it in two ways. First, separation is the process by which we distinguish between parts. There would be no relationship if we couldn't separate an "I" from a "you." Similarly, we are able to see because the eye can distinguish contrasting shades of light. *Separatio* is the fundamental operation that makes reality possible. In virtually every creation myth, a *separatio* process acts to divide land from bodies of water, animals from humans, etc. It also separates the unconscious from the conscious world, fantasy from reality.

This is the first meaning of *separatio*. When we fail to apply the operation we run the risk of becoming overwhelmed and confused by thoughts and emotions. Then, we must "sort things out." Another scene from *Amor and Psyche* illustrates this point and how a *separatio* helped save the young goddess—soul—from a suicidal depression. Psyche violated the condition of her relationship with Amor—she was never to see him at night.

When her curiosity could hold out no longer, Psyche lit an oil lamp and looked at her sleeping lover. In utter dismay, there before her she saw not a man, but a god. At once Amor flew away, leaving Psyche in a terrible state. At first she wanted to drown herself, but Pan talked her out of it. Having no one else to turn to, she appealed to Aphrodite, the goddess of love.

Aphrodite was harsh. She commanded Psyche to do a number of seemingly impossible tasks. I will only describe the first one since it involves the *separatio* operation. Psyche was ordered to sort out an enormous pile of mixed seeds by morning, or suffer the consequence of death. At first, this task seemed to only worsen her depression. On an ego level, the task could not be accomplished. Psyche was forced to give up and surrender her faith to destiny. But here is the wisdom of the myth: through her surrender, Psyche shifted to another order of reality. We might call this nature, god or Self. The name is less important than understanding the tremendous resources that become available through conscious submission. The *mortificatio* had obviously done its job. No amount of ego would help Psyche in this situation, and she knew it.

Through her despair and supplication, the energies of her psyche were activated. This is beautifully portrayed in the story with the arrival of ants that perform the task without any difficulty. The ants represent a woman's *animus,* the spiritual side of her personality. In Native American culture, ants symbolize patience. Psyche, in other words, is saved by her inner male and feminine resources, both doing what comes naturally to their nature: sorting and waiting, respectively. On the ego level, this task could never be done, but in concert with the unconscious, it was completed well before Aphrodite's return.

This aspect of the *separatio* teaches the wisdom of sorting to attain clarity and distinction. This is how we achieve meaning, for only by teasing apart the elements of a problem can we ever hope to find a solution. This is what the word "analysis" means. *Lysis* means to loosen. This *separatio* is also a process of purification. We separate out the good from the bad, the chaff from the wheat, the lead from the gold. We now address the second meaning of *separatio*.

The *separatio* operation is the preparation for the last stage of the work, *coniunctio*. There can be no union, until there is first a separation. We are separated at birth when the umbilical cord is cut. We are again separated from a complete state of unconsciousness when we become aware of others and ourselves. In a sense, we are psychologically born when this happens. We separate again when we leave home and begin living independently. There are many critical separations that occur throughout our lifetime. If we live our lives consciously, we will have a creative *separatio* experience long before the final separation: death of the physical body.

This experience is the separation from a dualistic way of living. Children live in such a world, but they do so unconsciously. *Separatio* at this stage means that we consciously separate from a frame of mind built on opposition. We are then able to separate at will from the demands of dualism. Dividing up the world between good and evil, right and wrong, correct and incorrect, are valuable activities we do most of the time. We are educated, even indoctrinated, into this particularly Western way of thinking. The problem is that we become identified with it to the exclusion of any other system of thought. Compensation through religion and even spiritual practice acts more as a "courtesy to god" than as the process of actually acquiring the complete experience of what god and gold represent. We will not have achieved the serenity of Buddha or accomplished what Christ taught: "Be in this world, but not of it."

The *separatio* experience frees us to shift between realities: doing ego work when necessary, playing as the spirit moves us. Work and play are of our choosing. In other words, we do not abandon all reason, but are not imprisoned by it either.

There's a time to work and there's a time to play!

The Seventh Operation: Coniunctio

Just as I have defined two levels of the *separatio* experience, alchemists referred to two types of *coniunctio*: a lesser and a greater *coniunctio*. In its first form, ego is still vulnerable to the lure of earthly delights. Reason, logic and rationality have a gravity that keeps ego's feet on the ground; instincts continue to offer immediate pleasure. What makes this *coniunctio* less is ego's repeated identifications with these conscious and unconscious activities. But, that we have already had one taste of the Individuated Self spurs us on toward adopting a self-orientation. Self-esteem, self-image, and self-confidence shift from deriving energy from the ego to tapping into the archetype of the Self. While we may not have yet stabilized the shift, the lesser *coniunctio* opens the doorway to the final level of conscious realization.

Alchemists chose the eyes in the peacock's tail to symbolize the opening conscious awareness that anticipates the greater *coniunctio*. Like a rainbow of colors, the whole spectrum of consciousness is simultaneously one and many dimensions. This symbolic eye, known in Hinduism as the Third Eye, sees both the individual and its collective experience. In this nondualism, ego and self have been merged and the alchemist can experience the two in one breathtaking way. It is extremely difficult, if not impossible, to express what this experience is without actually being in possession of it. Only symbols help give some sense of its nature.

The royal marriage of the Solar King and the Luna Queen is one example of this great *coniunctio* experience. In many traditions it is called the mystical marriage. In fact, this symbolic marriage is the cornerstone of all the great religions. It is the yin-yang of Tao, the Shakti-Shiva of Hinduism, Father Sky and Mother Moon of Native Americans, the union of Sefirot Tif'eret and Malkhut of Kabbala, the *heirosgamos* of alchemy, and the crucifixion of Christ. Each religion has a symbol that functions something like a doorway to this transpersonal experience. For Christians, it is the cross. "He (Christ) came to the marriage bed of the cross," wrote Augustine, "and there, in mounting it, he consummated his marriage."[14] If sin means missing the mark, then the cross is the target. At its center, where earth and heaven intersect, there is eternal peace and love.

On a more personal level, we find the experience of the *coniunctio* in the individual who has ready access to the transcendent function and makes regular use of active imagination in virtually every life situation. Whether symbolized by the cross or the merger of soul and spirit, the union of opposites means that the person has reached a very high degree of consciousness in their lives. As Jungian analyst von Franz tells us, once you've achieved this state of individuation "*you stay in the middle place . . . you stay within your active imagination, so to speak, and you have the feeling that this is where your life process goes on . . .*"[15] At this level you have the opportunity to go beyond the boundaries of the Individuated Self and experience the divine in every moment.

Chapter 7

Making Gold

The nature of infinity is this: That everything has its
Own vortex, and when once a traveller thro' Eternity
Has pass'd that Vortex, he perceives it roll backward behind
His path, into a globe itself unfolding like a sun . . .
Thus is the heaven a vortex pass'd already, and the earth
A vortex not yet pass'd by the traveller thro' Eternity.

WILLIAM BLAKE, MILTON

Throughout alchemy's illustrious history there were always those who doubted its incredible goals and others whose sole ambition was to profit from it. Until the late seventeenth century, science was principally based on observation. Only by firsthand witnessing of actual results could doubts be eliminated. There were no reliable scientific bodies or journals to attest to the veracity of claims, much less disseminate research findings. Like most scientists, alchemists relied on scarce papers and letters hand carried to them by messengers. Or, if they were lucky, they had personal friendships with other scholars with whom they shared their work. Even as late as the late nineteenth century, science was a personal affair where the person of the scientist was under as much scrutiny as his or her research. Human experience was as much a part of science as laboratory experiment.

All this changed with the advent of modern science. Experience was set aside, and even considered as a source of contamination. In establishing reliability and validity, all forms of error, including the "contaminants" of human experience, had to be eliminated. In order to produce objective findings, the laboratory experiment had to sterilize every possible source of human error. Thus, all emotions that might bias an investigator had to be identified and removed. These scientific methods produced objective results that then could be generalized to situations outside the laboratory.

Using this method, doubt became a number set by tables of probability. Modern science, unlike magic, could have its effect on as many people as possible, provided the stated conditions and limitations were adhered to. Where magic once served the good of the person, science was now put into public service. We have benefited enormously from empirical science. Ironically, the criticism that science tends to have an arrogant attitude toward nature was inaccurate: it was really magic that aimed to have nature serve human need through pure, passive domination. As a first step toward a more scientific approach, alchemy insisted on having a relationship with Nature, even joining with Her in pursuing common interests. The contemporary, material world was constructed using this scientific approach. But these rewards came with a high price. Modern science seemed to go too far in the other direction; in the extreme both animistic magic and modern science elevate human over nature and in the end incur severe consequences. It seemed the more science attempted to shut out personal factors, the more loudly nature objected, both within the realm of psyche and in that of the deteriorating ecology of the planet.

This reaction came in two ways. First, there arose a split between matter and mind that affected not only science, but with its technology and products, the general public. Human beings were being split in two. The spirit of knowledge was set at odds with the soul of belief. Secondly, modern science, having its own internal shortcomings, could not respond to bigger and bigger questions being put to it. This development gave way to a new science, which viewed the effects of human influences not as contaminants but as necessary for arriving at greater truths than could be established with traditional scientific methods. From these two consequences flowed two very important sciences that contribute to understanding alchemy as it is used in this book.

Jung, seeing the splits between mind and matter happening on the individual and collective level, responded by establishing a psychology to address the problem. Alchemy became the balm that soothed the wound, and the medicine that could in time be developed for re-integrating a divided consciousness growing ever wider apart in the arts, religion and science. In collaboration with Wolfgang Pauli, a brilliant physicist, Jung translated the old alchemy into a modern language that spoke to theologian and scientist alike.

- Use both halves of your brain, the artist and the scientist, in your personal alchemy. Be creative and inventive, explore and discover.
- Subjective and objective factors are two expressions of one consciousness. You can't remove one without influencing the other.
- Do not dismiss your doubts. Allow them to lead you to the unknown answers residing in the unconscious. In this frame of mind, a doubt becomes a revelation, and allows you to cross the threshold into the mysteries.

History shows that his efforts were occurring from within the scientific community itself. The advent of quantum physics broke ranks with an empirical model strictly based on a cause and effect paradigm of the universe. Rather than exclude human effects, or regard them in the idiosyncratic ways magic had done, quantum physics showed how these factors exert predictable effects. Mind was back in the picture. This time it wasn't an unaccounted-for variable, but one in which reliable laws could be established. Over the course of five centuries there was a radical shift from a paradigm based on magic, which was overpersonalized, to a mechanistic model, which was underpersonalized, to a new model, which promises to incorporate the best of both.

This model of science forms the cornerstone of a new model of alchemy. It values experience *and* experiment, both vital to the doubters who want to put this alchemy to the test.

As we move from theory to practice, this chapter provides some methods for doing personal alchemy. As a starting point, I hope it will spark your creative impulse and lead toward further research and experimentation.

Alchemists believed that all things having a circular form belong to the spiritual realm. Circles and cycles are therefore especially important in doing the work of alchemy. In this vision, creation begins as a swirl of cosmic dust that is energized by the sun. Out of this spiritual plasma, matter is born, taking on myriad sizes, textures, shapes and form. Rocks, oceans, trees and minerals—you and me—all began by this whirlpool of spiritual energy. This churning continues on in rhythms of time and space. The orbiting of planets, the changing of the seasons, the tides of the ocean are all a part of this cosmic dance.

Human consciousness follows along this same circular path. Our journey is anything but linear. Just as a spinning top has two forces, one drawing in, the other out, so consciousness moves in two directions at the same time. This is what the alchemists meant by the Ascent of Soul and the Descent of Spirit. This is a complex concept but because it offers a summary of some of the most important principles in alchemical psychology it will be worth our while to spend a few moments understanding its meaning.

In modern terms, consciousness develops along two lines: evolution, an upward (or, outward) movement, and involution, a downward (or inward) movement. Evolution literally means an "opening out" or "unfolding of a curve," while involution refers to a process of "curling or turning inward."[1] The actions required in the process of individuating consciousness are movements outward into the environment and inward in terms of developing the interior self. Interacting and communicating with others represents the behaviors of this outward movement and things like reflection and contemplation, the actions of involution.

CIRCULATION THROUGH THE ELEMENTS

Alchemists used Soul or Luna in referring to the *anima*, the feminine aspect that dwells both in a man's unconsciousness as well as representing the feminine forces in nature. In Taoist philosophy, this feminine aspect of nature is *yin* and the masculine counterpart is called *yang*. The Spirit comprises the masculine qualities of a woman's psyche (her *animus*) as well as the masculine aspects in nature.

As a man develops his feminine side he acquires a deeper capacity to relate and experience emotions. He becomes a more realized human being and in the process both helps evolve the species as well as further his own individuation. In a similar way, a woman develops consciousness by both evolving spirit (*yang*) and refining it through an inner process of involution. In the process, she learns to assert herself outward and at the same time, find herself more self-assured and independent. The alchemists envisioned this whole process of change occurring on the collective level as well as the individual level.

As a result, the Ascent of Soul represents the movements of the feminine forces of consciousness individually and collectively. As the feminine forces of individual and collective nature advance through cycles of individuation, there is a simultaneous countermovement in which the masculine spirit reciprocally reaches downward. At the nexus of their meeting, both Soul (*yin* or *Luna*) and Spirit (*yang* or *Sol*) intermingle and hopefully fuse to become "one thing." The process looks something like this:

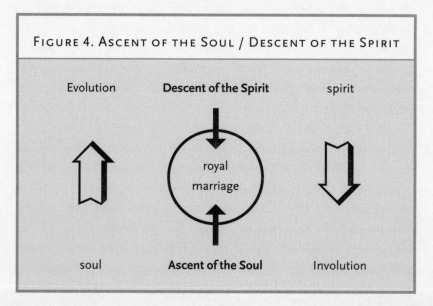

FIGURE 4. ASCENT OF THE SOUL / DESCENT OF THE SPIRIT

Evolution   **Descent of the Spirit**   spirit

royal
marriage

soul   **Ascent of the Soul**   Involution

There are three final points needed to understand this fascinating concept:

- The alchemist works to reverse Nature's soul and spiritual directions in order to facilitate both evolution and involution of consciousness.

- The advantage gained by reversing these cycles is that the opposites are more quickly brought into contact with the expectation that they will meet and marry in a Royal Marriage.

> How can we apply this dynamic action toward facilitating the conscious development of the personality? How do the elements fit into this model? What about the stages and operations?

- As a rule, the alchemist cannot work strictly on one (either Soul or Spirit) without its opposite *simultaneously* becoming activated.

We begin by using a technique known in alchemy as the circulation of the elements. I have taken this concept and provided examples drawn from psychology and physics to bring alchemy alive with exercises that get us doing the work. We start by moving through each of the elements, learning how each one serves to add, subtract and transform consciousness.

A.I.R.

Attention

Awareness is the function of consciousness that focuses attention on inner and outer perceptions. Attention is like a net cast out into the world in order to bring back a rich harvest of information. In every person, there is some proportion between how much attention is deliberate and how much unconscious. If your proportion is a 10:90 ratio, with 10 percent being conscious and the other 90 percent unconscious, then the first step is to work toward gradually shifting this ratio so that the number on the left grows.

Attention does for consciousness what our hands do for our bodies: it grabs hold of nature so that we can change it. This transformation of nature into meaningful reality begins by controlling attention. Paradoxically the way to begin is to pay attention to attention. Simply notice what you're attending to without analyzing or interpreting what you experience. A principle from quantum physics known as the observer effect (observer participantcy) states that the behavior of matter is *automatically* changed by merely attending to it. The first step in altering matter begins by increasing our awareness of where and when attention is focused.

Once you've improved this skill, then become aware of figure-ground relationships. The alchemists were masters of conceptualization. Their concept of the One and the Many is a good example of how they could think of life from two seemingly contrary perspectives. The One refers to the microcosm and the Many, the macrocosm. Simply put, this is the same as thinking of an individual as an entity unto herself and an individual as a member of a group. Gestalt psychologists attempted to put such concepts into figure-ground relationships that could be not only conceived but also perceived. They found that how we perceive something is oftentimes determined by what it means to us. If, for instance, we focus our attention strictly on ourselves, then we lose sight of other people and the collective group. When I am exclusively focused on myself, I lose a sense of membership. I am not thinking about myself as a member, a spouse, a citizen or an inhabitant of planet earth. All I know is that which is closest at hand: my appetites, my feelings, my urges, etc. The opposite is equally true. If I focused more on the background than on myself, then I run the risk of losing my personal identity. In Gestalt psychology, the interplay between figure and background gives meaning to life.

The task of alchemical psychology is always aimed at integration. Where attention is concerned, we try to become aware of figure and background simultaneously. This is no easy thing to do, but it is possible. With some practice you can master this skill. You might start with a simple perceptual task I call word-shape dissociation (Plates I and II on pages 163–164).

- In the first plate quickly read the word written in each shape. Ignore the shape and only READ the word.

- Then in the second plate IGNORE the word and identify only the shape.

In the second plate your rational mind wants to draw back to the safe harbor of words, but your creative mind needs to learn how to di-

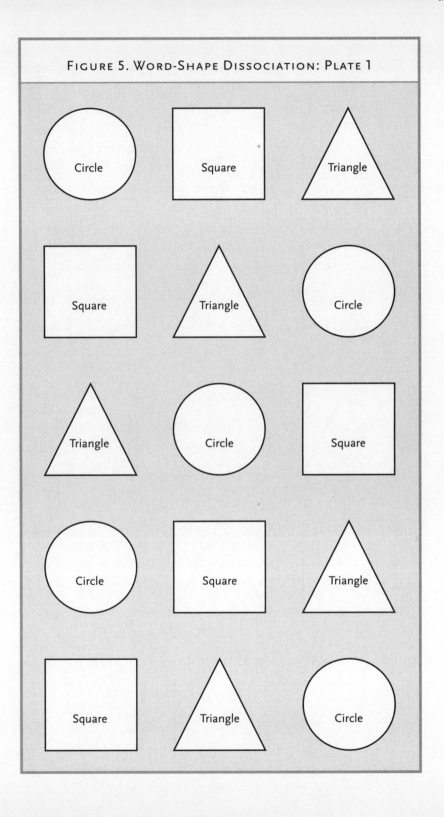

FIGURE 5. WORD-SHAPE DISSOCIATION: PLATE 1

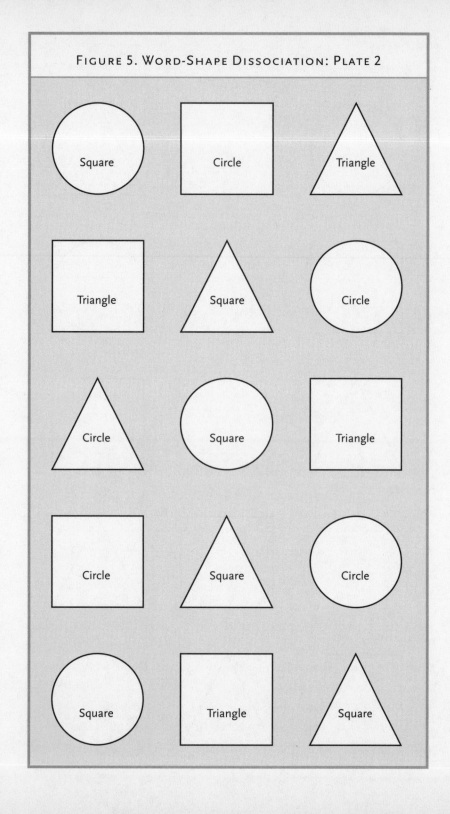

FIGURE 5. WORD-SHAPE DISSOCIATION: PLATE 2

vorce itself from the literal words in order to develop perceptual agility. This task is best undertaken with a partner who has a correct list of responses to the second plate. They should gently correct you when you err and have you begin again. Repeat until you are able to completely ignore all the words and correctly identify the shapes only in the second plate. Once you're able to do this task with success, make up your own chart using different combinations of words and shapes. Or, you can be even more creative by using other combinations, like words and colors, to design similar tasks that increase control over attention.

In *Mind into Matter,* theoretical physicist Fred Alan Wolf uses a more familiar exercise to help us master attention. We can look at the "shifting cube" in different ways. Either cube can be seen oriented up or down. If we shift our perception by focusing strictly on the white or black, we can make the cubes disappear altogether. All we then see are patches of white and black pieces.

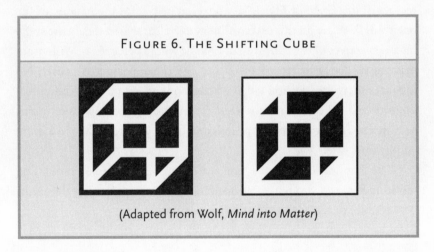

FIGURE 6. THE SHIFTING CUBE

(Adapted from Wolf, *Mind into Matter*)

The observer effect is a powerful tool of the conscious mind. As noted, some physicists claim that merely looking at something changes its physical properties. Physically as well as psychologically, seeing is an act of creation. "Remember," writes psychologist Paul Pearsall, "that the act of our observation creates what is observed."[2]

Another amazing ability that stems from the work of quantum physics is called the principle of complementarity. Simply put, this principle describes the universe as wholly interconnected, such "that the physical universe can never be known independently of the observer's choices of what to observe."[3] There is, in other words, an "infinite duality," or complementary action, response or behavior to everything we do. No matter how bad something may appear at this moment we can take comfort in knowing that there is complementary joy that is there to give us comfort. Complementarity, says Fred Alan Wolf, "affects how we all see, think about, and feel about the world and perhaps more importantly how we see, think about, and feel about ourselves."[4]

The shifting cube illustrates the parallel worlds that "pop" into and out of reality by shifting our attention between foreground and background elements. Now, I confess that I never understood Einstein's statement that parallel lines eventually merge until I began my alchemical studies. Such a feat can only be achieved cognitively by using both hemispheres of the brain. By training the mind to open up to multiple realities (any combination of competing elements in the cube) and seeing them at the same time, we accomplish perceptually one of the critical recipes of the *Emerald Tablet:* "as above, so below, for the making of the one thing." We are, in this extraordinary exercise, able to steady the shifting perspectives of the cube into one stable whole perception. With practice the tendency to return to one or the other perspective eases. No longer is there any tension when all components retain their individual identity *and* collective membership. By mastering the powers of attention we can harmonize the opposites and begin to perceive life in a more wholly integrated way.

The implications of this feat are enormous. Imagine eliminating tensions between thoughts and feelings, between competing thoughts, between the needs of the self and those of others.

Intention   In many alchemical images there are targets, bows and arrows used to illustrate the importance of concentrating our full, undivided intention. Once we've learned to focus attention we can then be more deliberate in what we want to do with what we observe. This is a powerful technique known not only to alchemists, but shamans, sages and saints throughout the ages. Intention adds purpose to attention. For example, if we want to stop smoking cigarettes, we must first increase our awareness of the behavior and then add our intention of quitting. Attention and intention lead us directly back to the awareness that nicotine is poisonous to the body and its natural reaction is to avoid, not invite, toxins. As in all of alchemy, this approach requires lots of practice. The more you repeat this simple recipe, the quicker the desired effect.

Previously, I mentioned that the word "sin" originally came from terms used in archery, where it means to miss the mark. Thus, the targets we see in alchemical pictures are there to remind us that by training our intention on our purpose, we reduce the likelihood of a sin. In an introduction to a book on Zen, D. T. Suzuki says that

> The hitter and the hit are no longer two opposing objects, but are one reality. The archer ceases to be conscious of himself as the one who is engaged in hitting the bull's-eye which confronts him. This state of unconsciousness is realized only when, completely empty and rid of the self, he becomes one with the perfecting of his technical skill, though there is in it something of a quite different order which cannot be attained by any progressive study of the art.[5]

We are faced, in other words, with a completely different challenge than that which is required in taking command of attention. While setting our intention begins in a very purposeful manner, it must dissolve in the end if our efforts are to become natural and fully integrated. We must rid ourselves of the self-consciousness that keeps us fixed on our goal, or at least the success we have attached to achieving it. Here it is not practice that makes perfect, but quite the opposite. By calming the mind the arrow of intention naturally finds its way to the target.

In practice, I have found no better way of achieving this calm than by deep breathing. Here is the procedure I use:

- Begin by sitting in a quiet place where you will not be distracted. Make sure your spine is erect and your eyes gently closed.

- Do no more in your first few sessions than simply notice the rhythm of your breath. Pay close attention to the in breath and how deep it descends into your lungs, then watch the out breath as it escapes through your mouth. Breathe in through your nose and out through your mouth.

- See if you can locate that point where your inhalation "turns" and the air is exhaled. Identify that place on your body where breath changes its flow. Do not, at this point, attempt to change your breathing, just notice where the turn occurs. Mind you, breathing doesn't stop and go. It is a continuous circulation.

- As you breathe out, place your tongue on the roof of your mouth, so that when the air is exhaled you make a whistling sound. Notice how steady and long the breath is by the sound it makes. You will want to make this sound even, long and diminutive as you go from being loud to cascading down to a whisper.

- With little effort, gently allow your breath to fall deeper so that the point of its turning is lower down on your body. Eventually, the breath falls below the level of the lungs and finds its "home" four finger widths below the navel.

- Imagine the air as it fills your lungs and begins to enter into the blood stream. Visualize oxygen being distributed throughout the body. Take one section at a time and imagine the billions of cells in each part being supplied with the life-giving breath. Once every section of your body has been filled in this way, imagine the outgoing breath leaving the cells, taking with it toxins, waste products, tensions, bad memories, etc.

- Imagine as you breathe more deeply that a circle of light is formed by the amount of air being inhaled and exhaled. The more air you then breath in, the larger the circle. Eventually this circle of breath will surround your entire body, like a halo.

- Practice this breathing "circulation" method in small increments. A circulation consists of one inhalation and one exhalation. Do no more than seven circulations at one sitting to start. Add one of the steps above only when you feel absolutely comfortable.

Retention   Alchemists worked as hard on learning how to suspend memory as they did on improving it. As with attention and intention, we must master the art of memory. This begins when we realize that memories are constructed out of conscious and unconscious experience. Fact and fantasy constitute the memory. By fantasy I include not only emotions and feelings, but the unconscious image stirred up by the event. Memories are different from fantasies in that they have been elevated to a level of consciousness that fixed them in our mind for later recall. They have a beginning and an end. With practice we can extend their boundaries or have them disappear altogether.

Memories are not all created equal. Some keep us bound to the past and others are little more than vague recollections of fact. If we are angry with someone or hurt by them, memory of the event not only keeps us stuck in the past, but it keeps us from being in the present. This explains the important role that forgiveness plays in allowing us to live wholly in present-time. Forgiveness is a way of disconnecting from the past. Unfortunately, the art of forgiveness has virtually been lost. For the most part, forgiveness oftentimes amounts to little more than an empty apology. Worse, we may carry around a sack filled with hurts and resentments that haven't even got to this point. We suffer guilt for the transgressions we've not expressed; resentment for all the injury done to us.

The Jungian analyst Clarrissa Pinkola-Estes recalls an old recipe for effective forgiveness. In her book, *Women Who Run with the Wolves,* she outlines four stages of forgiveness:

1. forego—leave it alone

2. forebear—abstain from punishing

3. forget—avert from memory, refuse to dwell

4. forgive—abandon the debt[6]

This is one of the most powerful recipes I know for healing the past and moving forward. This has been one of my most used remedies in helping people come to terms with the past, allowing them not only to forgive their aggressor but more often, themselves.

If forgiveness helps us disconnect from the past, recall allows us to remember it. While I have previously discussed the Art of Memory used by alchemists, here I want to add an important distinction between recall and reverie. Recall is recounting the factual parts of the memory. Word associations, acronyms and mnemonic devices are methods used to sharpen recall. Reverie, on the other hand, involves the fantastic part of memory. Among the words used to define the term in the OED, there is "rejoicing," a "state of delight," a "fit of abstracted musing." These are qualities that emanate from the unconscious. In mastering the ways of retention, we need both to experiment with recall and experience the past as an act of rejoicing with the Muses.[7]

Memory takes place at the point where the conscious and unconscious mind meet with something significant in nature. It is the birthplace of creation where nature is transmuted into reality. Like birth, the delivery comes with pain and delight.

WATER

Water is the special place where feelings enter our awareness. Just as water germinates seeds and brings them to flower, embryonic emotions begin in the watery element and gently find their way to the full expression of feelings. But, for anyone who has overwatered a plant knows, too much water kills. In alchemy, we work to inculcate feelings, moving them from seed to flower, without destroying them.

Feelings form a dimension that runs from coarse to fine. An infant is a ball of emotions, giggling one moment and screaming the next. Unconscious instincts rule their emotions. The child cries when she's hungry and laughs when her belly is full. In adolescence, emotions gradually become feelings that are more discriminating as ego begins to draw limits on demanding impulses. Many times, these feelings are experienced in very intense ways because they often pit instinctive impulses against the demands of civilized society. Feelings begin to have meaning. Love to an infant is mostly tactile, but for an adolescent, the words "I love you" begin to have meaning.

We would hope that this process is complete by the age of eighteen or twenty, but this seldom happens. Even adults who have achieved some success falter when met with unexpected challenges. Regressions back to earlier stages of life are not unusual. In fact, they are part of the circulation through which feelings must go in order to attain finer discrimination and stable, conscious control. Of course, from time to time we all lose ourselves to the heat of the moment, but, with mastery, we learn how to have the feeling instead of it having us. The aim is not to extinguish feelings or keep them locked up in a cage, but to respond appropriately with words that are accurate, assertive and clear. We do not then confuse feelings and thoughts, and we learn that feelings, not thoughts, are the source of our unique individuality.

The alchemy involved in the circulation through water works to transform impulsivity into spontaneity, rage into assertive anger, depression into reflective moments for meditation. The jumble of emotions that have young people acting out and confusing thought with sound judgment comes to rest when in the later stages of the work, they are able to stabilize their emotions and express what's in their heart effectively. The tug-of-war that precipitates emotional storms between married people subsides as they establish a context of love in which to argue and debate issues. Attaining this level of refinement requires constant vigilance and monitoring of feelings, their source and expression.

Water must be channeled, directed and even dammed up in order to be a useful source of energy. If allowed to flow unchecked, the nature of water is such that it pours into everything. The expression "our heart bleeds" means that we have lost words that can stem the flow of an overwhelmingly sad emotion. To learn how to control water we must become acquainted with the feminine.

When we "go with the flow" we learn what the Chinese meant by the concept of the feminine energy known as *yin*. This power is the equivalent of the alchemical Soul. The alchemy involved in taming this water energy requires a marriage between thought and feeling. The integration enables us to cease from identifying with every feeling that flows out of our heart by experiencing the feeling within a field of thought. This is the reason Jung placed the feeling function on the rational axis, connecting it to thinking. Within this context, a range is defined where on the inferior, unconscious end there are unbridled moods, and on a superior, conscious dimension we move to more refined, differentiated emotions and well-defined attitudes.

A good exercise to develop the feeling function is to keep a diary of emotions, monitor it weekly and identify the accuracy between objective events and your emotional response. Oftentimes we discover that a certain feeling was not prompted, or at least not adequately explained, by the current circumstance. These are marvelous opportunities to retrace the feeling to its true source. Like a well, we can draw up waters that dwell deep within the ground of Mother Earth. There we discover water that is pure and rectifying. We can use this water to wash clean the presenting situation of distortions. In other words, we see beneath the surface of a person's words and actions. There we discover the truth in what they give us, a truth they themselves might not even be aware of.

Mastering water empowers us with the ability to penetrate deeply into the soul. Like fish, we are freed from the tides and eddies that could smash us against rocks. When we are in the natural flow of life we discover the power of water to dissolve obstacles, germinate our dreams, and allow the tides of our emotions to cleanse the shores of old debris.

EARTH   Without the nooks and crannies formed by earth, there would be no ocean, lake or waterfall. Earth is the matrix that cradles water, giving it shape and direction. Since earth expresses consciousness in material form, it helps shape our life into vessels that contain emotions, or permit their outpouring when necessary. Thoughts are the channels formed by earth that guide feelings toward purposeful action.

Earth, too, is the ground of understanding. Galileo had an awful time convincing people that the earth was not fixed in its place, but that it was spinning in orbit around the sun. Despite his telescopic proof, he had to dislodge the belief that the earth was as immovable as the ground beneath their feet. Galileo caused a revolution in science, religion and psychology. Perhaps more than for his scientific discoveries, we are indebted to him for making the shift from a concrete, fixed world to one that is spherical and dynamic. To most of us, the fact that the earth moves about the sun is more a psychological truth than a scientific fact. No less than our sixteenth-century ancestors, we sense the earth being stationary. To understand earth in modern terms, we too must elevate reason to an abstract plane. I do not think most of us really accepted this new image of earth until we were awed by a photograph taken of our blue planet from the moon.

Elevating this understanding begins in the leaden, mundane activities of daily life, the place where we must obviously sense the weight of gravity. Perhaps because of the sedentary nature of my work as a therapist, I enjoy working with my hands during my off hours. Cleaning dishes is not a chore for me. Unlike the uncertainty of my therapeutic work, cleaning dishes offers a clear-cut task with a predictable outcome.

If you really want to know the source of all senses, then work with the elements of earth. Wood will teach you lessons about resistance. Cement teaches the alchemy of mixture, strength and durability. Like alchemical guildsmen, we learn the secrets of materials by trial and error. In this way we learn what the naked eye cannot teach. By the sweat of your labors you discover what goes into building a house, a bridge, a statue . . . a life.

FIRE

Through years spent tending their furnaces, alchemists developed a keen sense of fire. They intuitively knew how to measure heat, the different types of fire and what each could accomplish. Antoine-Joseph Pernety, author of *An Alchemical Treatise on the Great Art,* described three types of fire. These are: celestial, terrestrial (simple) and artificial. Knowing how and when to use each of these fires teaches us how to harness the power of this basic elemental force.

Celestial Fire

Alchemists regarded the moon as the source of water and the sun the source of fire. A rain brings down water from the skies and waterfalls do likewise on the earthly plane. As above, so below. And as the sun rains downs fire in the form of lightning, the alchemist's furnace captures this same furtive energy within his iron vessel. Water and fire, being so essential to life, led Hippocrates to credit these elements as having all that is necessary for creating everything in the universe. Celestial fire is the solar, archetypal energy that is composed of a sulfuric substance that ignites consciousness as well as the fire on our stoves. It is a creative, masculine force that causes all things to move and transform.

The best way to imagine celestial fire is to think of it as light. By light the alchemist meant an omnipresent spirit that need not be visible. According to Pernety, "When the lighted candle is extinguished the igneous and luminous spirit, which inflames the wick, is not lost, as is commonly believed. Its action simply disappears when food is lacking to it. It is diffused in the air, which is the receptacle of Light, and of the spiritual nature of the material world." He goes on to make it clear:

Light is for us a vivid image of Divinity. Divine love being unable, to speak thus, to contain itself in itself; has been diffused outside itself and multiplied in creation. So Light is not confined to luminous bodies: it is scattered, it is multiplied, it is as God, an inexhaustible source of benefit.[8]

In meditative practice, the image of white light can be used as a visual method of circulating this celestial energy throughout the body. In *The Secret of the Golden Flower,* an ancient alchemical text, methods are described for moving light in this way. Through the circulation of the spirit, the goal is to transmute dark, dense matter into light. The word "enlightenment" means to bring light into the darkness of our unconscious being.

Another method, employed by Tibetan shamans, used mandalas for circulating energy. The word "mandala" comes from the Sanskrit and simply means "circle." These magical pictures consist of a square drawn within a circle. In alchemy, the square represents earth and the circle, the realm of spirit. There are alchemical woodcuts showing the adept trying to "square the circle," meaning that he is working to transform matter into spirit. The mandala is a visual aid in guiding consciousness through the body and bringing it back to the source of its creation.

These magic circles are archetypal in that they can be found throughout history. Some of the oldest mandalas date back 25,000 to 30,000 years ago to Paleolithic times. They appear in Egyptian art in images depicting Horus surrounded by his four sons. This theme repeats itself centuries later in Christian mandalas, where Christ is shown at the center surrounded by the four Evangelists.

In his book *The Alchemical Mandala,* Adam McLean provides many beautiful examples of mandalas designed by alchemists. He suggests that these mandalas can be used "as Keys, as Doorways and as Pathways into our inner spiritual realm."[9] I have found that working with mandalas produces excellent results through both passive and active methods. Meditating on the mandalas in McLean's book, and following the course of imaginative concentration, can do more in gaining insight into alchemy than reading a hundred books on the subject. By passive I do not mean that nothing is going on. The celestial light is circulating, simultaneously bringing all opposites and their solutions to awareness. Thus, the mandala is often seen as an archetypal image of the Self. It recreates the churning movement of creation.

In his commentary to Wilhelm's interpretation of *The Secret of the Golden Flower,* Jung says, "As a rule, the phenomenon [of accessing this white light, the celestial fire] is spontaneous, coming and going on its own initiative. Its effect is astonishing in that it almost always brings about a solution of psychic complications, and imaginary entanglements, creating thus a unity of being, which is universally felt as a 're-lease.'"[10] The benefit of using a mandala is healing. Through the effort of drawing it and meditating on it, ego consciousness is transmuted into the healing energies of the Self.

Terrestrial (Simple) Fire

This type of fire is the one we are most familiar with. We use it in our fireplaces and stoves. It gives cars the power to move, furnaces the heat to warm our homes, and stoves the fire for cooking. Simple fire also has its symbolic uses. The lighting of candles represents the fire of the Holy Spirit for some, and a romantic evening for others. This fire is tangible and obvious, but should not be taken for granted. Regardless of what type of fire we consider, there is always a mystical source that accounts for its true power. Even a simple candle has its secret.

The eternal flame, the lighting of the menorah and Burning Man all represent more than what first meets the eye. Each contains a mystery and a promise. In these ways, ordinary fire is used for symbolic purpose. In a similar way, I invite you to light a candle to celebrate your initiation into the alchemical work. Remember, while the darkest place is beneath the candle, the brightest light of illumination is just above the flame.

Artificial Fire

Central to alchemy is the use of fire for transformation. This fire is called "artificial" because of its function, not its nature. When the fire of light can be focused like a laser beam it can do extraordinary things. What accounts for its efficiency is its purity. Excluding all but one band or vibration of light, energy produces laser light. Now, suppose that you could exclude all the elements that distract you from asserting your own firepower. Like a laser beam you too would be able to perform extraordinary feats.

The alchemical use of artificial fire acts to cleanse the mind, body and soul of its impurities. In the Christian concept of the afterlife, the flames of purgatory purify sinners so that they can enter the kingdom of heaven. So too on earth we can purge ourselves of sinning, not only morally, but like a shaft of laser light, hit the mark every time.

A second use of artificial fire is to transform natural materials into subtle forms in the blink of an eye. Terrestrial fire can reduce a forest to cinders within a few hours. We may or may not know the reason nature sets forests ablaze, but all can acknowledge the beautiful wild flowers that spring up from the ashes left behind. There is wisdom here, but it is one that goes beyond human comprehension. Is it only through devastation that new life can be borne? If this is so, then imitating her ways may ignite new life forms. Artificial fire is set for the purpose of rapidly reducing, distilling and transforming obstacles standing in the way of evolution and/or individuation.

Fire is the force that causes this facilitation in nature. "What nature made in the beginning, we can likewise make, by returning to the procedure she followed. What she is perhaps still making, by help of the centuries, in her subterranean solitude, we can cause her to finish in a *single instant,* by aiding her and surrounding her with better circumstances"[11] [emphasis mine].

I recall a woman who learned that her anger gave her the courage needed to burn off a victim role she had been unconsciously playing out for years. In another case, I saw how a young man transformed a suicidal use of psychostimulants into poetry I won't soon forget. What is often required in therapy is to fight fire with fire. In the first case, I directly confronted my patient with the destruction wrought upon others and herself as a consequence of self-immolation. Her anger eventually turned away from me and became the energy needed for a healing, *calcinatio* experience. A different fire was needed with my adolescent patient. For him, I applied a gentle fire. By identifying with the excitement induced by his years of drug use, we were able to transmute a reckless passion into blazing lines of poetry.

In yoga, the body is divided into "five parts," each corresponding to their system of elements: earth, water, fire, wind and ether. The region of the body that corresponds to fire (*agni*) is the area that extends from the rectum to the heart. By mediating on this area and repeating the sacred sound *ram,* yogins believe that they can master the fire element and even become incombustible. For our purpose, gaining mastery over fire means that we overcome our passions and find ways of sublimating their destructive force. With this skill we are immune to hostile intentions and aggressive behavior. Through the practice of concupiscence, the frustration of desire, we learn to master our impulses and put that energy to a higher purpose. As masters of fire, we blaze our individual paths through life and beyond.

The operation that describes this circulation of light is known in alchemy as the *circumnabulo* or *circulatio.* In describing how consciousness enters life and continues its development, Edinger writes, "psychologically, *circulatio,* is the repeated circuit of all aspects of one's being, which gradually generates awareness of a transpersonal center uniting the conflicting factors. There is a transit through the opposites, which are experienced alternately again and again, leading finally to their reconciliation."[12]

Edinger is describing a fundamental thought in Jungian psychology: that *"the purpose of human life is the creation of consciousness."*[13] The process of *circulatio* describes the cycles through which consciousness comes into full form. In this section, we will look at some of the images that describe this movement and how these look throughout the life cycle of individual development, and we will end with some practical methods for using this model to help in our individuation process.

In alchemy, the process begins with a spark of light called the *scintilla,* which is believed to be eternally looping in upon itself as it undergoes a process of evolution and involution. The Gnostics often used the image of the *ourborus* to symbolically describe this process. The *ourborus* image depicts a snake devouring its own tail. According to Cirlot's definition, the *ourborus* "biting its own tail is symbolic of self-fecundation, or the primitive idea of a self-sufficient Nature—a Nature that . . . continually returns, within a cyclic pattern, to its own beginning."[14] Alchemists equated the *ourborus* with the god Mercurius. He both participates in the process of transforming consciousness and at the same time is the template of wholeness that is the goal of the process. God then was alchemically defined as the "center of a circle whose center is everywhere and whose circumference is nowhere."[15]

LIFE CYCLES— TURNING OUT THE INDIVIDUATED SELF

Another very old symbol that describes the cycle of creation is the *spiral vortex*. Like mandalas, spirals are archetypal designs that symbolically express movements that cannot be fully expressed in words. Spirals are found everywhere. When we look out at the distant heavens—beyond the fixed stars of antiquity—we see the Spiral Nebula, a constellation formed by millions of stars swirling about one another in the form of a spiral. Closer to home, we find spirals appearing in the vortices created by water currents in ponds and eddies. As in nature, so too in art do spirals appear in works dating back to primitive times. From ancient art to modern science, the spiral represents the many vicissitudes of the creative process. Spirals are seen in Egyptian headdresses, East Indian paintings, Greek mosaics, Chinese lacquer vases, the stained glass windows of Christian cathedrals and Navajo sand paintings.

In 1988, Francis Crick and James Watson described the structure of the DNA molecule. Again we find a spiral pattern defining the basic blueprint of physical life. In his book *The Astonishing Hypothesis,* Crick shows how consciousness emanates from the living structure of DNA and our nervous system. The structure of DNA is a double helix, one that recalls the image of the two snakes coiled up around Hermes' magic wand, the *caduceus.* In these images we begin to see an interesting correspondence that connects the symbolic world with its material counterpart. Further, we find evidence suggesting that the creation and development of consciousness move in a circular fashion around some central point.

For our purpose, we can look at the double helix as representing spirit and soul as it moves through stages of evolution and involution around the central axis that is Mercury. In this image, the concept of "as above, so below" of the *Emerald Tablet* is held nicely together by the spiral that represents not only the development of human consciousness, but also the relationship between the parallel worlds of spirit and matter. Whether physical or psychological, the spiral describes the consciousness in its movement from unconsciousness to life.

In psychology, the spiral symbolizes cycles of life that are critical to periods of development. Life is the vessel in which consciousness becomes individuated from its gross state to something rare and refined. The same forces that act to move anything along a spiral course are active in this energy field of consciousness. Thus, consciousness moves by

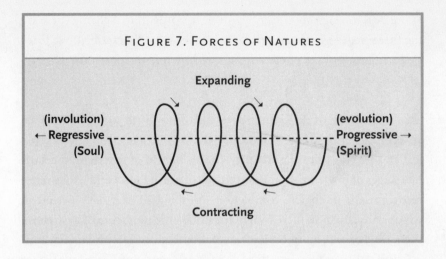

FIGURE 7. FORCES OF NATURES

forces that contract and expand, and other forces that draw it back by a retaining force and move it forward by an extending action. In Fred Alan Wolf's description of the elements and their function, he identifies four corresponding forces—time, motion, energy and space—that form the force field through which consciousness comes into the world and continues through successive series of development from gross to ever-more subtle forms. In Figure 7, I describe this model using the terms of alchemical psychology.

Soul (*luna*) and spirit (*sol*) intertwine as they form the basic spiral of consciousness. You will notice that spirit has the tendency to move toward the right, marked "evolution," and soul, the tendency to move toward the left, "involution." The psychological properties of soul help in this individuation process by causing us to dwell, look inward, reflect, contemplate—all words that describe involution. Spirit moves us outward in life. It extends consciousness into the world. In thinking of consciousness as a "substance, a psychic material usually but not always invisible and intangible to the senses,"[16] soul and spirit are the ingredients that transform this substance into matter. Psychologically, we would say that feminine and masculine consciousness are the stuff that constitute the visible manifestation of behavior.

Mercury is the axis around which these psychic substances move and are kept in harmony. Soul and spirit are opposites in nature, but through the intervention of Mercurius they are better thought of as forces that complement one another. As complements they move consciousness through specific stages of development. In alchemy these are the three stages of *nigredo, albedo* and *rubedo*. I will describe these three stages in terms of the psychological development of consciousness.

The Nigredo *Period*   This first period of development extends from birth to about eighteen years of age. Prior to eighteen the personality is in a relative state of physical and psychological immaturity. In this period of gestation, the various stages of birth, infancy and childhood, pre-puberty and adolescence move toward biological completion. Although it is a dark period in which consciousness increasingly achieves some modicum of awareness, it is a time of enormous biological activity. Beginning with infancy, consciousness undergoes an active process of separation (*separatio*) from the collective unconscious and the unconscious embrace of its host—mother.

The period that follows is regressive in the sense that there is a movement that returns consciousness to the grand cosmos, hopefully arriving in a more refined state than at its first taking leave.

This separation is initially unconscious with the infant needing to do no more than rely on nature as her guide. Alchemically we might say that soul predominates in this period while the forces of spirit are germinating. The first real breakthrough into consciousness comes when the child can form a lasting conscious memory. As adults we can mark this "psychological birthday" by recalling the very thing that we can consciously remember.

The second major development of consciousness comes when the spirit of adolescence takes the reins. The separation from parents is usually expressed in all kinds of oppositional behavior. This *separatio* varies from one adolescent to the next depending on how conscious they are of this separation-individuation process. It is typically a very difficult time for parents and adolescents.

The *nigredo* experience extends to young adulthood, where it is marked by a dramatic change from a condition in which the individual merely exists in the world to one where he or she increasingly engages with it. Up to that point the person has been primarily concerned with narcissistic needs to the virtual exclusion of everything (and everybody) else. Things really change only when individuals come to realize that they do not always get what they want and that gratification sometimes comes later, if at all—a sobering, if not depressing thought.

This period is well represented in alchemy by lead and its sullen, dark attributes. Alchemists describe lead as a base metal in which spirit is sleeping. Small wonder that children and many adolescents love to sleep, and when they are awake, they are seldom aware of anything other than the sensual pleasures of life—sex, drugs and rock and roll. The senses rule their worlds. As one television advertisement cleverly put it, "Obey your thirst" (and buy our soft drink!). The alchemical operation of *coagulatio* eventually brings a sense of order to the amorphous sleeping lead. Like lead poured into a mold, parents, teachers, employers and religious instructors provide this budding consciousness with a structure within which the person can shape up and take responsibility. The successful journey through the "dark night of the senses" comes with the individual's discovery of meaning and purpose of life as being more than simply responding to biological impulses. Failure during this period oftentimes leads to dreadful addictions that stymie development and true spiritual fulfillment. In essence the person unwittingly settles for the false gold rather than going on with the journey that will eventually bring him or her the real thing—ultimately discovering that one of life's prime mandates is the development of consciousness and refining it into ever higher levels of self.

The Albedo Period

As we recall, the *albedo* is the second stage of alchemy and its metal is silver. This whitening stage is the time when we psychologically come to "see the light" and must now take responsibility for ourselves. Spirit awakens in young adults during this time but unfortunately they usually do not like what they see. Reality has sharp edges. Demands are made and one is expected to carry his or her own weight. Life is no longer automatic and the young adult is faced with hard challenges in every direction. Family becomes less supportive, school more demanding, and hard work is required. There is a clear shift from merely existing in the world to a position where we're expected to do something productive. Rather than separate from the world, we are now forced into a relationship with it. The freedom of individual identity brings with it a host of duties and responsibilities.

In the best case scenario, the young adult takes heart and learns the skills necessary to gain mastery and competence. Just as the moon reflects and beams down to us its light, the young person receives guidance from others. The individual discovers the give and take of relationships not only to people in the immediate environment but increasingly to others not related to them. Recalling the first person you befriended who was not required by blood to be your friend marked another important shift in consciousness. The *albedo* experience is a time of great awakening to the world beyond one's ego, the family, the country, etc.

It is far easier to describe the work during the *albedo* experience than it is to accomplish its many tasks. In this period, as well as in all stages of the work, movement is a series of ups and downs, becoming more conscious one moment and regressing the next. Some never complete this part of the journey. Many people spend their whole lifetime struggling to come to terms with all that it means to be a responsible, loving adult. Ironically, it is the successful person, who has graduated college, married and raised a family, attained a stable and meaningful career, that spurs consciousness on toward further levels of individuation. This is our reward for all the hard work! For only when the individual has ceased deriving satisfaction from earthly ambitions can the spiritual aspirations that have been secretly at work all along come to fruition. At this point we begin turning away from the transitory pleasures of earthly rewards to the everlasting gold we call God, or the divine.

Toward the end of the *albedo* stage there is a contentment and even closure to life that we enjoy. Soul has countered its natural tendency to remain on the earth. It has reversed course, evolved and emerged into the light of day. As a result, soul finds its way into relationships with others. In the *albedo* experience, we sometimes attract soul mates who happen to be at the same place at the same time in their alchemy. Just as the soul extends outward in its Ascent, the spirit counters its nature to fly off in every direction. Its Descent means that spirit directs its energy downward into consciousness. The result is evident when young adults tame their wild energies and become productive. Labor acquires new meaning, careers begin to form and work takes its natural position in the life process.

The Ascent of Soul and Descent of Spirit occur during the *albedo* stage. This is the place where the two mighty forces of consciousness,

Soul and Spirit, come into conjunction with each other. I say conjunction because while they are aligned, or superimposed on each other, they may not join to become the One thing at this point. It is therefore awesome to behold the eventual coupling and better, the integration of these opposites of soul and spirit. For when joined, they form a marriage of opposites that signals the first real image of the philosopher's stone. Behaviorally, the individual in this position has acquired a Real Self who is neither bound to the dictates of biological impulses nor fooled by the demands of ego. A healthy personality that has been through the whitening stage of *albedo* thinks independently, acts responsibly, ethically and lovingly in the world.

Having met with some success in the *albedo* period, the individual begins to look beyond earthly experiences toward an even greater fulfillment that can only come in the final union of opposites—joining with God.

The Rubedo *Period*

Most of us like to think of our old age as the golden years. Since we are now at the level of the alchemical stage called the *rubedo,* gold is especially appropriate to symbolize the philosopher's stone that is the ultimate achievement of a life well lived. And here are the three basic steps that have brought us to the final stage of the individuation process:

- In the *nigredo,* consciousness discovers its own world. (the Real Self)

- In the *albedo,* consciousness discovers the world of others. (the Individuate Self)

- In the *rubedo,* consciousness discovers the divine world. (the Divine Self)

With each development, the scope of our vision enlarges. By the third stage we have the potential to take in the whole world. Zen monks tell their initiates to "swallow the ocean, drink in the stars." The poet William Blake put it in other words: "find infinity in a grain of sand." Unfortunately, none of this is possible until we first come to grips with our own mortality. Even then, fully achieving the goal of the *rubedo* stage is rare. Nevertheless, I believe there is no more worthwhile or any more meaningful work we can do in life than learning how to end it with grace.

At this stage perhaps more than ever we need to rely on the alchemical principle that matter is only the physical manifestation of consciousness and that death of the body does not mean extinction. Just as we saw in the case of celestial fire, life persists whether or not the candle is lit. A whole new vision of life opens to us when we are able to embrace death with this high level of awareness.

We are humbled by this vision. Nothing other than love can begin to describe it. The universe of possibilities is many more than even the parallel worlds described by physicists. Our imagination opens to an infinite range of potentialities.

At this high stage of development we are relating to the cosmos, transforming not only ourselves, but bringing order to the chaos that still exists in the world. The entire world benefits from our having become a better person; the power of an individual's presence in this state exerts positive influences in the whole world. Not only have we created consciousness but through the oscillations of these three stages we transform chaos into meaning—lead into gold. This is reflected in our personality in the form of contentment and generosity, compassion and selflessness, resignation and surrender. These are the indications that consciousness has achieved its golden state, the Individuated Self.

Is this then the end of the journey? Not quite. The net product of the *rubedo* period in alchemy is the production of a powder, known as the Red Tincture, another name for the philosopher's stone. It is a perfectly balanced substance that not only exists for the alchemist, but can also be used in helping others. For what purpose would anything of value be without sharing it. In *One Taste,* consciousness guru Ken Wilber answers the familiar question, "If God is so perfect, then why did He create us?" He answers by quoting an old Zen master, "It's no fun having dinner alone."[17]

The Individuated Self is a great achievement. But relative to humanity, not to mention the greater universe, even it is left wanting. There is a final step that precipitates Divine consciousness, or what I've called the Divine Self. This consciousness is what the alchemists meant by the philosopher's stone and why they had to use mystical terms in attempting to describe it. In the Eastern tradition, this supreme consciousness is simply referred to as "that," implying that the experience of the philosopher's stone embraces all to which "that" points, namely, everything. The alchemist who possesses the philosopher's stone perceives life through the eyes of the Divine Self. Through it he sees no distinctions between self and other, dark and light, this or that . . . the world has been made over into one whole and conscious being.

While we have seen how consciousness develops through the life cycle, we are left needing to know how to apply alchemy in our day-to-day lives. Before embarking on a more open discussion of some of the alchemical recipes, I offer the following guide as a means for achieving the best results in making gold:

FOR BEST RESULTS

1. IDENTIFY THE PRIMA MATERIA. Choose some dark aspect of your personality that needs attention. It may be a bad habit you want to stop or a lack of confidence or a depressed feeling that comes and goes. Write down the problem you want to work on as specifically as you can. This brackets off the problem and allows you to concentrate on it.

2. FRAME IT AS AN OBJECT OF STUDY. Adopt an unbiased, objective point of view. Pretend, if it helps, that you are talking about someone else.

3. EXPERIMENT WITH USING ALCHEMICAL METHODS. This can be done in a couple of ways.

   First, use the functions and the elemental power each represents to locate where the problem is. Let's take for example a bad habit of eating all the wrong things and consequently gaining weight. First I suggest you do an inventory of functions that use *circulatio*. Image a simple cross with thinking at top, feeling at the bottom, intuition on the right and sensate on the left. With this image in mind, or written down, go from one function to the next asking yourself how strong or weak each is with regard to the problem. Since overeating involves the sensate function, that is, receiving oral gratification from eating, you will probably want to begin there. This part of your psychological function probably needs attention. You do this by raising your level of awareness to every act involved in eating, from the moment you first notice a hunger pang all the way to the last bite. Just saying no doesn't help at this point. Simply take very close notice of the entire chain of behaviors that go into your compulsive eating. Pretend this is a movie that you're seeing in slow motion. This simple practice helps bring consciousness to the sensate function and sometimes it is all that is necessary to become more mindful and more in control of the situation.

Then move on to the other functions. Thinking will help you make a list of which foods to eat and which to avoid. The feeling function is extremely important in helping you examine your attitude toward food and eating habits. Oftentimes, the hunger that is being fed has nothing at all to do with food. It may represent a lack of warmth and affection in your life. Now take a look at the intuitive function. It can assist you by using the imagination to substitute images for actual eating. This is a regular part of hypnosis. Induce in yourself the image of having your belly completely full and you feeling great.

If your problem is with a lack of confidence, find the function in which you feel most deficient. In the case of depression, you may want to look first at the feeling function. Wherever you begin, simply move through each of the functions to find both strengths and weaknesses.

A second alchemical method relies on using the operations. You'll recall that the first four operations each connect with an element and an elemental being.

- CALCINATIO is the fire operation and its elemental is the salamander.

- SOLUTIO is the water operation and its elemental is the undine.

- COAGULATIO is the earth operation and its elemental is the gnome.

- SUBLIMATIO is the operation of air and its elemental being is the sylph.

To illustrate this method we will use another example. Let's say that you want to quit smoking cigarettes. Since smoke involves air, we will work with the operation that corresponds to the nature of the problem. In this case, that would be the air operation, *sublimatio*. Just as you were able to strength the sensate function in the previous example, here you will want to become more mindful of breathing in general. Deep breathing is an excellent example of *sublimatio*. Exercise, swimming and a brisk walk are also *sublimatio* behaviors that raise the level of our awareness of taking in and expelling air. When we deepen this consciousness sufficiently to the point that the body "remembers" that smoking cigarettes is unnatural and toxic, the habit "goes up in smoke." Don't forget to call upon the sylph or fairy that can connect your body with its spiritual power. You don't need to solely depend on sheer willpower to get the job done. Trust your guardian angel to lend a hand.

4. **PRACTICE THE CHANGES IN YOUR LIFE.** Alchemical changes involve endless practice. As a Zen Buddhist once said, "If something is boring after two minutes, try it for four. If still boring, try it for eight, sixteen, thirty-two, and so on. Eventually one discovers that it's not boring at all but very interesting."[18] Using any one of the above methods requires practice. Perhaps more important than the number of times you practice is the quality of the attention and intention you bring to each trial. I have seen cases where just one trial was enough to end years of a self-destructive habit.

5. **TRANSFORM YOURSELF.** Before something can be transformed, you have to raise the overall level of consciousness. Practice helps make change become a natural part of your behavior, but individual behavior must find its place in the world. Know that others will (unconsciously) work to repress your new self. Resist their efforts—gently. Surround yourself with people and things that accommodate your change. Follow the advice of one medieval alchemist: "Certain activities tend to draw to the soul particular kinds of spirits associated with that activity."[19]

6. **INTERNALIZE IT.** A clear indication that you have achieved this level is that you no longer think about the change, it is natural to you

and others. I quit smoking cigarettes many years ago. It took only one New Year's Eve resolution to quit, but another ten before I considered myself a nonsmoker. Smoking had dropped out of my identity.

7. **SHARE WHAT YOU HAVE LEARNED.** By helping others you remain part of the community (that's common unity); alchemy works to make the individual and the collective "One thing."

There is no one recipe that completely explains all the steps needed to ensure a progressive and satisfying course of individuation for everyone. Just as the cycle spirals up and down, you can expect the journey to be erratic, marked, I hope, by many more advances than setbacks. Much of what encourages the process is having the right attitude, and one that is accompanied by the sheer joy of participating in your own evolution. While we have focused on the life cycle of the individual, the larger, universal spiral that preceded us emerges out of the eternity of the past and will surely extend into the infinity of the future. Make your contribution count!

GOLDEN RULES   To further simplify the difficult process of transforming the lead of the natural self into the golden consciousness of the Divine Self, I offer the following fundamental principles that may guide you in the work:

1. Consciousness is the basis for all life. When we work with consciousness alchemically, we are transforming it into matter. Be sure to get it right: matter is the result, not the cause of consciousness.

2. We all have lead at the center of our being, but in it are found the seeds for making gold. Generate the gold. Greet everyone silently (or openly) with the salutation, "*Namaste,*" The god within me honors the god within you.

3. We all evolve and individuate and that is our destined purpose for having been born into this reality. Forgive those who are unconscious and surrender to those who have gone farther than you.

4. We are all one and many emanations of the One Thing. Spirit and matter are only two aspects of this supreme reality. See with your middle eye.

5. The act of transforming reality gives meaning to our lives, to the world and the universe—simultaneously!

6. The time to act is now. The present is the portal to infinity. It is where everything comes together, and therefore can be transmuted. Be fierce, be ready to live in this presence. Life is a paradox that can only be understood through the imaginal mind. It is a trick and a treat. Imagine That!

Chapter 8

Recipes

You think I'm torturing you.
I'm giving you flavor, so you can mix with rice and spices
and be the lovely vitality of a human being.

RUMI

Listen, undeceive yourself. Every housewife is a pharmacist,
every loaf of bread is a pharmaceutical preparation.

JOHN URI LLOYD,
AMERICAN JOURNAL OF PHARMACY, APRIL 1922

U p to this point we have discussed some of the key goals and operations of alchemy as they apply to the individuation process. Alchemy finds renewed relevance today particularly in psychological healing and consciousness transformation. Even a summary of alchemy suggests the enormity of its vision and the challenge of its work. Every great vision is a profound insight into the nature of reality. Sometimes insight comes without asking, but more often it results from years of dedicated work. Of course, many still question whether the alchemists, despite their labor, were either deceiving themselves or others. The only way to know whether their mission was misguided is to put their words into action.

Having briefly described their theories, we will now turn to ten recipes formulated by various alchemists in the course of their work. As you read them, keep in mind the following questions: How do these recipes apply to the common problems and issues we face in modern life? How do we use the elements, operations, forces and stages in putting these recipes into action? To these questions, I offer my own interpretations, but as with dreams, these recipes may be interpreted in many different ways. The missing ingredient that makes each recipe personally meaningful is the one you must add to it. That includes any personal associations, amplifications, "memories, dreams and reflections."

Each recipe can be read like an essay, independent of the others. I have added a keyword to each recipe should you want to go directly to any one that particularly appeals to you. However, there is a loose, underlying order to the sequence of the recipes that generally follows the three stages of the work. I therefore recommend reading them in order. If, in the future, any one of them is relevant to specific work you're doing, you can refer back to them using the keywords assigned to each in the table of contents.

Before going on to the recipes, it might be helpful to review, very briefly, connections between alchemy and psychology. Unlike scientific formulas, these recipes cannot be followed word for word. To understand them, we must peel away the symbolic skins that keep them pure and out of the wrong hands. Certainly we want to get as much out of these recipes as we can so that they speak not only to our heads but also to our souls and bodies. The know-how needed to put alchemy to work is found in the recipes. They contain, in capsule form, wisdom handed down through the ages to us. Receive them in the manner they were offered.

The personality is the vessel in which we experiment with life. Consciousness is the matter contained in the alchemist's vessel that we propose to transform from a state of chaos to one that is superbly organized. The transformation involves various processes that change the matter from its gross state, the *prima materia,* to its most refined form, the philosopher's stone. Psychologically, this development represents shifts in psychic orientations and stages. The movement goes through three stages and generally speaking three orientations: the *nigredo*/ego (me), the *albedo*/self (us), and the *rubedo*/collective us. We can summarize these changes using an old paradigm in which the first stage is one of unconscious perfection to the second, which is conscious imperfection, and finally to the third, which is conscious wholeness. Symbolically, the alchemists represented this movement as a progression in metals going from lead to gold.

The old practitioners believed that alchemy's methods could improve this natural development. Augmenting alchemy with principles borrowed from Jungian psychology and contemporary physics, the goal is to hasten the development of personality and extract an Individuated Self that lies hidden in nascent form within the *prima materia*. The work is taxing and arduous, often requiring a lifetime commitment. Fortunately, the process can be just as rewarding as the goal. At times, if we are fortunate enough, we get glimpses of the philosopher's stone long before we can stabilize and make permanent this incredible state of mind.

> Taking charge of our lives is inherently satisfying and growth producing. Despite its demands, this alchemy of individuating consciousness is a labor of love.

No one school of alchemy reveals a consistent, complete system for producing the true gold. Therefore, I have taken themes common to most systems, hoping to derive a model of alchemy that can respond to the needs of modern men and women. As we turn our attention to alchemical recipes, I continue with this strategy, extracting some powerful formulas concocted by alchemists in the course of their work. I recognize that the richness of any one theory, or school, of alchemy may be lost in this approach. Nonetheless, it gives us enough of an overview that will I hope encourage further research and personal exploration.

The recipes I have chosen come from many sources. Some were taken directly from texts, others from inscriptions in alchemical drawings. Each is a pearl of wisdom, timeless and pure.

Despite the many technological advances that have dramatically altered the outer landscape of our lives, the challenge of enhancing the beauty of body, mind and soul remains the same. Cosmetics were used by ancient Egyptians to adorn the body, but their philosophy was principally directed toward preparing the soul for the eternal afterlife. Understanding the temporality of life, great civilizations like ancient Egypt attempted to develop inner beauty. In this sense, alchemists were beauticians of the soul. Their Art aimed to make a masterpiece of all humanity.

Long ago, there were many kinds of recipes, not just those used for preparing meals. Recipes were prescriptions drawn up by witch doctors, shamans and healers. Today we watch our local pharmacist make up our medicine from a doctor's prescription by merely counting out pills. But, in past times, an apothecary mixed together plants, flowers and herbs. And before that, it was an alchemist poring over old recipes to find substances of every conceivable kind that possessed cures for everything from nightmares to syphilis. Many of their ingredients were quite unsavory, even disgusting. Human semen, blood and hair, urine, cow dung and rhinoceros horn were among the standard products taken from the shelves of the "dirt pharmacy." In addition to the differences in ingredients and different ways of dispensing medicine, the social act of healing has changed dramatically over the centuries.

The magic of modern-day prescriptions is gone. We simply take the medicine as directed and expect it will eliminate our symptoms. But, the further back you go, the more you find "added ingredients" of gods and spirits needed to make the magic work. Rituals aimed at empowering the potion with some supernatural spirit typically accompanied the recipes. It might involve an animal spirit, a god or even some alien creature. Without the agency of divine energies the potion was thought to be completely useless, dead and unable to cure anything. Many means were used to call forth an empowering god. The patient might have to do a sweat lodge, or make an offering, chant a healing song or even sacrifice an animal. Whatever the method, the potion would not have the desired effect without a personal contribution and a healthy dose of spiritual energy.

The word "pharmacy" originates in the Greek word *pharmakos,* meaning a symbolic substance that is empowered by "sacrificing parts of the community for the sake of regenerating its totality."[1] We can just as well understand community in terms of the collective as well as the community of mind, body and soul that makes up the individual. The important point here is the requirement of sacrifice that gave power to the medicine.

As we begin our study of recipes that were written during this magical, mythical era, we need to adopt the alchemists' psychology to liberate the power of their words. We must be willing to do all that is mentally, physically and spiritually necessary to empower the *pharmakon.* How, you need ask yourself, do each of these recipes help you become a more whole, complete individual? What sacrifice must be made to accomplish this goal?

Each of the ten recipes gives a partial answer to these questions, leaving you to put it all together. Only you can author the unique recipe that will bring good health and healing. Use your imagination!

THE FIRST RECIPE

Visit the Interior of the Earth and
Rectify what you find there,
and you will Discover the Hidden Stone

The alchemists were masters at keeping their sacred knowledge out of the hands of charlatans.[2] They resorted to misinformation, cryptic language, anagrams, symbolism and bizarre images to conceal their insights. This first recipe is an excellent example of how alchemists used an acronym to disguise an overall summary of the work. The recipe was originally written in Latin. The Latin translation reads, *visita interiora terrae rectificando occultum lapidem.* If you take the first letter of each Latin word as it appears in this recipe it spells out "vitriol," a word adopted into the English language to mean caustic speech, "virulence or acrimony of feeling." The etymology of this word, or acronym, makes an alchemical connection to its earlier meaning: "concentrated sulfuric acid."

This example gives us an excellent opportunity to show how trickster performs word magic. Alchemy made ample use of cover names and magical acronyms to protect its secrets. The path from a corrosive acid, like sulfuric acid, to caustic speech describes a complex psychic process that connects substance and language. We so often see this disconnect and use words without regard for their deeper significance. What acid and vitriol have in common can only be understood in the alchemical imagination. Rejoining word and image is a dynamic part of healing the split that's arisen between mind and soul. This recipe will only make sense if each word is examined with care.

Alchemists used this recipe as a template to describe the entire course of the work. To fully understand it, we must first consider the images used in the recipe. Images are the substance from which words issue. They depict an alchemical cosmology, one that draws little distinction between nature and human existence. In the alchemists' mind, there is a leaden stone at the center of the Earth's core. Minerals and gemstones filled other caverns throughout the earth's subterranean surface, but at its center was this stone. The sun, they thought, was the only agent that could directly penetrate this stone and other "dead," inferior substances and gradually transform them into gold. This gold is created by the sun's rotation around the earth. By virtue of this cosmic swirl, the sun's own image is imprinted both within the earth's core as well as at the very center of the human soul.

This cosmology is beautifully written in one of the oldest alchemical treatises, the *Emerald Tablet*. Referring to the *prima materia*, the *Tablet* describes its "father is the sun, its mother the moon; the wind has carried it in its belly; its nurse is the earth." The earth then forms the matrix, the basic structure, in which the inferior stone undergoes transformation. The sun fathers the stone in the sense that it brings vitalizing warmth and energy. The moon adds a silvery light to the dark stone that nurtures it and allows it to mature. The wind endows it with spiritual energy. These are the four elements at work on the stone, helping it "wake up" and evolve from its leaden sleepiness to its most purified form, gold.

Although the alchemists believed that everything in nature is conscious, they also thought that some things were more conscious than others. Lead, being the farthest removed from the sun, was the least awakened. Humans, on the other hand, possess the highest potential for becoming most fully alive, "living philosophical stones." In between these two ends were other metals, animals, minerals and vegetables that make up this evolutionary spectrum of consciousness. An old saying describes this spectrum in more poetic terms: the spirit wakes in the animal, dreams in the plant, but sleeps in the stone. Only humans have the requisite degree of self-reflective consciousness capable of becoming aware of spirit in all three dimensions and awakening the stone that "sleeps" within.

In this recipe, we are instructed to do a number of things. First, we are told to visit the interior earth. In psychological terms this translates to mean that our alchemical work begins by inspecting our unconscious life. In today's world, it is not considered aberrant to take seriously the unconscious. But, in historical context, this exercise is quite new. It was not until the late nineteenth century when science began to take seriously the possibility that there could be any such thing as an unconscious life beyond the magical world of ghosts and goblins.

Sigmund Freud was first to find his way into the interior earth of the unconscious by examining his dreams and those of his patients. His psychoanalysis cut like a surgeon's knife, opening the brain to expose the workings of the inner mind. But Freud's model of mind was fashioned after the type of laboratory work he was doing before establishing psychoanalysis: anatomically examining the spinal cords of fish. In addition to the empirical approach Freud took in describing interior reality, we must add the significant influences of the rigid moral climate of the late Victorian era. While to his credit Freud described the mechanics of the unconscious, he did so by very nearly equating ego with matter, thus leaving out critical contributions made by spirit.

It was precisely this myopia that led to his falling out with one of his most brilliant adherents, C. G. Jung. For this Swiss psychiatrist, the unconscious was broader and deeper than that conceived by Freud. For Jung, the unconscious was not simply a seething cauldron of repressed desires and impulses, but a world that connected the Self to nature. More than sexual fantasies lay hidden in its dark places. In Jung's view, darkness is an inescapable aspect of existence. Whether a man or woman is good or evil, standing there in the daylight, each casts a shadow. Every sin, indiscretion and immoral act goes into making up the shadow personality. And it was to this dark reality, that neither person nor even culture can escape, to which Jung gave the name Shadow archetype.

Entrance to the interior or unconscious life begins with discovering the shadow. Despite our resistance, shadow is in fact very accessible. It is our lead, that dim stratum of consciousness consisting of all those inferior qualities, that lies just beneath the surface of awareness. Shadow, being dark and dense, corresponds to the same qualities of lead. For this reason, alchemists assigned lead as the base metal and suggested that the work begin in the *nigredo,* the black first stage. As soon as we identify our shadow aspects, the lead is immediately elevated in status. It becomes the *prima materia,* a source for beginning the operations of the work. No longer are the leaden, shadowy aspects allowed to simply remain fixed and rock hard. Instead, the recipe requires us to take responsibility for our shadow, own it, and better, work to transform it. The shadow provides excellent material in beginning our alchemical work. Paradoxically, the worst of our nature serves our highest goal. In the lead and shadow, there is a bit of gold.

Most of us won't find it too difficult to identify the negative qualities that make up our personal shadow. If you do, just ask a few trusted friends to give you some clues. A good place to begin your own inventory is to draw up a list of habits. Whether good or bad, habits are mediated by the unconscious and therefore run contrary to raising our overall level of conscious awareness.

Habits are especially apparent in the unconscious workings of the body. With little effort we can see the body's automatic actions to internal as well as external demands. Pleasure and survival are not clearly distinguished by the body. Habits form when we fail to adequately differentiate survival needs from optional pleasures. As most of us know, breaking a habit is no easy task. Habits are extremely economical, always seeking the shortest distance between two points: need (real and/or imagined and satisfaction). Not that efficiency is bad in itself, but there is a huge difference between habits of impulse and those of intention. The former is blind, the second clearly sees the goal and object of its desires. Habits are the unexamined movements of spirit. Lacking imagination, they reduce us to mere automatons blindly carrying out nature's marching orders. While they feed the senses, they do nothing for the higher aspects of mind. Habits lead to mindless routines that

> Undoing habits means freedom and the place to start is simply (and ironically) by *validating* the habitual patterns that spew out of the body and its psychological equivalent, the shadow.

breed boredom, monotony and meaninglessness. In the worst case, body is enslaved by biological impulses that demand insatiable, instant gratification. In the case of addiction, people are forced to serve a selfish god who strips away dignity and returns them to Nature's chaos. In that state they spiral down, chase their own tail, go nowhere, endlessly left to pursue pleasure that neither offers love or meaning.

This recipe is reserved for those who wish to move their personal process forward, not because habits plague their lives but because they sense the gold hidden in the empty vacuum of their daily routines.

The second step in this recipe is rectification. Rectifying does not necessarily require analyzing dreams, doing active imagination or even eliminating a habit. While all these actions are fine, they require more sulfur than is yet available. Rely instead on the gentle heat of the sun as the source of consciousness to focus on the *prima materia*. Don't be in a rush to break every habit that jumps onto center stage. Instead, identify just one shadow element, or a habit, and simply train your attention on it until it begins to change of its own accord. At first, the change will be unnoticeable, but in reality the situation is completely different. In fact, the change is immediate. The minute we bring consciousness to bear on any unconscious element, the whole condition is revolutionized. We open new pathways for shadow to take, ones that ever so gently transform its darkness into creative expression.

My mother lives in the beautiful Catskill Mountains in upstate New York. Being a nervous individual, she seldom ventures out much beyond her property, and when she does, there are only a few safe routes she dares to take. During a visit, I suggested we go for a drive. I sat behind the wheel of her car and simply began driving in no particular direction. Even before we were out of the driveway, my mother asked where we were going. I simply told her that we were going to get lost. Of course this unnerved her and I had to reassure her over and over again that we would eventually find our way back home.

It was a lovely fall day and the leaves fell like golden wings along the country roads. After about thirty minutes we came to a dirt road marked by a sign that read STORM KING. I had no idea what this might lead us to, but in the spirit of adventure and despite a fearful mother, we ventured down the country lane. As it turned out, Storm King is an enormous sculpture park. It encloses hundreds of acres of beautiful rolling hills covered with gigantic sculptures. The view was spectacular. Only later did I learn how famous a place this was, and only later did my mother learn the value of taking roads never traveled.

> Habits are not adventuresome. The way we rectify habits is by taking bold steps into the unknown.
>
> Humor has a way of turning situations upside down and thereby creating new connections. Sometimes the alchemical vessel needs a good shaking to break up the mindless routines that drain its lifeblood. Laugh with, not at, your habitual way of doing things.

The third step in this recipe calls for discovering the hidden stone. The fact that it is hidden tells us that it is not familiar or that it may be disguised. This stone is not a concrete object and it may well be different in the eyes of those who behold it. The stone has this paradoxical quality: "It is a stone," Zosimos said, "that is not a stone." The stone that makes up the *prima materia* is the same as that which makes up the philosopher's stone, and yet, one lays dormant in the unconscious while the other has been fully refined and infused with consciousness. Confusing the latter with the former only delays the work needed to change lead into gold. Beware: *By idealizing the philosopher's stone, we run the risk of never attaining it*. In fact, the stone is not to be attained at all. Instead, it must be realized through conscious development. Unfortunately, the desire to attain full consciousness is oftentimes so great that it unwittingly leads some people to getting stoned with drugs rather than taking up the conscious work of individuation.

This recipe calls for imagination and cultivation of vision. Alchemical imagery challenges us to see the most ordinary things in unusual ways. Kings and queens are joined in one body. A tree grows out of a person's arm. An old man soars up above a city, spewing out a large rock from his mouth. On first inspection, these surrealistic images look like the work of children and mad men. When at first we descend into the unconscious, our ego cannot make heads or tails of anything. We look for logic where none exists. Often, I caution patients, "don't try making sense out of nonsense." In other words, we must accept the unconscious on its own terms, warts and all.

> Your intention might be stated, "I intend to look for the sources behind my _____." (state an unwanted behavior) You might further assert your willingness to suspend judgment and remain fully receptive to any and all shadow images that arise.

Now this does not mean relinquishing our will, but rather applying it with knowledge, foresight and persistence. Especially in the beginning stage of the work, there is a danger of becoming identified with the contents of the unconscious. It therefore behooves us to anchor ourselves by holding firmly to our stated intention. It is the baseline to which we return, again and again, to remind us of our goal.

The ego is repulsed by irrationality. It behaves in much the same way Hercules did when he descended into the Underworld. Rather than pay homage to King Hades, he attacked him. The object is not to destroy either the ego or the unconscious. Transformation means changing form, not eliminating it. Finding the hidden stone therefore requires paying attention to sidestepping the ego. Never challenge the ego directly. Rather, work on the conditions that surround ego. Occupy the ego with those tasks that it does well and leave the greater part of the alchemical work to the Self. Since consciousness circumscribes the ego, inspect what lies outside the scope of ego's concern.

> Imagine that area described by a cone of light emitted by a flashlight to be filled with ego's attention. Now look to see what lies in the shadows. At first, this may be difficult to see, but with practice, your eyes will adjust and the darkness will reveal the shadow.

Discovering the hidden stone signifies success in releasing consciousness from Nature's grip. When we contact the stone at the core of our life we have connected consciously to the vast realm of the unconscious as it resides in us and beyond us. Thus, the process of transformation has begun and you can now rightfully call yourself an initiate.

THE SECOND RECIPE

Dissolve the Matter in its own Water

There was a time when we looked to our own inner counsel before turning to others for advice. In the past century, we have fallen into a terrible state of overdependence on specialists, consultants and therapists. On the other hand, the spirit of invention seems to hover above those who maintain an independent mind and have the courage of their convictions. These people know when to turn to others for help, but by and large they deal with challenge on their own terms. I can think of no other group that more exemplifies this spirit than the alchemists. Risking social isolation, public scorn, scientific condemnation, religious persecution and even execution, alchemists marched to their own drummer.

Such independence can just as easily describe madness as more positive virtues like individualism, genius and dedication. And certainly many examples could be cited to support any of these possibilities. Often, no clear line separates the two. Some of the greatest minds have shown a "method in their madness," which paved the way to brilliant invention and discovery. The recipe that combines the two is a prescription not just for the eccentric genius, but for everyone. At the heart of the individuation theory is the notion that genius is not the province for the select few. Collectively speaking, genius refers only to those gains that benefit the whole. The paradox is this: as members of collective society, we are making an invaluable contribution to the whole world. At the same time, the deeper we go in our individuation process the more we naturally open to the world and want to give more to it. In this way, the Individuated Self is a gift we bring to the celebration of life.

> The ultimate expression of individuality is a state in which every cell, thought and feeling has been transmuted into an indivisible part of the whole world. Every realized soul then contributes to the individuation of the entire planet.

In the process of individuation we must give up some part of ourselves. It is a necessary sacrifice, one that we do consciously and for the good of self and others. Sacrifice of this kind is always about gaining something special and never about loss. What we gain adds to our individuating process. For example, in sacrificing narcissism we gain love and respect for others. This sacrifice leads to selfless service and a deep appreciation for the sacred interconnectedness of all living beings. To love with deep compassion requires dissolving the walls that separate "me" from "us," leading then toward a conscious embrace of the entire universe.

Dissolving does not mean eliminating. Actually, quite the opposite is true. A grain of salt dissolved in a cup of hot water does not result in the salt being eliminated. The salt has changed its condition by undergoing a process of dissolution; it has become part of every water molecule in the cup. One grain of salt has seemingly disappeared but in fact, it has permeated every water molecule.

To understand this recipe we must then know the nature of water and how it facilitates conscious development. To summarize the three important points made so far:

1. In the individuation process, the most powerful changes begin from within.

2. An excellent catalyst for change is water and its psychological equivalent, feeling.

3. Even a tiny dose of conscious feeling can change the overall disposition of the person.

Water is a symbol of the unconscious because of the special qualities and behaviors it shares with nature. Both are amorphous and ubiquitous. Each is fluid, gentle and powerful. Water is a mysterious element within whose depths even light disappears. This is the reason I tell patients to honor their feelings more than their thoughts. Feelings are unique, give depth and define who we are. They need no defense or explanation provided we own them and take responsibility for them.

In alchemy, every element has an accompanying action or operation that acts on the *prima materia* to transform it in some special way. The water operation is *solutio* and the process of dissolution derives from the action of this element. The present recipe advises the initiate to use this water operation to dissolve the *prima materia*. *Solutio* initially works to break down the walls separating ego from its shadow, thereby making the unconscious more conscious. The last thing on earth that ego wants to admit are its weaknesses, but with *solutio* even ego's defenses melt.

The corrosive ability of water to penetrate virtually all matter reduces gross matter to its essential form. Psychologically, water transforms shadow elements by breaking it up into bits that can be "digested" by the ego. I have seen this happen many times in therapy. When a patient undergoes a *solutio* process, both the tendency of shadow to remain hidden and the ego's tendency to deny shadow begin to dissolve. This paves the way for transformation. A patient who accepts that his shadow consists of old hurts learns to forgive. Another, quick to anger, learns to assert negative feelings in appropriate ways. And still others, whose shadows are constricted by perfectionism, learn the wisdom of insecurity, spontaneity, and trial

> "The drop," said Rumi, "becomes the ocean, the ocean becomes the drop."

and error. These are hard-won lessons and *solutio* is a slow process. It takes a lot of convincing for the ego to realize that there is a shadow. Water gently allows ego to acknowledge its dark side and gradually begin the process of dissolving the inferior matter.

Water is the only element capable of simultaneously existing in three states: solid, liquid and gas. Ice melting on a frozen pond illustrates this special aspect of water. The ice is solid, the water liquid and the evaporation is gaseous. Water also has the unique feature of expanding rather than contracting as its temperature cools. For these reasons, water shares many of the same characteristics attributed to Mercurius. For this reason, alchemists referred to mercury as living water, *aqua permanens*. This god is the "spirit that moves upon the face of the waters."[3]

The dissolving power of water comes from its ability to seep into things, soften them up and gradually reduce them to a liquid. Creation myths describe water as the primordial element from which the world emerged. *Solutio* then has the effect of returning matter to water, a rebirth that renews and refreshes the soul. In the work of individuation, this return plunges us back into the depths of existence. Ironically, only by returning to the original state of chaos are we able to create cosmic order. We must, in other words, dissolve in order to individuate consciously.

There is no escaping this existential requirement. Those who avoid it are left to suffer either neurosis or addiction. The neurotic is plagued with anxiety stemming from the false belief of being alone and cut off from nature. For him, the chaos is kept buried and out of conscious awareness. The addict, on the other hand, struggles to simulate the watery womb, but being unconscious of a spiritual craving for conscious wholeness, she is only left with a false *coniunctio,* one that does no more than stimulate the senses.

Only by making the return consciously can we shed light on the unknown—in ourselves by way of the unconscious, in the world by way of the universe, in god by way of the transpersonal. But, entering these unknown regions requires enormous courage. Within a few seconds after submerging ego beneath the waters of the conscious realm, panic sets in. It takes a lot of cajoling to have ego realize that it can swim like a fish. The metaphor in this case carries an important symbolic meaning. While the unconscious is symbolized by water, the symbol of the fish represents consciousness. With its ever-opened eyes, the fish has been a symbol used throughout the ages to signify a consciousness capable of penetrating the blackness of its own depths.

Baptism, a *solutio* ritual in the Christian faith, serves this very purpose. The baptismal water touches the unconscious, reminding it of its origin as well as the journey ego must take back home in order to discover its true parent, the Self. The journey is fraught with fear and danger. We fear drowning in the emotional waters of unbidden moods. Tumultuous feelings can inundate ego consciousness and loosen its moorings to everyday reality.

> Mercurius, the living water, gives us the power necessary to submerge ourselves in this great ocean and discover its secrets.

Anxiety, fear and panic, mood swings and nameless feelings can come upon us like a tidal wave. They cannot be avoided anymore than life can without water. Every tear and raindrop reminds us of the infinite ocean from which we all come and to which we will all someday return. Our personal unconscious is like a tiny stream leading to this great ocean of the unconscious. All peoples, all countries, all planets and stars—everything—is contained in this vast ocean.

Water is archetypally feminine in nature. This element, having no form of its own, goes whichever way the wind blows. In its human form, moods and the tides of emotions have this same quality. Water also conforms to all containers regardless of size and shape. Just as water takes the shape of oceans, lakes and streams, containers provided by Mother Earth—brains, bodies and buildings—hold and organize thoughts. And just as physical structures give shape to thoughts, feelings conform to the shape of their environment.

Wind and earth are necessary for structuring and channeling feelings. Air gives feelings the ability to move, and earth, the channels through which they become felt experiences. Without these elements, feelings are little more than a flood of emotions causing all sorts of problems. Hysteria, panic disorder, depression and codependency result from disturbances in this area. By coordinating the elements, we create a psychological world that is alive with feeling and the means of expressing thoughts with heartfelt conviction.

The association between the feminine and the water element has created confusion for both men and women. Feminine consciousness is not limited to females. It is contained within the psyches of men as well and takes the form of an inner feminine soul, or *anima*. Further confusion exists in concluding that the feminine must be weak since its associations with water (soft, nurturing, pliable) appear to lack power. Nothing could be further from the truth. Water's power is underestimated because its force is slow and invisible. We cannot, for example, see the force that drives an ocean wave, but anyone who has ever been knocked off his or her feet by one knows how powerful water can be. Even solid rock cannot withstand the dissolving power of water. Drip by drip, water is slow, patient and penetrating.

Feelings work in the same way. With love and enduring patience, even tyrants are made to fall. The gentle tear that falls from our eye is the same water that goes into making a hurricane. The Great Flood was the cataclysm sent by God to wipe out evil. In the same way, feelings cause things to change first by dissolving them, then by helping them grow. How often do we see parents spanking their children one minute and consoling them the next? Feelings have the force of water in all its many forms, colors and apparent contradictions. We must take care in using this element.

Mahatma Gandhi gave us a beautiful example that illustrates the power of this recipe. His famous march to the sea teaches us another *solutio* lesson, what came to be called nonviolent passive resistance. Although Gandhi regarded the British as a "curse," he wished not one of them any harm. Rather, he held them accountable for their actions and the oppression of his people. Despite a frail body, withered by repeated incarcerations, voluntary fasts and old age, Gandhi responded with passion. He used the tax on salt as his target because salt, he said "is as essential as air and water, and in India all the more essential to the hardworking, perspiring poor man and his beasts because of the tropical heat."[4]

Without a shot being fired, Gandhi forced the British Empire not only to repeal the dreaded salt tax, but in the end, lead them to evacuate the subcontinent altogether. His victory was spurred on by leading a group of seventy-eight members of his ashram 224 miles to the sea. In defiance of British rule, Gandhi simply picked up some salt left by the waves. In this bold gesture, Gandhi violated the law that made it a "punishable crime to possess salt not obtained from the British government salt monopoly."[5]

> Gandhi's philosophy embraces the alchemical concept of *luna,* the feminine, and its power to bring harmony to the world. Here are his seven sins:
>
> > Wealth without work
> > Pleasure without conscience
> > Knowledge without character
> > Commerce without morality
> > Science without humanity
> > Worship without sacrifice
> > Politics without principle

Too often people think they must quickly dissolve anything and everything that gets in the way of inner experience. Be it a family matter, a sexual matter or a money matter standing in the way of growth, people demand a quick fix. They want to turn on the fire hose and blast through the problem. This approach often creates more problems than solutions. Instead, we sometimes need to "go with the flow." Water may be slow, but it is powerful. It works gently to dissolve and transform. Attitude makes all the difference in learning and mastering this recipe. Like the reflections on a pool of water, the unconscious mirrors back what it sees. A very important aspect of water and the unconscious is well stated by Jungian analyst Edward Edinger: "the unconscious takes the same attitude toward the ego as the ego takes toward it."[6]

There is no magic, no rescue, when we find ourselves blocked and unable to navigate through dangerous straits. At times we find ourselves in the same mythic drama that Ulysses, the heroic ego, found himself when caught between Scylla and Charybdis. Like him, the initiate is put to the test at this desperate hour: will feelings overwhelm him and devour him whole, or will he be sucked up into the vortex of unconsciousness? Ulysses narrowly escaped dangers that lesser men could not survive. It is the same in life. When the tides of powerful emotions threaten, we must hold steady to our course. With compass in hand, a chart before us and most importantly, a determined will, we cut through the stormy currents of moods and emotions.

In alchemy, every element is essentially neutral and only acquires a helpful or destructive energy once it enters the human realm. Water can be soft and flexible or hard and rigid depending on its form and how it is used. Similarly, when unadulterated emotions become feelings, they can either work for or against us. Unchecked emotions inundate the psyche, causing it to drown in a sea of impulses and sensations. By contrast, living water animates the elements and their associated functions. Thoughts acquire conviction; intuitions inspire empathy; and the body is hydrated with soul.

> When we resolve to do something, every molecule of our body is changed by our will. The force of will is like a jet of high-pressured water passing through a hose. In making resolutions, the body responds with unbending strength.

"The Red Sea," wrote Jung, "is a water of death for those that are 'unconscious,' but for those that are 'conscious' it is a baptismal water of rebirth and transcendence."[7] We are born in a watery womb of unconsciousness and ascend, in the course of our lives, to a distant shore that promises new life. Nine months before birth we are bathed in amniotic fluid, and nine months after, we float in a sea of oceanic bliss. But, as Shakespeare has Hamlet lamenting, ". . . and in that sleep what dreams may come." The fetus's kicks can be felt in utero, and close attention to its perinatal life reveals stirrings of an individuating child. Instinct drives them both; nature gives the call; "It's time to wake up." Both child and parent need to hear the wake-up call, because a birth is never singular: it presents parents and child with the challenge of advancing to a new level of consciousness. The family line goes from me to us to everyone.

Parents go to extraordinary lengths to teach children how to walk and talk, but do far less to engender the individuation process. And yet, it is more difficult to learn emotional balance than to learn the balance necessary to walk. When we fall emotionally, the injury is more painful and lasting. More than thoughts, feelings and bodily sensation maintain primacy until the brain is sufficiently developed. Meanwhile the child has to establish a secure place for itself, separating and individuating from its hosts: Nature and parents. Without sufficient attention paid to emotional development, the walls defining personal space can dissolve even *before* they've been firmly established. In the worst case scenario, personality completely dissolves in its own water and individuality is either never established or at best, only tentatively formed.

During my years working with psychotic patients in a state hospital, I saw what happens when people fail to individuate in the first months of life. These unhappy people were fixated in their *solutio* process, replete with all the hallucinations and delusions of that watery womb. It was a strange experience seeing the chaos of nature displayed so openly in human form. Without defenses against the storms of affects and tidal waves of emotions, these unfortunate patients suffered dearly. Having only enough consciousness to know pain, they were heavily medicated by well-meaning doctors. Unfortunately there was no medicine that could ameliorate their worst suffering: loneliness. The waters of feelings could not, in these people, flow and mix with others. They were dammed up, boiling, as it were, in their own juices.

In less severe cases, we find other damage that is not nearly as visible but much more common. Without adequate boundaries, problems of codependence crop up. The worst part of this disorder is almost the reverse of the psychotic. Unlike the psychotic, who cannot attach to anyone, the codependent attaches to everyone. Their attention is riveted on other people's needs to such a dire extent that they all but ignore what is best for them. The dependency is so great that even pleasure and joy devolve into a vortex of masochistic perversion. Masochism is another example of the *solutio* fixation, where the matrix that forms personality is on weak soil.

The secret transformative power of this recipe is found in its direction to find solutions within our own water. R. D. Laing, John Weir Perry and Stanislav Grof attempted to use this recipe in treating psychotic patients. Treating functional psychosis as a process of spiritual awakening rather than a well-defined psychiatric disorder "often culminates," wrote Stanislav and Christina Grof, "in the experience of 'sacred marriage' . . . [that] usually reflects that the masculine and the feminine aspects of the personality are reaching a new balance."[8]

In a similar way, alchemical healing facilitates the dissolving/resolving aspects of *solutio*. Where nature is stuck, alchemy can redirect its currents. By building a dike, a river's flow is redirected, and barren lands are transformed into rich farm fields. So too must we at times disturb Nature, even violate her, in order to put her resources to good use. When the codependent refocuses his attention in building up from within, he learns the true joy of love.

While I have only mentioned these two problems, we can easily add more. Hysteria, addiction and borderline personality disorder are some other examples. Despite the seemingly impossible symptoms caused by these disturbances, I always find hope in knowing that the very thing that created the problem can just as well be used to cure it. "Like cures like" is the recipe used by homeopaths in treating physical illnesses. The same principle applies in caring for those suffering from these early psychological traumas. The spirit that dwells in the living water must be enlisted to revive the drowning psychotic, the exhausted addict and the lovelorn codependent. "The mystery of everything in life," quotes Jung from the *Gloria mundi* (The Glory of the Word), "is water; for water dissolves the body into spirit and summons a spirit from the dead."[9]

Healing enables suffering individuals to redirect attention away from others and discover for themselves the spirit dwelling in their own depths. Then, rather than nature dissolving them, they dissolve the delusions and dependencies that threaten individuation. At the start, turning inward means facing one's own doubts and fears. This is a painful process. The automatic tendency of relying on someone else to take care of us must be sacrificed to the higher purpose of establishing an individual identity. This requires us to do something that is contrary to our nature: we must turn toward the pain. As this recipe illustrates, alchemical healing is an *opus contra naturum*, a work contrary to nature.

This is, of course, a risky venture because nature is blind to the needs of the person; it looks out for the whole and sometimes cares little for the individual. It can just as well suck us back into itself as activate the instincts needed for individual growth and survival. Alchemy, in this case, picks up where nature leaves off. It is a David and Goliath story replete with all the same risks. But there is no getting around this part of the work. "When danger is there," wrote Hölderlin, "Arises salvation also."[10] Water is dangerous, but it is also the source of all living life.

THE THIRD RECIPE

Keep Vigilant even while Asleep

Most everything about alchemy is like a dream: its surrealistic symbols, puzzling ciphers and cryptic anagrams. Fortunately, we've learned a great deal about the nature and function of dreams. Still we will need to understand dreams in the context of alchemy and how they amplify concepts that transcend words. Dreams are the quantum artworks produced by the alchemical intersection between different realms of time. First, there was Picasso, who brought the visual illusion of movement to the flat surface of the canvas. Then, there was the surrealist Salvador Dali, who expressed Einstein's new concept of time-space in an image of melting watches. Such images redefined our psychological sense of the world.

This is what a brilliant image can do when created by a master. In his own way, Jung too was an artist. He liberated the unconscious from the confines of the Freudian model, where id, ego and superego worked more to limit the human mind than set it free. The picture Jung paints is one where dreaming is so much a part of the creative process that without it reality would not exist at all.

Alchemy is a myth that interlaces extraordinary events with the unconscious world of dream, myth and magic. As I've shown, even the history of alchemy is best understood from an ahistoric perspective—that is, seen through the lens of the unconscious. Otherwise, its history would be reduced to a simple, conventional interpretation: alchemy was the forerunner of chemistry. By now we know that alchemy is very much more than an attempt by early chemists to turn lead into gold. But, without a mythic perspective, we would be left with a paltry, anachronistic definition of the Royal Art.

While the study of dreams and other research into the world of the unconscious changed the scientific landscape dramatically, dreamers just went on dreaming—all the while knowing how elusive and difficult an experience dreams can be to understand and master. Today we may be more willing to take dreams seriously, but often do little beyond keeping a dream journal. We shy away from the real work that can bring dreams into physical form. This is a modern problem, one not shared by our ancestors. For them, there was no separation between dream and reality. They did not analyze dreams because in a very real sense they were living out their dreams. They did not have to contend with a science that places stringent criteria on the acceptance of things into the collective myth.

By definition, a dream is unique and very personal; it doesn't lend itself to normative statistical analysis—thank goodness. Science today is by and large at the service of the collective. In so doing, it oftentimes overlooks individual, idiosyncratic experience. In past times, the situation was just the reverse. Yesterday's science was magic and it emphasized individual experience over collective need. We should not glorify one or the other. While, for the most part, our ancestors could dream away without having to prove anything, they lacked a sophisticated technology that facilitates the transformation of fantasy into reality. For the few that had "big dreams" and felt compelled to openly share their vision, the political establishment was in many cases no less harsh than today's scientific community.

Technology is providing us with imaging machines that reveal the invisible world in unprecedented ways. I doubt that it will be very long before we will be able to see our dreams displayed on a monitor. But for now, dreams are more often treated like an extension of television shows than gateways into the unconscious. Invisible to anyone but their owners, dreams light up the night with sights and sounds of this world and others. We intuitively know dreams must mean something, but their meaning is elusive. To discern what they are telling us requires a certain objective detachment from them, reflection, association and active imagination. It's like sorting out and putting together the pieces of a jigsaw puzzle, but in this case, one dream puzzle fits into a larger puzzle, ad infinitum. It is regrettable that this imaginal work is not attempted and dreams are regarded as little more than nightly entertainment.

Numbed by the magic of technology we can easily fall victim to passivity, leaving the real adventure of doing dream work to those courageous few who refuse to do anything that might jeopardize the creative urge to individuate. Science is not the enemy. On the contrary, it may well be the last stronghold of the imagination, especially for those looking for something more than mere narcissistic amusement. Science, as a tool and in the right hands, can and must be part of the modern alchemists' resources.

The viewpoint of a scientist requires as much attention to beauty as to theory and calculation. Sending up an astronaut-artist in a space shuttle is a small token of appreciation for the vast artistry that describes the starry firmament. Modern science is light-years away from discovering the mystery that captivated the imagination of the old scientists. For the alchemists, the grandeur of nature was a sublime, transcendent experience. They took the dream as a living part of reality without sacrificing sanity or perspective. This required skill and determined effort.

This old recipe tells us where to begin in this great experiment with nature. It instructs the alchemist to be vigilant during the night hours. As with so much of alchemy, this recipe presents us with a paradox. We typically associate sleep with being unconscious. The idea of being vigilant and consciously attentive during the night befuddles the modern mind. So how can we be both conscious and unconscious, or conscious while being unconscious? This was not a problem for the alchemist because such sharp distinctions as conscious and unconscious did not exist. But for us they are huge obstacles and they create contradictions that make recipes like this one seem impossible to carry out. With the help of modern science, however, we can clarify the situation and then use this recipe to advance our work.

Dream recall is evidence that sleep is not an activity in which we are completely shut off from consciousness. In recalling a dream, we are reminded of bizarre and unusual situations; doing extraordinary things we cannot do during the day. We can fly, change shape and travel backward or forward in time. Dream recall varies from one person to the next. Many do not recall dreams at all. But whether or not we remember our dreams, the fact remains that dreaming goes on in waves of four cycles every night. Cumulatively we dream approximately ninety minutes each night during these four cycles of rapid eye movement (REM). These cycles are interesting in terms of this recipe because we now know that dreaming only takes place as we are moving toward a wakeful state. We must then retain a certain amount of consciousness even while we are sleeping, as evidenced by dream recall and those semiconscious periods when dreams occur.

The alchemists did not have sleep labs or EEGs to measure these things and yet they were correct in the instruction given in this recipe. If we were completely unconscious during sleep we would not be able to have the conscious awareness required for vigilance during night hours. Nor would we be able to recall anything, much less make sense of it. This is not to say that dreamless sleep doesn't occur, but that at this stage in the work, some amount of consciousness is necessary night and day.

Stephen LaBerge, who did pioneering work in lucid dreaming,[11] performed an experiment to show that the mind could be conditioned in such a way that conscious control could be asserted during sleep. He instructed his subjects to give a signal in the course of their sleep to indicate that they were at that moment experiencing a dream. On the basis of his laboratory experiments, LaBerge then developed a behavioral program that, when practiced during the day, would enhance one's ability to exercise some conscious control during dream states. Such exercises, however, are not new. In many religious and spiritual traditions, an initiate was required to learn methods for increasing the ability to assert conscious will while dreaming. For example, under the tutelage of a Yaqui Indian shaman named Don Juan, the anthropologist Carlos Castenada learned lucid dreaming.[12] The Dalai Lama described similar methods drawn from teachings on dream yoga.[13] This practice has been used in Tibet for thousands of years. Then there is the example of the Senoi Indians of the South Pacific islands. In this culture, dreams are a communal activity used to protect the tribe and maintain harmony with nature. In this case, each member of the tribe brings his or her dream to a shaman, who not only interprets the dream but also prescribes ways to enact the dream in order to derive its full benefit. When we consider these examples, this old alchemical recipe does not appear so unusual or impossible.

Actually, the recipe identifies the first step in manifesting and transforming the imaginal world into physical reality by concentrated effort. To manifest means to "make evident to the eye or to the mind." We generally associate sleep with darkness and dreaming with confusion. For the alchemist, this darkness was associated with the *nigredo,* the first stage in the work. In the *nigredo* period, we begin sorting out the confused images of mind and nature, the former goes by the name *massa confusa* and the latter, in this case, are dreams. We see this same process of sorting going on in creation myths. The book of Genesis describes this *nigredo* experience beautifully:

> In the beginning of creation, when God made heaven and earth, the earth
> was without form and void, with darkness over the face of the abyss, and
> a mighty wind that swept over the surface of the waters. God said, "Let

there be light," and there was light; and God saw that the light was good, and he separated light from darkness. He called the light day, and the darkness night. So evening came, and morning came, the first day.[14]

Vigilance is the focused light of consciousness, that when applied to the unconscious darkness not only makes it visible but also changes the physical structure of what is seen. Magicians intuitively knew this; contemporary physicists are proving it.

This last statement rests on evidence provided by quantum mechanics, which both proves retrospectively the alchemist's claims and proposes ways to go beyond what is possible even in lucid dreaming.

Quantum physicists have demonstrated that accurate measurement can only be accomplished by including the effect an observer has on the object being measured. In other words, we cannot exclude ourselves from the equation without distorting nature. Not including the effect our very presence has on nature is unscientific. It is a distortion of nature that produces a false representation of the real world. We are, as the alchemists believed, an inextricable part of nature and cannot therefore know nature without

> Vigilance is the first step in transforming dreams into physical reality.

knowing and including the effects of our presence in the work we do with nature. Whether we are performing a scientific experiment or taking a walk in the park, we cannot exclude the undeniable effects of simply being part of the overall situation. Cutting-edge science attempts to tell us what the nature of this contribution is and how we can modify our effect in the total scheme of things.

Earlier I mentioned two principles from quantum physics known as observer participantcy and complementarity. In summary, these principles mean that human observation changes physical matter and "that the physical universe can never be known independently of the observer's choices of what to observe."[15] In other words, the physical universe is changed by our observing it as well as by what we choose to focus on. The physical world is therefore inescapably defined by the presence of human consciousness and specifically by its ability to choose what will be observed. In this light, vigilance can be seen as a powerful tool that changes the structure of reality. At the same time, as we focus on something, something else is automatically changed elsewhere in the world.

Vigilance is a method that amplifies the effects of consciousness. Fred Alan Wolf believes that we can influence nature and even direct it in much the same way an artist uses her hands to create a sculpture out of clay:

> Whatever you can imagine begins to appear as if we called it into existence. We are creating these images as realities because the universe is ambivalent and paradoxical. It doesn't care what you produce. It doesn't say to you that you can't do this and you can do that. It is like a mother who loves all her children . . . it doesn't care. It says whatever you create is imagery, so will it be. Why? Because at the core of the universe, at its most fundamental level, it is not solid stuff. It is not hard reality. It is capable of forming reality into whatever *our* images produce.[16]

This is a radical formulation for us, but an alchemist visiting from the fourteenth century would view it quite differently. On hearing such things, he would probably smile at our ignorance. However, an important distinction must be made between the quantum physicist and the old alchemist before we can make good use of this recipe.

From the quantum physicist's point of view, the alchemist was practicing magic, and for our visiting alchemist the physicist has merely discovered a new way to make the magic work. In human experience we find that both magic and science exist simultaneously, with magic being chiefly mediated through the unconscious and science via conscious processes. We are physiologically programmed to operate in both realms of experience; in our right brain resides the magician, and in the left, there is a scientist. Somewhere in between there is a modern-day alchemist trying to fuse the best of old and new, magic and science.

Paradoxically, there are multiple ways of viewing nature; one and many images that while true are difficult to capture in a single thought. Just as light can be seen as both particle and wave, the psyche can be simultaneously both conscious and unconscious. The sun (consciousness) does not disappear at night and the moon (unconsciousness) is visible even during daytime hours. Our inner sun and moon, not to mention the planets, are constant in their effects on psyche. The blackness associated with the *nigredo* stage is not one that disappears with the light of the *albedo*. The darkness is coincidental with the light just as our earthly life

would not be possible without the moon. Lucid dreaming as well as alchemical vigilance in general helps us attain what Jung termed the *coincidentia oppositorum;* that is, the simultaneous apprehension of the one
and many facets of nature.

In this state of mind, intense vigilance dissolves the divisions that
ego imposes on nature. This expansive state of consciousness gives us a
glimpse of the psychological experience of the philosopher's stone. Increasingly, modern science is demonstrating the multidimensional functioning of the human brain and correlate states of consciousness.
Scientists describe various stages of consciousness by tracing brain wave
activity using electroencephalograms (EEG). Longtime expert in consciousness studies Ken Wilber cites some remarkable findings in this
area of research. In his book *One Taste* he describes how "subjects report
being 'conscious' during sleep, and the EEG seems to support this, in that
alpha (waking), theta (dreaming), and delta (deep sleep) patterns are *all
simultaneously present*—this is 'constant consciousness' through all three
states."[17]

Again, science confirms what alchemists were saying centuries ago.
If we still find this difficult to do at night, imagine the task of being fully
conscious during the day. Most of our daily be-
havior is driven by blind habitual routines. How
much theta activity is going on in broad daylight? We have the mistaken notion that night
is the exclusive home for dreams. In reality,
not only do we daydream, but much of our daytime is actually spent in a trancelike state. Perhaps "constant consciousness" is a good term for
describing a lucid life.

We have the potential for lucid living, but
that does not mean we use it. Our bodies are
mostly run by autonomic activities that require no conscious direction.
Breathing, digestion and even the blinking of our eyes are under the involuntary control of the autonomic nervous system. We can access these
functions just as we can access our dream states, but in general we entrust them to our unconscious nature with nearly complete abandon.

Vigilance is the conduit of awareness streaming directly from the
Self. It is the eye of self and its vision transforms by way of the *calcinatio*

> How much time do you spend consciously aware of your actions? Your environment? People around you? What was your first thought on awakening from sleep? Your last thought before falling asleep? What color are your bosses' eyes? How many times did you use the restroom? What music did you hear? Did you even once think of God?

operation. When we master the art of sustained attention, both conscious and unconscious experiences change radically. There are many ways to learn this skill. Meditation that focuses on a single word or sound produces mind-altering effects. Concentrating exclusively on a character in a dream brings that figure to life. In addition to spiritual and psychological disciplines, body methods can also activate the unconscious, raising the threshold of awareness and producing extraordinary states of consciousness.

Beginning with the work of Roger Penfield in 1988, the science of brain mapping exploded into a whole new dimension of medical engineering. Using maps supplied by Penfield and his associates, electrical stimulation can now be applied to particular areas of the brain with pinpoint accuracy, resulting in very predictable responses. In recent years, this technique has been used to arrest the tremors associated with Parkinson's disease and other debilitating neurological disorders. But, again, we even find the roots of physical stimulation deeply embedded in an ancient, magical tradition.

Acupuncture, a method that uses thin needles applied to various parts of the body, has been in use since 200 B.C.[18] In theory these needles open/close the channel through which *Qi* or *chi,* life energy, flows.[19] In this way, proper balance is restored to the two poles of life—yin and yang—causing a healing response. Moxibusion goes even further in stimulating the flow of *Qi* by adding heat and burning herbs to the needles. Unlike brain stimulation, these ancient methods include the unconscious life of the body. Perhaps we may someday find the joining of old and new ways in creating an alchemical science that goes beyond the treatment of disease to opening up the vast (and rapidly growing) field of consciousness research.

There are down sides to both approaches. If the old way lacked enough ego, the new methods have too much of it. It seems to me that one good approach requires us to maintain a healthy level of ego while allowing the powers of self to guide our work. Too much magic and we dissolve into a morass of psychobabbling nonsense; too much science and we arrogantly seek to dominate nature, forgetting that we are an implicit part of it. For this reason, alchemy seeks to transcend the extremes

> Regardless of what method we use, the trick in sustaining attention lies in voluntarily surrendering to the experience without giving up more than we possess.

of magic and science, finding a third alternative that integrates the best of both approaches.

Maintaining vigilance of this magnitude may seem obsessive and even paranoid. Certainly there are pathological variations and misdirected attempts at grasping numinous experiences: the obsessive aims to control a world filled with endless possibilities; the paranoid loses sense of individual identity and sees instead the unmitigated power of the universe. Both have acute perception and persistent vigilance, but neither has a healthy enough ego to integrate the experience. In similar ways, drug abuse, schizophrenia and delusional behavior overwhelm the resources of ego, leaving little more than fantasies, hallucinations and broken dreams.

This recipe was taken from the old engraving that begins this section. It shows an elaborate alchemical laboratory. The recipe is located in the inscription just above the doorway leading into the laboratory. To the left there is a bed and to the right, scientific equipment. The engraving is a perfect circle with an alchemist kneeling at his bedside, looking upward at other inscriptions above his bed that read,

- Happy the one who follows the advice of the Lord.

- Do not speak of God without enlightenment.

- When we attend strictly to our work God himself will help us.

These additional recipes provide further steps needed to transform dreams and aspirations into reality. I would also like to point out another very important detail. There is, in the very center of the picture, a table on which sit a number of musical instruments. This is a wonderful image that portrays alchemy as the art and science of transforming nature's ambient sounds into beautiful music. What comes through clearly in this remarkable picture is a richly textured symbolism that depicts the human mind as an exquisite alchemical instrument.

THE FOURTH RECIPE

The Mind must be in Harmony with the Work

In some 30 million years we have built an impressive world. On the backs of mountains, there are great castles and monasteries. In arid deserts, giant pyramids jut high into the sky. Along the shores of rivers and oceans, wonderful villas and retreat centers offer sanctuary. There are few places in this good earth that have not been touched by human hands. We have sculpted beauty out of earth's abundant resources.

Long before the builder, *homo faber,* came of age, nature was the only artist. We call her Mother Nature for she gave birth to trees, deserts, rocks, caves, clouds, sky and of course, human beings. She is the *Anima Mundi,* soul of the world. With the rapid growth of civilization she has taken refuge in the woods, far from the maddening crowds of cities and towns. We visit her occasionally to refresh our soul. Her retreat came as a result of finding no place for her in our hearts. Unfortunately, it takes a flood to wipe away villages and earthquakes to rock the ground beneath our feet, to have us realize she is still very much with us and that her power is not the least diminished by our neglect.

This recipe is about how nature moves through our bodies, silently giving it the orders of the day. Building strong bodies and minds, buildings and bridges, nature moves through us like a great wave bringing creativity one moment and destruction the next. What remains is an indomitable urge we have to build, repair, restore, invent and create. What will we build today? A house? A business? A baby? A poem? Whatever it is, the process involves a transformation from the imaginal world of the unconscious to the substantial reality of matter. Images wash up on the shores of reality, where we use mud and water to build places to live, work and worship. Some amount of consciousness passes through us and is held in all that we create.

Unfortunately, this old notion of work is seldom appreciated in modern society. To our children, work is a bad, four-letter word that spells out something to be avoided at all cost. Even adults regard work as an activity devoid of imagination, pleasure and meaning. In either case, work is associated with pain and discomfort. Some of the confusion derives from a single Latin root word that gives work a double meaning. This root accounts for both *ponos,* the Greek word for work, and *poena,* meaning penalty and punishment. Word origins, being the inner structures that go into the process of translating image into action, shape the world we create. In this case, etymology restores work to a place where it has positive and negative connotations. In the confusion, the sacred element of work is lost.

Work had an entirely different meaning for the alchemists. For them, work was an interactive process involving spiritual agents (elementals) that were necessary to get the job done properly. Gnomes, fairies, sylphs and salamanders were the names given to beings that inhabit the elements. Those who work with their hands intuitively know that their materials have life. Oak's strength lends itself well to floor construction, the scent of cedar is ideal for closets and the beauty of rosewood makes for excellent furniture. Each type of wood, metal, even plastic behaves differently. But, far from green forests, the only wood an office worker has is her pencil, a sad souvenir indeed. It is easy to forget that the desk, ceiling, light fixtures and tiled floors all came from some faraway place in meadows, groves, mines and forests. It is extremely difficult to remember soul in this situation. Work, in this case, is just a job.

It is not that Nature is geographically distant from us, but that we are distant from her. In the linear structures that make up the Western world, she may be harder to see, but she is there. Hendricks and Ludeman, in their book the *Corporate Mystic,* tell a story that illustrates different ways of seeing the situation.

> One man was working listlessly, with a sullen expression on his face, while the other man was cheerfully singing as he busily carried stone after stone. "What are you doing?" asked the traveler of the sullen worker. "Laying stone" was his reply. "What are you doing?" the industrious worker was asked. "Building a cathedral" was his reply.[20]

The image of the cathedral emanates from the rich soil of psyche and psyche is Nature existing in and through us. A job is drudgery when there is no soul in it. But when the soul of matter is present and we go about our work with spirit, Nature appears in our labor and she is beautiful.

When we see soul and spirit in the things we build, they take on a divine quality. This is how we animate the world and make it a sacred place. Then, rocks are no longer lifeless stones. They are the building blocks used to create a cathedral. This alchemical vision takes in all levels of seeing: gross (the object itself) and the subtle (symbolic, metaphoric). When, for example, we look at van Gogh's last painting in this way, we appreciate the rich colors and his free-flowing brush strokes, but we also smell the field and hear the crows heralding his death. With alchemical vision we cease being voyeurs and actually participate in making the image come to life.

> The old monks would chant, *"laborare est orare,"* working is praying.

As image makers, the world is our palette and reality the result. Our tools are extensions of our hands; being and doing are no longer separate categories. "To labor," wrote the French writer Simone Weil, "is to place one's own being, body and soul, in the circuit of inert matter, turn it into an intermediary between one state and another of a fragment of matter, to make of it an instrument . . . an appendage of the tool."[21] We become, in other words, one with the work, the "Great Work."

A job is not a career, it's an occupation; something we do to pay the bills. It demands little of us save "clocking in" the time required to get paid. A career, on the other hand, is time well spent in a meaningful activity. It is both a means and an end to which we devote our lives in recreating something personally important. Its demands are not external. There is no need for any form of control when the desire to work comes from within. Work, in the form of a job, involves doing with little regard for the worker. Career is doing, but it also includes our being. The alchemy of work blends these two aspects of psyche: doing and being.

How is it that some people have jobs and others have careers? Psychological type, level of consciousness, dependency needs, locus of control, leader/follower traits, cultural and developmental factors all go into the path each decides to take. The satisfaction of a job is typically found in external rewards, and meaning therefore must be found outside the workplace. If the soul is not being fed by work, look for it elsewhere. Without meaningful work, people dry up inside. Even their work environments become toxic. Violence in the workplace provides a painful reminder that mind is not

> Human beings are a paradox, combining what appear to be two contrary elements: the experience of being fully human and the work involved in simply being. The joy of meaning and the satisfaction of building a happy existence give us a good recipe for making a successful life.

in harmony with the work; that, in fact, it is totally absent. When competition and control threaten to dehumanize us, the mind goes out of control.

The career path has its own dangers. Great compromises must be made between personal needs and the unavoidable demand to meet the bottom line. Divided loyalties pull the career person in two directions. Who I work for comes into question. Should I be loyal to the university, or is this research MINE? Personal profit or corporate gain? Protecting the environment or company compliance? These tensions cause an inner violence that eats away at soul.

Whether our path leads to job or career, these problems contribute to an old problem with a new name. In my practice, I have seen a dramatic increase in cases of agoraphobia, a dreadful disorder that literally means "fear of the marketplace." Its symptoms include intense anxiety, fear, dizziness, depersonalization and avoidance behavior. From time immemorial, the marketplace has been the center of civilized society; psychically, it represents the Self. If we run from the market, then we also find ourselves fleeing from Self. Where then do we turn to get help for this awful problem?

Mercurius, Lord of the Marketplace, is the great reconciler. Occupational medicine is his trade. But how, we ask, can Mercurius bring healing to a mind that is out of tune with the work? Ironically, his odd, strange and extraordinary nature offers us some clues. Certainly his swiftness and shape-shifting agility are essential qualities that assist in putting mind and work together in happy compliance. He gets right to the point, by deftly changing into whatever garb is necessary to get the job done well. Mercurius is an inventor who is especially adept at making things he can barter for greater gain. He loves to bargain and strike deals that serve all parties. He is not afraid of taking risks, and often his path is pitted with every imaginable accident. And it is especially this quixotic quality that brings us to the essence of his nature: he resides at the intersection between nature's chaos and the cosmic order we make of her.

In an article I wrote entitled "The Cosmology of Chance," I described a variety of methods used by many trickster figures in making order out of chaos. Mercurius especially figures into this cadre of archetypal magicians. "In doing psychological alchemy," I wrote, "the work of individuation, a sensitivity to change, both in oneself (involution) and in the world (evolution) develops. Merely discovering that there are soul operations and spirit operations, and operations conjoining both aspects of consciousness, already facilitates the work. It is like knowing what tools you have for a certain job. As this sensitivity expands, an awareness of good timing also develops, a coordinating of your changes to coincide with the milieu."[22] This sensitivity has its origin in what James Joyce described as a Hermetic "invisible influence (prayer, chance, agility, *presence of mind, power of recuperation*)."[23] This trickster's presence of mind is the invisible catalyst that harmonizes the mind with the work.

One of Jung's favorite tales was told to him by his friend, Richard Wilhelm. The story illustrates how a disciplined mind can bring harmony to the work. This is from one of Jung's last books, found in a footnote in *Mysterium Coniunctionis:*

> There was a great draught where Wilhelm lived; for months there had not been a drop of rain and the situation became catastrophic. The Catholics made processions, the Protestants made prayers, and the Chinese burned joss-sticks and shot off guns to frighten away the demons of the draught, but with no result. Finally, the Chinese said, "We will fetch the rainmaker." And from another province a dried up old man appeared. The only thing he asked for was a quiet little house somewhere, and there he locked himself in for three days. On the fourth day the clouds gathered and there was a great snow-storm at the time of the year when no snow was expected. An unusual amount, and the town was so full of rumors about the wonderful rain-maker that Wilhelm went to ask the man how he did it. In true European fashion he said: "They call you the rain-maker, will you tell me how you made the snow?" And the little Chinese said: "I did not make the snow, I am not responsible." "But what have you done these three days?" "Oh, I can explain that, I come from another country where things are in order. Here they are out of order, they are not as they should be by the ordinance of heaven. Therefore the whole country is not in Tao, and I also am not in the natural order of things because I am in a disordered country. So, I had to wait three days until I was back in Tao and then naturally the rain came."[24]

Making order out of chaos requires the mind to be in harmony with the work. In this story, the rainmaker did the inner work necessary to achieve that goal. In alchemy, Mercurius is the spiritual god that presides over this state of mind, and he draws as much from chaos, in the form of chance, as he does from an orderly, concentrated mind.

In his book *Trickster Makes This World*, Lewis Hyde captures this mercurial quality in a paradox. "Hermes," he writes, "is a god of luck, but more than that, he stands for what might be called 'smart luck' rather than dumb luck."[25] Hermes and Mercurius constantly work and play a cosmic game of chance. They are relentless, fearless jugglers of endless possibilities. They set up the circumstances where the possibility for wholeness may occur. More than hard work and even clarity are needed to bring confusion into order. "Mercurius," Hyde suggests, "stands for the smart [luck] and Hercules for the dumb."[26] He points out that ego alone can never do the trick of balancing mind with work. We cannot strong-arm this state of mind; it needs finessing and a healthy dose of good luck.

In recalling Louis Pasteur's famous aphorism, "Chance favors the prepared mind,"[27] Hyde gives us a clue as to how we might decrease the risk associated with trickster's folly and improve our chances of bringing mind and work into conformity. There are at least three things that will help us do this:

1. Embrace the unknown with a daring, trusting and receptive attitude.

    Hyde: "It might even be better to drop 'cosmos' and 'chaos,' and simply say that a chance event is a little bit of the world as it is—a world always larger and more complicated than our cosmologies—and that smart luck is a kind of responsive intelligence invoked by whatever happens."[28]

2. Allow the worst to enter into your affairs. Give the devil his due!

    Jung: Mercurius "is the devil, a redeeming psychopomp, an evasive trickster, and God's reflection in physical matter."[29]

3. Don't allow yourself to be sidetracked by falling victim to this fool's show, embarrassed by what he shoves in your face, or even amused by his pranks. Create and recreate by bringing invention to the matter at hand.

    Hyde: ". . . the mind that has smart luck makes meaning from unlikely coincidences and juxtapositions."[30]

At the very end of their work, alchemists offered a prayer to Mercurius with the hope that he might cause the efforts of mind and work to yield the precious stone. With this in mind, I recall that special moment I mentioned in my introduction when my good friend placed a pile of rocks at the edge of a stream in hopes that some spirit might provide us with a safe journey. What better god to make such a request than Mercurius, Lord of the Roads! When mind is not in harmony with the work of creation, we unwittingly invite chaos into our lives; we forfeit our destiny by casting it out to the winds of chance. "Going on a journey without consulting the god of the roads," Hyde cautions, "invites dumb luck; taking the god into account summons the presence of mind that can work with whatever happens. The first lucky find (or unlucky loss!) will reveal whether or not anything has responded to the summons."[31]

THE FIFTH RECIPE

The Sun and the Shadow Complete the Work

The human organism is a masterpiece of biological alchemy. Hundreds of operations take place every moment to keep the body functioning, safe and able to meet the demands of daily living. Sugars are transmuted into energy; oxygen is broken down and distributed to every cell in the body. These are silent processes that, for the most part, go on without requiring any awareness from us. We can, to some degree, make ourselves aware of these operations and even, with some effort, change them. These autonomic functions are about as close as we come to witnessing the ongoing activities of nature in human beings.

By contrast, the central nervous system is more conscious. The two parts of this system, brain and spinal cord, are responsible for executive functions that put us at the apex of the Great Chain of Being.[32] Abstract reasoning and the ability to walk upright are the mechanics that elevate us above the animal, vegetable and mineral kingdoms. But even more important than these functions are the abilities to control and regulate consciousness, as well as make the unconscious conscious, that legitimates our unique status. Wired into our psychobiology are these two modes of being: the unconscious autonomic nervous system and an unparalleled conscious central nervous system. In myth, these divisions are respectively referred to as the dark and light aspects of human life.

The relationship between the conscious mind and its dark regions is an archetypal theme found in art and literature. Artists from time immemorial have personified and projected these two aspects in countless ways. Over time, the light aspect became associated with good because of the trust we inherently have with things we can see and control. But goodness doesn't exist alone; darkness adds a tension that gives it meaning. Art creates a tension between these two forces and its appeal comes from the thrill of seeing whether the good guy will, in the end, triumph over evil. We delight in seeing movies and reading books that pit good against the dark forces. There is no end to our fascination with this mythic theme. The story has been told throughout the ages. Myths are filled with adventure stories of heroes and heroines pitted against some dark, mysterious force that must be vanquished in order for them to gain favor with the king.

The contest between good and evil is really about our personal struggle to individuate consciousness. The hero is the unproved ego (the initiate) who seeks to gain recognition from the Self (the king) by undergoing a trial by fire. Lacking this awareness, many a fight has led to empty victories. When we mistakenly declare war on others or ourselves, a neurosis develops. We point our weapons at phantom warriors and fret when they refuse to die. Anxiety is inevitable in this situation, but all the worry in the world will not accomplish anything. Nothing will change the truth that the real enemy is not somewhere out there, but instead can only be found within us. Even in heroic tales, it often happens that the villain transforms into some aspect of the hero, or the witch turns into a lovely princess. Transmuting lead into gold is the alchemical equivalent of the frog turning into the prince.

The dark matter is the *prima materia* and its primary substance consists of the Shadow elements of personality, all those inferior, unrefined traits of character. These amoral, uncivilized characteristics sneak up on us when we're not looking. They are the foibles of human behavior that we laugh at, deny and suffer. Alchemy begins its work by focusing its attention directly at bringing to light these dark aspects.

Our current recipe moves us from the discovery of shadow to operations that help complete the work. We move, in other words, out of the chaos of complete darkness (the unknown, the unconscious) and into the light of day, where conscious processes immediately set to work transforming the darkness into light.

The recipe mentions that both sun and shadow are important. The sun represents the light that shines through psyche. When we have been in darkness a long time, even a glimmer of light blinds us. We need to adjust our eyes in order to see clearly. The source of sun is *Sol,* the archetype of Self. So powerful are its rays that we may feel the impulse to run and hide. Our first encounter with Self can be a frightening experience because once our eyes are open we see everything, including shadow.

Having been born in darkness we must learn to live life consciously. The prospect of having to make decisions, think for ourselves and take responsibility are daunting challenges. Individuation requires courage, trust and fortitude. Poet and philosopher John O'Donohue suggests that this work begin "in the invisible realm. When you work in the territory of mind, you see nothing. Only sometimes are you given the slightest little glimpse of the ripples from your effort. You need great patience and self-trust to sense the invisible harvest in the territory of the mind. You need to train the inner eye for the invisible realms where thoughts can grow, and where feelings put down their roots."[33]

By gently letting go of ego's identification with the body, we become aware of other ways to orient ourselves so that we can assimilate shadow and transform it's energy into the light of consciousness. Letting go does not mean getting rid of shadow. Since the ego's fight with shadow is founded on fear, any action of letting go only activates its defenses. Rather, as the Beatles song title suggests, "Let It Be." Some part of shadow represents the unknown void that cannot be grasped, much less assimilated, by ego. The shadow is black and its absence of life equates with death. Ego exists in time and space; whereas archetypes are impervious to earth's conditions. From the ego's standpoint, death is the annihilation of time and space; succumbing to anything that even remotely resembles death is tantamount to suicide.

The work involved in simply letting ego and shadow exist as they are corresponds to an alchemist putting two substances into a vessel and applying heat. The heat represents consciousness used as a force that causes the two substances to shed their inferior elements and start a process where they begin to interact and absorb into one another. If the experiment is successful there is a great discovery: Ego and Shadow are part of the same thing—Self. This is very disorienting for ego since the laws that govern Self are completely different than its own.

From the Self's perspective, mind, soul and spirit do not exclusively localize within the confines of any one of them. O'Donohue makes this point by describing soul as something we are in, rather than something that is in us. Anthropologist Evan Harris Walker describes a model in which "our 'minds' do not reside in our brains but non-locally permeate and/or transcend space-time entirely. Our brains, then, merely 'tune in' to this non-local consciousness."[34] If mind and soul are in and around us, so too is Self. Ken Wilber further refines this concept by describing the functions of three different orientations. *"As the ego orients consciousness to the gross, and the soul orients consciousness to the subtle, the Self orients consciousness to the causal."* [Wilber's emphasis][35] By causal, Wilber means consciousness that we are here equating with those advanced levels of self that begin with the Individuated Self and progress to the Divine Self and beyond.

From the alchemist's point of view, shadow, in the form of the *prima materia,* is not necessarily bad or evil. Rather, it consists of inferior elements needing work. Ego too often identifies with matter, and without different perspectives, neither consciousness nor the Self would ever be given the opportunity to quickly evolve. We can never see the gold in the lead if all we're looking at is its superficial characteristics. It is essential to adopt different ways of thinking and seeing in order to advance the work; otherwise ego behaves like a lead soldier shooting at everything that moves.

In alchemy, sun and shadow are not opposites. They are two expressions of the same energy. Just like male and female describe two aspects of human consciousness, sun and shadow express two aspects of nature. This is paradoxical to the ego, whose job it is to break nature down into pairs of opposites that we can then use to discriminate and make decisions. But the ego can be deceived by it own good intentions. I recall a well-known Sufi story:

> The wise fool Nasrudin is looking for his keys under a lamppost. When asked where he may have lost them, he points to an area some distance away. He explains that he is looking under the lamppost because it is easier to see.

If we stay in this ego orientation, we make foolish mistakes. It does no good to punish the ego, for that only gives it the idea that it might really be as powerful as it already thinks it is. This is why we must talk about a shift in consciousness rather than one that develops along the lines of the Freudian paradigm. We need to shift our awareness from a narcissistic, ego orientation to one that allows us to apprehend more subtle phenomena. Lead to gold requires this shift from matter to spirit.

Shadow is not the enemy but a reflection of other worlds yet to be lived.

Many myths have it that the sun was born in some dark underground world. In some cases, the sun even has to be cajoled out of darkness. As the sun breaks the plane of the horizon, it takes some of the darkness with it. Shadow is this invisible aspect of the sun. Such thoughts boggle the modern mind and only in myth and fairy tale do we allow for mystery of this kind to go unquestioned. The metaphor and images protect us from the full realization that myths are really describing the inner workings of the mind.

In myth there is no difference between sun and shadow, their substances—a *homousia*—consist of one substance. Only when the sun—conscious light—enters the human realm does it take on a decidedly different *appearance* than shadow. Ego consciousness reacts to this superficial appearance, and without intervention, misses the massive reality of the Self. Crisis sometimes cracks open the ego to Self. Miracles are also sudden expansions of ego's awareness. Alchemy typically takes a gentler, more gradual approach in preparing the initiate for ego's introduction to Self (beginning with Shadow) and ultimately integrating it.

Science is another myth that opens ego to the wonders of nature and the Self. It appeals directly to the intellect and the senses, both of which are very attractive to the ego and its kinship with rationality. Contradictions are acceptable to the ego, even permitted, provided they do not involve us in any deeply personal way. The fact that dark matter, for example, makes up most of the night sky has little if any reality for us. That gaping holes exist in matter and that we are somehow held together by unseen forces are mysteries we blithely accept. For the most part, we rely on astrophysicists and biochemists to reassure us that these things really do exist and that everything is okay. Lost is the firsthand experience and joy of Gnostic knowing. (We believe in God, but do we know God?)[36]

Alchemists were first and foremost scientists, but the scope of their work included direct experience of the unknown. Increasingly, modern science is closing the gap between the object world and inner experience. Ultimately, the region above and below, light and dark, like sun and shadow, are one substance. "The common background of microphysics and depth-psychology," wrote Jung, "is as much physical as psychic and therefore neither, but rather a third thing, a neutral nature which can at most be grasped in hints since in essence it is transcendental."[37]

This third, transcendent position is difficult to imagine because it forces us out of the ego orientation where things are mostly rational and neatly organized. In alchemy, this is a rare event. It begins at the ego-matter-gross orientation but moves us into a field of consciousness where soul and self take precedence. Most alchemical recipes therefore seem paradoxical from the ego level. The only sense we can initially make of alchemy comes from the unconscious world of childhood. There, the magical mind, having poorly defined boundaries, merged things together without any real consequence. The consciousness needed to protect the child resides in the parents. From this perspective, alchemy is nothing more than magic. There is no third, transcendental orientation. But, as we have seen, alchemy goes much further. It methodically fuses opposites together in order to take us out of the magical mind, pass ego and straight into the orientation of Self. For the ego, this journey is disorienting and oftentimes treacherous. In the *nigredo* this awful experience is symbolized by the total eclipse of ego consciousness and is visualized as the black sun. Paradoxically, this image of the *sol niger* is both a problem and a solution for the ego.

The task of the *nigredo* is how to integrate forces of darkness and light. Jungian psychology has us symbolize the process or use art as a way of fusing shadow and substance. As a therapist, I have seen the tremendous change such methods have in helping patients shift orientations. Therapy sometimes requires heating up the relationship between therapist and patient to such intensity that the two are joined by a mutual problem. Jung said that no healing takes place until both therapist and patient reach this sort of therapeutic crisis. Then, in the heat of the moment, the selves of healer and patient, being of one substance, are each transmuted into something more whole.

I recall vividly the terrible feeling I had in treating a young woman. This turned out to be a *nigredo* experience for both of us, one that reined in the healing energy needed for change. My patient was very bright, articulate and fond of pinning me to the wall. While therapy helped her enormously, we'd not gotten to the core of her difficulties. Having just returned from a very stressful business trip, I did not have much patience for her sharp-tongued attacks. Exhausted, I made it clear, in no uncertain terms, how much I cared for her, that I was doing the best I could for her, and if that weren't good enough, it was her problem, not mine. At that moment there was a silence in that room so deep and penetrating you could cut it with a knife.

At the end of the hour and in many more sessions since then, our relationship took a dramatic change for the better. It was as if a bright light went on. We'd cut through the darkness and for a moment that seemed like an eternity, we saw each other's soul. This is not to say that she didn't continue to have problems in her life, but clearly, she sees them from the orientation of the Self, and that makes all the difference in the healing process.

Alchemy doesn't just happen in therapy. Another example comes to mind that illustrates contact made with my own shadow. Once when I was late for a medical appointment, I pulled into an underground parking spot a little too quickly. It was dark and in my haste I didn't notice a man just getting out of the car next to where I'd parked. I didn't hit him or the opening door, but I sensed he was upset with me. I raced up to the tenth floor, greeted the receptionist and took my seat. A few minutes later, a huge, burly man with tattoos and cowboy hat walked in. When the receptionist greeted him and asked how his day was going, he launched into a verbal tirade that was obviously meant for my ears. This was the guy parked next to me in the garage!

As I sat and listened to him vicariously berating me, I felt all sorts of feelings surge through my veins, each competing to have me say something. Anger took the lead and eventually won out over guilt. I simply couldn't stomach this unmanly attack. From the bowels of my gut issued the sounds of an animal. "That's a lot of hooey!" I shouted. The words bellowed out of my mouth. All ego defenses shut down. The gloves were off. I was one with my anger! Despite his intimidating bulk, I felt no fear. Surprisingly, nothing happened. There was only a pensive silence. And there we sat, just the two of us, in this waiting room.

In many years of personal therapy, I never had this kind of visceral encounter with my own dark self. All my civility went right out the window, and I felt refreshed. For just a few minutes I was transformed, and I would like to believe, so was the gentleman sitting across from me.

Alchemy deals with psyche from this level of orientation. The only way to integrate the darkness is to live it. The difference between the psychopath and the initiate depends on the different orientations of each. If we identify with the gross substance, we never integrate it, much less transcend it. While resisting the forces of darkness does have collective value, it often comes at a very high price for the individual. The initiate goes into darkness with detachment from the aggressive and sexual impulses of the body. Fighting with the shadow or

> Paradoxically, alchemy is about doing by way of being. When we raise consciousness to the level of Self, there is no difference between doing and being; we are one with the action.

with one's enemy is not productive. My intention was not to do battle with this man. On some instinctive level, I think he knew this. (Thank god!)

My interpretation of this recipe draws from Tantric alchemy. Its practice emphasizes mastery over the body and willful assertion of actions that rapidly disintegrate false divisions of mind. The way of Tantric alchemy directs us to the heart of an experience. Only by consciously living the experience fully can we pierce through it and gain clarity. "In the center of anger," wrote Ken Wilber, "is clarity; in the middle of lust is compassion; in the heart of fear is freedom."[38]

When we avoid the darkness, a black hole forms in our psyche. This lacuna has a dense mass, the gravity of which is tremendously intense. It sucks in everything. In order to complete the work, we have to see the light in the darkness. Only by living out the darkness in an ethical, responsible way can we assimilate, sublimate and eventually transcend it. To do this safely we must understand the nature of darkness and also have a level of sophistication that permits a passionate display of emotion without losing one's grip on reality. The sun, the symbol of eternal spirit, is in everything. That includes the darkness.

St. John of the Cross described the work of *nigredo* as the dark night of the soul. He understood darkness as the condition in which ego discovers a critically important secret: *darkness has no power!* It is the absence of light, consciousness, knowledge and substance. As such, it absorbs light, projections, images and fantasies. If we are unaware of these characteristics, the mind automatically projects its fears onto the blank screen of the unknown, giving it a power it does not inherently possess. Rajneesh, a Tantric master, tells us that "Darkness does not exist, it only appears to be. In fact it is just an absence of light. Light exists; remove the light—there is darkness . . . Do whatsoever you want to do, you cannot remove darkness. You cannot bring it, you cannot throw it. If you want to do something with darkness, you will have to do something with light, because only something that has existence can be related to. Put the light off, darkness is there; put the light on, darkness is not there—but you do something with light. You cannot do anything with darkness."[39]

As alchemists, we work on lead and shadow always bearing in mind the power that light has to assimilate darkness and transmute consciousness into a new and more enlightened form.

THE SIXTH RECIPE

Sow your Gold in White Foliated Earth

Pastoral scenes, resting-places and themes of farming, tending gardens and horticulture are beautifully depicted in many alchemical woodcuts. Images of trees, planting and pruning shears, harvesting, crypts and graves, mountains, scythes, axes and shovels are all commonly found in alchemical art. The alchemists followed Mother Nature through dense forests and along country lanes in hopes of learning her secrets. These images were used as visual recipes to describe the stages and operations of their work. Although the images are static, their messages suggest dynamic cycles of birth, death and resurrection. These images were never intended to be taken at face value. We must understand them with a symbolic appreciation for nature and psyche. Sowing seed, for example, expresses sexual communion with the soil, and because we carry nature within us, it also expresses a sexual awakening of consciousness.

Depositing seeds into Mother Earth infers sexual activity. In the *Picatrix,* an Arabian Hermetic text,[40] this intercourse is described in rich mythic detail. This creation story depicts Father God making man in his own likeness. Man is so beautiful that God falls in love with his creation. In this way, man comes to know the power that God has to create and love. Man shares this knowledge with Nature, who in turn sees "his beautiful features reflected in the water and his shadow on earth." She falls in love with him too. Man, seeing his form on earth, wishes to unite with it. "Nature and man are united in love." As a result, man acquires a dual nature, becoming half-mortal, half-divine. Alchemists in other places summarize this duality in saying, "Nature takes pleasure in Nature."

Psychologically, these images are filled with narcissistic themes. The Greek myth of Narcissus tells a very similar story. We generally think of narcissism in a very negative way. When someone is narcissistic, they have inflated egos and think nothing of anyone else's needs but their own. Narcissism, however, is just the kind of energy needed for body and soul to find its way into life. At the outset of any project we need lots of energy to get things started. Of course, early (primary) narcissism must wane and transform as the individual develops. Pride and reality-based confidence must in time replace self-love. The seed, in other words, sheds its outer covering and a well-formed plant eventually takes root in the firm soil of reality. In the alchemical imagination, earth and human images merge into one another.

In Eliade's classic work *The Forge and the Crucible,* we are reminded of what the simple act of seeding the fields meant to early farmers. Themes of sexuality are found throughout the work of miners as well as farmers because in early times primitive projections of life onto nature had the effect of sexualizing it. Rocks and soil had immediate importance to basic survival needs. Perhaps even projection is too sophisticated a word to describe the *participation mystique* that existed between the sexual impulse and the identification with nature's body parts. In any event, Eliade beautifully described this intimate relationship and the mythic implications for human alchemy:

> If streams, galleries of mines, and caves are compared to the vagina of the Earth-Mother, everything that lies in the belly of the earth is alive, albeit in the state of gestation. In other words, ores extracted from the mines are in some way embryos: they grow slowly as though in obedience to some temporal rhythm other than that of vegetable and animal organisms. They nevertheless grow—they "grow ripe" in their telluric darkness. Their extraction from the bowels of the earth is thus an operation executed before its due time. If they had been permitted the time to develop . . . the ores would have become ripe metals, having reached a state of "perfection."[41]

We can see why seeding in these times was no simple act. Seeding is one example where humans intervened in Nature, facilitating her process for gain. Thus, sacrifices, some even human, were made in the same way we sacrifice things in our own lives. Eliade shows how some of these ancient sacrificial rituals still survive today. The rekindling fire on New Year's Day is "an enactment of the Cosmogony, the rebirth of the world."[42]

Sacrifice is a voluntary act in which we give something small and personal in exchange for something much greater. We see this in our own lives. When we give from the heart, we benefit from both the giving and the receiving.

> The scent of the rose remains on the hand that gave it.

Some amount of pain is attached to the gift we give. True sacrifice involves giving something personal. In sacrifice we consciously allow ourselves to suffer a symbolic loss in service to some higher order or purpose. Accordingly, it is common to find images of maimed limbs, crutches, torture and even punishment in alchemical art. Giving in this spirit requires hard mental and physical work. Farmers don't just throw seeds around. They strike the earth, tear it apart and dig holes.

In the same way, our process begins by violating psyche's earth, disturbing it, awakening it to our purpose. The seeds we sow are pregnant with spiritual energy and possibility, each containing a dream. Without human effort, seeds don't get planted, fields aren't cultivated and plants are left to the winds of chance. "Without us," writes Jean Reynand in his eighteenth-century encyclopedia, "the harvest would not ripen in the fields; . . . nor the flour to bread by stirring and baking."[43]

Seeding is an imaginal image buried deep in our unconscious. Historically, farming was the principal occupation that gave rise to civilized society. With farming, hunters and gatherers could settle down, work the land and begin building towns, villages and cities. The work of transforming virgin land into organized communities began by drilling a well. Psychically, drilling, farming and mining belong to a common family of archetypal images. Each describes a mythology that is repeated over and over again with the birth and individuation of every new child. Each time we work psyche's soil in hopes of producing the "philosophical egg."[44] The seeds we plant in that child's unconscious are critically important to the outcome.

The earth is made golden by the quality of seeds placed into her womb. If, as the alchemists tell us, "it takes gold to make gold," then our seeds must contain some precious ingredient. What will give our seeds the power to transmute lead into gold? Americans are hard workers, industrious and inventive. Material possessions and financial worth are the things they most value. Are these the golden seeds? No, neither objects nor cash have the power to transform earthly experience into something divine. What about time? I might volunteer time to some worthy cause. As valuable and necessary as volunteering surely can be, it is still not the most important thing I have to give.

> Our most prized possession is none other than ourselves, nothing less will do. When asked, Christ said the greatest commandment is to love with your whole heart, mind and soul. We must be willing to give it all in exchange for a new, and more perfect, Self.

In the story of Abraham, we see this depth of commitment. Abraham is asked by God to give up his son Isaac as proof of his devotion.

This scene is a favorite among Renaissance painters. Just at the moment when Abraham raises his knife, God sends an angel to intervene. So great was Abraham's love that he was willing to give his son to his Lord. Every parent knows that their children are part of themselves. To sacrifice a child is more painful than even giving up one's own life.

The greatest Christian sacrifice was Christ's crucifixion. The transmutation of Christ's body and blood is symbolically re-enacted at each and every mass. While these examples are drawn from Christianity, sacrifice is not unique to any one faith. Every great religion involves some form of sacrifice, be it human or animal, material or symbolic. In order to sow our seeds properly we need to understand that sacrifice is an act that gives seeds their transformative power.

Ancient sacrificial rites are an affront to the modern imagination. Very unpleasant images arise when we think about martyrs and even animals being sacrificed. It all sounds so primitive. Yet, while we may have lost our taste for blood, psyche has become anemic without the practice of sacrifice in our lives. To the extent that religions have been secularized, the act of sacrifice has been diluted, expunged of virtually all sacred meaning. Certainly, if we consider the story of Abraham as no more than a test of character, we are left with a pretty ugly impression of the Christian God. But from the perspective of the Self, the story tells us something very different. In order for Abraham to murder his son, he must completely surrender his will to a higher power. He must think from a completely different orientation, one that puts him "in this world, but not of it." Anything less would make him a murderer. Only when he is acting in the service of a divine cause does sacrifice move to the ethics of a different dimension.

This point is poignantly told in another story. This one is from Japan. In it, an assassin manages to get past a sleeping samurai who is supposed to be guarding the emperor. The assassin kills the emperor and escapes. In the code of the ancient samurai warriors, this is the ultimate humiliation. Insulted, the offended samurai pursues the assassin for many years, vowing to avenge the death of his emperor. When at last the samurai catches up with the assassin, something extraordinary happens. As the samurai lifts his razor-sharp sword to kill the assassin, he is stopped dead in his tracks by something he'd not anticipated. The assassin spits in his face! As swiftly as he drew his sword from its scabbard, the samurai replaces it and departs without as much as leaving a scratch on the assassin. What's going on here?

The moral to the story is that when we act out of our lower animal/human nature we are judged accordingly. But when we are acting from the level of our highest human/divine nature there is no judgment. The samurai rightly leaves the assassin without killing him because to do so would have been unjustifiable murder, an act in retaliation for the insult he'd received due, in part, to his own negligence. Duty, not personal anger, is the code of the warrior. This is the sword of life, not death. The samurai correctly understood that at the very moment of the kill, his high-minded sense of duty was replaced by his lower instincts by the humiliating gesture. Never does a true samurai kill; it is the sword of justice that removes evil from the world.

The lesson in this story and in that of Abraham is learned by identifying the degree of intention and consciousness in which either act could have been performed. Abraham's willingness to kill his son was enough for God to see that he had shed his earthly attachment; thus actually killing was unnecessary. The sacrificial act was the quickening moment that made Abraham's union with God permanent.

From these golden seeds spring golden flowers. When we give something sacred we do it with the right intention, then amazing results happen. Sacrifice is an inherent part of every creative act. Just as both Abraham and the samurai intuitively came to understand that child and assassin are not really separate from them, but are, from a Self orientation, an implicit part of them, so too are all Nature's creatures. "Creation is sacrifice," writes Eliade, "One can put life into what one has created only by giving to it one's own life (blood, tears, sperm, 'soul', etc.)."[45] So it is plain to see that even the things we create must always involve sacrifice.

The recipe gives us a clue as to how we can sharpen intention and prepare ourselves for making a meaningful sacrifice. The earth in which these seeds are planted must first be foliated. To foliate means to hammer out material until it is paper thin. The *prima materia* is made so thin that any further effort would result in its transition to a gaseous state. Psychologically, the process involves a special process known as concupiscence, which means frustrating desire right up to the point where any further effort results in

> By sacrificing the pleasure we get from acting something out, we turn consciousness in upon itself. The liquid of our emotions is heated up to a boiling point, but not allowed to completely turn into a gaseous form. What is released are the dangerous vapors that make aggression evil and sexuality a heartless impulse.

its being acted out. As a practice, concupiscence offers us the opportunity to develop control of desire and steadfast allegiance to a higher purpose.

The result of our present recipe is white ash. This is matter that has been purified of random thoughts and emotions. Just as ash can no longer burn, our soul is immune from the flames of desire. It has been liberated from all attachment to instinct and ego. "Psychologically," explains Edward Edinger, "this means the possibility of a new and purified attitude toward materiality. It means the discovery of the transpersonal value of the ego. What purifies is consciousness. The black earth of ego desirousness becomes the white foliated earth that incarnates the Self."[46]

There are many impurities that must be eliminated before the white ash can form. Impure desires must be burned off, wrongful thoughts dried up and demanding impulses transformed into purposeful behavior. Our golden seeds can only take root in specially prepared earth. This white earth takes us into the second stage of the work, the *albedo*. It is produced from the salt of the earth where all impurities have been burned off by the sulfuric operation of *calcinatio* and ultimately transformed into a spiritual substance through the actions of mercury.

The *albedo* is a transitional stage and the time it is most likely to occur is during midlife. This time is typically called a crisis because the psyche undergoes a tremendous change from its preoccupation with mundane matters to a deeper interest in pursuing spiritual aspirations. By midlife, most people have married, had children, settled in their careers and begun focusing on a higher, more spiritual agenda. They have matured and know the great treasures awaiting discovery in their inner life.

> A crisis often marks the transition into a more spiritual dimension of existence. Practice gains depth once this occurs. "True prayer and love," said Thomas Merton, "are learned in the hour when prayer becomes impossible and the heart has turned to stone."[47]

The *albedo* is visualized as a pure white goddess. Quan Yin and the Blessed Virgin Mary are beautiful examples. A blossoming of the different fragrances of love marks this period in our lives. The second half of life is a time when the work of *albedo* becomes fully engaged. This is a great achievement that is visualized as a translucent white stone. Like *Luna,* this stone reflects the salt of all our wisdom and the deepest depths of our soul. At this point in the work there is no turning back. For even a moment spent in such purity leaves one with an eternal feeling.

THE SEVENTH RECIPE

The Rose Gives Honey to the Bee

Everything about this recipe seems wrong. Roses do not give honey to bees. To make any sense of this recipe we need to interpret it in a symbolic way. Alchemical recipes are written in symbolic language because of the alchemists' code of silence. Only those who possess a deep understanding and respect for the inner value of alchemy will be able to unlock the riddles tied up in an old recipe like this one. This recipe is taken from the Rosicrucian Order, a very old secret society that has long been associated with alchemy.[48]

To begin with, let us examine the symbolic meaning of the rose. Although roses come in many colors, red is the most important symbolic color of the rose. In modern times, red is typically associated with blood. In the American flag, the color represents the blood shed for freedom, liberty and justice. But the older meaning of red had to do with its connection to spirit and soul. In the Middles Ages, it was a commonly held belief that the soul resides in the blood. So when we hear of the blood of Christ, the reference is actually to his soul. In alchemy, red carries other symbolic meanings. It is particularly associated with the final stage of the work; *rubedo* means red.

As we decipher these recipes, we move through a spectrum of color: from the black of the *nigredo* to the white *albedo* and finally, into the *rubedo* stage. We shall again find meaningful connections between these stages and the individuation process. Psychologically, the rose is an archetypal symbol of the Self. The image of the rose is as important to the symbol as its color. The rose design is a mandala, a beautiful form that is often used in cathedral windows as a means of lifting our spirits and elevating the soul. The lovely scent of the rose adds a special fragrance to this same sense of eternity.

Jung made important distinctions between the Self and the ego that help unlock the secrets contained in this recipe. He pointed out that ego is a perceptive organ, not a decision maker. It gives us the information we need in order to make wise decisions. Unfortunately, we often rely on the ego to make decisions rather than simply relying on it for gathering and analyzing data. As a result, we mistake information and even knowledge for wisdom. In the information age, even raw data is sometimes treated like true knowledge. Information, we say, is power. This is so because data gives us an edge, an opportunity to act before others. This kind of thinking is the province of ego, whose primary mandate is to insure survival, not transcend it. In this recipe, the bee represents the ego and this kind of limited thinking.

Often we associate qualities of industriousness with the bee.[49] We say a person is as "busy as a bee" when we see them immersed in work. Some people are constantly busy with something. They are a buzz of activity. Ego and brain are very much alike in this way; both thrive on activity. It is hard to imagine a bee either quiet or at rest. They are noisy and constantly moving around. Their entire world seems devoted to organization and service to a group mind. The hive is their universe and their primary allegiance is to the queen. The bee, like most animals and insects, can teach us a lot about the world of instinct and how, in this case, to extract insight from honey.

In a conversation with Gregory Bateson, the great anthropologist Margaret Mead listed the following ways to find insight:

> To study infants; to study animals; to study primitive people; to be psychoanalyzed; to have a religious conversion and get over it; to have a psychotic episode and get over it; or to have a love affair with an Old Russian. (And I stopped saying that when a little dancer in the front row put up her hand and said, "Does he have to be old?")[50]

All humor aside, Mead's suggestions have much to offer, especially the overlooked wisdom of the animal kingdom. Following all but her last piece of advice, let's look more closely at the bee's world and what it can tell us about this recipe.

Bees live in a matriarchal society. All bees worship the queen. The queen is selected in a manner more common to choosing a Tibetan avatar than a British member of royalty. Common bees carefully choose the egg that will serve as the host for their new queen. She doesn't descend from a long line of royalty. Instead, the chosen one is fed *lebensraum,* a special jelly that sounds very much like an alchemical elixir of immortality. In fact, a queen bee lives on average six to eight years longer than the typical six-week life span of most worker bees. This royal gel is a secretion that flows out of the head of a nurse bee. The queen bee's birth recalls the birth of Venus, who was born out of the head, or thoughts, of Zeus.

After fighting off jealous admirers, the queen takes her maiden voyage to firmly announce her royalty. In flight the fastest flying drone impregnates her. Far from being a royal marriage, the drone explodes after depositing millions of spermatozoa in the queen's body. Fortunately for drones, the queen generally only mates once in her life. She is a queen like no other. Forty-eight hours after mating, the queen gets busy laying eggs. She carefully inspects each cell to see if it's ready to receive one of her precious eggs. The queen determines the sex of each egg by inserting it with some of the drone's sperm, creating either a sterile female or a male drone. Although she lays millions of eggs in her lifetime, she does not get to choose when or how many eggs will be laid each time. The nurses control the number of eggs by feeding or withholding the royal jelly from the queen.

Added to these complex organizational dynamics is a nonverbal communication among bees that is, as far as we know, virtually unparalleled in the insect kingdom. These intricate details explain why alchemists were so interested in bees and why they so often used them in their images and recipes. Although I know of no instance where Sigmund Freud connected bee behavior with his concept of ego, the two are in some ways very much alike. The German word *ego* is neither masculine nor feminine, but neutral. Having no gender, it characterizes pure organization devoid of soul and spirit. Like the bee, the ego is an expert communicator and as mentioned, both are forever busy doing something. But unlike the bee, whose status is well defined and subservient to the group mind, the ego often acts like a pretender to the throne.

The work of ego is vitally important, but it should not be confused with the authority of the Self. Hard work alone cannot turn lead into gold. Activity is not the same as conscious action. "The Golden World cannot be acquired," wrote Robert Johnson in *Balancing Heaven and Earth*, "like a possession, and enlightenment cannot be turned into a project. We do not select

A good practice is to spend some time watching the ego mind at work, without making any effort to alter its course or modify it in any way. How often does it exceed its primary job of orienting, testing reality and defending against threat? Simply notice when ego begins to make decisions. Is it overstepping its bounds? Does it really have the wisdom to take command of the entire kingdom?

an ecstatic experience; rather, it is delivered upon us as a state of grace. However, we can do the necessary inner work so that we are open to and prepared for such experiences when they arrive."[51]

Compared with the bee, the rose has a quiet elegance. It is a mandala that reflects the beauty of the Self. Unlike ego, the Self is not made or earned. It just is. In Christ's words, "I am that I am," we discover the true nature of the Self; it is an end unto itself. The ego, borne of reality, communicates in logical, linear sentences in order to express coherent meaning. Without ego we would not be able to create a coherent narrative of our life. While this narrative is important in giving life continuity and meaning, it is only description at the ego level. By contrast, the Self speaks in poetry. It expresses a transpersonal reality that only begins to have definition with symbolic and metaphoric language.

This recipe is like a haiku poem. Brief, but filled with symbolic meaning. On the ego level, it makes no sense. It reverses logic, and thereby confuses the rational mind. While the words of the recipe follow the form of a sentence having subject, verb and object, they fall short of having anything useful to say to the ego. Instead, the recipe confounds our brain, and the more we try and make sense of it, the more irrational it seems to be. Alchemical recipes are designed exactly to do this very thing. Like Zen *koans,* they are used to trick the brain and force it into thinking at the metaphorical level of Self.

> Likuko said to Nansen, "In my house there is a stone that sits up and lies down. I intend to carve it as a Buddha. Can I do it?" Nansen answered, "Yes, you can." Likuko persisted, "Can I really do it?" Nansen answered, "No, you can not!"[52] The ego that doubts hesitates. To make a stone Buddha requires the kind of action and confidence that comes only from the Self.

We typically think of the bee taking pollen *from* the flower to make honey and not the flower giving honey to the bee. This taking and giving points to an important difference. When a flower gives something of itself there is a sacrifice being made. When we forget that all nature is imbued with consciousness, we cannot imagine flowers, rocks and animals as making a sacrifice that supports humankind. In Native American culture, animals are believed to surrender their lives to the noble hunter, who acknowledges their precious gift. "According to Zuni myths," writes Eliade, "primitive humanity was born (as a result of the heaven-earth hierogamy) in the deepest of the four chthonian 'cavern-wombs.' Guided by mythical twins, humans climb from one of these 'wombs' to another until they reach the earth's surface."[53]

In this cosmology, humans, animals and even metal ores are capable of making sacrifices. Eliade describes the "animal behavior of the ore: it is alive, it moves at will, hides, shows sympathy or antipathy to human beings—a conduct not dissimilar from that shown by game toward its hunter."[54] We do not generally think in this sacred way. More often, animals are no more than prey; roses used for sentimental reasons and diamonds, a guarantee of commitment. Return to a primitive way of living is of course ridiculous, but adopting our ancestors reverence for life would do more to feed the soul than anything ego could ever possibly provide. Without sacredness, the spirit of sacrifice is lost and as a result, we are more often left with sacrilege. Whereas sacrifice requires willful surrender, sacrilege is like stealing. The consequences of such wrongful thinking are amply illustrated in the pollution of our air and contamination of our water.

The Self connects us to nature and ego connects us to reality. The ego equips us with the means necessary for physical survival and the tools for making meaning. The Self enables us to acquire wisdom and thereby live a spiritually fulfilling life. Honey is the divine food, the manna, which is provided by the Self to the ego for this purpose. In myth and fairy tale, honey is often the favorite food of beloved characters that personify our finest values. Pooh Bear, with his quiet and innocent wisdom, loves honey. Baby Krishna, the god who saves and heals, feasts on honey. In marriage, we call our beloved "honey."

In alchemy, the preserving qualities of honey make it an excellent symbol for representing the enduring presence of the Self. When the ego receives honey from the Self, it is like a sacrament in which we celebrate a royal marriage of heaven and earth. This doesn't happen automatically. Something is required of both parties. Each must take the other as its beloved, something that is difficult for each for very different reasons. The eyes of Self see psyche as a small part of a gigantic whole. Ego primarily sees only itself. The biggest challenge in alchemical psychology is getting these two to align their sights on a common goal. We begin life without sight (unconsciousness), are then blinded by the first rays of consciousness (conscious imperfection) and if successful achieve full consciousness (conscious wholeness) before taking our leave. The operation of *coniunctio* brings ego and Self into union in the *rubedo* stage. The philosopher's stone symbolizes the animating and spiritual power that is achieved by the Royal Marriage of these two great realms of existence.

Roses are used to celebrate union. We give our beloved roses as an expression of everlasting love. Roses are placed on graves to celebrate union of matter and spirit. In each, there is the hint that something has died. Dissolving the separation between two people is a voluntary surrender of some part of each person. In death, we surrender our bodies to nature. In each there is the opportunity to make a sacrifice. If we willingly surrender ourselves, we need not fear death. For ego, this is the most difficult thing to do. Antagonism naturally exists between ego and self because of their different orientations. Again, the *experience of the self is always a defeat for ego,*" wrote Jung in *Mysterium Coniunctionis*.[55] When we put aside the communications received from the ego and make decisions from our center, the Self, the experience is akin to dying. Since we are conditioned to rely on ego for self-preservation, ignoring its data feels like an invitation for disaster. The major purpose of ego is to "serve and protect"; relaxing its defenses, and worse, abandoning them altogether, feels like death from the ego's point of view. But no sacrifice, no roses.

Letting go of ego is the equivalent of letting go of reality. While we may have varying degrees of desire to do this, it requires courage and enormous trust in oneself and the universe to drop the ego orientation and adopt the orientation of the Self. For this reason, I sometimes give patients permission to do some crazy things that help transit from one orientation to another. Trust in the process, trust in yourself, trust in me, trust in your god, trust nature, and trust the Kosmos.[56] These are all very important if we artfully act to preserve the ego (not destroy it) as we move into the province of spirit and self. The flowering of the rose gives us the first real hint of divine love and the Divine Self.

In my experience, we will all learn to let go someday. The reality is that death is the final point at which we let go of life. During the course of everyday living we are presented with this reality in small ways. Life is often a battle between what we hold onto and what we let go of. Insomnia, for example, is a problem in which the person can't let go of the day. Conversely, someone with hypersomnia (oversleeping) can't let go of the unconscious state. The fact is that, short of dying, we will let go. The question is whether we do it willingly or submit by default. I suggest that the former brings greater rewards. When we willingly allow ourselves to let go of things we do not need we make new discoveries. In other words, when we let go of ego, we entrust ourselves to the embrace of Self. Then, quite the opposite of what ego expected happens: rather than suffer a defeat we enjoy victory. Voluntary surrender to the Self is like rose petals unfolding in the warmth of the sun. When we allow the ego to release its grip on reality, our world opens up wide and we can see things that we could not see before.

To illustrate how this letting-go process works and how we might find the courage needed to surrender to the Self, I recall a beautiful story I read in one of Richard Bach's magical storybooks. Over the years I've modified his story to amplify its rich meaning. In the story, Bach described a civilization of creatures—I call them cling-ons—that live on a rock at the bottom of a stream. The cling-ons *believe* that without holding onto their rock, they would be quickly swept away by fast-moving currents. This is normal for them. For as long as anyone can remember, it has always been this way. But one day something unbelievable happened: a cling-on wondered what would happen if he just let go? This was a revolutionary question, for no one had ever dared have such dangerous thoughts.

The question persisted despite efforts by others to quell such thoughts. It rooted in his being, and when it flowered he was ready to face the unknown. He was prepared to make the ultimate sacrifice by letting go of the only world he'd ever known. So great had his trust grown, that suddenly one day he simply stopped holding on. He surrendered himself to the mighty forces of nature. Immediately he was lifted up by the powerful currents and swept far away from his home. To the other cling-ons, he disappeared in an instant, leaving them only to tighten their grip. This, they thought, is what happens when you let go.

> Messiah is a Hebrew word that means "one that is anointed, enlightened and endowed with a special mission."[57] We all have the potential and even the mandate, to realize ourselves as messiahs, but only those who are willing to consciously let go will bring others into full awareness.

What they did not know, and would never know until they too let go, is that other civilizations, just like theirs, existed farther downstream. Now, we must use our imagination to appreciate the sight of the one cling-on brave enough to undertake this dangerous journey. Another race, which I call flatlanders, lived in very much the same way as the cling-ons. Being no more enlightened than their neighbors, they too hung on to their rock world. Neither could they ever imagine letting go. So when, out of their watery sky, they saw a flying cling-on, they could only arrive at one conclusion: this must be the messiah. And, in many ways, they were right.

How often do we hear that letting go is the ultimate expression of love? Or, we read bumper stickers that instruct us to LET GO, LET GOD. Easier said than done. To the ego, which holds tightly to the rock of reality, letting go means giving up its matter-oriented way of thinking for some sort of invisible reward. Its allegiance is to a collective that is very limited. Ego has collective value but no real symbolic worth. If we settle for the benefits that ego provides we get fool's gold instead of the real thing.

Acting from an ego orientation, we cannot experience the fruits of a transpersonal dimension; this can only come from the orientation of Self. Letting go of money, material possessions, information, etc., are very much defeats to the ego because without consciously understanding the symbolic necessity of sacrifice, loss is seen as giving in to death. Whatever exchange takes place in sacrificial offerings depends on the limits we impose on reality. If it extends only as far as a hive or a rock, there can be no transpersonal exchange, no communion with the divine.

As we move into the *rubedo* stage, sacrifice means more than letting go of material possessions. At this point, the tenor of the work shifts from the ego orientation, where even soul is anchored in matter, to a Self orientation, which embraces spirit. The alchemists conceived of this tremendous shift as the middle ground where the Ascent of Soul and the Descent of Spirit bring ego and Self together for the purpose of transformation. The busy bee, ego, is embraced by its spiritual mother, the Self. The rose gives honey to the bee. It offers it what it truly desires—eternity—but only if it is willing to let go first.

In some forms of meditation, initiates are instructed to keep their eyes half-opened. In this way, their eyes focus on both the material world as well as the realm of spirit. This practice engenders the right attitude, one that embraces heaven and earth. In this way, ego is not overwhelmed by the vastness of nature, nor by its more immediate environment, the Self. Still, this is no easy task to accomplish. The ego cling-on holds tightly to reality, and relaxing its grip requires great love and patience. It alone does not have the power to release itself. Spirit must come to its

From Edwin Abbot's *Flatland* we learn that the discovery of other dimensions is not easily accepted. In this scene we pick up with an argument that is used to illustrate the resistance against surrendering one's ordinary perspective in order to gain a greater field of vision.

"At the word I began to move my body out of Lineland. As long as any part of me remained in his dominion and in his view, the King kept exclaiming, 'I see you, I see you still; you are not moving.' But when I had at last moved myself out of his Line, he cried in his shrillest voice, 'She is vanished; she is dead.' 'I am not dead,' replied I; 'I am simply out of Lineland, that is to say, out of the Straight Line which you call Space, and in the true Space, where I can see things as they are . . .'

"When I had done this at great length, I cried triumphantly, 'Does that at last convince you?'

". . . But the Monarch replied, 'If you were a Man of sense . . . you would listen to reason . . . Instead of moving, you merely exercise some magic art of vanishing and returning to sight; and instead of any lucid description of your new World, you simply tell me the numbers and sizes of . . . my retinue. Can anything be more irrational or audacious? Acknowledge your folly or depart from my dominions.'

". . . I retorted in no measured terms, 'Besotted Being! You think yourself the perfection of existence, while you are in reality the most imperfect and imbecile. You profess to see, whereas you can see nothing but a Point! You plume yourself on inferring the existence of a Straight Line; but I *can see* Straight Lines, and infer the existence of Angels, Triangles, Squares, Pentagons, Hexagon, and even Circles. Why waste more words? Suffice it that I am the completion of your incomplete self. You are a Line, but I am a Line of Lines, called in your country a Square: and even I, infinitely superior though I am to you, am of little account among the great nobles of Flatland, whence I have come to visit you, in the hope of enlightening your ignorance.' "[58]

aid. Only when being and doing are in sympathy do the lines separating ego and Self begin to fade.

Without help from spirit, ego clings to the known world. Mistakenly, many people demonize the ego and through meditation and therapy, work to destroy it. This is foolishness. Rather, we need to adopt an attitude of love that appreciates ego for what it is and what it is not. The self, in alliance with spirit, must work to individuate the ego; nursing it as if it were a young, very smart child. It needs attention and tender loving care.

When we adopt this loving attitude and practice it throughout the day, life becomes a meditation on the self. In our busy Western world there is little left of the Old World that supports this approach. However, in other parts of the world, I have seen how wonderfully this viewpoint is woven into the fabric of society. In Japan, for instance, people go to great lengths to ritualize nearly every daily activity as a constant reminder that the divinity of nature is ubiquitous. A simple flower arrangement expresses the feelings of nature; a rock garden displays the permanence of spirit. In India, people seem to be in constant celebration. They have a god for nearly every occasion, all reflecting the god dwelling within each of them. Africans honor spirit through music and dance; the aboriginal people of Australia still see spirit dreaming the universe.

Rituals and celebrations are graceful ways of inviting spirit into our lives. If we push ourselves toward individuation, we fail miserably. The ego will only tighten its grip. Similarly, intoxicating ego is no shortcut for consciously realizing the Divine Self. One cannot fake the genuine experience of living in a state of grace. When we've had even a glimpse of this reality, love transcends temporary pleasure and blooms into lasting fragrances. Real gold shines through those who delight in sharing their honey with everyone.

There is another association with the image of the rose that must be included in the work during the *rubedo* stage. The Latin *ros* means both rose and dew. In alchemy, dew serves the ego in much the same way as honey. The alchemists believed dew comes from the moon. Like a mist, it gently showers the earth with grace. This grace carries with it a special wisdom they called the *aqua sapientiae*.

May, being the fifth month, was especially known to bring this wisdom to earth. Some alchemists described this blessed shower as a quintessence, or fifth element, that joins and transcends all four elements. Dew, thought the alchemists, possesses the salt needed to activate the sulfur and mercury contained in the *prima materia*. It acts in much the same way as the honey in this recipe does in connecting Self with ego.

It is significant that dew, not rain, brings this special wisdom to earth. Dew has a dampening effect on us. It slows things down but doesn't drown them out. It gives just enough moisture to stimulate and quietly keep all things refreshed. The tiny dew drops that form on rose petals remind us of the sweat on our brow from a long day's work, or the tears of joy that well up in our eyes when beholding great beauty. Interestingly, the shortest verse in the Christian bible is simply, "Jesus wept." (John 11:35) This came when he was just about to raise Lazarus from the dead. Hearing his family's moans, Christ felt their despair and in sympathy cried with them.

Dew is the visible form of grace. It relates to the dissolving/resolving power of *solutio,* where water breaks up dense thoughts, and prepares the *prima materia* for further operations in the *albedo* stage. In this we find a connection between the fiery aspect of the rose and the softness of dew and honey. The contrast juxtaposes fire and water, the mercurial aspect that invites the different aspects of Self and ego to commingle and hopefully integrate.

The work of the *rubedo* requires the *coniunctio* operation to join these disparate elements. In gross nature, fire and water do not mix. We use water to put out fires. But just as we could not understand this recipe in a literal way neither can we comprehend how fire could ever be mixed with water without one being destroyed by the other.

The work of alchemy, according to Jung, requires "not only laboratory work, the reading of books, meditation, and patience, but also love."[59] Love is the medium in which elements surrender themselves and ultimately have a chance to combine into One thing. What better expression of love do we have than giving a dozen roses to our beloved! This is a recipe of love and for those who understand it well, dreams do come true.

> First, imagine that such a thing is possible. Identify an experience you have had in which the seemingly impossible happened. Have you ever had the experience where you undertook something and found it impossible? You might have tried countless times to understand how to do it, but failed each time. The ego worked hard, but each time you fell short of the mark. Then one day, long after you'd thought it could ever be done, you returned to the task and did it successfully without any difficulty. Ego set the stage for the eventual appearance of the Self, but only once it got off the stage could Self perform the act. This is how it is when fire and water are mixed in an alchemical way!

THE EIGHTH RECIPE

Dissolve and Coagulate

Solve et coagula

This is one of the oldest alchemical recipes. To understand its meaning we must return to the image of the stone. No one knows with certainty why the image of a stone was chosen to symbolize the entire opus from beginning to end—from *prima materia* to *lapis philosophorum* (the philosopher's stone). Most likely it emerged autonomously from the collective unconscious. Untouched stone features a lifeless landscape, solid, dense, appearing uninhabitable. This is a timeless place of origin. So it is that we come into the world *tabula rasa,* our minds a blank slate, having virtually no consciousness or any knowledge. Allowing nature simply to take its course assures merely that the species will go on through a pattern of competing genes and the survival of the fittest. But, in order to advance beyond stone-age consciousness and mature into fully individuated human beings, more is needed.

This recipe has two parts: dissolution and coagulation. We will discuss each part of this recipe in order to understand the psychological and alchemical operations involved in each process.

In the beginning stages of the work, the alchemist would dissolve (*solve* in Latin) the *prima materia* into its component parts. This required repeated efforts to break down the *prima materia* into smaller and ever-more refined parts. The first operation in this recipe recalls the *separatio* operation. Psychologically, *separatio* signifies the embryonic birth of consciousness, because only once we split from the unconscious do we become self-aware.

Dissolution involves a number of separations, each of which is critical in transforming the *prima materia* into increasingly more refined states of consciousness. I summarize these separations as follows:

- In the first division, there is a split from unconsciousness with nature that forms a microcosmic being that is mostly unconscious but has the potential to gain fully conscious sense of self and nature. In other words, a baby is born.

- The second division causes a split between consciousness and unconsciousness—the child gains awareness of him or herself and soon becomes aware of the distinction between "I" and "it."

- The third split results in the formation of the two primary psychological functions (rational and nonrational) and a subset of four more refined functions (thinking and feeling, intuition and sensate).

- The fourth *separatio* has the potential of elevating conscious functions to the level of the transcendental. At this stage the Individuated Self is established and the person makes full use of active imagination and the transcendental function.

- The fifth division results in a final split between self and other. Perceiving boundaries between self and other people occurs to varying degrees with this division. Clear and stable boundaries are necessary for living a healthy psychological existence. Beyond this, however, much more can be gained. With this *separatio* comes the potential for the Divine Self to be born. The rare individual who achieves this level gains a sense of universal, or divine, consciousness.

Each of these successive divisions advances consciousness to a higher level of self. This grooming process that uses *separatio* to individuate consciousness is known in psychology as differentiation. Jung defined individuation as "a process of differentiation having for its goal the development of the individual personality."[60] Differentiation simply refers to the process of splitting gross, dense areas of personality into smaller, more functional units. As you might have already guessed there must be a corresponding reciprocal process that also integrates the pieces in order to establish the goal of the individuation—a fully functional individual personality. We will describe integration when we come to the second part of the recipe.

The alchemists stated the necessity of breaking down the crude stone before consciousness would be able to advance to higher levels of organization. In a related recipe, they succinctly put it this way: *No generation without corruption.* Dissolving the stone using *separatio* and differentiation allows for other operations to come into play. The work of *separatio* is to split apart the stone through its evolution; differentiation psychologically reorganizes the stone so that it becomes more conscious and functional. These processes are particularly important in dissolving the real impediments to individuation—extremely dense areas of psyche known as complexes.

This recipe reduces alchemy down to its core. When we strive to understand how to dissolve the complexes that obstruct growth and rebuild the personality we are responding to a natural urge or impulse toward individuation. The urge to individuate compels us toward action, both conscious and unconscious, that will assist in having us express our fullest potential. Before presenting examples of how a complex dissolves and how the personality then reconstitutes, we need to know more about the nature of a complex, what they are and how they work.

Jungian psychology was originally known as a complex psychology because it initially focused its attention on the study of psychological complexes. A complex is that part of psyche that has neither been separated nor differentiated from nature or the conscious mind. A complex is the psychological equivalent of the alchemist's lead. Both are the dense, base matter that must be separated and repeatedly differentiated before the individual becomes consciously aware of them.

We are seldom aware of complexes. We sometimes laughingly say that he or she has a mother complex or a power complex but in fact we are rarely able to see our own complexes. Complexes form early in life and being unconscious are usually filled with lots of instinctual and emotional energy. A complex is like a knot whose many strands are connected to our biological drives and instincts as well as to people representing powerful sources of primary gratification. When a complex dominates the personality it is like being possessed. We can hardly think about what we're doing and even when we know that our actions may be self-defeating we are not able to stop, look and change. Rather, we are simply carrying out nature's prime mandate to survive by any and all means. Thus, habits and impulses are the behaviors that keep us trapped in a complex.

An example will help us understand how a complex interferes in the individuation process and how differentiation works in resolving the problem. In the following example I will describe a mother complex and then present a detailed example of a father complex.

If a mother has not sufficiently established a stable independent life, she may unconsciously interfere with the separation-individuation process of her child. Separation involves both the mother freeing herself physically and emotionally from the child and the child doing likewise in order to achieve autonomy and independence. But, if the child is not allowed to adequately separate, she may never become her own person. Even when the child grows up and moves out of the family home she takes with her the psychology of her mother. This unconscious psychology becomes part of her adult psyche. A complex is formed that has deep-rooted ties to the mother and the instinctual world she represents.

This complex is particularly damaging because of its interference with a person's ability to establish clear boundaries. While there are

> If you are not master of your own mind, you will be a slave to the mind of others.

many different types of symptoms that may result from a mother complex, the most common are low self-esteem, passivity, false accommodation, inappropriate dependency needs, hypersensitivity to rejection, depression, alcohol abuse and other addictive behaviors. The colloquial names given to the problem should sound familiar: the doormat syndrome, codependence, women (or men) who love too much. Mother complexes are blind to gender. Just as many men can suffer from this problem as women.

In the most severe cases, a person who has suffered traumatic psychological damage in the earliest stages of life may not individuate at all. In this event the second *separatio* did not occur adequately and the infant's psyche fails to achieve a consistent, stable form of identity. It can not distinguish self from other, or for that matter any boundaries. Consequently, the infant remains in a state of deep psychosis, meaning that it is completely cut off from the world. Yet even in these psychotic states I have observed how psyche struggles to find the lost mother. Unfortunately, she may appear in shattered pieces among the many bits of hallucination and delusional beliefs. Such distortion deprives the person from developing any coherent image of the mother. She is completely mean and hideous one moment, and a goddess the next. Differentiation, in this case, is left to the random, unconscious forces of nature, and as a result, there is virtually no ability to draw the pieces together into any meaningful whole.

Although this awful condition may sound unfamiliar, some small measure of it exists in all of us. In times of disorientation, intoxication, shock or crisis, we are rudely reminded of this embryonic consciousness. Fortunately, most of us move past the second *separatio* and then deal with other, less damaging complexes. Another way of understanding this dynamic concept of personality lies in the realization that we are each a bundle of complexes. Individuation works at untying this bundle in an effort to bring stabilized order to the organization of the mind. Our chief ally in this process is the Self. While the ego typically becomes ensnared in these psychic knots, the Self remains constant and untouched. It is the principle attributes of the Real Self that allow us to maintain stability as the ego wrestles with obstructive complexes. Health (meaning whole) describes the ability to resolve complexes using the powers of the Self to bring the many pieces of psyche together into a cohesive individual personality.

Another ally in the process of resolving complexes is psychotherapy. Therapy aims to resolve complexes and further the work of individuation.

In fact, the term "analysis" derives its meaning from *lysis,* a Greek word meaning "to loosen." A therapy that works on differentiation therefore involves loosening the tight knot holding a complex together. This is, of course, no easy process. The complex is cloaked in all kinds of unconscious images that are guarded by ego defenses and charged with lots of emotion. Without the use of finesse to tease these elements apart, both therapist and patient can easily slip into a tug-of-war with one holding on to old, maladaptive behaviors while the other encourages individuation. This is difficult work for therapist and patient, but the resolution of a complex is a beautiful thing to behold. When the complex resolves, it is often accompanied by a burst of energy and insight, an unburdening that frees the individual from the past. This is what happened with a gentleman I treated for several years.

The patient was a late-middle-aged man who suffered from a terrible father complex that caused him to have intense panic attacks. While still an infant he was abandoned by his father. Soon after, his mother married an abusive, alcoholic man who stood over six feet tall and was a professional boxer. In addition to abusing my patient emotionally, the stepfather often challenged the young boy to fight him. My patient only accepted the challenge once with the result that, "he knocked me out cold."

By the time my patient arrived at my office, his stepfather was long dead and only terrible memories remained. Despite a traumatic childhood, he had managed to have a very successful career and retired with a good deal of money, but now was trying to figure out what to do with the rest of his life. He had four failed marriages and two sons whom he had not seen since they were children. In addition to suffering severe panic attacks, he stuttered and was obsessed with dividing numbers, reducing them to their lowest common denominator.[61] With therapy he learned that these symptoms were ways to displace his aggression and represented a surefire way to psychically cut his cruel stepfather down to size.

In the process of gaining a healthier perspective toward the abuse he suffered as a child, a weight seemed to be lifted from his shoulders. An enormous flood of emotional energy was released in the form of tears and a newborn vitality for life. Although his energy seemed to explode, he had not yet garnered insight or the means to destroy the evil memory of his stepfather that even now, years later, seemed to possess him. The real turning point in his therapy came when he realized that the source of his panic attacks was the father complex that had haunted him throughout his life. He even understood that many of his actions had been unconsciously determined by emotions tied to this complex. Don't get close, don't trust, don't lose control—these were some of the silent messages dictating his actions.

In therapy, he was encouraged to do an active imagination exercise in which he asked his unconscious to reveal the fear underlying his panic attacks. To his surprise, he received an answer within a week: "I'm afraid of dying when I'm alone."

In further dissolving the source of his fear, he discovered its infantile origin. Being a bright, well-aged man, he fully understood that we all die alone; his was not a fear of mortality, but was an infant's cry of neglect. The panic attacks were the writhing of a child being helplessly beaten, alone and terrified. The anger was his wish to eliminate the source of his terror, his abusive stepfather.

As the complex dissolved, he discovered that the fear and anger were the components of the internal rage and desperation he'd suffered as a child. With intense therapy, he learned he no longer had to fear that he might murder himself or anyone else. He did not have to hide the shame of his murderous thoughts and abuse of alcohol. The image of the beast had been assassinated! Henceforth, he could express his anger responsibly and assertively. As other symptoms remitted, he became more genuinely loving both toward himself and others. He began seriously loving a woman who had for years been more of a fantasy object than a real, live person. In the process, he "adopted" her family and learned to love them as well. The more he opened to them, the less alone he felt; he had become part of a family. The healing energies of the unconscious were deconstructing his infantile fear of dying alone, unloved and unwanted. Fear of death was not the problem. Living in desperate fear of being helpless and alone was the real source of his pain.

The old cruel stepfather had first to be destroyed before the lost father could surface. Fear had kept this man from discovering the feelings of remorse for having lost his biological father. He could not, of course, remember his real father, but even without the memories, the psyche can imagine how much that loss meant. It can even invent the father, the one he never had but always yearned for. Once my patient was able to let his imagination loose, he was able to find his long lost dad in dreams, fantasies and, most importantly, in the parenting he now offered to the children in his newfound family. He ceased being a tree without roots, a father and husband who lacked the psychic depth to really know how to raise children or be responsible to the women he'd married. When the psychic connection was made after a prolonged course of achieving the necessary separations, a new masculine identity emerged, one that was solid and capable of further individuation.

Psychotherapy served this patient well. It acted like a hermetic vessel in which his individuation, part of which had been paralyzed in childhood, could be cleared of psychic trauma and dissolution of complexes. In this case, psychotherapy provided a womb, the "philosophical egg," in which the fixations of early childhood trauma could gestate and mature. Just as alchemists used their vessel to contain the gross elements of the *prima materia,* therapy offered a strong and safe container in which to do the necessary work. In confronting his complex, he drew courage from his higher self. He was able to coagulate the shattered images of the complex and re-member them into a mature picture of manhood.

As we see in this example, both the dissolving and resolution of complexes is a difficult and often painful procedure. In various traditions, the images used to symbolize this process are gruesome. In alchemy, images of dismemberment, cutting and division illustrate this aspect of the *separatio* operation. In this case the patient's obsession with division represents a process of *separatio* that was not under his conscious control. Therapy aims to make the unconscious conscious. When this gentleman was able to gain perspective of the life circumstances contributing to his father complex, true healing began. In other words, he had undergone the initial *separatio,* whereby he could see how early trauma was being kept alive through his current behavior. The more he was able to deepen this awareness, the more he was able to curtail inappropriate behaviors and more accurately identify and express long repressed feelings.

The second part of the recipe, *coagulatio,* is illustrated in this example by the restoration of his personality. Having undergone an arduous process of differentiation, he then had to do the psychological work of integrating new and more adaptive views of his traumatized childhood. In our recipe, this integrating work is called *coagulatio*. Like the various stages of differentiation, integration involves a series of joining reworked memories and emotions. Each *coagulatio* experience raises consciousness and brings deeper insights and improved levels of functioning.

In terms of my patient, we have seen how he worked through breaking down the complex and the integration needed to reassemble his personality into one that freed him from the past. Using the alchemical recipe in therapy relieved him of all those horrible messages that had kept him internalizing aggression, numbing pain with alcohol and keeping him from love. The release was dramatic. In therapy he would burst out crying, bitterly condemn his stepfather and accuse his mother, while expressing a deep longing for his real father. As each painful memory surfaced he was able to increasingly sort out the facts and feelings based on the intelligent, successful man he had become despite the many odds against him. His integrative work was fantastic. I marveled at the new man I was seeing and how, with each new insight, he was capable of giving and receiving more love. He was no longer afraid of dying because now, surrounded by people who loved him, he was never alone.

Coagulatio derives its power directly from the earth element. As we have already discussed, the earth element is concrete and immediate in its effect on consciousness. This operation enables us to translate what we know into what we do. In therapy, the true test of insight is behavior change. A complex cannot be resolved in the mind alone. Unless we have internalized knowledge so that our whole personality is changed in the process, the complex still lives on in the unconscious.

In reality, it is rare that we are ever completely free of all complexes. In this way, the philosopher's stone represents the rare personality that has been completely liberated from everything that keeps it from achieving the highest levels of Self. Nevertheless, the arduous journey of individuation is worth the effort because it may be the closest we will ever get to our destination. Jungian analyst Edward Whitmont writes:

> We are challenged to try to reach a sort of conscious, affirmative partnership with our own complexes and biological shortcomings in which they are neither idealistically denied and suppressed nor allowed to overwhelm us. This can be a formidable task indeed. It amounts to a constant struggle with ourselves in which the balance always keeps tipping, asking ever again to be resolved. But the discovery of meaning in this tug of war of conflicting impulses and needs might also be the most central task of human creativity, perhaps even the reason and purpose of life and our cosmic contribution to being alive.[62]

Coagulatio brings this sobering reality to the forefront of our awareness. We come to it by a series of differentiations and integrations of the psychic material that make up our inner world. In the process of doing the individuation work of personal alchemy, we realize that life is an endless process of many separations and reunions.

THE NINTH RECIPE

It Takes Mercury to Make Mercury

Mercurius and his metal, mercury, are the symbol and substance of change. You can no more catch hold of mercury than you can pin down change. Both are elusive to grasp and hold. Paradoxically, however, the only constant in change is its permanence. We can always count on change happening. Nothing is impervious to change. We only delude ourselves in thinking we are the same person today as we were a year ago, or even a minute ago. In fact, we only know this precious moment; behind us stand memories and before us are endless fantasies waiting to open.

> Keep time by breathing
> What I exhale is past
> The next breath is all I know
> Of the future.

I wrote this verse bearing in mind that Mercurius is a spirit, and the element in which all spirits thrive is air. Breathing and digestion are two processes that alchemists often mentioned in describing Mercurius. In order to understand this recipe, we must know the rules that govern this elusive spirit.

The Doctrine of Correspondence is a central, underlying theory in alchemy that explains paradoxical sayings such as the one in our present recipe. Simply put, this doctrine holds that there is a fundamental symmetry between all things, regardless of how small or large or different they appear. Hippocrates, the father of modern medicine, described this doctrine as a "sympathy" between all living things:

There is one common flow, one common breathing, all things are in sympathy. The whole organism and each one of its parts are working in conjunction for the same purpose . . . the great principle extends to the extremest part, and from the extremest part it returns to the great principle, to the one nature, being and not-being.[63]

This Doctrine has survived throughout the ages and can, with a little effort, be seen even in modern times. It is central to sympathetic magic as well as occupying the interest of some of the world's foremost philosophers and scientists. Aristotle, Leibniz, Copernicus, Newton, Pauli and Jung described the doctrine and its implications in philosophy, mathematics, astronomy, physics and psychology. I believe that the doctrine is one of the cornerstones of all the great philosophies, arts, sciences and religions. It is therefore to this doctrine that we turn in trying to understand the riddle contained in this recipe.

Just as there are grades that signify the quality between various products, there are grades or degrees of consciousness that describe the qualities of a spirit. Lucifer and the archangel Gabriel are both spirits but where the former occupies the lowest level of awareness, the latter reflects pure consciousness. What makes Mercurius so special is that he embodies every possible grade. At one moment, he is a royal imp, devious and mischievous, the next, a divine psychopomp who inspires, guides and brings insight to the mind. No less an image better captures the essence of change than Mercurius.

Applying then the Doctrine of Correspondence to Mercurius we discover a split in his nature between a lowly trickster and a divine spirit. These two cannot be allowed to exist side by side if we hope to make gold out of lead. The alchemist brings these two aspects of his own consciousness into juxtaposition, and with fire, causes them to unite.

The lowly trickster's cunning appears in myths and legends throughout the world. The Grimms' fairy tale "The Spirit in the Bottle" features Mercurius as a neglected spirit demanding attention. In the story, a poor woodcutter's son roams through the woods. Hearing a voice calling out, "Let me out, let me out!" the boy discovers an old bottle lying beneath an oak tree. Opening the bottle, a spirit, half as large as the tree, rushes out and declares, "I have had my punishment and I will be revenged! I am the great and mighty spirit Mercurius, and now you shall have your reward. Whoso releases me, him I must strangle."[64]

Obviously, this Mercurius is not a very nice spirit. The reason for his rage lies in the fact that he has been neglected. In other words, the mercurial/spiritual aspects of the boy have not been well attended, and if he is to be saved he must act quickly to address this need. The boy plays a trick on Mercurius by asking him to prove that he is really the spirit that emerged from the old bottle; only then will he oblige his would-be murderer. Offended, Mercurius rushes back into the bottle, whereupon the boy quickly seals it tightly.

Were the story to end here, the boy would have proven himself a man and would find his rewards in this life. At the level of ego, he would have accomplished the great separation from nature by initiating change in a clever and expedient way. But, Mercurius is not content to leave it there. He cries out for release and offers a rich reward if the boy will let him out. At the ego level, this would of course make no sense, but a critical transition has taken place. The boy shifts from the ego to the higher level of the Self. From this perspective, he recognizes the higher mercurial element in his own psyche.

The boy releases Mercurius and in exchange receives a magic rag. Mercurius says, "If you spread one end of this over a wound it will heal, and if you rub steel or iron with the other end it will turn into silver."[65] Sure enough, when the boy rubs the cloth on his rusted ax, it turns into silver. With the money he gets from selling the ax he is able to return to school and eventually become a medical doctor.

The magic rag is emblematic of Mercurius's power to change matter and mind into precious things. It is interesting however, that the ax is turned into silver and not gold. Apparently there is work still to be done. Becoming a doctor is good for the boy, but applying his skills as a healer is the real test of his mettle.

While the ego picks and chooses what it will allow into reality, the Self embraces the entire universe. As a healer, a doctor must be willing to give equal treatment to saints and murderers alike. The healer applies him- or herself, while the doctor uses technique and clinical know-how to help patients. Ego enables us to develop technical skills, but Self elevates our vision to a spiritual height. By tricks and treachery, Mercurius forces us into discovering these powerful differences. This tale illustrates how the Doctrine of Correspondences works both within psyche as well as in the psychology between people.

Many presidencies show evidence of the trickster at work. At one moment a president is the king of the hill, the next, he's the fool on the hill. Politics and the marketplace are some of trickster's favorite places because with so much change going on, there is sure to be lots of opportunity for him to influence consciousness for better or worse. Psychology is another place where trickster loves to get involved. Even the likes of Jung were no match for this archetypal spirit. Like all of us, Jung was bedeviled from time to time by this wily spirit. The old expression, "always keep one eye on the devil," is good advice in dealing with trickster. Jung was sure to include Trickster in the stone carvings he made for his retreat house in Bollingen along the shores of Lake Zurich. No person, regardless of his or her station in life, is exempt from the influence of this spirit. Just as we all have a shadow we also have in our psyche a trickster, who bargains, cajoles, wheels and deals, turning our dirt into fertile ground.

> Trickster is no more evil than shadow. It is not picking and choosing the good that elevates depth psychology to the level that alchemy demands but rather its willingness to accept the bad with the good in order to make things whole.

"Mercurius," wrote Jung, "consists of all conceivable opposites . . . He is the process by which the lower and material is transformed into the higher and spiritual, and vice versa . . . He is the devil, a redeeming psychopomp, an evasive trickster, and God's reflection in physical nature."[66] If, as Freud wrote in his *Interpretation of Dreams,* the dream is the *via regalia* (the royal road) to the unconscious, then surely Mercurius is our guide.

Following the law of correspondence, Mercurius enables us to see life without prejudice. Kings and fools, rich and poor are all equal from this perspective. In this way, the world is made "One Thing"—conscious, alive and filled with meaningful potential. The alchemists believed that Mercurius resides in mercury, or what they called quicksilver. For them, mercury was an excellent agent to use in fusing metals. The only metal that resists mercury is iron. These two metals have very contrary natures and for good reason.

Change alone apparently is meaningless unless there exists something that can fixate the endless mutations of matter and mind. There must, in other words, be something that can cause things to stabilize and manifest as a concrete substance. From our earlier discussion we will recall that iron had dual citizenship: it comes to us from above in the form of meteors and from the deep mines below the surface of the earth. Forged on the anvils of heaven and earth, iron is a metal having strength and inflexibility. As such, it provides the necessary counterpart to mercury and its power to transform. Together the two form a concept known as the fixed-volatile, wherein the fixed, symbolized by iron, stands for solidity and the volatile mercury for change.

Where iron acts to consolidate and embody, mercury, with its energetic spirit, breaks things up and causes them to unite. Together iron and mercury form a powerful set of complementary opposites. In human terms, where an "'iron will' and the 'mercurial temperament' work harmoniously together, they produce capable and well-rounded personalities with social gifts."[67]

In another Grimms' fairy tale, named "Iron John," an old, rusty giant is dredged up from a pond. Like Mercurius, he too had a murderous impulse for having been neglected. But, instead of change, Iron John represents raw, primitive aggression. The hero in that story becomes a man when he becomes acquainted with this power and how to control it. He learns that there is nothing inherently wrong with aggression when it is appropriately and justly applied. In both myths, it is clear that ignoring these powerful gods and the psychological potentials they represent causes them to act out in unconscious, dangerous ways.

Two methods we can use to master mercury and iron come from understanding how our bodies operate. Let us consider breathing and digestion in terms of these metals and how each plays a crucial role in the alchemical process of transforming physical and psychological elements.

As I've already mentioned, mercury shares a close affinity with the air element. Breath is the medium of thoughts and communication. Thus, Mercurius is god of language and the interpretative arts. When we are in good relationship with him, the correspondence between image and word is very nearly identical. Language reaches a pinnacle of conscious expression in poetry. In both sound and substance, poetry expresses a truth that embraces the macrocosm and microcosm of experience, even at times transcending them.

As we move toward one world we are beginning to find poetry even in the most advanced forms of mathematics and physics. The search for a "theory of everything" is this same truth that might express in one elegant recipe the workings of all physical matter. Yet, we do not have to be poets or physicists to participate in these great experiments. Psychologically, each breath represents a world replete with past, present and future all rolled up into the only true reality we know and yet, rarely live in. Mercurius is most palpably felt in breath, language and thought; he provides the means by which we can fuse all worlds into one.

A second means of using Mercurius in the work is digestion. The alchemists used this term to describe all forms of processes that involve the movement and transformation of matter. They did not restrict it to its biological meaning. Minerals, for example, were thought to undergo a process of digestion, moving from crude, dense matter toward a more subtle form. The object is always centered on how to facilitate this digestive process and move the opposites existing within and around the elements into a harmonious whole. A clue to how this is done can be found by carefully examining the picture that introduces this recipe.

There are clearly two images of Mercurius, one seated and the other standing. Mercurius, being a ubiquitous spirit, is used here to represent the opposites. Since he is shown splendidly adorned in both images, I suggest that he represents the ego, seated, and the self, standing—both gods ruling over a dominion and a world, respectively. Having brought them together, the alchemist must now find a way to fuse them. You will notice that he holds a lit torch and is standing in front of a blazing furnace. Fire is the medium he will use in causing these opposites to be digested into one harmonious being. This is no easy task. Ego resists with all its might to give up its empire and spirit would sooner fly off than have to deal with this unwilling partner. In therapy, I see many obstacles that get in the way of bringing these two together, much less having them combine.

In treating a woman who suffered from an eating disorder, I discovered that the source of her digestive difficulties was more psychological in origin than having anything to do with a strictly physical cause. I use the word digestive in this case in both its physical and psychological meaning; the division between the two was not at all as clearly defined as the opposites illustrated by the two images of Mercurius. I offer this clinical example to show how I, as a therapist, was working much like the alchemist in this picture, trying to bring the opposites together in an attempt to restore health.

At first my patient had no idea of the source of her chronic binging and purging. We initially used behavioral techniques to help her gain some control, but the results were erratic. She would have control for one week and then lose all control the next. She was miserable to say the least. Then, one day she reported a dream.

I was at a gas station.[68] My brother was there and he was very angry with me. The night before, I'd refused to do something for him. We got into a fight. This time I wasn't going to back down. I took the nozzle from the pump and lit the gas with a match. I wanted to destroy him.

As we investigated her associations to this dream, lots of memories surfaced. She described in vivid details years of physical and emotional abuse she had suffered at the hands of her older brother during their adolescence. Her emotions shifted from fear to utter despair as she recalled these traumatic memories. As we worked further to understand the connection between feelings and body states the opposites became increasingly clear. We discovered the mechanism by which she either tried to seize control or relinquish it. When she felt fear, she unconsciously asserted control in the only way she (as a child) knew how— withholding food or voiding it. At other times her anger dominated. But, again, lacking the ability to express rage outwardly, she took her vengeance out on herself by gorging food, leaving her feeling guilty, depressed and inadequate.

The therapy aimed at elevating her conscious ability to outwardly express feelings in appropriate ways. Fire was the medium and the consulting room the furnace in which she would learn to extinguish these dysfunctional behaviors. Her dream showed us her unconscious wish to destroy her brother, and fire the means by which she would do this. As she became better at expressing her emotions, the body responded favorably. Her symptoms diminished. She learned to separate her unconscious wishes from her conscious desire to get well. Rather than take out her anger or sadness on herself, she found better channels of expression. Increasingly, she felt that there was some hope for changing her lifelong battle with food.

The torch held by the alchemist not only represents the method used in joining opposites but also the hope of his success. Whether in therapy or elsewhere, healing does not occur without hope. The symbolic image of fire reflects this paradoxical meaning: it destroys in order to create. The torch is the light of hope. For my patient, therapy initially offered some dim hope of success, but only by tending the fire and helping her see the split that had been formed between her healthy and unhealthy self would that light of hope grow stronger.

The patient's dreams offered enormous help in this process. They shed light on the rage and humiliation she felt as a vulnerable adolescent who unwittingly internalizes a battle not of her making. Consequently, she could no more digest the abuse levied upon her by her brother than follow a normal diet. Worse, she'd adopted his image of herself in lieu of her own truly beautiful body. She became her own worst enemy. With extensive therapy she garnered the insight necessary to see more clearly her Real Self and begin healing the split that had cleaved her reality in two.

Breathing and digestion are two methods of controlling the fires of the body and mind. The master alchemist is one who knows the nature of fire and how to use it constructively. What's more, he knows that Mercurius is the spirit that dwells in the parts needing to be joined as well as being the agent that will cause them to unify. This recipe is a prescription that describes the basic elements involved in changing our lives. With it comes hope!

THE TENTH RECIPE

Without Divine Inspiration,
No One Is Great

INSIGHT   In the original *Frankenstein* movie, we are told the grisly story of a monster made from human body parts. The movie is based on Mary Shelley's *Frankenstein,* a book she wrote at the tender young age of nineteen. Despite her youth, some speculate that she was well informed on matters of alchemy and even perhaps knowledge of the alleged creation of a *golem*[69] by sixteenth-century Jewish alchemists.[70] In the movie, lightning is the animating force that brings the monster to life. This feature corresponds with the alchemist's attempt to invoke transpersonal energies to animate their concoctions. In many alchemical formulas, there are even less savory ingredients than those used by Dr. Frankenstein in creating *homunculii.* Paracelsus, for example, lists urine, semen and dung as ingredients in his recipe for making an artificial man. From these examples, it is obvious that light and dark elements are necessary in equal measure for creating synthetic as well as human life.

Literary works like *Frankenstein* and *The Golem* by G. Meyer are of course pure fiction. Along with alchemist's claims of creating *homunculii,* it might well be easy to dismiss them as being no more than fanciful stories if it weren't for the extraordinary work being done in the field of cloning today. How often have we seen how "yesterday's magic becomes tomorrow's science"? I will leave this lofty pursuit to physical scientists and alchemists currently working in these fields. However, what is germane to understanding this recipe is identifying the force needed to spark one form of life into another.

This same question challenged physicists for more than a century and more recently psychologists interested in the relationship between mind and matter. As early as 1900, Max Planck, the father of modern physics, described packages of light known as quanta. His quantum hypothesis led other leading physicists to new conceptions of energy and atomic structure. By 1911, Niels Bohr and others knew that electrons jump from one state to another by some mysterious means. They further understood that without this transition, energy would remain potential and not yield any usable (kinetic) energy. How electrons pop out and into existence still remains a mystery. However, what we do know is that these transitions do not occur without consciousness. In other words, these transitions happen because we observe them. It doesn't require us to be mindful or hopeful or anything; electrons pop in and out of existence simply when we focus our attention on matter. This effect has been documented many times and as discussed represents observer participantcy.[71]

This connection between mind and matter launched a whole new field called quantum physics. As incredible as the theory sounds, the modern world would be dramatically different without discoveries made from quantum research. Quantum physics paved the way for cell phones, high-speed computers and the Internet. It literally ushered in a whole new world. We are not dealing with magic, but hard science. Know it or not, quantum physics brought us back to the basic alchemical vision of a world where the role humans play is critical in the behavior of matter. I only wished psychology had kept pace with the marvelous advances of quantum physics. In some small way, I hope this book gets people thinking about the incredible opportunities of merging psychology with other branches of hard science.

Despite painstaking effort made by alchemists in the laboratory, the work could not yield the philosopher's stone without an infusion of transpersonal power. This explains the religious and spiritual language of alchemical texts and the importance placed on prayer and meditation in conducting laboratory experiments. The adept thought of himself as a conduit through which divine energy flowed into the chemicals, exciting them and causing them to behave in extraordinary ways. We can immediately see why their recipes and procedures were kept secret and out of the reach of unworthy individuals. But even if unsavory characters were to steal the alchemist's secrets, they would still lack the presence of mind necessary to bring Mercurius into the work.

This leads us to some very important questions: What conditions are necessary in personal alchemy that might bring the unconscious to life? How might we further facilitate the work? What is this spark that is needed to complete the work? Do we have to be religious in order for this spiritual spark to ignite?

While I have already mentioned qualities alchemists need to have in their personal affairs, I would like to elaborate on one that is central to our present recipe. Divine inspiration is the spark that causes common things to come to life and become great.

Alchemy is a labor of love and it requires hard work. To find success there must be a discipline that balances the inspiration of heaven with the perspiration of earth. In the *I Ching*, an ancient Chinese book of change, it is the Superior Man who possesses great wisdom and the discipline needed to combine these forces. Transmuting metals, creating healing elixirs and potions of immortality are certainly lofty endeavors that require no less than the powers of a superior human being. These pursuits can easily give way to false ambition and superficial pride. This special work is reserved for those who can do the work of gods with the hands of a common craftsman and the gentle humor of a saint.

Jungian analyst Robert Johnson describes this balance between heaven and earth as arising out of common everyday experience. "It is ironic," he writes, "that often our breakthroughs into consciousness of the divine grow out of breakdowns in ordinary consciousness. Contacts with the divine may at the time feel like pure suffering, and I sometimes wonder if all suffering is a vision of God too great to bear."[72] Divine inspiration doesn't, in other words, come out of the mouths of saints, but from the very words that issue from us during the course of an ordinary day. Haven't you noticed those times when, out of great compassion or even mindlessness, you say things that are wise and true? Can we cultivate this faculty? Certainly, such wisdom hardly comes from the ego. Rather, it issues from the Self, which alone is in connection with nature and with some divine realm.

Personal alchemy also requires one to suffer, not the ordinary kind of suffering, but one that is noble and even ecstatic. When we experience ecstatic suffering, there is a silent joy even in our most desperate moments. So great is our desire to possess the philosopher's stone that our bodies physically ache. The human body can tolerate enormous pain and suffering if the mind is deeply committed to a meaningful purpose.

Every alchemist has some lead in her head and some gold in her feet. In this way, she anchors her dreams in earthly reality, but at the same time does not find herself bogged down by the weight of tedious, endless operations. In personal alchemy, human qualities, like the alchemist's metals, either coagulate or sublimate. These are the respective operations of earth and heaven. The process of *coagulatio* has the effect

> It is a good exercise to inventory your pain and suffering and ask whether they rise to this level. I assign the ones that don't to problems that are typically associated with the ego and are therefore best addressed at that level. But what problems have a deeper source? Don't be too much in a rush to dismiss the first set of problems, because more often than not, they give us hints to more deeply pressing issues.

of fixating lofty fantasies, runaway emotions and high-flown ideals. *Sublimatio,* on the other hand, liberates attitudes that are too earthbound and stagnant. We see how these operations mirror their symbolic counterparts—iron and mercury. As we master these operations, we create a sacred space that invites divine inspiration.

In alchemical symbolism, inspiration is often signified as a rain shower, and its manifest experience as dew. These images are drawn from the water element and are both known as the *aqua sapientiae,* a taste of divine wisdom. Rain, of course, is water from the heavens. It fertilizes the field of our imagination, enabling us to have ecstatic vision and do creative work. Dew is very much like the sweat of our brow that bears evidence of honest work and purpose. These symbols suggest the special kind of grace that derives from devotion to work and love. For every ounce of perspiration there had to be an ounce of inspiration in doing the work.

Even with careful attention paid to suffering in love and work, we cannot predict when, or if ever, we will be struck with a spark of divine inspiration. In the biblical story of Paul, we see that God doesn't reserve inspiration for the most holy. Paul persecuted Christians before he was struck by lightning and came to know a higher, transcendental wisdom. The conversion was instantaneous and so complete that it caused this Jewish man from Tarsus to change his name. He became known as one of Christ's greatest apostles. Paul, meaning "little, restrained, lessened, made small," gives us a good indication of what was needed for him to open up to divine inspiration. Clearly, a prejudiced, tyrannical ego with a domineering will and narrow perception of the world had to be "made small" so that Paul might open his eyes to a consciousness greater than his own.

Without good reasons to explain why divine interventions occur, we sometimes treat synchronistic events as if they were miracles. While this very well might be the case, we still want to know how to optimize the conditions that invite divinity into our lives. Rather than be passive voyeurs of unconscious occurrences, alchemy invites full participation. In my experience, I find that miracles do not always come in dramatic ways. Flashes of insight and synchronistic events oftentimes are the minor miracles that take place in everyday experiences. Jung suspects that these kinds of "illumination and inspiration . . . are sudden expansions of consciousness [having] a subject that is not the ego."[73] Well then, if not ego and not god, we are led once more to the Self, which is neither fully human nor wholly divine.

What are the qualities of Self that cause us to receive ecstasy, miracles, insight and experience synchronistic events? The Self is our interface with nature. It is simultaneously an experience that is comprised of natural and human elements. It connects us to a wisdom that is far greater than the ego mind could ever hope to have. At the same time, it relies on ego consciousness for the discipline necessary to successfully navigate the world of reality and experience it fully. This understanding is missed from a strictly egoistic perspective.

If the ego is not adequately secure and properly individuated, it often thinks of itself as the source of wisdom. This is a grave mistake. We need ego to see the wisdom Self alone has to offer, but without ego dropping its false claim, the true source of its greatest ally will never be had. Ego must, therefore, rescind its claim on things greater than itself. It must behold the mystery and allow itself to be infused with spirit. Ramakrishna says that we must make ego a "servant of God."[74]

"One allows oneself to be less in order to be more—less nearly perfect, but more nearly whole."[75]

Inspiration comes to ego when we lighten up and don't take ourselves too seriously. When the ego can turn around and see through its own defenses, it begins to detach from the fears that went into its own making. Clarity comes to the ego mind when it is willing to embrace the "small" but vital part it plays in life. As Jung points out, the "'little god of the world' is consciousness," and consciousness is experienced first and foremost through the agency of the ego.

The superiority of the Self rests on its inclusion of ego within its purview and its affinity to nature. Jung explains:

> However one may define the self, it is always something other than the ego, and inasmuch as a higher insight of the ego leads over to the self, the self is a more comprehensive thing which includes the experience of the ego and therefore transcends it. Just as the ego is a certain experience I have of myself, so is the self an experience of my ego. It is, however, no longer experienced in the form of a broader or higher ego, but in the form of a non-ego."[76]

When ego matures to this level of insight, it sees nature not as something to be dominated, but more accurately, as a screen upon which greater truths are reflected. "Nature," writes Ken Wilber, "is the outer form of Buddha, nature is the corporeal body of Christ . . . For those who do not know the Timeless, nature is all they have; for those who do not taste Infinity, nature serves its last supper. For those in need of redemption, nature tricks you into thinking it alone is real. But, for those who have found release, nature is the radiant shell in which a deeper truth resides." [77]

Mary Shelley's book *Frankenstein,* or *The New Prometheus,* is a cautionary tale whose message has proven to be prophetic in our New World. On the surface, there is Victor Frankenstein, whose chemical knowledge comes by way of two alchemists, Agrippa and Paracelsus. He creates his monster only to find himself reviled by "the creature." Scientist and monster appear to be two antithetical halves of one individual, the former representing pure intellect, the latter pure feeling. As a result, Dr. Frankenstein loathes his creature, leaving it isolated and left to its own devices. The creature laments, "I ought to be thy Adam, but I am rather the fallen angel, whom thou drivest from joy for no misdeed. Everywhere I see bliss, from which I alone am irrevocably excluded. I was benevolent and good; misery made me a fiend." [78]

Sadly, Frankenstein turns his back on the creature, and in the end, lacking integration between feeling and thought, the story ends in tragedy. Abandoned and left to die, the creature cries out, "The light of that conflagration will fade away; my ashes will be swept into the sea by the winds."[79] Recalling the Promethean myth gives us a deeper perspective, which helps add meaning to this disturbing story.

Out of his love for humankind, this trickster god, Prometheus, stole fire from the gods. As punishment for his transgression, the gods had him chained to a rock, whereupon vultures fed on his liver. To make matters worse, his liver magically regenerated each morning. Eventually, Prometheus was freed on the condition that he wear a ring of iron, a sign of wrongdoing, and Chiron, the wounded healer (half-animal, half-human) be sacrificed. And finally, as Edward Whitmont explains, his liberation required that he "reveal to the gods a vital secret upon which the continuity of the world depended, that only he, the representative of mankind, not the gods, knew about. This secret referred to the need for having the great goddess joined in marriage to a human mortal, not to another god." [80]

Against this mythological backdrop, what was Mary Shelley telling us in this gruesome tale? What does it have to do with divine inspiration? We need to make several important points clear in order to understand the alchemy of the situation and be able to apply this recipe in our lives:

1. Feelings and thoughts do not exist independently of each other. While one may be less developed than the other, both must be brought into conscious alliance in order for feelings to be made meaningful and thoughts to acquire conviction and resolve.

2. Excessive consciousness is no better than a paucity of consciousness. Too much does not necessarily mean better; it only leads to problems of the kind suffered in mania (expansiveness), narcissism (omnipotence) and sleepless nights. For this reason, the creature becomes a maniacal monster who is unable, owing to a lack of love, to control his murderous impulses. Without the necessary work to change the quality of consciousness, its increase or decrease only causes problems.

3. While ego must expand its consciousness to include itself within the Self, in the process not only does it forfeit some of its power, but also loses a connection to its natural, perfect state in the unconscious. "The ego's attempt to abrogate to itself the powers of the transpersonal Self," explains Whitmont, "separate it from feeling contained in its divine origin."[81] Paradoxically, the ego gives up its hold on the natural order, which leads to a state of alienation, only to merge in the end with a Divine Self.

4. Divine envy is a necessary sin for the development of consciousness. Humans envied the fire of consciousness possessed by the gods in the Prometheus myth and by God in the story of Adam and Eve. The creature, envious of its maker's capacity to feel, compares its plight to Adam and in desperation admits, "Many times I considered Satan as the fitter emblem of my condition, for often like him, when I viewed the bliss of my protectors, the bitter gall of envy rose within me."[82] In addition to shame, envy too is an original sin.

5. The final condition of Prometheus's release suggests that the "transpersonal (the Goddess) must connect with the individuating human consciousness."[83] Rejected and alone, the creature threatens revenge with the words, "I will be with you on your wedding-night."[84]

In alchemical language, this amounts to the critical *coniunctio* that must occur in order to complete the work. But, it can only happen if there is a true and loving dialogue between feelings and thoughts, ego and self, and Self and Kosmos. When we turn our back on any one or the other of these, the whole process collapses and we are thrown back into the unconscious only to begin anew.

Finally, this recipe teaches us that sometimes things cannot be expressed in words. Spiritual insight more often comes to us through a sudden spark of illumination. The fire that Prometheus stole from the gods symbolizes the spark needed to change dead matter into new life. We can understand the Frankenstein creature as both our shadow and our higher self. Without love and relationship he is no more than a walking automaton. But, when we, in cocreation with god, give love to that part of ourselves that we have made, a new self is born into the world.

So, we end our recipes where we began them—with the shadow. But, now we have the knowledge to see that shadow is not something entirely separate from the Self and that whatever space we might imagine separates them is not much at all. It is a paradox that when we focus our attention on one, immediately its opposite comes into being. Wholeness is not a matter of selecting one part or another, but rather embracing all that we are and all that we can become.

Chapter 9

God Is in the Recipe

The scientist does not study Nature because it is useful; he studies it because he delights in it, and he delights in it because it is beautiful. If Nature were not beautiful, it would not be worth knowing, and if Nature were not worth knowing, life would not be worth living.

JULES-HENRI POINCARÉ

We are here face to face with the very old symbolism of the coincidentia oppositorum, *universally widespread, well attested in primitive stages of culture, and which served more or less to define both the fundamental reality . . . and the paradoxical state of totality, the perfection and consequently the sacredness of God.*

MIRCEA ELIADE

Alchemy delights us with the expected. Who would have thought that porcelain and phosphorus, brandy and smelling salts come right out of the alchemical laboratory?[1] Who would have suspected that saints and popes, scholars and artists would be found in the secret societies, guilds and brethren of the alchemical order? But history records the superlative contributions made by alchemists in virtually every field of art and science.

More than the actual writings of alchemists, it was their fantastic ideas and concepts that influenced some of the greatest philosophers. From Plato's eternal forms to Heraclitus' *logos,* alchemy left its indelible mark. At times, attempts were made to establish an alchemical philosophy that stood on its own two feet. The Hermetic texts, for example, are a compendium of alchemical philosophy, but even these fail to capture the full breadth of the Art. More often, alchemical thought is found in artistic and literary themes.

Virgil and Homer sang alchemy's praises in verse and rhyme. The *Odyssey* depicts the journey of the hero in the course of individuation. Numerous references in Shakespeare reflect the poet's deep insights into the Art. Ben Jonson authored a play called *The Alchemists,* in which a homunculus has a leading role. Chaucer too "studied the Art with close attention, and certain rather bitter remarks suggest that he had himself lost time and money in unsuccessful attempts at transmutation."[2] The great German writer Goethe based his tragic alchemical tale *Faust* on the life of a "conjurer of air," fire and water. Like Marlowe before him, Goethe described what often happens in the pursuit of immortality. From his deathbed, Henry Wadsworth Longfellow memorialized alchemy's legendary Hermes Trismegistus in a poem by the same name. "Trismegistus!" he wrote, "Three times greatest!/How thy name sublime/Has descended to this latest/Progeny of time!"[3]

Alchemists used images as well as words to express (and conceal) their mind-boggling ideas. Today, no less than in centuries past, alchemists shy away from revealing who they are and what wisdom they possess. One of the most mysterious alchemists who some say was living during the years of the First World War and is alleged to still be living despite having the appearance of a man in his forties goes by the name Fulcanelli. One alleged encounter describes him as an expert in Hermetic lore and the driving force behind a group (the Brothers of Heliopolis), who dedicated itself to unveiling the alchemical secrets carved into the stone facades of Medieval homes and cathedrals. Chartres and Nôtre Dame are excellent examples of Gothic cathedrals. We do better to acquaint ourselves with Fulcanelli from his two most famous books, *Le Mystère des Cathédrales* and *The Dwellings of the Philosophers*, the latter dedicated to the Brothers of Heliopolis.

In *Le Mystère des Cathédrales*, Fulcanelli reveals the secrets used in Gothic architecture to hide occult formulas in the walls and galleys of Nôtre Dame.[4] In *The Dwellings of the Philosophers*, he interprets in intricate detail signs and symbols etched into doorways, walls and porticos of medieval castles and places once occupied by alchemists. No doubt similar artistic devices like these were employed in building the pyramids of Egypt and Mexico. Still many mysteries remain.

What can explain the relatively sudden explosion in building these awesome structures? Where did the designs and methods needed to support massive tons of stones come from?

In his book *The Philosopher's Stone*, Peter Marshall suggests that the methods used by the Goths in building Chartres possibly came from the Knights Templar, a group sworn to protect Christian highways during the crusades.[5]

As we have seen the use of symbolic imagery filled the pages of many fourteenth- and fifteenth-century woodcuts. To the discerning eye, these works present us with a cookbook filled with visual recipes, each expressing some operation, stage or occult aspect of the Art. In this book, I have purposefully included some examples of the wonderful woodcuts executed by artists under the direction of master alchemists. In the history of visual art, this type of art is unparalleled and very much underrepresented. Although the British Museum possesses rare alchemical pieces, it was only in Prague that I found alchemical art on display as a special exhibition. Several museums were filled with books, laboratory equipment and other artifacts from alchemical works.

By design, these artists relied on symbols and metaphor to move the eye from the flat, two-dimensional surface to multidimensional space. Their skill came by way of combining ordinary objects in very unusual ways, a technique that would be used centuries later by the surrealists. In alchemical art, common things like trees, fish, tools and musical instruments, are never simply used to illustrate a scene. Instead, the alchemists were fond of fusing and juxtaposing common objects to create mysteries that ignite the imagination. The puzzle leaves one perplexed and looking for answers in a deeper, cosmic reality. This talent, and the effect it has on us, lends justification for alchemy truly being a Royal Art.

In music and mathematics, alchemy gained lyrical expression in musical composition and numerical formulation. In fact, these related disciplines continue to influence modern physics. Music and number are the sounds of the eternal soul. Their joint expression is heard in the ancient "music of the spheres," and in future, the vibrations coming from superstring theory.

Jung's intensive studies of the collective unconscious drew the attention of scholars working in diverse fields; theologians, mythologists and anthropologists, sharing his interest in consciousness studies, met regularly with him at Eranos, Switzerland. In essence, they shared a common bond that aimed at creating a new alchemy of consciousness. Historically, the Eranos conference and others like it represent an invisible college much like that of the Rosicrucians and the Royal Society. Through collegial discussion and scholarly presentation, alchemy shifted from secrets etched in stone to theoretical developments in modern fields of study. Particularly important to this development was Jung's collaboration with the enigmatic physicist Wolfgang Pauli, famous for his discovery of the neutrino, the exclusion principle and the mysterious Pauli effect.[6] Their work represents a modern dialogue between psyche (soul) and *physis* (matter), one that went a long way toward establishing a New World.

Pauli was among the leading physicists establishing quantum theory in the early twentieth century. Being an open-minded professor at the University of Zurich, Pauli met with Jung and "became convinced that the unconscious was far more instrumental in making theories about matter than most physicists would have even contemplated." Pauli was certain that a "new conception of reality had to include matter and spirit as complementary aspects of the one world." [7]

As evidenced by the growing acceptance of quantum theory, Pauli was not alone in his thinking. By the middle of the last century, it seemed that physics embraced psychology to such an extent that accurate measurement could not be made without including the laws of perception. Heisenberg's uncertainty principle, Einstein's theory of relativity and Schrödinger paradoxes represent the products of disciplines studying this new field of mind and matter. Today, the search for a "Theory of Everything" recapitulates in many ways the timeless recipe of the *Emerald Tablet,* "As above, so below for the making of the One Thing."

Artists, anthropologists, magicians, mythologists, musicians, physicists, poets and psychologists are all part of the alchemical family. As I mentioned earlier, change any one part and the overall story is never quite the same.

In this brief accounting of alchemy's influence, we discover a museum made not of bricks and mortar, but one that exists principally in the minds of enlightened souls who understand alchemy as an archetypal art. True adepts seldom sought fame or glory, for their prize could never be weighed in common gold. Though alchemy's inventions are many, its goal has always remained the same: *to capture the essence of divine being in mind and matter.* In a word, alchemists sought ways to find god through art and experiment. Each and every recipe must therefore be considered a formula constructed precisely for this purpose. In each, there is some operation that draws us closer to divine experience.

> • Gold is God in earthly matter.
> • Recipes are ways of experiencing God.
> • "God is an alchemist," declares Fulcanelli in *Le Mystère des Cathédrales.*
> • "Summoned or not the god will be there," writes Jung.

Breaking free from traditional aesthetics, these artists thought nothing of combining disgusting details with images of kings and queens. The symbols they invented were made to represent creation in all its gory and glorious detail. As a result, alchemy remains an art practiced by dedicated individuals declaring, *"Ecce homo."* ("Here is man.") Its aesthetic rests on the principle that the lowest serves the highest, and the highest serves the lowest—the "One thing" excludes nothing. To make any sense of the Royal Art we must accept creation, "warts and all." Neither can anyone, from the lowliest peasant to rulers of state, be excluded from its school of art. Its only membership requires a mind that embraces life without allowing prejudice or limitations to restrict the nature of god.

From gods to common people, alchemy is still practiced by some in secret, solitary ways, and by many more in the laboratories of everyday life. Whether cooking a meal, blending perfumes, cloning animals or making movies, alchemical work is taking place. For this reason, I chance to label its influence on humanity a truly vital archetypal force.

With this being the case, ancient and modern people are equally touched by the power of this archetype. Time and space have us expressing alchemy in countless ways, but the voice is singular to all who "have ears to hear." One purpose in writing this book has been to contemporize alchemy by recognizing and appreciating its influence in the activities of ordinary citizens as well as the untapped potential reserved for individuals seeking to make a significant contribution to the global evolution of consciousness. While we may not all be enlightened masters of the Art, or even realize we are practicing alchemy, the changes made when minds mix with matter have an incalculable effect on each and every one of us. Conscious practice, of course, enhances the positive effects of the work. Especially for those who take their individuation process seriously, these recipes and the psychological skills they require, offer powerful ways to change the human condition at every level of society.

A recipe is only as good as the cook. Alchemical literature abounds with good counsel for the making of a master alchemist. But, more than character goes into training the initiate. In researching the subject, Manly P. Hall discovered a book that delineates three degrees of alchemists. These include:

- the *Adept,* a "master alchemist . . . who is fully possessed of the mysteries of the Art" and has performed it;

- the *Illuminate,* who has "experienced the mystery of the work but doesn't know how it is performed";

- the *Initiate,* who has "attained to the knowledge of the method but hasn't performed the work."[8]

Based on this scheme, Moses, Hermes and Solomon are adepts of the highest order; John the Apostle and Ptolemy were Illuminates; and

Homer, Thomas Aquinas, Michael Maier and Thomas Bacon held the rank of Initiates.

Although Jung was not mentioned in this old book, he would probably belong to the Initiate class. Despite his immense knowledge of the subject, Jung never practiced laboratory alchemy and arguably never advanced to the level of Illuminate. Instead, his alchemy shines through many of his psychological theories. Admittedly, he was not interested in chemical experiment and in fact felt that the alchemist's real worth was not to be found in this field of study. Rather, Jung used alchemy as a historic model to illustrate par excellence the unfolding development of the unconscious within the context of the individuation process. For him, the past offered a profound resource to prove that culture, as much as individuals, moves through predictable stages of development that mirror the course of natural evolution. Moreover, alchemy offered a method for facilitating this process by synthetic technique.

The alchemists had one foot in the ancient past and one foot in the distant future. They were idealists struggling to find ways of making matter conform to wild speculations bubbling up from the collective unconscious. They often described the results of their works as miracles. As a result, their language was oftentimes lofty and incomprehensible, more suited to madmen than scientists. As a psychologist, I can only explain miracles as transpersonal experiences having a stimulus derived from some extraordinary, unseen source whose effects are nonetheless felt to be meaningful. I recognize that much of what I've offered in this book may leave some skeptical, especially for those having little experience with the old science, magic. Well might they ask: Did alchemists really transmute substances? Do miracles really happen? In response, I suggest keeping an open mind and consider what follows.

> After a century of general acceptance that unconscious stimuli can produce physical and psychological reaction, it shouldn't take a leap of faith to accept that a stimulus can just as well spring from an unseen spiritual source.

The following is a schematic that describes these unconscious and superconscious dynamics:

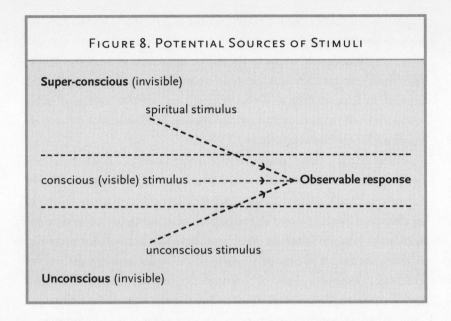

FIGURE 8. POTENTIAL SOURCES OF STIMULI

Super-conscious (invisible)

spiritual stimulus

conscious (visible) stimulus ----------> **Observable response**

unconscious stimulus

Unconscious (invisible)

Neither spiritual nor unconscious stimuli are visible and yet we accept that the latter has a very real effect on the consequences of our actions. Hasn't the time arrived to accept that spiritual stimuli might also have a direct influence on our behavior, well beyond that which is postulated by religion and denied by orthodox science?

MAKING MIRACLES, MAKING MISTAKES

At the turn of the nineteenth century, Sigmund Freud caused a revolution in science by introducing the concept of unconscious motivation. In a way, he took the magic out of life by introducing a science of mind called psychoanalysis. At about the same time, James Watson introduced his own school of psychology, known as behaviorism. With these two schools, psychology dominated Western thought for the better part of the last century. Alongside these schools, the works of Carl Jung, Abraham Maslow and Roberto Assagioli presented a more holistic, spiritual model of human psychology.

These two main schools viewed consciousness from very different perspectives. Freud's interests lead to an intense exploration of the unconscious workings of the psyche. Like Newton before him, Freud described the unconscious in mechanistic terms. Freud, we must remember, did laboratory work before taking up his psychoanalytic research. For him, the unconscious was principally based in biology and the world of instincts. He was a biologist of the mind, interested in what lies within psyche. By contrast, Watson focused on what lies outside the mind. That is to say, he focused exclusively on behavior and action. Both approaches reduced psyche to the level of matter, leaving little room for a more expansive vision of human beings.

Jung held a much broader view of human beings, one that includes body, soul and mind, but also emphasizes the spiritual aspects of consciousness in all three. While great debates have taken place as to who of all these theorists is (most) right, the real issue facing us now is whether another revolution is taking place, one that must account for great discoveries coming from modern physics, molecular biology, astronomy and cognitive science. In this revolution, not one of these pioneers owns the whole truth. They are all right! Its like the old story of the three blind Indians, each describing some part of an elephant and insisting they've discovered a different creature.

Now the real question is whether we can accept a model of consciousness that embraces an integral or unitive consciousness that allows for qualities drawn from different parts of the same elephant and ones that we may at present be too blind to explain. To do so requires a leap of faith most scientists are not willing to take: they must accept the limits of their models and return to the mystery of the unknown, not as something quantifiable but as a numinous experience. Are we ready to bring back the imagination as used by the great sages of the past? Are we prepared to let go of the egotism that attaches itself to discovery and allow for possibilities that multiple truths exist simultaneously?

Were we to recognize that a revolution is in fact already underway, then a new view of consciousness opens up to us that is simultaneously integral and differentiated. And yes, it does defy rational comprehension. The concept is not new. Alchemists and philosophers described it as the "One and the Many." The symbolism of the philosopher's stone encompasses both the contradictory and complementary aspects of a unitive conception of nature. In the history of philosophy, this leap is actually a return to the primitive past by one fully equipped with the technology available to us today.

In this context, a miracle is an experience in which we witness manifestations that result from dimensions of parallel worlds breaking into the one we happen to be in at the moment. From this perspective, miracles are the rule rather than the exception; only perceptual prejudice keeps us from seeing them. Alchemy goes further and suggests that we can master miracles by using its operations and formulas. While a miracle can occur suddenly even in alchemy, more often the work generates a slow miracle, one that may not be as dramatic in its immediate effect but is nonetheless spectacular in its results.

At the ego level, the philosopher's stone is a boiling mass of opposites that eventually give way to the production of a solid, stable identity. Out of the confusion a personality is born. This, in itself, is a miracle! In the *albedo* stage, we develop a sense of self that recognizes and appreciates the world beyond ego. And finally, the *rubedo* represents a consciousness that appreciates the whole world.

There is a god in each level and each has a recipe for knowing that god. This god is spirit and it supplies the motivating force that drives the individuation process. The old gods provide us with reflections of all three levels. Each one captures a piece of the divinity. They are emanations of the One and the Many aspects of the transpersonal world. A quick review will help remind us that alchemy is the overarching concept that draws these images of god under one roof without denying the omnipotence of each.

Christian mythology is filled with many examples of miracles. Each one reflects a different aspect of alchemy, but all tell us something special about the "making of the One thing." The Last Supper, where Christ transforms bread into his body, wine into his blood is an act of transmutation that is central to the ritual re-enactment of the Mass. The multiplication of the loaves of bread and jugs of wine at the Marriage of Cana reminds us of the regenerative property of the philosopher's stone and the alchemical operation known as *multipicatio*. Even the words from the Lord's Prayer, "on earth as it is in Heaven," recall the words from the *Emerald Tablet;* "as above, so below."

In some stories, Jesus is described as the "master of fire"[9] who said clearly, "He who is near to me is near the fire." Fire, of course, is the

> Miracles represent a state of mind where there are no contradictions. Imagination, not reason, is the medium by which miracles can best be experienced. Miracles do not necessarily require religion for their occurrence, only faith in the mystery of the universe as something immense and divine. Recall Gandhi's insight, "God has no religion."

essence of change as well as the source by which all things are transmuted from one state to another. "All things," said Heraclitus, "change to fire, and fire exhausted falls back into things."[10] Jung equated Christ with the philosopher's stone, combining as it were the fixed substance with its volatile ability to change all things. Thus, when Christ says, "I am that I am," he means that he represents the alchemical fixed-volatile *in toto*. From the Christian perspective, Christ is the alpha and the omega, the keystone that supports the world. We need not, however, restrict ourselves to examples drawn from the Judeo-Christian religions to evidence the underlying structure of god consciousness.

At Buddha's "Last Supper," the master summoned a smith to prepare his final meal on earth. When it was done, Buddha gave the sweetest portions to his disciples and ate the bitter leftovers. As a result, he became gravely ill and in the last moments before his death remarked on the bitterness of this physical life. His death corresponds to Jesus' crucifixion: both offered the gross, earthly body as a sacrificial death for the sins (unconsciousness) of humankind. Out of compassion, they sought to redeem humanity by releasing it from the prisons of time and space, and the unconscious guards holding it captive. This same theme is central to alchemy, where redemption plays a critical role. We will recall that the alchemists embraced the Gnostic conception of a spirit trapped in matter that could only find release through human intervention.

These themes of redemption and release are an essential part of every great religion and spiritual philosophy. As Buddhism spread to China, it took with it elements of alchemical psychology. As we have seen in Taoism, the feminine yin and the masculine yang correspond to the alchemical *luna* and *sol*. Redemption is achieved by consciously integrating each pair of opposites. When an initiate consciously realizes Tao, he or she is redeemed from their unconscious fate and released from the Wheel of Karma. Where Christian alchemy placed emphasis on spiritual transubstantiation in the symbolism of the Mass, Chinese alchemy took a more practical approach, aimed at bodily transformation. Taoist priests, for instance, sought physical immortality through an *opus contra naturam,* in which they attempted to withhold the "seeds of life"—breath and semen. Taoist practice, like alchemy, aimed at nothing short of an *apotheosis,* in which human flesh is transmuted into godly substance.

Zen Buddhism also embraced the central concept of the "One and the Many." In their version, it became known as "One in All and All in One." Like Tao, Zen stressed the importance of action over analysis. "Zen," explains Daisetz Suzuki, "would never hypostatize the One or the All as a thing to be grasped by the senses. The phrase . . . is to be understood as an expression of absolute *prajna* intuition and is not to be conceptually analyzed."[11] Zen, like alchemy, not only allows for but even encourages paradox and contradiction. A special state of mind, *wabi*, enables the mind to maintain unity amidst the ever-changing forms that constitute reality.

As mentioned earlier, many alchemists also used Kabbala in their practice. The language, symbolism and vision of this mystical form of Judaism were in many ways similar to alchemy. Likewise, Sufism expressed an Islamic conception not unlike that found in the Royal Art. For this reason, I have often quoted the great Persian poet Rumi, whose verses read like verses from an alchemical manuscript.

We can also find alchemical truths in spiritualism. I have already made many references to the practice of shamans and the parallels in alchemy. While shamanism is practiced worldwide, we in the Western world are most familiar with it in Native American culture. In Black Elk's famous vision, he saw the integration of all the world's tribes, a theme that resonates with the final *coniunctio* of alchemy. There is no country that I am aware of that doesn't express alchemy in its own indigenous way. The reason for this is simple: *we all take god as a basis for understanding nature and feel compelled to simulate the divine in the things we say and do.*

> From the Talmud:
>> "Greater than the first miracle is the last."
>
> From ninth century Sufi master Abu Yazid al-Bistami:
>> "Try to gain one moment in which you see only God in heaven and earth."
>
> From Rumi:
>> "Please come in, my Self. There's no place in this house for two."[12]

These many examples make the point that the *psychological* experience of god (the philosopher's stone seen from the third level) is the same regardless of the particular way that god might be imagined by people throughout the world. We find "god in the details" when we embrace particular gods and their unique way of connecting us with a divine reality. Each is simultaneously unique and pluralistic. I emphasize again that the view I offer is psychologically, not theologically, based. God, from this perspective, begins and ends in the mind.

When we think of god we conceive of a transpersonal presence that possesses extraordinary powers. The alchemists believed that humans, being "little gods" in this world, have the potential to acquire these supernatural abilities. By supernatural, alchemists meant that these powers were already present in the lead of human consciousness and with careful experiment these abilities can be released, developed and eventually mastered. This feature of the philosopher's stone explains why it was often referred to as a miraculous and supernatural object. In addition to clairvoyance, the practice of intentionally "projecting" thoughts and emotions onto others and appearing simultaneously in many different places, one contemporary alchemist adds the following description of the stone's amazing abilities:

> Finally, when dissociation, purification and reconstitution vest the same cohesive telluric structure in the body-apart from the possibility of transporting into the invisible everything that makes up visible man, (invisibility, death without leaving a body—"raising the whole body to heaven by Assumption," "the body raising itself, by its own power, to the region of Brahma," etc.) and apart from the possibility of magically dissolving the body in one given place in order to recompose it and cause it to appear intact in another, and not just in its double . . . beyond all that, is the not inconsiderable power to act on substances and on the laws of external minerality, on the occult forces active in them, that henceforth the initiate has activated within his own magically enlivened organism.[13]

Attaining any one of these extraordinary abilities satisfies Saint Thomas Aquinas's definition of what constitutes a miracle. According to him, a miracle is an event that is set "apart from the generally established order of things."[14] Its effect is met with astonishment precisely because its cause remains unknown.

These are godlike powers. Whether or not we can really acquire any of them, the fact remains that most of us have to go to work the next day. In his book *After the Ecstasy, the Laundry,* longtime meditater Jack Kornfield writes, "Enlightenment flowers not as an ideal, but in the miraculous reality of the human form, with its pleasures and pains. No master can escape this truth, nor does enlightenment make the vulnerability of our body go away. The Buddha had illnesses and backaches."[15]

To pursue alchemy for the mere acquisition of power only leads to failure. Suspicious of such misuse, the *Course in Miracles,* a Christian mystical book, suggests that "Miracles should be involuntary. They should not be under conscious control. Consciously selected miracles can be misguided."[16] Involuntary does not psychologically equate with habit. Instead, the *Course* is describing a voluntary forgetfulness that allows an action to be internalized and expressed naturally.

> "Draw bamboos for ten years, become a bamboo, then forget all about bamboos when you are drawing. In possession of an infallible technique, the individual places himself at the mercy of inspiration."[17]

At the same time, we must also distinguish between acquired abilities and natural ones. The recipe of the *Emerald Tablet* calls for an "adaptation" of consciousness that ignites the seeds of nature vested in human nature. The Hermetic texts recommend that "if you don't make yourself equal to God, you can't perceive God; for like is known to like."[18] These, being potentially dangerous propositions, lead me to add a caution: *making yourself equal to God does not mean identification with God.* This is the difference between the narcissist and the saint.

To illustrate this point I recall a delightful story that Ram Dass tells in his seminars of a visit he made to a friend suffering from a severe mental disorder. To appreciate this story we have to recall the garb worn by hippies during the 1960s. So imagine Ram Dass, at the time a full-fledged hippie, dressed in clothes from India, adorned with beads, long hair and a straggly beard. The oddity of the situation was not lost on his friend. "How can this be? There you are," said his friend, "dressed in those weird clothes, and here I am locked up in this loony bin." Ram Dass smiled and responded by saying, "I talk of god and find god in every human being, but you think you alone are god." Therein lies the difference between wisdom and folly.

We need to carefully examine these differences in order to prevent a false *coniunctio* from occurring. Risks abound at every step of the way. In the *nigredo* stage, sudden acquisition of supernatural abilities often throws the initiate back into a magical world of instincts. Such a state lacks the boundaries that only come with *coagulatio*. The initiate experiences a phantasmagoria of sensations and dazzling images; every idea easily gains behavioral expression because there are no separations distinguishing thought from action. Just wishing it makes it so. The god of this world is a nature god who rules by chance and circumstance. This state of consciousness holds such power that some (psychotics) never want or know how to leave it, while others (addicts) are unconsciously trying to return to it. Before *coagulatio* can put in place solid boundaries, *calcinatio* is needed to burn away the primitive desires keeping ego bound to the instinctual, magical realm of the unconscious.

In the *albedo*, we develop a container that adds integrity to the *prima materia*. Thoughts separate from feelings, feelings differentiate from sensations, and intuitions are distinguished from thoughts. These differentiations must take place in order for us to define an identity that is cohesive and distinct from others. As identity consolidates, we develop capacities for sympathy and empathy, both of which form the essential basis for mature love. God in this stage is more benevolent.

Finally, in the last stage of the work, god takes on more global significance. This god embraces everyone and everything. Paradoxically, as the world becomes much larger, the individual becomes smaller. But, as we saw with Paul, smaller does not mean weaker. This smallness achieves an intensity that has powerful effects on the person and everyone in his or her company. This "charge" comes about through a number of operations that work to diminish unhealthy narcissism. At this point, god and Self are in close proximity, but they are never the same.

Another important distinction that should be taken into consideration in practicing alchemy is the difference between the Individuated Self and enlightenment. The concepts of individuation and enlightenment stem from two different but related points of view. Jung gave us the first term to describe the development of the personality throughout a person's lifetime. It is a scientific term based on evidence drawn from a body of research that includes alchemy and behavioral science. Jung anchored individuation in a psychology that describes ego and self in functional terms. "The Self," Jung wrote, "is not only the center, but also the whole circumference which embraces both conscious and unconscious; it is the center of this totality; just as the ego is the center of consciousness."[19]

By contrast, enlightenment comes from religious practices, espe-

> One way to distinguish between the Divine Self and God is to recall that individuation is a process that can precipitate divine and ecstatic experience. By contrast, enlightenment is a condition of being. One then emphasizes doing, the other being. Many alchemists did not draw this distinction but rather equated the philosopher's stone with a divine and gnostic experience of human being.

cially Eastern spiritual beliefs. Whereas Jung placed ego at the center of his individuation process, enlightenment encircles much more of psyche and takes self as its starting point. Using theological terms to explain these different perspectives, Jung quotes Paracelsus, who described "God the Father [as the one who] created man 'from below upwards,' but God the Son 'from above downwards.'"[20] In other words, individuation works from the bottom up while enlightenment works from the top down.

Alchemy attempts to integrate earth-ego consciousness with the heaven-self totality. It works bottom up and top down (ascent of the soul, descent of the spirit). From the ego perspective, we perceive the material aspect of nature and from the self-viewpoint, we apprehend its magnificence. Ego and self are then not enemies, but like the Tao, they represent two critically important perspectives produced by mind in its attempt to leave out nothing. "Nature (god and human consciousness) abhors a vacuum." Like an adventurer, the human mind seeks to establish its home in every corner of the universe.

Even Jung comes close to this gnostic interpretation of the *lapis*. In old age, when asked whether he believed in God, he responded by saying, "I know God." It is indeed only one small step further that leads us back to a *participation mystique,* where the distinctions between human and divine collapse and we can speak of a fully aware state of mind that lives in divine consciousness. In alchemy, the image that best symbolized what Dorn called the *unus mundus* is the *lapis philosophorum*. Again, we come back to Mercurius, adventurer and this time discoverer of a New World.

> The *Individuated Self,* being both process and state, represents a temporary experience of an enlightened condition of conscious development.
>
> The *Divine Self* is the permanent, living manifestation of god expressed within and through the human psyche.

The restless mind is filled with his mercurial spirit. When we consider the god of this metal, we immediately see how the mind operates. Mercurius is as quick to tear down boundaries as he is in erecting them. He is a shape-shifter who transforms mind and matter into whatever it takes to promote growth-producing change. His forms are many. As a vapor, mercury becomes the spirit Mercurius; as a solvent, he fuses, decomposes and transmutes substances; as quicksilver, Mercurius is the water of death and resurrection.

Mercurius is a ubiquitous god who resides in all metals. Change, in other words, is present in all forms of life. Alchemists also observed how this *aqua permanens,* being elusive to touch and sensitive to temperature, aptly represents the various solid and liquid forms (juices and elixirs) of the philosopher's stone.

Does not our mind operate in similar ways? The mind defines and transforms our perceptions and sensations into meaningful forms and shapes. At the same time, the mind is elusive, quick and like most tricksters, perennially hungry. It also has a sense of humor.

Mercurius loves good jokes and playing pranks. For the one who thinks he's achieved some sort of divine status, this trickster can be counted on to hold his feet to the fire. An old saying put it this way: My head fits through the window, but my tail gets stuck. The wily trickster has a tail as wide as a man's shadow, and until he integrates the shadow, he will surely make a fool of himself. No less does the mind squeeze into realities that its lower body might not quite be ready to accommodate.

This brings up another important distinction between individuation and enlightenment. Individuation is subject to the same twists and turns of every other developmental process. Developmental psychologists have shown that development is a diverse process where different systems advance at different rates. Life is like a river whose tributaries follow different currents in hopes of finding again a common source. In the same way, consciousness advances quickly here, slowly there, running up against rocks and stumps, causing as many problems as solutions. "For each stage of development," writes Wilber in *The Theory of Everything,* "brings not only new capacities but the possibility of new disasters; not just novel potentials but novel pathologies; new strengths, new diseases."[21]

While individuation creates all sorts of difficulties, enlightenment is the absence of problems. In alchemical psychology, every advance is met with a new problem. Fortunately, as consciousness progresses, the level of its pathology becomes divine madness, the diseases of which we use to further illuminate the soul.

And what might these new diseases be? With the magic of technology, we run a serious risk of forgetting the old recipes that went into the making of a foundational consciousness on which the modern world rests. Spirit without soul is meaningless, vacant and empty. The Royal Marriage brings spirit and soul to the altar. Here's an example of what I mean. In the Fiji Islands, nearly everyone has a cell phone, and yet, they have not lost touch with their traditions. Mercurius, in this case, facilitates the celebration, the dance and the sacred rituals by getting the message out faster than word of mouth. He knows his place as long as we know ours. Perhaps the so-called third world refuses to die because without its daily reminders (awful though they sometimes may be), we in the so-called first world might well forget where our soul finds itself most alive.

In many of his books, Wilber described another symptom that illustrates the tendency consciousness has of regressing in upon itself. He calls this problem the "pre/trans fallacy." This fallacy happens when people mistake the magical qualities of the *nigredo* for the truly supernatural properties of the philosopher's stone. While the two may seem very much alike, there's a dimension separating them that is as wide as the Grand Canyon. In the first place, magical thinking is mediated by the unconscious, and its functions are passive, nonproductive. By comparison, supernatural powers function under the sway of a conscious self. These powers can be put to good use and they are seldom used for individual good. Mistaking the one for the other produces fool's gold.

A third symptom comes from a failure to adequately sublimate the work to a symbolic, spiritual level. If we take the goals of alchemy on a literal level, we achieve no more than what any flat dimension can offer. At these times, the Zen master takes his stick to the initiate in an attempt to shake the lead out of him. Do not mistake the pointing finger for the moon. Without vision and insight, no one is great! Physical immortality without spiritual understanding is eternal damnation. "Eternity," Wilber writes, "does not mean living forever in time—a rather horrible notion—but living in the *timeless* moment, prior to time and its turmoils altogether. Likewise, infinity does not mean a really big space, it means completely *spaceless*."[22] In other words, in our haste to achieve heaven, gold or the philosopher's stone, we run the risk of chasing after empty dreams. The alchemical gold can only be produced in the mind, while its evidence is found in behavior and experience.

These three symptoms do not begin to cover all the possible "new diseases" to which Ken Wilber refers. In your personal alchemy, you will undoubtedly discover others that must be addressed. Each new mistake opens up a mystery that leads to a grander view of alchemy and the extraordinary world it holds for us. If we talk of disease, then what is the source of our illness? Rather than remedies that come *after* the fact, how can we start off on the right foot? What are things that go into generating higher levels of Self?

Some answers to these questions come out of the latest brain-mind research. The most exciting work in alchemy is actually being done today in developmental research, consciousness studies and many other related disciplines. It appears that the parallel lines between body and mind are coming to a focus in ways that defy reason, but nonetheless prove that truly miraculous breakthroughs in modern-day alchemy are happening.

GOD'S RECIPE

I believe that wisdom comes from a communion between minds, human and divine. The recipes we've studied are fragments of wisdom, each reflecting some truth of what it means to become a whole, individuated person. It is our job to put the pieces together and read "god's recipe" as it is inscribed in nature and known in the depths of our being.

Alchemists struggled just as hard to get the elements of mind to separate and unite as they did working with chemicals. They knew all too well how the dark side of the masculine—the impulse to dominate, impatience, demanding results—put them further from their goal. The feminine shadow fared no better: all process and no results lead nowhere. As if getting the *Solar* King and the *Lunar* Queen to meet, mate and marry weren't difficult enough, the Royal Marriage could not be consecrated without the intervention of some spirit or god. For many alchemists this god was Mercurius, the divine spirit who connects all spheres of existence. Enticing this wily god to preside over the work required prayer and good luck.

After a lifetime of hard work, alchemists hermetically sealed their vessel with wax. They stamped it with the symbol of Mercurius, a figure that signified the conjunction of *sol* and *luna*

Alchemists taught the subtleties of the Art. The work involved was a process of endless refinement. Like them, we should do the best we can reasonably expect of ourselves, remain steadfast in our purpose, stay true to our intention and, most importantly, create a sacred space that invites nonhuman, transpersonal energies to consummate the work. When we embrace this attitude, the Kosmos and all that it holds—elements and elementals, gods above and spirits below—conspire to help us.

One indication that we are on the right track is an inevitable increase of synchronistic events, mystical manifestations, lucid dreams, and even miracles in our lives. These are only signs. Don't stop there!

in human form. Next they offered a prayer to Mercurius in hopes that he and all attendant gods might bless the alchemist, transmuting him or her into a "living philosophical stone."

The final act is then a prayer of your own making. Here is one from Black Elk's vision: [23]

> *With visible face I am appearing.*
> *In a sacred manner I appear.*
> *For the greening earth a pleasantness I make.*
> *The center of the nation's hoop*
> *I have made pleasant.*
> *With visible face, behold me!*
> *The four-leggeds and two-leggeds,*
> *I have made them to walk;*
> *The wings of the air,*
> *I have made them to fly.*
> *With visible face I appear.*
> *My day, I have made it holy.*

Chapter 10

The Heart of the Matter

God turns you from one feeling to another
And teaches you by means of opposites
So that you will have two wings to fly,
Not one.
RUMI

I began this book by proposing that alchemy is much more than a procedure for changing lead into gold. While it may be true that alchemy is a dead science, it is alive in the soul and its study—psychology. Alchemy is an eternal metaphor that lives on in the passions and dreams of the soul. But, where can soul be found?

Over the centuries, the soul has found residence in many parts of the body. Descartes located it in the pineal gland within the center of the brain. In his book *Anam Cara*, Celtic scholar O'Donohue tells us that soul is not within us, but rather that we are completely enshrouded by soul. I think the soul is in all matter and that it becomes a deeply felt experience within the human heart.

The heart is more than the organ that keeps us alive. It is a dynamic concept that embraces our whole existence. In this chapter, we look at some of the feelings that obstruct the full release of alchemy's ambrosia. Doubt and fear are two formidable impediments to the heart's release. When we investigate doubt we come to see that it is less an impediment than a potential source for transformation. To this I add some cautions and clarifications to ensure success in future alchemical endeavors. We then take up a less obvious problem: how even methods sometimes get in the way of individuation. Finally, we end with a paradox that captures what alchemy is really all about: at the center of the heart is a consciousness that knows no distinctions between inner and outer, above and below. At the heart of the matter, alchemy is about coming to the realization that we already possess the philosopher's stone and its name is love.

DOUBT AND DESIRE

Fear lies at the very heart of much of ego's driving force. As much as it may disguise, delude and deceive itself, fear is what drives the ego toward narcissism (control), arrogance (compensation) and defense. A line from the Bible helps us understand the necessity for this dreadful feeling. "Fear of the Lord is the beginning of wisdom." Without fear we are not awakened to the awesome realities of omnipotence, much less equipped to acquire such power. Unless we humble ourselves, or be humbled by fear, we cannot envision something greater than we are. Fear signifies a tremendous transition in consciousness between a mind lacking self-awareness to one beginning the long journey of increased self-consciousness. Often, when we recognize the vastness of consciousness, we act to deny the awareness in every possible way.

Doubt is a symptom of this problem as well as the first sign of its solution. In order to doubt something, we must first sufficiently develop a sense of self that can recognize fear when we are threatened. At the most primitive level of consciousness, fear takes on ominous appearances. Goblins, demons and bogeymen are evil spirits that haunt people day and night. They each have a name and work their evil deeds in any number of demonic ways. Doubt and denial only result in empowering them further. Magic used to be the scientific method for dispelling evil demons in the Old World. Nowadays, our more sophisticated society does not believe in ghosts and goblins and turns to science in lieu of magic. It is interesting how doubt, in the new age, has been turned inside out and at least on the surface, given the appearance of something useful.

> To the extent that we deny fear, and banish all imagining where it might safely reside, we externally fear in both seemingly good ways (science as defense and control) and bad ones (terrorists as enemies in resistance to law and order).

For Descartes, father of dualism, doubt turns out to be the one thing that can most reliably prove existence. Because I can recognize not only fear, but also other feelings and thoughts, I must therefore possess a conscious mind capable of such perception. Or, as he said it, "I think therefore I am." Descartes refashioned doubt into the basis of proving we are conscious beings. So successful was this argument that doubt became the basis of modern scientific inquiry. Only by repeated proofs will doubt give way to a predictable occurrence. If something happens nine out of ten times then we might conclude that the result is proven to be real. At the same time, doubt forms the basis of control. If I play the odds right, I will be in control. Notice the shift we've made from heart to head. Fears exist in the body and the realm of feeling, but prediction and control are products of the intellect. With this shift, goblins of old change their appearance and manifest in the New World as psychological symptoms.

Fear of the unknown causes doubt and control to come into existence. Too much doubt leaves one plagued with anxiety, too little invites gullibility, passivity and magical thinking. It is the same whether our need to control is excessively great or not adequate enough. Just as we can become frozen with fear, we can be devoured by doubt. Too much or too little of either disables the ego. Neither extreme promotes individuation.

Alchemical practice involves respect for unknown things and especially requires learning to use the imagination in working with unseen phenomena. At the same time, it also seeks to establish a healthy middle position in all our thoughts and emotions. Alchemical psychology attempts to blend the best of magic and science. It seeks to bring the leaden qualities of fear and doubt to a place where they can be subjected to the transformative powers of mind.

Ambivalence represents the alchemical middle ground between doubt and certainty. With ambivalence there is the recognition on a feeling level (usually anxiety) that there might be something real about my unseen fears. The mind weighs its options, "Should I go with this unproven option or not?" Now, it is not a simple matter of whether the choice is a simple yes or good or bad. I have to decide which way to go. This forces me to recognize that no choice is perfect or without risks. There is some error attached to all possibilities. As consciousness matures, we realize that the only thing that really makes choice right is the fact that I made the choice at all. By cutting through the fear of making a mistake, I have asserted myself and whether I suffer the consequence or enjoy the benefit, at least I know I have the power to decide— a sure sign that ego is beginning to trust itself and its Self.

> When we are in harmony with the Self, we act in complete accordance with the ways of nature. "The man emptied of all thoughts, all emotions originating from fear, all sense of insecurity, all desire to win, is not conscious of using the sword; both man and sword turn into instruments in the hands, as it were, of the unconscious, and it is this unconscious that achieves wonders of creativity."[1] In Zen practice, this is the "everyday mind" (*heijo-shin*).

With courage and some humor, doubt eventually gives way to revelation. This transition requires dissolving the things that obstruct the flow of life. Then it is possible to open the heart and mind to creative possibility. The spirit I have found most helpful in this process is the trickster. I have found that when I am willing to be a fool, trickster appears ready to engage me in my process. He spurs me on to greater adventures into the unknown, not just as a playful frolic but also with divine purpose and guidance.

When doubt and fear hold me back, I also turn to dreams. They invariably come to my aid. While writing this book, I had a dream that symbolically illustrates many of these developments.

I dreamt that I was giving a party. Despite the fact that I was expecting a special woman, I was dressed in dirty rags. My face and hands were covered in dirt and plaster. I was extremely delighted when the beautiful woman arrived. In fact, I was "smitten" by her good looks. Perhaps because of my attire I hesitated to approach her. But, by the time some of the guests began to leave, I realized I was missing my chance. I cleaned up and put on some fresh clothes. As she was getting ready to leave, some of the guests asked if she would play her guitar. She was obviously shy, but nevertheless agreed to play one song. It was wonderful. I didn't want her to go, and so I asked if she would play another. To ease her shyness I offered to stand in front of her if she would play just one more song. She agreed. As the melody of her song captured my heart I spontaneously began to sing the words, "I'm imperiled, imperiled by your beauty." These were the only lyrics and as I repeated them many times, they took on the sound of a sacred chant. Before I knew it, there were thousands of people in an audience in front of me, chanting along, "I'm imperiled, imperiled by your beauty . . ."

This dream has a number of important alchemical elements. To my mind, the woman is Mother Nature, *Anima Mundi*. I am infatuated with her mysterious beauty. In the beginning of the dream, my ego consciousness is mired in soot (shadow) and plaster (white ash). I have to clean up my other garments (persona) in order to be fully in her presence. Only then will she play her music. She gives two songs, one unaccompanied, the second accompanied by me. Her need for mystery (shyness) is revealed to me, and if I do not honor it (standing in front of her) she will leave. Then, in harmony with her, I express both pain and joy (the opposites) of being in her presence. I'm afraid and yet long to become one with her. The feeling is too precious to be experienced alone, and so the dream invites the whole world to join in the celebration.

This revelatory dream has done much to change me. I, the perennial "doubting Thomas," need dreams like this one to reveal truths greater than my ego can ever hope to receive.

In addition to doubt and fear, another emotional symptom that gets in the way of transformation is desire. Along with fear, desire captivates the ego's interests and drives it toward endless ambition, activity and aspiration. A good practice in dealing with these excesses is to separate what we need from what we want. When needs disguise themselves as wants, we act as if we could not live without them. Needs serve our survival and ignoring them means physical death. On the other hand, we can do without many wants. My life does not depend on my long list of wants. This list therefore carries the potential to create meaning. Needs, on the other hand, do not have this quality. They are heavy like lead; demanding appetites that must be fed. They require little of me. On the other hand, we can choose the things we want, and even sacrifice them. "I do this for him out of love." Whereas needs are regressive, wants lead us in the direction of the Self.

In the end, the *only* worthwhile desire that allows ever-greater degrees of individuation is the desire for god. When I set my mind solely on the divine, all lesser desires go up in flames. Dedicating myself to the service of god means that I recognize the divinity that exists in all things.

When we feel passion about something our heart tends to soar away. Alchemy is my passion and to prevent any inflated thought that might have slipped in, I offer the following clarifications as cautionary measures against getting carried away.

USE ONLY AS DIRECTED

1. Nature is not god. It is only one expression of the transpersonal.

2. God, as used in this book, is a nonreligious term. It represents a psychological expression of divine experience.

3. Alchemical psychology primarily aims at integration, not transcendence. However, an integrated self can more readily precipitate a conscious transcendent experience.

4. Gold and the philosopher's stone are terms used in this book to denote highly refined and fully integrated psychological states of consciousness, not physical objects.

5. Spiritual development does not necessarily follow along the same lines as psychological development (individuation). From the ego's point of view, spirit is defined in materialistic, linear, reductionistic terms. Thus, ego equates with the concrete nature of matter. Spirit, as a transpersonal concept, begins to come into

proper view at the level of the Individuated Self. Spirit is autonomous, ubiquitous, constant, persistent and clear.

ALCHEMICAL
PRACTICE

Some researchers stress the importance of practice in the course of developing consciousness. Most notably, consciousness researcher Ken Wilber suggests a wide variety of practices that go a long way in achieving wholeness, or what he calls the Integral mind. Given the many exercises I have suggested throughout this book, it should come as no surprise that I too think practice (doing) is everywhere as important as being. I certainly think that the disciplines that Wilber and others recommend are excellent practices. In addition to Wilber's list, I think the exercises in Andrew Harvey's book *The Direct Path,* and Roger Walsh's *Essential Spirituality* are good sources from which to draw.

> The Five Hearts—Geisha House Motto
> 1. A gentle and obedient heart—to have the heart to say "Yes"
> 2. An apologetic heart—to say "I'm sorry," and admit and reflect on mistakes
> 3. A modest heart—to give credit to others for any accomplishments
> 4. A volunteer heart—to say "I will do it" without thought of benefit
> 5. An appreciative heart—to say "Thank you."

Alchemy, being the first laboratory science, certainly placed a great deal of emphasis on doing. Perhaps less known were the psychological practices, including prayer, meditation, focused attention and lucid dreaming, that were part of their work. I also support these practices. Where I differ slightly from modern alchemists like Wilber is in seeing the downside to practice. All too often we forget that practice, technique and exercise are activities that appeal to the ego. They give ego something (hopefully worthwhile) to do. My concern is that the attention given to daily practices not captivate the ego to such an extent that the real purpose of these activities is forgotten. Excellence in practice may have nothing to do with changing the heart's disposition toward others. Ironically, if there were indeed a breakthrough in consciousness, there would be no need for practice. As the husband of my minister once said to his wife, "If you were so successful this church would be empty!"

Let me be clear that I am not opposed to practice. Alchemy, as I have said many times throughout this book, is about doing. When we use practice as a means to an end, and not as an end to itself, then the real gold is a state and process of being and doing—in a word, becoming. We must not let practice mislead, deceive or detract us from the goal of establishing individuated consciousness. Practice adds a sense of joy to the journey, but it is never the sole destination.

Make no mistake that yoga and meditation are noble practices and they too have their place in refining consciousness, but unless the "mind *be* in harmony with the work," not much will come of the endless hours spent doing deep breathing and meditating. Doing these without the right intention will do little to achieve their higher goals. Mind, body and soul must always be in sympathy for these techniques to do their magic. Another concern I have is the appeal Eastern practice has for Westerners and vice versa.[2] Curiosity, novelty and experimentation do not go very far in fusing the best that each hemisphere has to offer to individuating world consciousness.

> Intense practice gives one a moment of liberation, one taste, but the real joy comes when life itself becomes a practice and we feast for all the days of our lives.

Finally, I have had a number of patients in psychotherapy suffering from illnesses that cannot be medically defined. Rather, the cause of these patients' problems is what psychiatrist Stanislav Grof calls "spiritual emergency." He and his colleagues describe serious psychological disturbances caused by a "crisis of the evolution of consciousness."[3] These crises can be precipitated by all kinds of extreme life situations, such as "disease, accident, or operation," as well as "various forms of meditation and spiritual practice." He reports having been "contacted by persons whose unusual experiences occurred during the pursuit of Zen, *Vipassana* Buddhist meditation, *Kundalini* yoga, Sufi exercises or Christian prayer and monastic contemplation."[4]

I suggest that Self, not ego, be at the center of all practice. In our haste to excel at practice we sometimes overlook this obvious fact. Rather than strict reliance on ego-driven exercises, we might instead look to the resources of the Self. When we see through the single eye of Self, even for moments at a time, life comes into sharp focus and priorities naturally fall into place. A practice based on Self is easier and often more powerful than those with greater complexity and requiring hard work. What I have in mind is so ridiculously simple that I have hesitated to mention it until now, as we are drawing close to the end of this book.

> Practice, yes, but do it with guidance and with the right attitude. Keep two eyes on ego, and the third on Self.

Here is the secret: *simply live life with an open heart, then living life consciously becomes the best practice of all.*

Living with an open heart is an alchemical practice that is expedient, economical and elegant.

WHAT THE HEART KNOWS

We have spent a great deal of time discussing abstract concepts like ego and self in order to understand the nature of psyche and human consciousness. Helpful as these concepts are, they are not a substitute for the wisdom contained in the central organ of life: the heart. It is the place from which all life—physical, psychic and spiritual—emanates, transforms and connects us with other dimensions.

Science has shown us that the heart, the first fully functioning organ in the body, is the "Seed of Existence." It pumps 15 million gallons of blood and beats 2.5 billion times over the course of an average person's lifetime. There are many experiments showing physical evidence that the heart is also the seat of emotional consciousness, the true "House of God," having very real, physical effects on people and the world. While these facts are interesting they are not new. Virtually every religion and spiritual practice knows the significance that heart has to the well-being of body, mind, soul, spirit and Kosmos.[5]

Wise alchemists also understood that no transmutation of metallic and spiritual bodies is possible without a pure heart. They embraced the

---

Do nothing. Open up, swallow, digest. The alchemical experience is no different from other experiences we have and know enough NOT to question. Questioning breaks its spell. Remember: "Life is a spell so exquisite that everything conspires to break it." When Spirit moves us, we simply take in the experience wholeheartedly. Some things should not be questioned, at least not initially. It's a wonderful time just after lovemaking to be quiet. Or, having seen a brilliant sunset allow memory to take shape from the image, not the words.

Once, while in Big Sur, I found myself high atop a mountain in a place called Las Ventanas (the windows). I saw one of the most glorious sunsets I'd ever seen. Just after the sun sank below the horizon my hands started clapping involuntarily. The gesture was odd, humorous, but not insincere. It was infectious and people around me began clapping too. Not a word was mentioned as we applauded this wonderful experience. This silent moment was an alchemical experience that required no words.

heart's innocence as well as its enigmatic language in their work. Unlike science, the heart has no problem with contradictions that exist only in the province of mind. The heart's language has no problem with riddles and paradox. Putting alchemy into daily practice means that the heart knows that doing and not doing are not at odds with each other. The heart makes no distinction between the practice and the one doing the practice; they are one.

Love is not required to do anything. A heart filled with love automatically dissolves every barrier separating the world. There is no effort involved. In this fulfillment, we meet the beloved as embodied in everyone and everything. When we acquire the wisdom of the philosopher's stone we know this truth is real.

CONCLUSION

While all the operations I have described in this book are powerful methods, not one of them will do much good if we get caught up in doing and never arrive at being fully alive in the ever-present moment. To be sure, the future exists in the moment, and each breath makes it real. Breath opens our heart to the fullness of life. The heart's joys enable us to celebrate existence. Its despair brings shadow to light. Its wounds allow us to discover the gift of healing. Again, Rumi captures the essence of an open heart and its kinship with self and spirit in a lovely poem, "Only Breath."[6]

> *Not Christian or Jew or Muslim, not Hindu,*
> *Buddhist, sufi, or zen. Not any religion*
>
> *or cultural system. I am not from the East*
> *or the West, not out of the ocean or up*
>
> *from the ground, not natural or ethereal, not*
> *composed of elements at all. I do not exist,*
>
> *am not an entity in this world or the next,*
> *did not descend from Adam and Eve or any*
>
> *origin story. My place is placeless, a trace*
> *of the traceless. Neither body or soul.*
>
> *I belong to the beloved, have seen the two*
> *worlds as one and that one call to and know,*

first, last, outer, inner, only that
breath breathing human being

There is a way between voice and presence
where information flows.

In disciplined silence it opens.
With wandering talk it closes.

In conscious silence, without words to disturb the peace or even well-intentioned practice, there the extraordinary may happen.

The heart of the matter is that opposites *only* exist in a newly awakened mind. As Rumi said, God provides us with two wings so that we might learn to fly. But, having penetrated the depths of soul and soared to the heights of spirit, having married the opposites and embraced ourselves wholly, we enter an entirely new dimension of being. There the angels wait to spirit us away to a golden consciousness where we once again take our place beyond the stars.

NOTES ON THE IMAGES AND RECIPES

Text Notes and References

The Emerald Tablet

Tabula Smaragdina Hermetis

The woodcuts displayed in this book are examples of alchemical master-pieces. There are three ways art can be classified, each according to how the image impacts our eyes. Wilber speaks of these perspectives as "the eye of flesh . . . the eye of mind . . . [and] the eye of spirit."[1] Alchemical art impacts us in all three ways. Their designs are like puzzles for the mind. They get us thinking and trying to put odd pieces together. There is a latent spirituality about them that doesn't jump out at you like most religious art works. Even where sex and violence are part of the image we are forced to accept that this too is an important aspect of spirit. Like the beautiful mandalas and *yantras* of Buddhist art, these alchemical pictures move the mind toward a spiritual dimension. The images become icons that change us at the physical level. By meditating on them long enough you begin to feel the artist reaching into your mind, sharing ancient secrets and inviting you into his brotherhood.

IMAGE FOR
CHAPTER 1,
PAGE 15

De Chemis Strasburg, Zadith Senior, 1566.

This picture shows Hermes holding open a book of wisdom. His posture is not unlike the one we often see in Christian renderings of the Virgin Mary and Jesus. The pages depict an ouroboric creature on the left and the sun on the right. They suggest the eternal essence from which alchemy derives its power.

IMAGE FOR
CHAPTER 2,
PAGE 37

Utriusque cosmi, II, tractatus primus, M. Merian

According to Fabricius this picture "shows the alchemist-as-astrologer seated at his celestial globe and pointing to the Fishes. In this sign, the old philosopher beholds the splendor of the last *coniunctio solis et lunae* bursting to illuminate the heavens at the end of his opus."[2] As with many alchemical plates we see both moon and sun in the heavens. In this image, they are divided by a column that frames each of them. The dynamics of the work are circular. It begins with the adept sitting on the right who points to the astrologer on the left. He in turn points upward to the moon. The eye then continues its course clockwise, caught by the large sun on the extreme right. The three orbs, moon, sun and globe not only secure this movement but also intimate a earth-spirit connection between them.

Emblem XXVII from *Atalanta fugiens,* Michael Maier, Oppenheim, 1618

IMAGE FOR CHAPTER 3, PAGE 63

Maier was the personal physician to Rudolf II as well as being a celebrated alchemist. He was instrumental in the Rosicrucian movement and authored many significant alchemical books. Many of the images used in the present work are drawn from his most important work, *Atalanta Fugiens* (Escaping Atalanta).

In this picture, the young adept is confronted with a bolted door with three locks, suggesting that there are secrets that must be unlocked within each of the three stages of the work. The spires atop the door show the three different fires to be used. Beyond the gate is a beautiful garden with a special tree in its center. This garden is a mandala and the lone tree at its center contains the green rose. This rose is plucked by the wise man without being pricked but false alchemists "have nothing but pain from it." Notice also how the adept's feet are sunk into the earth. Maier goes on to say, "Whosoever wishes to enter the Philosophical Rose-Garden without the key is like a man who wishes to walk without feet." Yet, this intrepid young man has left his party, which consists of five men and four women (seen in the upper righthand corner), to enter the mysteries. He, being the tenth, represents the summation of all that is possible, a good sign for someone who is preparing to undertake the Great Work.

Hand der Philosophen, J. Isaak Hollandus, 1667

IMAGE FOR CHAPTER 4, PAGE 79

Here we see Saturn holding a sword in one hand and an orb in the other. He is standing naked in a large metal vessel. There are many important meanings in this picture. To begin with, we are reminded that all transmutation requires changing oneself. As Dorn said, "Thou wilt never make the One which thou seekest, except first there be made one thing of thyself"[3] Before any transmutation of substances can occur, the alchemist must first transform himself. In this alembic the alchemist, appearing as Saturn, undergoes the process of self-transformation. His sword is not the sword of reason but of *mens,* a power that transcends Mercury's rationality and even *Sol's* spirituality. This is the sword of transformation that "turns something infinitesimally small into the infinitely great."[4] By cutting the cord that binds us to ordinary life, we literally have the whole world in our hands. The crowned orb symbolizes power and authority.

IMAGE FOR CHAPTER 5, PAGE 103

Auslegun von 30 magischen Figuren, Paracelsus

This remarkable picture shows a salamander with wings and a magical cap. His body appears muscular, like that of a lion, with a tail of a dragon's head. The dragon has a sword in its jaws. This picture is different from others in that the salamander seems to be pouncing on the flames, displaying its triumph over fire. This theme is enhanced by the suggestive elements of the dragon and the sword. The former symbolizes attachment to the mother that must be overcome in order to establish an independent spirit. The sword then is grasped by the dragon to be used to vanquish any obstacle that stands in the way of finding wholeness. Its placement in the tail suggests that this development has been reached and now must be elevated by *sublimatio* to a subtler dimension.

The picture is taken from Manly P. Hall's *The Secret Teachings of All Ages.* Under the picture he adds, "The Greeks, following the example of earlier nations, deified the fire spirits and in their honor kept incense and altar fires burning perpetually."[5]

IMAGE FOR CHAPTER 6, PAGE 133

Viridarium chymicum, D. Stolcius von Stolcenberg, Frankfurt, 1624

This image shows the *sol niger,* that terrifying moment when *sol* and *luna* coincide for the first time at the end of the *nigredo.* At this point, the heroic ego has been stripped of its former "sceptre and apple," which are replaced with the black crow. In other words, the ego confronts its shadow and the process of removing all outer elements of the persona begins in earnest.

Putrefaction is the process that causes this critically important action to occur. The heroic ego, stripped to the bone, is surrounded by two angels, one on the right touching the skeleton's left finger, a gesture reminiscent of Michelangelo's *Creation of Adam* in the main fresco in the Sistine Chapel. Both signify the giving of new life from a divine power. But this image goes further. It makes the point that consciousness begins only when we relinquish all desires and appetites of the body. We must die first in order to be born anew.

Emblem XVIII from *Atalanta fugiens,* Michael Maier, Oppenheim, 1618

IMAGE FOR CHAPTER 7, PAGE 155

In this image we see the alchemist making coins from a golden rod. The woodcut illustrates the recipe "It takes gold to make gold." This picture also shows the operation of *multiplicatio* that enables the adept to produce innumerable amounts of gold from a substance that possesses the power of the philosopher's stone.

Intergrum Morborum Mysterium: Sive Medicinae Catholicae, Robert Fludd

IMAGE FOR CHAPTER 8, PAGE 191

Robert Fludd was a physician, philosopher and alchemist. He studied at Oxford and was a staunch follower of Paracelsus. In this picture, taken from one of his books, we see his teacher, Paracelsus, the famous Swiss physician and alchemist. Here, Paracelsus is shown uncapping some unknown substance (azoth?) surrounded by numbered squares within which are texts drawn from Kabbabla.

Although Paracelsus was believed to have transmuted metals, his chief aim was concocting healing elixirs. Contrary to traditional alchemical theory, Paracelsus believed that disease did not result from an imbalance of the four humors. Instead, he thought that there were bad "seeds" that attack the body's vital organs. Only by concoction and intense understanding of the patient's misalignment with God is the "Great Physician" able to restore health. His reliance on alchemically produced *arcana* (chemical medicines) set the stage for modern pharmacological treatment of disease.

Cababa, S. Michelspacher, Augsburg, 1616

IMAGE FOR THE FIRST RECIPE, PAGE 197

This work by Michelspacher is a masterpiece that incorporates an enormous amount of symbolism, including alchemical, astrological and Kabbalistic principles. The male figures in the bottom foreground illus-

trate the different approaches taken to the work of alchemy. The left figure symbolizes an experimental approach and the right an intuitive,
spiritual approach. The figures on the mountain steps show the seven
gods who represent the seven metals, with mercury standing at the apex.
Beyond them is a ring of astrological images indicating that the work begins in May in the sign of Taurus. Spring is the time of new beginnings.
And in each corner are named each of the four elements. Directly at the
center we see a magical room, above which are the symbols for *Sol* and
Luna, and above that the crowned Mercury bird. The room is a bridal
chamber where the king and queen prepare to be joined in holy matri-
mony; the Royal Marriage of opposites.

IMAGE FOR
THE SECOND RECIPE,
PAGE 204

Atalanta fugiens, Michael Maier, Oppenheim, 1618

The heroic ego, in the form of the royal king, submits to the feminine
waters of the unconscious *solutio,* which will purify and dissolve all
traces of leaden matter. This picture is remarkable for at least two reasons. First, it graphically illustrates a chemical process using an actual
human figure instead of a physical substance. In other words, solid matter cannot dissolve until the psychic material has submitted to the acid
bath of the Mercurial waters. Secondly, the king, even in this act of dissolution, retains his crown. "One should be careful," writes Maier, "that
he does not lose his crown, for with its stones one could heal illnesses."[6]
The radiant crown says Jung "is the symbol par excellence of reaching
the highest goal in evolution: for he who conquers himself wins the
crown of eternal life."[7]

IMAGE FOR
THE THIRD RECIPE,
PAGE 214

Amphitheatrum sapienhtiae aeternae, Heinrich Khunrath, 1602

In addition to the numerous alchemical symbols contained in this picture, we can also appreciate the dramatic use of perspective. Previously,
most works of art lacked this method of creating the illusion of a third
dimension on a flat surface. We can see how consciousness was developing as much in art as it was in Galileo's new concept of a heliocentric universe. As space was being redefined cosmologically, so too was it being
rendered in a bold relief in all forms of art.

The various details in this picture indicate that the alchemical work requires experience and reason, prayer and experiment. This is emphasized by the dramatic symmetry of the image with the left depicting the oratory and the right, the alchemist's laboratory. The oven in the foreground is inscribed with the call for patience: "Hasten slowly."

In addition to the inscription above the doorway, which reads, "While sleeping, watch!," there are two other noteworthy recipes. Above the tabernacle before which the alchemist kneels and prays other messages read, "Happy the one who follows the advice of the Lord," "Do not speak of God without enlightenment" and "When we attend strictly to our work God himself will help us."

Viridarium chymicum, D. Stolcius von Stolcenber, Frankfurt, 1624

IMAGE FOR
THE FOURTH RECIPE,
PAGE 224

Alexander Roob describes the main elements of this picture in these words, "When lion/sun and serpent/moon are fully united, the *lapis* is complete. But so that it may have the power to increase, and Mercury can bear fruits, it must be heated and fermented in a melding-pot with three parts purified gold."[8] *Sol* and *Luna* are boxed in a window frame just above the alchemist and his furnace. In the lower righthand part of the image there is a lion devouring a snake or serpent. The lion often represents gold and the snake transformation. In order for gold to "bear fruits," that is, multiply itself, there must be a transformation of the metal to the philosopher's stone. Then it possesses the ability, *multiplactio,* to regenerate itself infinitely. I choose this particular image to represent this recipe because of the intensity in the alchemist's gaze at the fire. His gesture connects the lion image with the source of its transformation through and by him.

Atalanta fugiens, Michael Maier, Oppenheim, 1618

IMAGE FOR
THE FIFTH RECIPE,
PAGE 232

To fully appreciate this picture, we should recall some of the critical events that took place during this period. In the early 1600s, the authority of the Catholic Church was threatened by the Reformation movement. Giordano Bruno was burned at the stake for his beliefs in an infinite universe filled with planets and stars in constant movement. His death may have contributed to Galileo's retraction of his own belief that the sun, not the earth, was the true center of the cosmos; a doctrine diametrically opposite to the one held by the Catholic Church where God and Church coincide.

In this picture we then see the earth directly placed in the center of the image, with the sun much smaller in the extreme upper left corner. Aesthetically, as with many alchemical drawings, the design is in the shape of a mandala; all the elements are connected by a ring of celestial stars well contained within the square of the picture. We should also recall that Sulfur (*Sol*) and Mercurius (*Luna*) are also known as "the sun and its shadow." The shadow, cast by the earth, does not cover the moon. Without a lunar eclipse, *sol* and *luna* maintain their influence on earth; emphasis is given to *sol* in the many rays that emanate from it.

IMAGE FOR THE SIXTH RECIPE, PAGE 241

Atalanta fugiens, **Michael Maier, Oppenheim, 1618**

In explaining the meaning of this picture, Frabricius quotes Senior:

> The foliate water, which is the gold of the philosophers, Lord Hermes called the egg with many names. The lower world is the body and the burnt ashes, to which they reduce the venerable soul. And the burnt ashes and the soul are the gold of the sages which they sow in their white earth, and in the earth scattered with stars, foliate, blessed and thirsting, which he called the earth of leaves and the earth of silver and the earth of gold . . . [Wherefore] Hermes said: Sow the gold in the white foliated earth. For the white foliated earth is the crown of victory, which is ashes extracted from ashes."[9]

IMAGE FOR THE SEVENTH RECIPE, PAGE 248

Summum Bonum, **Robert Fludd, Frankfurt, 1629**

The rose is a very old symbol of the Christ-Lapis, used especially by the Rosicrucians. In this picture, we see the image of the cross fashioned from the stem of a branch. The Latin words *Dat Rosa Mel Apibus* above the rose mean "the Rose gives honey to the bees." Roob quotes Goethe, from *Die Geheimnisse,* in describing the symbolic significance of this image.

> *The cross stands wound densely round with roses.*
> *Who has put roses on the cross?*

And from the middle springs a holy life
Of threefold rays from a single point.[10]

In *The Encyclopedia of Secret Knowledge,* Charles Walker elaborates this mystical meaning of the rosy-cross. "The bees," he writes, "are taking nourishment from the rosy-cross, which symbolizes a renewed Christ impulse: the rose is Christ growing upon the painful, spiny cross."[11] He also points out the seven petals surrounded by bees, which he says represent human souls.

Besondere Chymische Schriften, Baro Urbigerus, Hamburg, 1705

Again we find a globe being held in an outstretched hand, this time by Mercurius, so named in Latin, *Filius Noster,* Our Son. Above the mercurial waters are *Sol* and *Luna.* The picture essentially shows Mercurius as both the medium in which the masculine Sulfur and the feminine Salt are conjoined and Mercurius as the product of their union. The caduceus represents the union of these opposites.

IMAGE FOR
THE EIGHTH RECIPE,
PAGE 260

Atalanta fugiens, Michael Maier, Oppenheim, 1618

In this picture, we see two identical images of Mercury with an alchemist in between them holding a lit torch before his furnace. The image expresses the principle of "like cures like" and the significance of fire as the means of unifying ego and self, consciousness and unconscious, or, in other words, the opposites. There are many kinds of fire and mercury. For example, it is the mercury of water that produces matter and the mercury of sulfur that produces form. There are also different types of fire. Through inner heat, a *calcinatio* unifies psychic opposites by heating up the *prima materia* and causing it to shed its shadowy elements, desires and unwanted emotions. In a similar way, external heat causes metals of different natures to "meet and marry" in order to make new alloys.

The idea of inner heat is not just a psychological notion. In her book *Magic and Mystery in Tibet,* Alexandra David-Neel describes a method called *tumo,* used by some yogis for producing inner heat. Some are so proficient at this art that they can live unclothed year-round in the frigid

IMAGE FOR
THE NINTH RECIPE,
PAGE 270

climate of the Himalayan Mountains. By contrast, fire can go out of control, both with humans and in nature. For example, there are many bizarre reports of people dying of spontaneous combustion. And in nature, we regularly observe forest fires claiming hundreds of acres of land. Interestingly, one method of combating these infernos involves fighting fire with fire. By intentionally setting fires in strategic locations, a backdraft forms that literally consumes or steals the energy feeding the blaze. Perhaps, in some psychologically equivalent way, fakirs who've mastered the art of walking on beds of burning coals use a similar technique. Such are the many dimensions of Mercury's fire.

IMAGE FOR
THE TENTH RECIPE,
PAGE 279

Practicing Alchemist (so called Faust), etching by Rembrandt

In addition to the woodcuts produced by alchemists, fine artists captured the various aspects of the Royal Art in etchings and colorful paintings.

Some well-known paintings include *Distillatio* by Jan van der Straet (late sixteenth century); *The Alchemists* by Adran van Ostade, 1757; *The Alchymist* by Pietro Longhi, 1661; two paintings by David Teniers's named *The Alchemist,* c. 1645 and 1680; *The Village Alchemist* by Jan Steen; *The Alchemist's Experiment Takes Fire* by Heindrik Heerschop from the late seventeenth century; Sir William Fettes Douglas's *The Alchemist,* nineteenth century; *Paracelsus Lecturing on the Elixir Vitae,* by David Scott, nineteenth century. For a more complete list, go to www.levity.com/alchemy. Also see Brueghel's magnificent paintings of the four seasons replete with all the elements portrayed in all their resplendent beauty. I should also mention Hieronymus Bosch, whose works depict alchemical themes. Rudolf II was an avid collector of his paintings.

IMAGE FOR
CHAPTER 9,
PAGE 289

Utriusque Cosmi Historia, Robert Fludd, 1617–1618

Along with his friend and colleague Michael Maier, Robert Fludd worked ardently to advance the theories of the Rosicrucians. This image, entitled *Picture of the Art and Mirror of all Nature, Anima Mundi* is personified as a woman from whose breast flows a liquid that links all realms of being, connecting animal, mineral and vegetable to God. "On her breast is the true sun, on her belly is the moon . . . her right foot stands on the earth, her left foot in the water, thus showing the connection between Sulphur and Mercury, without which nothing can be created."[12] Note that each kingdom has its assigned position in the cosmological order of nature and that the outermost rings represent paradise.

Fludd was suspicious of the growing interest in empirical science. He advocated moving science, including alchemy, away from laboratory practice and back to the mystical traditions of Hermetics and the Kabbala. I refer the interested reader to William Huffman's book *Robert Fludd, Essential Readings,* in which Huffman discusses Fludd's works and his debate with Kepler over the disparate theories of the structure of the universe as well as Fludd's defense of the Rosicrucians.

Theosophische Wercke, Jakob Bohme, Amsterdam, 1682

IMAGE FOR CHAPTER 10, PAGE 311

Jakob Boehme (1575–1624) was a spiritual alchemist. He was an avid follower of the works of Paracelsus. In 1598, he believed he had seen into the heart of nature, or what Paracelsus called the *lumen naturae* in his *The Book of Nature.* Boehme revitalized Christian mysticism through his many visions and writings. "Alchemy," wrote Mark Haeffner, the author of *The Dictionary of Alchemy,* "with Boehme has left the laboratory to become a system of mystical, transcendent symbolism."[13]

The Emerald Tablet, from Amphitheatrum sapientiae aeternae, Heinrich Khunrath, Hanover, 1606

CLOSING IMAGE, PAGE 323

The *Emerald Tablet* of Hermes Trismegistus is perhaps the oldest collection of alchemical recipes known to us. Its thirteen recipes are a prescription for developing consciousness that has endured for thousands of years. No one truly knows its origin and some believe its message came from Atlantis or possibly other worlds. In any event, the tablet is a dynamic document that has been interpreted thousands of times and become the cornerstone of the Hermetic tradition. Much of its philosophy was taken up and put into practice in the United States of America, whose national motto is *E Pluribus Unum,* "One out of Many." The ancients believed that America would become a mighty nation long before Native Americans inhabited the continent or Viking sailors pointed their vessels westward. In this same vision, the New World was seen as the staging area that would take humankind to its new home. Thus spoke Hermes:

Stop and become sober: perceive with the eyes of your heart again! And if all of you cannot do this, then at least let those who are able to do so. For the wickedness of ignorance floods the whole world, destroys the soul which is locked in the body and prevents it from completing its journey and docking into the port of the stars.[14]

REFERENCES

1 Wilber, Ken. *One Taste*. Boston and London: Shambala, 1999, p. 6.
2 Frabricus, Johannes. *Alchemy: The Medieval Alchemists and Their Royal Art*. London: Diamond Books, 1976, p. 190.
3 Jung, C. J. *Mysterium Coniunctionis, An Inquiry into the Separation and Synthesis of Psychic Opposites in Alchemy,* vol. 14. New York: Bollingen Foundation, 1963, p. 235.
4 ———. *Psychology and Religion: West and East,* vol. 11. New York: Bollingen Foundation, 1958, p. 359.
5 Hall, Manly P. *The Secret Teachings of All Ages*. Los Angeles: The Philosophical Research Society, 1978, p. CV.
6 Roob, Alexander. *The Hermetic Museum: Alchemy & Mysticism*. London, New York and Paris: Taschen, 1996, p. 214
7 Cirlot, J. E. *A Dictionary of Symbols*. New York: The Philosophical Society, 1962, p. 70.
8 Roob. *The Hermetic Museum,* p. 370.
9 Frabricus. *Alchemy,* p. 142.
10 Roob. *The Hermetic Museum,* p. 690.
11 Walker, Charles. *The Encyclopedia of Secret Knowledge*. London: Limited Editions, 1995, p. 8
12 Roob. *The Hermetic Museum,* p. 501.
13 Haeffner, Mark. *The Dictionary of Alchemy: From Maria Prophetissa to Isaac Newton*. London: The Aquarian Press, 1971, p. 74.
14 Hauck, Dennis. *The Emerald Tablet: Alchemy for Personal Transformation*. New York: Penguin Putnam Inc., 1999, p. 400.

NOTES ON THE TEN RECIPES

Visit the Interior of the Earth and Rectify what you find there, and you will Discover the Hidden Stone

THE FIRST RECIPE

This recipe comes from the alchemist Basil Valentinus (1394–1413). It is an alchemical maxim that uses "the first letters of an alchemical Latin adage found in many occult texts:

Visita Interiora Terrae; Rectificandoque Invenies Occultum Lapidem.

Some claim that all alchemical secrets are contained in this adage . . .[1]

THE SECOND RECIPE

Dissolve the Matter in its own Water

This old maxim is taken from Edinger's book but its theme is repeated in many alchemical texts.[2]

Keep Vigilant even while Asleep   THE THIRD RECIPE

This inscription comes from Heinrich Khunrath's *Amphitheatrum sapienhtiae aeternae,* 1602.

The Mind must be in Harmony with the Work   THE FOURTH RECIPE

From Norton's *Ordinale of Alchemy* (*Museum Hermitica,* p. 519) which reads, "*nam mens eius cum opere consentiat. . . .*"[3]

The Sun and the Shadow Complete the Work   THE FIFTH RECIPE

"The sun and its shadow bring the work to perfection."[4] Jung also notes that this same idea occurs in the *Turba*: "But he who hath tinged the poison of the sages with the sun and its shadow, hath attained to the greatest secret."[5]

Sow your Gold in White Foliated Earth   THE SIXTH RECIPE

In Michael Maier, *emblema VI in Scrutinium chymicrum,* (pp. 16ff). Also see Jung; "The symbol probably derives from Senior, *De chemia,* where it is written, '[Wherefore] Hermes said, "Sow the gold in white foliated earth. For white foliate earth is the crown of victory, which is ashes extracted from ashes."'"[6]

The Rose gives Honey to the Bee   THE SEVENTH RECIPE

From the Latin words, "*dat rosa mel apibus,*" written above the image of the Rosy Cross. From Robert Fludd's *Clavis Philosphiae et Alchymiae,* 1633.

Dissolve and Coagulate (*Solve et coagula*)   THE EIGHT RECIPE

So ancient and common is this motto that it is difficult to say with absolute certainty whose name should bear credit for its wisdom. Perhaps Geber or even Hermes Trismegistus is the rightful author of this timeless recipe. In any event, other versions of this recipe include, "fixate the Spirit, volatize matter," "that which has not been separated cannot be joined" and "no generation without corruption." Richard and Iona Miller put it well, "We need to find connections between spirit's upward drive and matter's encumbering embrace."[7]

THE NINTH RECIPE   **It Takes Mercury to Make Mercury**

"Make mercury with mercury." Khunrath, (*Von hylealischen Chaos,* p. 224).[8]

THE TENTH RECIPE   **Without Divine Inspiration, No One is Great**

This inscription is also taken (like the third recipe) from Heinrich Khunrath, *Amphitheatrum sapienhtiae aeternae,* 1602. As Charles Walker tells us it is located "on the ceiling above the table, [and] is the most important of all occult maxims."[9]

REFERENCES

1 Walker, Charles. *The Encyclopedia of Secret Knowledge.* London: Limited Editions, 1995, p. 25.
2 Edinger, Edward F. *Anatomy of the Psyche: Alchemical Symbolism in Psychotherapy.* La Salle, Illinois: Open Court, 1985, p. 1.
3 Jung, C. G. *Psychology and Alchemy,* p. 270. See footnote 79.
4 ———. *Mysterium Coniunctionis,* p. 97.
5 ibid., p. 97. See footnote 38.
6 ibid., p. 438. See footnote 270.
7 Miller, Richard and Iona Miller. *The Modern Alchemist: A Guide to Personal Transformation.* Grand Rapids, Mich: Phanes Press, 1994, p. 15.
8 Jung. *Mysterium Coniunctionis,* 1963, p. 43. See footnote 17.
9 Walker, p. 37.

Notes and References

1 Raff, Jeffrey. *Jung and the Alchemical Imagination*. York Beach, Maine: Nicolas-Hays, Inc., 2000, p. xvi.

2 Eliade, Mircea. *The Forge and the Crucible: The Origins and Structures of Alchemy*. Chicago, Ill: The University of Chicago Press, 1962, p. 24.

3 Hauck, Dennis. *The Emerald Tablet: Alchemy for Personal Transformation*. New York: Penguin Putnam Inc., 1999. According to Hauck, sources say "the tablet was in Egypt about 10,000 years ago, though some historians point to a date around 300 B.C.E. . . . Egyptian papyri dating as far back as 2000 B.C.E. contain many of the same phrases and principles stated in the *Emerald Tablet* . . ." p. 32.
Marshall, Peter. *The Philosopher's Stone*. London: Macmillan, 2001. Marshall says that "the exact date and authorship of the *Emerald Tablet* are . . . unknown." p. 353.

4 Marshall, *The Philosopher's Stone*. Based on Egyptian and Chinese tradition, Marshall suggests that this mysterious knowledge originally came from a long lost Atlantean civilization.

5 ibid., p. 17.

6 ibid., p. 97.

7 ibid., p. 112–113.

8 Cavendish, Richard, ed. *Man, Myth & Magic: An Illustrated Encyclopedia of the Supernatural*. New York: Marshall Cavendish Corporation, 1970. Quote is from an essay by Benjamin Walker under the heading "Tantrism," p. 2780.

9 Fernadando, Diana. *Alchemy: An Illustrated A to Z*. Great Britain: Blandford, 1998, p. 78.

10 Cooper, David. *God Is a Verb: Kabbalah and the Practice of Mystical Judaism*. New York: Riverside Books, 1997, p. 37.

11 ibid., p. 50.

12 Jung, C. G. *Mysterium Coniunctionis: An Inquiry into the Separation and Synthesis of Psychic Opposites in Alchemy*. New York: Bollingen Foundation, 1963, p. 501.

13 Marshall. *The Philosopher's Stone*, p. 217.

14 White, Michael. *Isaac Newton: The Last Sorcerer*. Cambridge, Mass.: Perseus Books, 1997, p. 188.

15 Keynes, John Maynard, from his essay *The World of Mathematics*, edited by James R. Newman, p. 279.

16   Gilchrist, Cherry. *Elements of Alchemy*. Shaftesbury, Dorset: Element Books, 1991, p. 1.

17   Marshall. *The Philosopher's Stone,* p. 251.

18   Jung, C. G. *Memories, Dreams, Reflections,* ed. A. Jaffe. New York: Pantheon Books, 1961, p. 400.

19   ibid., p. 401.

20   While no one knows for sure who authored the *Emerald Tablet,* Hermes Trismegitus is typically given credit. Other legends have it that Sara, the wife of Abraham, discovered the tablet in a cave, while still others believed it was the work of either Alexander the Great or Apollonius of Tyana. An abridged version also appears in Jabir's work, and there is an even earlier Syriac translation. The text was eventually translated into Latin by Hugh of Santillana in the twelfth century, making it available to European scholars, and of course alchemists, who prized it as dearly as their bibles. See Peter Marshall's *The Philosopher's Stone,* p. 253.

21   These texts originated in Alexandria and therefore represent a lost ancient wisdom tradition. The famous library of Alexandria was burnt to the ground by Christians in 391. Many centuries later they were brought to Florence from Byzantium, where the Renaissance alchemist Ficino was ordered to translate the texts by Cosimo de' Medici. Ficino's translation of the first fourteen treatises, named the *Pimander* (1471), became well known throughout Europe. "It remained," writes Peter Marshall, "the most influential presentation of the *Corpus Hermeticum* until the nineteenth century." (*The Philosopher's Stone,* p. 340) Eventually, the Hermetic text contributed to the formulation of the perennial philosophy, first mentioned by Agostino Steuco and later popularized in the twentieth century by Aldous Huxley in his book by the same title.

22   Mitchell, Stephen, ed. *The Enlightened Mind: An Anthology of Sacred Prose*. New York: HarperCollins, 1991, p.34. This quote is taken from a "collection of short essays and dialogues by Egyptian philosophers of the neo-Platonic school." See also p. 208.

23   Evola, Julius. *The Hermetic Tradition: Symbols and Teachings of the Royal Art*. Rochester, Vt.: Inner Traditions, 1971, p. 21.

24   In Lurianic Kabbalah, the concept of Adam Kadmon refers to an archetypal first man from whom emanates sparks (*scintilla* in alchemy), which ignite life in all other beings. In this way, Nature will receive all beings on their death regardless of where they happen to die. The concept recalls the Buddhist idea that we are all one soul and cannot therefore achieve enlightenment until all peoples have achieved this exalted state. The notion of a synthetic being, a clone, differs from the alchemical *homunculus* in that this "little man" was believed to possess a soul. It's an open question as to whether a human clone will have a soul. Perhaps part of the debate will stem from the basic definition of Adam as spirit in flesh and whether humans alone can not only create a cloned being but also infuse it with spirit. The etymology of the name Adam means spirit in matter.

      In alchemy, Adam is considered the first adept. As Mylius says, "And therefore it is said that the stone is in every man. And Adam brought it forth with him from Paradise, from which material our stone or Elixir is produced in every man." Jung. *Mysterium Coniunctionis,* footnote 88 on p. 397.

CHAPTER 2

1   Jung, Carl. *Memories, Dreams, Reflections,* p. 202.

2   ibid., p. 204.

3   ibid., p. 205.

4   Jaffe, Aniela, ed. *C.G. Jung: Word and Image*. Princeton, N.J.: Princeton University Press, 1979, p. 103.

5 Jung. *Two Essays on Analytical Psychology,* vol. 7. New York: Bollingen Foundation, 1953, p. 171.

6 Marshall. *The Philosopher's Stone,* p. 355.

7 From a memorial pamphlet, p. 20, Curatorium of the C. G. Institute.

8 I use the word "synthetic" not to mean something artificially concocted in a chemical laboratory. Rather I use the word to mean "put together" (Gr. *syntithenia*) into a composition (Gr. *synthetikos*).

9 Jung. *Mysterium Coniunctionis,* p. 497.

10 ibid., p. 526.

11 Raff. *Jung and the Alchemical Imagination,* p. 31

12 Avens, Roberts. *Imagination is Reality: Western Nirvana in Jung, Hillman, Barfield & Cassirer.* Dallas: Spring Publications, 1980, p. 38.

13 Berman, Morris. *The Reenchantment of the World.* Ithaca and London: Cornell University Press, 1981, p. 93.

14 Jung, C. G. *Aion.* Princeton, N.J.: Princeton University Press, 1959, p. 170.

15 In a revealing footnote provided by Edward Whitmont, we find Jung's hesitation to either take alchemists as serious chemists or himself as one who might have undertaken the laboratory work of alchemy. Whitmont: "I had the opportunity of personally bringing the fact of such actual functional correspondences to Jung's attention. The information evoked Jung's interest and approval, but apparently, because of his exclusive preoccupation with the psyche, was not of sufficient interest to him to explore it further psychosomatically. Instead he suggest that I try to do it!" Whitmont, Edward C. *The Alchemy of Healing, Psyche and Soma.* Berkeley, Calif.: North Atlantic Books, 1993, p. 47.

16 Berman. *Reenchantment of the World,* p. 93.

17 Avens. *Imagination is Reality,* p. 38.

18 Masterson, James. *In Search of the Real Self: Unmasking the Personality Disorders of Our Age.* New York: The Free Press, 1988, pp. 38–50.

19 Kiersey, David and Marilyn Bates. *Please Understand Me: Character and Temperament Types.* Delmar, Calif.: Promethius Nemesis Book Company, 1978, p. 27.

20 ibid., p. 27.

21 Jung, C. G. *Psychological Types: The Psychology of Individuation,* vol. 6. New York: Pantheon Books, 1953, p. 545.

22 In addition to the inventory provided by Kiersey and Bates, there is the Myers-Briggs™ Personality Inventory.

23 Von Franz, Marie-Louise. *Projection and Re-collection in Jungian Psychology: Reflections of the Soul.* LaSalle, Ill.: Open Court, 1980, p. 108.

24 Jung, ed. *Man and His Symbols.* New York: Doubleday & Company, Inc., 1964. Quote is from Marie Louise von Franz's essay "The Process of Individuation," p. 162.

25 ibid., p. 164.

26 Jung, C. G. *Psychology and Religion: West and East,* vol. 11. New York: Bollingen Foundation, 1958, p. 35.

27 Godwin, Joscelyn. "The Meaning of the Rose Cross," in *The Rosicrucian Enlightenment Revisited,* ed. Ralph White. Hudson, New York: Lindisfarne Books, 1999, p. 60. The *Summa Perfectionis* is attributed to Geber but as Godwin suggests may have been authored by Paul of Taranto.

28 Chopra, Deepak, ed. *Love Poems of Rumi.* New York: Harmony Books, 1998, pp. 18–19.

CHAPTER 3

1   Hall, Manly. *The Secret Destiny of America*. Los Angeles: The Philosophical Research Society, 1941, pp. 87–88.

2   Hence the word "disaster" literally means "bad star." This particular star has an interesting history. The comet that had so fascinated Tycho Brahe caught the attention of Isaac Newton centuries later, leading Newton ultimately to devise his famous laws of gravitation. Beginning in November 1680, a number of astronomers observed what they initially thought were a series of comets sighted over Europe. Robert Hooke, Edmund Haley, John Flamsteed and finally Newton all observed these comets appearing, then disappearing. It was Flamsteed who first realized that these observations were one and the same comet. In 1682, Newton again sighted the comet, this time brighter than its appearance two years before. He collected reports from astronomers all over Europe in an attempt to define the comet's orbit. The comet again disappeared after two months but not without Giovanni Domenico Cassini publishing an astonishing paper ("Observations on the Comet") that suggested that this comet was the very same one observed by Tycho Brahe in 1577!

3   Marshall. *The Philosopher's Stone,* p. 397.

4   Vurm, Robert. *Rudolf II and His Prague*. Prague: Robert Vurm, 1997, p. 14.

5   ibid., p. 19.

6   ibid. p. 20.

7   Edinger, Edward F. *Anatomy of the Psyche: Alchemical Symbolism in Psychotherapy*. La Salle, Ill.: Open Court, 1985, p. 230.

8   In Richard Rudgley's book *Essential Substances,* he points out in his chapter Stone Age Alchemy that hemp "was being used as an intoxicant by the Iron Age" (p. 31). While we know some alchemists either discovered and/or prescribed psychoactive substances there is, says Dennis Hauck, "no direct references that such compounds were ever used by them in their work. "Raymond Lully was first to make brandy which he called burnt wine, and Paracelsus often prescribed laudanum, i.e., opium. But "certainly," Hauck continues, "had the alchemists used psychoactive compounds, they would have approached them in the sacred way of shamans traveling to nonordinary reality in search of spiritual truth and not in the 'recreational' use we see today." (*The Emerald Tablet,* pp. 243–244.) I agree with this wholeheartedly, especially given that the effects of psychoactive chemicals in reducing consciousness runs exactly opposite to the goals of alchemical experimental practices. Without a doubt, however, I am sure there were some false alchemists (e.g., Edward Kelly) who used drugs to circumvent the demands of true alchemy. However, we must not be naive about the possible use of psychoactive agents by sincere alchemists. About the best argument to substantiate this theory is found in Clark Heinrich's *Strange Fruit: Alchemy, Religion and Magical Foods: A Speculative History*. London: Bloomsbury, 1995.

9   Jung, C. G. *Alchemical Studies*. New Jersey: Princeton University Press, 1967, p. 18.

CHAPTER 4

1   Burland, C. A. *The Arts of the Alchemists*. New York: Macmillan, 1967, p. 158. Hathor, one of the most revered of the Egyptian gods, is best known for her healing and creative powers. As "mother of the world" and "creator of the heavens" we can easily equate her with the archetype of the Great Mother. See *The Healing Gods of Ancient Civilizations* by Walter Addison Jayne, pp. 57–58. For a splendid description of the derivation of the word alchemy see the chapter entitled The Name Alchemy in *The Origins of Alchemy in Graeco-Roman Egypt* by Jack Lindsay, pp. 68–89. As Jack Lindsay points out, there are a number of ways to etymologically derive the original meaning of the word alchemy, including tracing it back to one of its roots, *km* (with *km*=chem), meaning black. This is, he further points out, not to confuse alchemy as a black art versus a white art, but rather meaning a "sense of fulfillment." See p. 74.

2 Lindsay, Jack. *The Origins of Alchemy in Graeco-Roman Egypt*. London: Frederick Muller, 1970, p. 73.

3 ibid., p. 74.

4 Eliade, Mircea. *Forge and the Crucible*. p. 43.

5 White, Michael. *Isaac Newton*.

6 Ulam, S. M. *Adventures of a Mathematician*. New York: Charles Scribner's Sons, 1987, p. 289.

7 Brown, Joseph Epes. "The Wisdom of the Contrary," *Parabola*, volume IV, No. 1, February 1979, p. 58.

8 The women alchemists most often mentioned in literature are Moses' sister, Maria Prophetessa, who invented the baine Marie, and Cleopatra.

9 LaBerge, Stephen, and Howard Rheingold. *Exploring the World of Lucid Dreaming*. New York: Ballantine Books, 1990, p. 234.

10 Berman, Morris. *The Reenchantment of the World*. Ithaca and London: Cornell University Press, 1981, p. 95.

11 Magus, Albertus, and Jay Ramsay. *Alchemy: the Art of Transformation*. London: Thorsons, 1997, p. 22.

12 Harding, M. Esther. *Psychic Energy: Its Source and Its Transformation*. Washington, D. C.: The Bollingen Foundatioin, 1947, p. 466.

13 Walsh, Roger. *Essential Spirituality*. New York: John Wiley & Sons, 1999.

14 Taylor, F. Sherwood. *The Alchemists: Founders of Modern Chemistry*. New York: Collier Books, 1949, pp. 233–234.

15 Lindsay, Jack. *Origins of Alchemy*, p. 74.

16 Grossinger, Richard. *Planet Medicine: From Stone Age Shamanism to Post-Industrial Healing*. Boulder: Shambala, 1982, p. 133.

17 Psychotherapy is an excellent adjunct to the growing medical treatment known as complementary medicine.

18 Haggard, H. *Devils, Drugs and Doctors: The Story of the Science of Healing from Medicine Man to Doctor*. New York: Harper & Row, 1929, p. 143. Jupiter, writes Thomas Moore, "the god of tempering is known in the image of the peacock's tail, which, Jung informs us, is an alchemical image of spring, *primavera*, the arrival of new life . . . If psychology as a discipline," he continues, "were to value finally the variety in psychological life the peacock represents, then maybe that long-sought elixir of the 'liberated life' might be found." Moore, Thomas. *The Planets Within: The Astrological Psychology of Marsilio Ficino*. Maine: Lindisfarne Press, 1982, p. 207.

19 Godwin, Joscelyn. *Harmonies of Heaven and Earth from Antiquity to Avant-Garde*. Rochester, Vt.: Inner Traditions International, 1995, p. 158.

20 Moore, Thomas. *The Planets Within*, pp. 86–87. Also see Godwin where he quotes Ficino from his book *De vita coelitus comparanda*: "Musical sound by the movement of the air moves the body: by purified air it excites the aerial *spiritus* which is the bond of body and soul: by emotion it affects the senses and at the same time the soul." (p. 17.)

21 Godwin, Joscelyn. *Harmonies of Heaven and Earth*, p. 5.

22 ibid., p. 6. Note also that some alchemists conceived of the ether as being the fifth element, the quintessence. The possibility of the existence of the ether has challenged alchemists and modern scientists. Even Newton and Einstein would at various times in their research either admit or dismiss its existence.

23 Eliade, Mircea. *Forge and the Crucible*. p. 99.

24 Burckhardt, Titus. *Alchemy*. Great Britain: Element Books, 1967, p. 157.

25 Neiman, Carol. *Miracles: The Extraordinary, the Impossible, and the Divine*. United Kingdom: Labrynth Publishing Ltd., 1995, p. 220.

26 ibid., p. 220.

27 Evola, *The Hermetic Tradition,* p. 16.

28 Mitchell, Stephen, ed. *The Enlightened Mind,* p. 34.

29 Leo, William. *Alchemy.* Los Angeles: Sherbourne Press, 1972, p. 121.

CHAPTER 5   1 Godwin, Joscelyn. *Harmonies of Heaven and Earth,* p. 47.

2 ibid., p. 58.

3 ibid., p. 75.

4 Quarks was the name given to the smallest components of matter by physicist Murray Gell-Mann in 1963.

5 Watson, Lyall. *The Nature of Things: The Secret Life of Inanimate Objects.* Rochester, Vt.: Destiny Books, 1990, p. 47.

6 ibid., p. 47.

7 This concept is also seen in *Aurora Consurgens,* a fourteenth-century alchemical text attributed to Thomas Aquinus. In it, the Goddess of Wisdom enters the body of the deceased to bring about the creation of a new and whole self. The reference may well come from an old medieval theory in which it was believed that Christ's conception originates at the Annunciation via Mary's ear after being told by an angel that she would bear the Christ child.

8 Whitmont, Edward C. *The Alchemy of Healing,* p. 71.

9 Moore. *The Planets Within,* p. 75.

10 Hall, Manly P. *The Secret Teachings of All Ages.* Los Angeles: The Philosophical Research Society, 1978, p. CVII.

11 ibid., p. CVI.

12 ibid., p. CV.

13 Edinger, Edward. *The Anatomy of the Psyche,* p. 114.

14 Hall, Manly. *Secret Teachings of All Ages,* p. CVIII.

15 Evola. *The Hermetic Tradition,* p. 197.

16 Moore. *The Planets Within,* p. 167.

17 Walker, Charles. *The Encyclopedia of Secret Knowledge.* London: Limited Editions, 1995, p. 21.

18 Hermes is often called "Thrice Greatest," referring to his domination over the three realms of Heaven, Earth and the Underworld. The name Hermes Trismegistus signifies Hermes's rulership over these three kingdoms, powers every alchemist sought to possess through their work.

19 Moore. *The Planets Within,* p 188.

20 The Tarot has direct connections with alchemy and Kabbala. It is believed that the Tarot was invented on the heels of the collapse of Alexandria and that the twenty-two enigmas were a sort of universal shorthand, mnemonic device, abbreviating ancient wisdom. The Tarot connects past with present. For example, the four suits of the Tarot—swords, clubs, goblets and diamonds—associate with the four elements as well as the four suits we have in modern playing cards. This subject did not escape the interests of Jung and much of modern interpretation of the cards follow along Jungian lines. While there are many books written on the subject, I would recommend Sallie Nichols's *Jung and Tarot* for obvious reasons and Richard Cavendish's book, *The Tarot,* for its research and beautiful pictures.

21 Moore. *The Planets Within,* p. 142.

22 Burckhardt. *Alchemy,* p. 91.

23 Jung. *Mysterium Coniunctionis,* p. 230.

24 Godwin. *Harmonies of Heaven and Earth,* p. 49.

25 ibid., p. 49.

26 Edinger. *Anatomy of the Psyche,* p. 134.

27 Brown, Norman O. *Hermes the Thief.* New York: Vintage, 1969, p. 20.

28 To give some sense of the fullness of the symbolic expression of Mercurius, consider a few of his "aliases" mentioned in Holmyard: "the silvery water, the ever-fugitive, the divine water, the masculine-feminine, the seed of the dragon, the bile of the dragon, divine dew, Scythian water, sea-water, water of the moon, and milk of a black cow." Holmyard, E. J. *Alchemy,* New York: Dover, 1990, p. 27.

29 Godwin. *Harmonies of Heaven and Earth,* p. 39.

30 ibid., p. 39.

CHAPTER 6

1   See Robert Johnson's book *She!* for a full analysis of this beautiful story.

2   White. *The Rosicrucian Enlightenment Revisited,* p. 54.

3   Paracelsus is fabled to have carried around a small amount of this precious azoth in the hilt of his walking stick. With it he could transmute any metal into gold.

4   Hillman, James. "Salt: A Chapter in Alchemical Psychology." Marlan, Stanton, ed. *Salt and the Alchemical Soul.* Woodstock, Conn.: Spring Publications, 1995, p. 170.

5   Following the theory laid out by Ficino, Paracelsus popularized the tripartite theory, in which salt equates with soul, sulfur with body and mercury with spirit. Unable to avoid a literal comparison, Hillman points out the parallel between salt's nature and Paracelsus's salty disposition. Moreover, he reminds us that Paracelsus died in Salzburg.

6   Denise Hauk reminds us that "the Medieval alchemists believed the salt in tears was the actual remnant of crystallized thoughts broken down by crying." See Hauck. *The Emerald Tablet,* p. 197.

7   *Metaphysical Bible Dictionary*. Missouri: Unity Books, 1931, p. 217.

8   Chopra, Deepak. *The Seven Laws of Success.* San Rafael, Calif.: Amber-Allen, 1994, p. 20.

9   Moore. *The Planets Within,* p. 71.

10 Edinger. *Anatomy of the Psyche,* p. 85.

11 ibid., p. 117.

12 Goethe's work, *Faust,* is regarded by many as an excellent example of alchemical writing. See Joseph Mast's *The Emerging Self* for some poignant passages from this great work that directly relate to alchemy, pp. 160–162.

13 Jung. *Mysterium Coniunctionis,* p. 546.

14 Edinger. *Anatomy of the Psyche,* p. 218.

15 Raff, Jeffrey. *Jung and the Alchemical Imagination,* p. 24.

CHAPTER 7

1   *Oxford English Dictionary,* Third Edition, pp. 644, 1042.

2   Pearsall, Paul. *Making Miracles.* New York: Prentice Hall Press, 1991, p. 34

3   Wolf, Fred Alan. *Mind into Matter: A New Alchemy of Science and Spirit.* New Hampshire: Moment Point Press, 2001, p. 73.

4   ibid., p. 74.

5   Herrigel, Eugen. *Zen.* New York: McGraw-Hill Book Company, 1964, p. 13.

6   Pinkola-Estes, Clarissa. *Women Who Run with the Wolves: Myths and Stories of the Wild Woman Archetype.* New York: Ballantine Books, 1992, p. 370.

7   Mnemosyne is mother to the muses. "The Memory of which Mnemsosyne is patroness is not the everyday memory that recalls things from the past, but the power of recapturing our other modes of being: of remembering whence we came, who we really are, and where we are going." Godwin. *Harmonies of Heaven and Earth,* p. 73.

8 Pernety, Antoine-Joseph. *An Alchemical Treatise on the Great Art*. New York: Samuel Weiser, 1973, p. 103.

9 McLean, Adam. *The Alchemical Mandala*. Grand Rapids, Mich.: Phanes, 1989, p. 15.

10 Jung. *The Secret of the Golden Flower*. Wilhelm, Richard, trans. New York: Causeway Books, 1975, p. 105.

11 Edinger, Edward F. *Yoga, Immortality and Freedom*. Princeton, N.J.: Princeton University Press, 1958, p. 291.

12 Edinger. *Anatomy of the Psyche*, p. 143.

13 Edinger, Edward. *The Creation of Consciousness: Jung's Myth of Modern Man*. Toronto: Inner City Books, 1984, p. 17.

14 Cirlot, J. E. *A Dictionary of Symbols*. New York: Philosophical Library, 1962, p. 235.

15 Moore. *The Planets Within*, p. 128.

16 Edinger. *The Creation of Consciousness*, p. 17.

17 Wilber, Ken. *One Taste*. Boston and London: Shambala, 1999, p. 207.

18 Godwin. *Harmonies of Heaven and Earth*, p. 24.

19 Moore. *The Planets Within*, p. 171.

CHAPTER 8

1 Whitmont. *Alchemy of Healing*, p. 161. The *pharmakon* was a voluntary sacrifice of a chief, a king or even a special child that served to rid the community of its sins, diseases, and/or wrongdoings. Christ would be considered a collective *pharmakon* who served as a "substitute for the inability of the human state in Original Sin to surrender itself to the Divine." Healing in this manner involves the doctor sacrificing something of himself, the patient or even the community to restore health.

2 It is believed that Steffan Michelspacher, the artist who designed the accompanying alchemical masterpiece, intentionally misordered the operations leading to the sanctuary in order to detract false alchemists.

3 Hall, Manly P. *Secret Teachings of All Ages*, p. 172.

4 Fischer, Louis, ed. *The Essential Gandhi: His Life, Work, and Ideas*. New York: Vintage Books, 1962, p. 262.

5 ibid., p. 262.

6 Edinger. *Anatomy of the Psyche*, p. 230.

7 Jung. *Mysterium Coniunctionis*, p. 199.

8 Grof, Stanislav and Christina Grof, eds. *Spiritual Emergency: When Personal Transformation Becomes a Crisis*. New York: Jeremy P. Tarcher/Perigee Books, 1989, p. 17.

9 Haeffner, Mark. *The Dictionary of Alchemy: From Maria Prophetissa to Isaac Newton*. London: The Aquarian Press, 1971, p. 51.

10 Jung. *Mysterium Coniunctionis*, p. 222.

11 Stephen LaBerge. *Lucid Dreaming*. Los Angeles: J. P. Tarcher, 1985.

12 Casteneda, Carlos. *The Art of Dreaming*. New York: HarperCollins, 1993.

13 Varela, Francisco, ed. *Sleeping, Dreaming, and Dying: An Exploration of Consciousness with the Dalai Lama*. Boston: Wisdom Publications, 1997.

14 Bible, chapters 1 and 2.

15 Einstein would sarcastically say that if quantum theory held true then even the gaze of a mouse would change the universe. Fred Alan Wolf much later responded by saying that Einstein, while correct, neglected the fact that given the relatively small amount of brain matter contained in a mouse, the effect would in consequence be so slight as to be considered negligible.

16 Wolf, Fred Alan. *The Dreaming Universe: A Mind Exploring Journey into the Realm Where Psyche and Physics Meet*. New York: Simon & Schuster, 1994, pp. 347–348.

17   Wilber, Ken. *One Taste*, p. 277.

18   It is believed that acupuncture "developed when people noticed that a warrior slightly wounded in battle by a blow from a stone or sharp weapon, might be cured of some ailment by the wound." Cavendish, Richard. *Man, Myth and Magic,* vol. 1. New York: BPC Publishing, 1972, p. 20. Such a suggestion recalls the sympathetic magic associated with the sword. As Eliade points out, "The Bedouins of Sinai are convinced that the man who is successful in making a sword of meteoric iron becomes invulnerable in battle and assured of overcoming all his opponents. The celestial metal is foreign to earth, hence it is 'transcendent'; it comes from 'up above.'" *Forge and Crucible,* p. 28. In other words, the combination of spiritual and earthly power makes the warrior invincible. This is an alchemical concept and indeed, acupuncture, in attempting to balance the forces of yin and yang—the dynamic of which produces the five basic elements—is little different than what we find in classic alchemical theory.

19   *Qi,* or *Chi* means air or breath, which is one of the chief characteristics of spirit. That the spirit heals is a familiar theme found in many religious traditions. Eliade recalls the "myth of dismemberment of Indra, [where] we are told that, intoxicated by an excess of soma, the body of the god began to 'flow out', giving birth to every kind of creature, plant and metal. [and] From his navel, his life-breath flowed out and became lead, not iron, not silver; from his seed his form flowed out and became gold.'" *Forge and Crucible,* p. 69.

20   Hendricks, Gay, and Kate Ludeman. *The Corporate Mystic.* New York: Bantam Books, 1996, p. 61.

21   Dooling, D.M., ed. *A Way of Working: The Spiritual Dimension of Craft.* New York: Parabola Books, 1979, p. 9.

22   Doty, Sheelan, Carol and Donald, eds. Notes and papers on *Archaic Studies, Transformations of Archaic Images,* p. 142.

23   Hyde, Lewis. *Trickster Makes This World.* New York: North Point Press, 1998, p. 141.

24   Jung. *Mysterium Coniunctionis,* fn found on p. 420.

25   Hyde. *Trickster Makes This World,* p. 138.

26   ibid., p. 138.

27   ibid., p. 140.

28   ibid., pp. 139–140.

29   Jung, C. G. *Alchemical Studies,* p. 237.

30   Hyde. *Trickster Makes This World,* p. 141.

31   ibid., p. 141.

32   The Great Chain of Being is a concept that states that consciousness is multidimensional, continuous and all-inclusive. In his book *Forgotten Truth,* Houston Smith describes how all the great religions and wisdom traditions fit into this paradigm. The Great Chain is thought to be central to the perennial philosophy and has been expanded in the work done by Ken Wilber, who prefers to call it the Great Holarchy of Being. We are reminded of a deeper alchemical structure where he describes these concepts: "Central to the perennial philosophy is the notion of the Great Chain of Being. . . . Reality, according to the perennial philosophy, is not one-dimensional; it is not a flatland of uniform substance stretching monotonously before the eye. Rather, reality is composed of several different but continuous dimensions. Manifest reality, that is, consists of different grades or levels, reaching from the lowest and most dense and least conscious to the highest and most subtle and most conscious. At one end of this continuum of being or spectrum of consciousness is what we in the West would call "matter" or the insentient and the nonconscious, and at the other end is "spirit" or "godhead" or the "superconscious." . . . Arrayed in between are the other dimensions of being arranged according to their individual degrees of reality (Plato), actuality (Aristotle), inclusiveness (Hegel), consciousness (Aurobindo), clarity

(Leibniz), embrace (Plotinus), or knowingness (Garab Dorje)." *The Eye of Spirit.* Boston and London: Shambala, 1998, p. 39.

33   O'Donohue, John. *Anam Cara: A Book of Celtic Wisdom.* New York: Cliff Street Books, 1997, pp. 134–135.

34   Wilson, Robert Anton. *Quantum Psychology.* Phoenix: New Falcon Publications, 1990, pp. 185–186.

35   Wilber, Ken. *One Taste,* p. 296.

36   Toward the end of his life Jung was asked by a reporter whether he believed in god. Jung said, "No, I know there is a god."

37   Jung. *Mysterium Coniunctionis,* 1963, p. 538.

38   Wilber, Ken. *One Taste,* p. 135.

39   Osho (a title Rajneesh used toward the end of his life). *Courage: The Joy of Living Dangerously.* New York: St. Martin's Griffin, 1999, p. 63.

40   This magical text was translated from the tenth-century Arabic *Gayat al-hakim* (*The Final Aim of the Wise*), attributed to the alchemist Al-Majriti. See Marshall. *The Philosopher's Stone,* pp. 261–263.

41   Eliade. *Forge and the Crucible,* p. 42.

42   ibid., p. 40.

43   ibid., p. 47. In this same sense, Paracelsus felt that every baker and wine maker were in their manner of transmuting substance, true alchemists.

44   The philosophical egg was literally a glass flask, but its imagery recalls the four elements of an egg: its shell, skin, yoke and fluid.

45   Eliade. *Forge and the Crucible,* p. 32.

46   Edinger. *Anatomy of the Psyche,* pp. 104–105.

47   Kornfield, Jack, "Obstacles and Vicissitudes in Spiritual Practice," as quoted in Grof, Stanislav and Christina Grof, eds. *Spiritual Emergency,* p. 142.

48   The Rosicrucians organized in 1614, when their first manifesto, the *Fama Fraternitatis,* appeared in Cassel. The order was originally known as the Brotherhood of the Rose and Cross, founded by a German monk named Christian Rosenkreutz. Two additional manifestos, the *Confessio* and the *Chymische Hochzeit Christiani Rosenfreutz, Anno 1459,* were published in 1615 and 1617. These works had a profound influence on philosophers and leading scientists. The fraternity spread throughout the European intelligensia and attracted the interest and membership of such famous people as Fludd, Khunrach, Maier, Bacon, Boyle, and Newton. Special secret societies sprouted out of the Rosicrucians, including the elite invisible college and the mysterious band of thirty-six Invisible Ones, known as the Illuminati, who were supposed to disseminate Hermetic truths throughout the world. The invisible college eventually developed into the Royal Society of England, of which, many years later, Isaac Newton would become president.

49   For a thorough analysis of the sacred significance of the bee, refer to Hilda Ransome's book *The Sacred Bee: In Ancient Times and Folklore.* New York: Ballantine Reprints, 1996.

50   The reference for this story is uncertain since it came via E-mail distribution. But in a personal conversation I had with one of Dr. Margaret Mead's former students, the story seems to be quite plausible.

51   Johnson, Robert with Jerry Ruhl. *Balancing Heaven and Earth: A Memoir of Visions, Dreams, and Realizations.* San Francisco: HarperSan Francisco, 1998, p. 12.

52   Kubose, Gyomay. *Zen Koans.* Chicago: Henry Regnery Company, 1973, p. 86.

53   Eliade. *Forge and the Crucible,* p. 40.

54   ibid., p. 54.

55   Jung. *Mysterium Coniunctionis,* p. 546. The superiority of the self rests on its inclusion of ego within its purview and its affinity to nature. In this regard, Jung writes, "However one

may define the self, it is always something other than the ego, and inasmuch as a higher insight of the ego leads over to the self, the self is a more comprehensive thing which includes the experience of the ego and therefore transcends it. Just as the ego is a certain experience I have of myself, so is the self an experience of my ego. It is, however, no longer experienced in the form of a broader or higher ego, but in the form of a non-ego." *Psychology and Religion,* p. 542.

56 When Ken Wilber was asked by a reporter why he preferred to use the word "Kosmos" instead of "cosmos," he responded,

> *Kosmos* is an old Pythagorean term, which means the entire universe in all it many dimensions—physical, emotional, mental, and spiritual. Cosmos today usually means just the physical universe or physical dimension. So we might say the Kosmos includes the physiosphere or cosmos, the biosphere or life, the nooshphere or mind, all of which are radiant manifestation of pure Emptiness, and are not other to that Emptiness." (*One Taste,* p. 352.)

I agree. The word cosmos has fallen back, this time in an unfortunate way, to its original meaning—*ornament*—something that is far short of the more inclusive meaning I, and Ken Wilber, wish to convey in our respective writings.

57 *Metaphysical Bible Dictionary,* p. 446.

58 Abbot, Edwin A. *Flatland.* New York: Dover Publications, 1952, p. 64.

59 Jung, C. G. *The Practice of Psychotherapy,* vol. 16. New York: Bollingen Foundation, 1954, p. 280.

60 Jung. *Psychological Types,* p. 561.

61 An alternative interpretation might be that the patient's unconscious was striving to derive a truth that symbolized the lost, idealized father. I should add that the patient was a nonpracticing Jew, thereby adding possible Kabbalistic influences to this play on numbers.

62 Whitmont. *The Alchemy of Healing,* p. 139.

63 Jung, C. G. *The Structure and Dynamics of the Psyche,* vol. 8. New York: Pantheon Books, 1960, p. 490.

64 Jung. *Alchemical Studies,* p. 193.

65 ibid., p. 194.

66 ibid., p. 237.

67 Hauschka, R. From Richard Grossinger, ed. *The Alchemical Tradition in the Late Twentieth Century.* Berkeley, California: North American Books, 1983. Quote taken from Rudolf Hauschka's essay "The Vital Properties of the Metals," p. 83.

68 The word gas comes from a Greek root meaning "chaos." In the language of the unconscious, archaic meanings often give us important clues, especially when interpreting dreams. In this case, the patient was indeed struggling with feelings stemming from an old, unresolved traumatic (chaotic) memory.

69 The *golem* is a small clay figure that is brought to life through alchemy. Perhaps the most famous of these was created by Rabbi Judah Loew of Prague in the sixteenth century. Animating the figure involved burying it, walking in a clockwise direction around it and chanting recipes from the Sepher Yetzirah. The ability to create and destroy a *golem* was a test of the alchemist's progress in the work.

70 According to Charles Walker, the origin of Mary Shelley's *Frankenstein* came from the work of an alchemist named Konrad Dippel. He was born in Castle Frankenstein, near Darmstadt. "One important difference between the historical Dippel and Mary Shelley's doctor," writes Walker, "was that Dippel believed that life could be injected into dead bodies by magical means. He therefore belonged to the ancient tradition of black magic,

while the doctor of the story was an unconventional scientist, seeking for life secrets in the world of chemistry and physics." Walker, Charles. *The Encyclopedia of Secret Knowledge*. London: Limited Editions, 1995, p. 33.

71   At about the same time that this principle was being accepted by orthodox science, Jacques Bergier recalls in his book *The Morning of the Magicians,* an unusual meeting with a stranger (who he supposes might be the mysterious Fulcanelli) in which he is told:

> The secret of alchemy is this: there is a way of manipulating matter and energy so as to produce what modern scientists call "a field of force." This field acts on the observer and puts him in a privileged position vis-à-vis the Universe. From this position he has access to the realities which are ordinarily hidden from us by time and space, matter and energy. This is what we call 'The Great Work.' p. 78.

Also see Peter Marshall's *The Philosopher's Stone,* pp. 415–416 for more information on Fulcanelli.

72   Robert Johnson, quoted in Jerry Ruhl's *Balancing Heaven and Earth,* p. 12.

73   Jung. *Mysterium Coniunctionis,* footnote 67 on p. 108.

74   Jung. *Psychology and Religion,* p. 582.

75   Edinger. *Anatomy of the Psyche,* p. 161.

76   Jung. *Psychology and Religion,* p. 542.

77   Wilber, Ken. *One Taste,* p. 73.

78   Shelley, Mary. *Frankenstein,* p. 219.

79   ibid., p. 222.

80   Whitmont. *Alchemy of Healing,* p. 221.

81   ibid., p. 111.

82   Shelley, Mary. *Frankenstein,* p. 221.

83   Whitmont. *Alchemy of Healing,* p. 221.

84   Shelley, Mary. *Frankenstein,* p. 161.

CHAPTER 9

1   Added to these are a whole range of compounds developed by alchemists in their laboratories, including "sulphur, nitric acid (Geber), mercuric oxide, calomel, potassium sulphate, hydrochloride acid, (Valentinus)." Ramsey, Jay. *Alchemy: the Art of Transformation*. London: Thorsons, 1997, pp. 38–39.

2   Holmyard, E. J. *Alchemy*. New York: Dover, 1990, p. 171.

3   "Hermes Trismegistus," a poem by Longfellow, as quoted in Dennis Hauck's *The Emerald Tablet*. p. 31.

4   Some believe that the Goths acquired their knowledge of sacred geometry from the Ark of the Covenant, which somehow escaped the flames that destroyed the Temple of Solomon. For information on this interesting theory see Marshall. *The Philosopher's Stone,* pp. 267–269.

5   Marshall. *The Philosopher's Stone,* p. 268.

6   As George Gamow defines it, the Pauli Effect is "a mysterious phenomenon which is not, and probably never will, be understood on a purely materialistic basis." In essence, this German physicist, best known for his Exclusion Principle and conceiving of neutrino decades before their existence could be proven, had a strange effect on the very equipment he (and others) used in their experiments. Gamow relates this amusing and amazing story:

> It is well known that theoretical physicists cannot handle experimental equipment; it breaks whenever they touch it. Pauli was such a good theo-

retical physicist that something usually broke in the lab whenever he merely stepped across the threshold. A mysterious event that did not seem at first to be connected with Pauli's presence once occurred in Professor J. Franck's laboratory in Gottingen. Early one afternoon, without apparent cause, a complicated apparatus for the study of atomic phenomena collapsed. Franck wrote humorously about this to Pauli at his Zurich address and, after some delay, received an answer in an envelope with a Danish stamp. Pauli wrote that he had gone to visit Bohr and at the time of the mishap in Franck's laboratory his train was stopped for a few minutes at the Gottingen railroad station. You may believe this anecdote or not, but there are many other observations concerning the reality of the Pauli Effect!" Synchronicity?!!

Note: Dr. Gamow was himself a theoretical physicist who wrote with Niels Bohr and Ernest Rutherford. Gamow, George. *Thirty Years that Shock Physics: the Story of Quantum Theory*. New York: Dover Publications, 1966, p. 64.

7   Wolf. *The Dreaming Universe,* p. 285.
8   An audiotaped lecture by Manly P. Hall, "Alchemy," The Philosophical Research Society, 1998.
9   Jung goes even further by suggesting that Christ is the equivalent of the philosopher's stone. See *Psychology and Alchemy,* p. 469.
10 Haxton, Brook, trans. *Fragments: The Collected Wisdom of Heralitus.* New York: Viking, 2001, p. 15.
11 Suzuki, Daisetz T. *Zen and Japanese Culture.* New Jersey: Princeton University Press, 1959, p. 32.
12 Mitchell, ed. *The Enlightened Mind,* pp. 155, 77, 103.
13 Evola. *The Hermetic Tradition,* p. 195.
14 Neiman. *Miracles,* p. 8.
15 Kornfield, Jack. *After the Ecstasy, the Laundry.* New York: Bantam Books, 2000, p. 179.
16 Neiman. *Miracles,* p. 220.
17 Suzuki. *Zen and Japanese Culture,* p. 31. Suzuki is quoting George Duthuit in *Chinese Mysticism and Modern Painting* (London: A Zwemmer, 1936).
18 Mitchell, ed. *The Enlightened Mind,* p. 34.
19 Jung. *Psychology and Alchemy,* Vol. 12, p. 41.
20 Jung. *Alchemical Studies,* p. 116.
21 Wilber, Ken. *The Theory of Everything.* Boston: Shambala, 2000, p. 22.
22 Wilber, Ken. *One Taste,* p. 113.
23 Neihardt, John G. *Black Elk Speaks: Being the Life Story of a Holy Man of the Oglala Sioux.* Lincoln: University of Nebraska Press, 1961, p 46. Black Elk had this vision at the age of nine. He kept it to himself until he developed an intense fear of thunder. He then told the medicine man of his vision. The shaman instructed him to tell the people of the tribe. After having done so, Black Elk's thunder phobia disappeared. Recall that some things come to us through illumination and that holding back our "thunder" will sometimes cause us problems.

CHAPTER 10

1   Suzuki. *Zen and Japanese Culture,* p. 146.

2   On this point, Jung wrote, "There could be no greater mistake than for a Westerner to take up the direct practice of Chinese yoga, for that would merely strengthen his will and consciousness against the unconscious and bring about the very effect to be avoided. The neurosis would then simply be intensified. It cannot be emphasized enough that we are not Orientals, and that we have an entirely different point of departure in these matters." *Alchemical Studies,* vol. 13, p. 14. To this I would add by way of a reminder that Jung was not American but European. While his interpretations of the alchemical opus were brilliant, there remains for us to draw our own conclusions and set about establishing our own unique understanding of the Royal Art.

3   Grof, Stanislav and Christina Grof, eds. *Spiritual Emergency,* p. 3.

4   ibid., p. 8.

5   Most religions and spiritual practices emphasize the importance of the heart and its association with love and compassion. In ancient Egypt, the heart was the only organ not removed from the mummified body. On it was placed an emerald stone, which was meant to transport the *baa* soul to heaven. In Hinduism, *bhati* (mystical devotion) is an integral aspect of yoga and the center of such devotion in the *chakra* system is located in the heart. The Tantrics describe the second stage of transformation as a *bodhicitta,* "heart opening," in which a person begins to see beyond him or herself to the interconnectedness between all living beings. The six transcendental actions of the heart, the *paramitas,* include generosity, harmonious conduct, endurance, enthusiasm, concentration and insight.

In the Arahamic religions, the heart is the place of feelings and emotional intelligence. Muhammad said, "Wisdom is a light in the heart that distinguishes between truth and falsehood." The esoteric order of the Sufis adopted the winged heart as their emblem to symbolize and celebrate spiritual essence. "And once a person understands," writes Sufi master Hazrat Inayat Khan, "the nature, the character and the mystery of the heart, he understands . . . the language of the whole universe." *The Sufi Message of Hazarat Inayat Khan,* vol. II. London: International Headquarters of the Sufi Movement, 1969, p. 352.

In Hebrew scripture and Christian text, the heart plays a dominant role. It is the most important word in Hebrew scripture, mentioned 814 times to describe everything from joy (Deut 28:47; Acts 2:26) and courage (2 Sam. 17:10; Ps. 27:14) to wisdom and conscience (1 Kings 3:12; 10:24) Traditionally, the heart is viewed as having a higher intelligence than the brain. Where the mind divides, the heart tends to open and embrace differences.

6   Barks, Coleman. *The Essential Rumi.* John Moyne, trans. New Jersey: Castle Book, 1995, p. 32.

Bibliography

Abbot, Edwin A. *Flatland*. New York: Dover Publications, 1952.

Agrippa, Henry Cornelius, *Three Books of Occult Philosophy*. Donald Tyson, ed. Minnesota: Llewllyn Publications, 1995.

Avens, Roberts. *Imagination Is Reality: Western Nirvana in Jung, Hillman, Barfield & Cassirer*. Dallas: Spring Publications, 1980.

Bachelard, Gaston. *The Psychoanalysis of Fire*. Boston: Beacon Press, 1964.

Barks, Coleman. John Moyne, trans. *The Essential Rumi*. Edison, New Jersey: Castle Books, 1995.

Berman, Morris. *The Reenchantment of the World*. Ithaca and London: Cornell University Press, 1981.

Bly, Robert. *Iron John*. New York: Vintage Books, 1992.

Brown, Norman O. *Hermes, the Thief*. New York: Vintage, 1969.

Burckhardt, Titus. *Alchemy*. Shaftsbury, Dorset: Element Books, 1967.

Burland, C. A. *The Arts of the Alchemists*. New York: MacMillan, 1967.

Castenada, Carlos. *The Art of Dreaming*. New York: HarperCollins, 1993.

Cavendish, Richard. *The Tarot*. New York: Harper & Row, 1975.

Cavendish, Richard, ed. *Man, Myth & Magic*. New York: BPC Publishing, 1972.

Chopra, Deepak, ed. *Love Poems of Rumi*. New York: Harmony Books, 1998.

———. *The Seven Spiritual Laws of Success*. San Rafael, Calif., Amber-Allen, 1994.

Cirlot, J. E. *A Dictionary of Symbols*. New York: The Philosophical Library, 1962.

Cobb, Jodi. *Geisha, The Life, The Voices, The Art*. New York: Alfred A. Knopf, 2000.

Cooper, David. *God is a Verb: Kabbalah and the Practice of Mystical Judaism*. New York: Riverside Books, 1997.

Course in Miracles. New York: Viking/Penguin, 1975.

Crick, Francis. *The Astonishing Hypothesis, the Scientific Search for the Soul*. New York: Charles Scribner's Sons, 1994.

Curatorium of the C. G. Institute, Gemeindestrasse 27m CG-8032, Zurich. Memorial pamphlet entitled "C. G. Jung."

David-Neel, Alexandra. *Magic and Mystery in Tibet*. New York: Dover Publications, 1971.

Dooling, D. M., ed. *A Way of Working, The Spiritual Dimension of Craft*. Parabola Books, 1979.

Doty, Sheehan, ed. *Notes and Papers on Archaic Studies: Transformations of Archaic Images*. Franconia, N.H.: Center for Archaic Studies, 1981.

Edinger, Edward F. *Anatomy of the Psyche: Alchemical Symbolism in Psychotherapy*. La Salle, Illinois: Open Court, 1985.

———. *The Creation of Consciousness: Jung's Myth of Modern Man*. Toronto: Inner City Books, 1984.

Eliade, Mircea. *The Forge and the Crucible, The Origins and Structures of Alchemy*. Chicago, Illinois: The University of Chicago Press, 1962.

———. *Yoga, Immortality and Freedom*. Princeton, N.J.: Princeton University Press, 1958.

Epes, Joseph. "The Wisdom of the Contrary," *Parabola,* volume IV, no. 1. New York: The Tamarack Press, February 1979.

Evola, Julius. *The Hermetic Tradition: Symbols and Teachings of the Royal Art*. Rochester, Vt.: Inner Traditions, 1971.

Fauvel, John, ed., et.al. *Let Newton Be! A New Perspective on His Life and Works*. Oxford: Oxford University Press, 1988.

Fernadando, Diana. *Alchemy, An Illustrated A to Z*. Great Britain: Blandford, 1998.

Fischer, Louis, ed. *The Essential Gandhi: His Life, Work, and Ideas*. New York: Vintage Books, 1962.

Frabricius, Johannes. *Alchemy: The Medieval Alchemists and Their Royal Art*. London: Diamond Books, 1976.

Freud, Sigmund. *The Interpretation of Dreams*. New York: Basic Books, 1953.

Fulcanelli, Master Alchemist. *The Dwellings of the Philosophers*. Boulder: Archive Press and Communications, 1999.

———. *Le Mystère des Cathédrales: Esoteric Interpretation of the Hermetic Symbols of the Great Work*. Suffolk: Neville Spearman, 1971.

Gamow, George. *Thirty Years that Shocked Physics: the Story of Quantum Theory*. New York: Dover Publications, 1966.

Gell-Mann, Murray. *The Quark and the Jaguar: Adventures in the Simple and the Complex*. New York: W. H. Freeman and Company, 1994.

Gilchrist, Cherry. *Elements of Alchemy*. Shaftesbury, Dorset: Element, 1991.

Godwin, Joscelyn. *Harmonies of Heaven and Earth from Antiquity to Avant-Garde*. Rochester, Vt.: Inner Traditions International, 1995.

Goethe, Johann Wolfgang von. *Faust*. Indianapolis: The Bobbs-Merrill Company, 1965.

Grof, Stanislav and Christina Grof, eds. *Spiritual Emergency: When Personal Transformation Becomes a Crisis*. New York: Jeremy P. Tarcher/Perigee Books, 1989.

Grossinger, Richard. *Planet Medicine: From Stone Age Shamanism to Post-Industrial Healing*. Boulder: Shambala, 1982.

Grossinger, Richard, ed. *The Alchemical Tradition in the Late Twentieth Century*. Berkeley, Calif.: North Atlantic Books, 1983.

Haeffner, Mark. *The Dictionary of Alchemy: From Maria Prophetissa to Isaac Newton*. London: The Aquarian Press, 1971.

Haggard, Howard. *Devils, Drugs and Doctors: The Story of the Science of Healing from Medicine-Man to Doctor*. New York: Harper & Row, 1929.

Hall, Manly, P. *The Secret Destiny of America*. Los Angeles: The Philosophical Research Society, 1944.

———. *The Secret Teachings of All Ages*. Los Angeles: The Philosophical Research Society, 1978.

———. Audiotaped lecture, "Alchemy." Los Angeles: The Philosophical Research Society, 1998.

Harding, M. Esther. *Psychic Energy: Its Source and Its Transformation*. Washington, D. C.: The Bollingen Foundation, 1947.

Harvey, Andrew. *The Direct Path*. New York: Broadway Books, 2000.

Hauck, Dennis William. *The Emerald Tablet: Alchemy for Personal Transformation*. New York: Penguin Putnam Inc., 1999.

Haxton, Brooks, trans. *Fragments: the Collected Wisdom of Heraclitus*. New York: Viking, 2001.

Hazrat Inayat Khan. *The Sufi Message of Hazrat Inayat Khan*, vol. II. London: International Headquarters of the Sufi Movement, 1969.

Heinrich, Clark. *Strange Fruit: Alchemy, Religion and Magical Foods, A Speculative History*. London: Bloomsbury, 1995.

Hendricks, Gay, and Kate Ludeman. *The Corporate Mystic*. New York: Bantam Books, 1996.

Herbert, Nick. *Quantum Reality: Beyond the New Physics*. New York: Anchor Press/Doubleday, 1985.

Herrigel, Eugen. *Zen*. New York: McGraw-Hill Book Company, 1964.

Holmyard, E. J. *Alchemy*. New York: Dover, 1990.

Huffman, William H., ed. *Robert Fludd: Essential Readings*. London: The Aquarian Press, 1992.

Huygen, Wil. *Gnomes*. New York: Harry N. Abrams, 1976.

Hyde, Lewis. *Trickster Makes This World*. New York: North Point Press, 1998.

Jacobi, Jolande. *Complex/Archetype/Symbol*. Princeton, N.J.: Princeton University Press, 1959.

Jaffe, Aniela, ed. *C. G. Jung: Word and Image*. Princeton, New Jersey: Princeton University Press. 1979.

Jayne, Walter Addison. *The Healing Gods of Ancient Civilizations*. New Hyde Park, New York: University Books, 1962.

Johnson, Robert. *Ecstasy, Understanding the Psychology of Joy*. San Francisco: Harper & Row, 1987.

———. *Lying with the Heavenly Woman: Understanding and Integrating the Feminine Archetypes in Men's Lives*. San Francisco: Harper San Francisco, 1994.

———. *She! Understanding Feminine Psychology*. New York: Harper & Row, 1976.

Johnson, Robert with Jerry Ruhl. *Balancing Heaven and Earth: A Memoir of Visions, Dreams, and Realizations*. San Francisco: HarperSan Francisco, 1998.

Jung, C. G. *Aion*, vol. 9, part II. Princeton, N.J.: Princeton University Press, 1959.

———. *Alchemical Studies*, vol. 13. Princeton: Princeton University Press, 1967.

———. *The Archetypes of the Collective Unconscious*, vol. 9, part I. New York: Pantheon Books, 1959.

———. *Mysterium Coniunctionis: An Inquiry into the Separation and Synthesis of Psychic Opposites in Alchemy*, vol. 14. New York: Bollingen Foundation, 1963.

———. *The Practice of Psychotherapy*, vol. 16. New York: Bollingen Foundation, 1954.

———. *Psychological Types: The Psychology of Individuation*, vol. 6. New York: Pantheon Books, 1953.

———. *Psychology and Alchemy*, vol. 12. Princeton, N.J.: Princeton University Press, 1968.

———. *Psychology and Religion: West and East*, vol. 11. New York: Bollingen Foundation, 1958.

———. *The Structure and Dynamics of the Psyche*, vol. 8. New York: Pantheon Books, 1960.

———. *Two Essays on Analytical Psychology*, vol. 7. New York: Bollingen Foundation, 1953.

Jung, Carl Gustav and Wolfgang Pauli. *The Interpretation of Nature and the Psyche*. New York: Pantheon, 1955.

Jung, Carl Gustav *Memories, Dreams, Reflections*. A. Jaffe, ed. New York: Pantheon Books, 1961.

Jung, Carl Gustav, ed. *Man and his Symbols*. New York: Doubleday & Company. 1964.

Kazantzakis, Nikos. *Zorba, the Greek*. New York: Ballantine Book, 1952.

Keirsey, David and Marilyn Bates. *Please Understand Me: Character and Temperament Types*. Del Mar, Calif.: Promethius Nemesis Book Company, 1978.

Kornfield, Jack. *After the Ecstasy, the Laundry*. New York: Bantam Books, 2000.

Kubose, Gyomay. *Zen Koans*. Chicago: Henry Regnery Company, 1973.

LaBerge, Stephen. *Lucid Dreaming*. Los Angeles: J. P. Tarcher, 1985.

LaBerge, Stephen, and Howard Rheingold. *Exploring the World of Lucid Dreaming*. New York: Ballantine Books, 1990.

Lindsay, Jack. *The Origins of Alchemy in Graeco-Roman Egypt.* London: Frederick Muller, 1970.

Maier, Michael. *Atalanta Fugiens: An Edition of the Fugues, Emblems and Epigrams.* Grand Rapids, Mich.: Phanes Press, 1989.

Marlan, Stanton, ed. *Salt and the Alchemical Soul.* Woodstock, Conn.: Spring Publications, 1995.

Marshall, Peter. *The Philosopher's Stone.* London: Macmillan, 2001.

Mast, Joseph. *The Emerging Self.* Santa Barbara, Calif.: Fithian Press, 1991.

Masterson, James. *The Search for the Real Self: Unmasking the Personality Disorders of Our Age.* New York: The Free Press, 1988.

Metaphysical Bible Dictionary. Missouri: Unity Books, 1931.

Meyer, G. *The Golem.* Boston: Houghton Mifflin, 1928.

McArthur, Margie. *Wisdom of the Elements.* Freedom, Calif.: The Crossing Press, 1998.

McLean, Adam. *The Alchemical Mandala.* Grand Rapids, Mich.: Phanes Press, 1989.

Miller, Richard and Iona Miller. *The Modern Alchemist: A Guide to Personal Transformation.* Grand Rapids, Mich.: Phanes Press, 1994.

Mitchell, Stephen, ed. *The Enlightened Mind: An Anthology of Sacred Prose.* New York: HarperCollins, 1991.

Moore, Thomas. *The Planets Within: The Astrological Psychology of Marsilio Ficino.* Great Barrington, Maine: Lindisfarne Press, 1982.

Neihardt, John G. *Black Elk Speaks: Being the Life Story of a Holy Man of the Oglala Sioux.* Lincoln, Nebr.: University of Nebraska Press, 1961

Neiman, Carol. *Miracles: The Extraordinary, the Impossible, and the Divine.* United Kingdom: Labyrinth Publishing Ltd., 1995.

New English Bible, The. Oxford Study Edition. New York: Oxford University Press, 1976.

Newman, James R., ed. *The World of Mathematics,* vol. 1. New York: Simon & Schuster, 1956.

Nichols, Sallie. *Jung and Tarot: An Archetypal Journey.* York Beach, Maine: Samuel Weiser, 1980.

O'Donohue, John. *Anam Cara: A Book of Celtic Wisdom.* New York: Cliff Street Books, 1997.

Ornstein, Robert. *The Right Mind: Making Sense of the Hemispheres.* New York: Harcourt Brace and Company, 1997.

Osho. *Courage: The Joy of Living Dangerously.* New York: St. Martin's Griffin, 1999.

Oxford English Dictionary.

Parabola, vol. XX, no. 1. New York: The Tamarack Press, February 1995.

———. vol. IV, no. 1. New York: The Tamarack Press, February 1979.

Pauwels, Louis and Jacques Bergier. *The Morning of the Magicians.* London: Avon Books.

Pearsall, Paul. *Making Miracles.* New York: Prentice Hall Press, 1991.

Pernety, Antoine-Joseph. *An Alchemical Treatise on The Great Art.* New York: Samuel Weiser, 1973.

Pinkola-Estes, Clarissa. *Women Who Run with the Wolves: Myths and Stories of the Wild Woman Archetype.* New York: Ballantine Books, 1992.

Raff, Jeffrey. *Jung and the Alchemical Imagination.* York Beach, Maine: Nicolas-Hays, Inc., 2000.

Ramsay, Jay. *Alchemy: the Art of Transformation.* London: Thorsons, 1997.

Ransome, Hilda. *The Sacred Bee: In Ancient Times and Folklore.* New York: Ballantine Reprints, 1996.

Roob, Alexander. *The Hermetic Museum: Alchemy & Mysticism.* London, New York and Paris: Taschen, 1996.

Rudgley, Richard. *Essential Substances: A Cultural History of Intoxicants in Society.* New York: Kodansha America, 1993.

Schwartz-Salant, Nathan. *Jung on Alchemy.* Princeton, N.J.: Princeton University Press, 1995.

Shelley, Mary. *Frankenstein, or the Modern Prometheus.* New York: Signet Classic, 1983.

Smith, Houston. *Forgotten Truth.* New York: Harper, 1976.

Suzuki, Daisetz T. *Zen and Japanese Culture*. Princeton, N.J.: Princeton University Priess, 1959.

Taylor, F. Sherwood. *The Alchemists: Founders of Modern Chemistry*. New York: Collier Books, 1949.

Ulam, S. M. *Adventures of a Mathematician*. New York: Charles Scribner's Sons, 1976.

VandenBroeck, Andre. *Al-kemi: a Memoir*. Hudson, New York: Lindisfarne Press, 1987.

Varela, Francisco, ed. *Sleeping, Dreaming, and Dying: An Exploration of Conscioiusness with the Dalai Lama*. Boston: Wisdom Publications, 1997.

Von Franz, Marie-Louise. *Alchemical Active Imagination*. Irving, Tex., Spring Publications, 1979.

———. *Projection and Re-collection in Jungian Psychology: Reflections of the Soul*. La Salle, Ill.: Open Court, 1980.

Vurm, Robert B. *Rudolf II and his Prague: Mysteries and Curiosities of Rudolfine Prague during the Period 1550–1650*. Prague: Robert Vurm, 1997.

Waite, Arthur Edward. *Alchemists Through the Ages*. New York: Rudolf Steiner Publications, 1970.

Walker, Charles. *The Encyclopedia of Secret Knowledge*. London: Limited Editions, 1995.

Walsh, Roger. *Essential Spirituality*. New York: John Wiley & Sons, 1999.

Watson, Lyall. *The Nature of Things: The Secret Life of Inanimate Objects*. Rochester, Vt.: Destiny Books, 1990.

White, Michael. *Isaac Newton: The Last Sorcerer*. Cambridge, Mass.: Perseus Books, 1997.

White, Ralph, ed. *The Rosicrucian Enlightenment Revisited*. Hudson, New York: Lindisfarne Books, 1999.

Whitmont, Edward C. *The Alchemy of Healing, Psyche and Soma*. Berkeley, Calif.: North Atlantic Books, 1993.

Wilbur, Ken. *The Eye of Spirit*. Boston and London: Shambala, 1998.

———. *One Taste*. Boston and London: Shambala, 1999.

———. *The Theory of Everything*. Boston: Shambala, 2000.

Wilhelm, Richard, trans. *The I Ching or Book of Changes*. Princeton, N.J.: Princeton University Press, 1950.

———. *The Secret of the Golden Flower*. New York: Causeway Books, 1975.

Wilson, Robert Anton. *Quantum Psychology*. Phoenix: New Falcon Publications, 1990.

Wolf, Fred Alan. *The Dreaming Universe: A Mind-Expanding Journey into the Realm Where Psyche and Physics Meet*. New York: Simon & Schuster, 1994.

———. *Mind into Matter: a New Alchemy of Science and Spirit*. Portsmouth, N.H.: Moment Point Press, 2001.

Yates, Francis, A. *The Art of Memory*. Chicago: The University of Chicago Press, 1966.

———. *Giordano Bruno and the Hermetic Tradition*. Chicago: University of Chicago Press, 1991.

Acknowledgments

I am blessed to have had so many wonderful people supporting me throughout the writing of this book. The list stretches from earth to heaven.

I am grateful for the love my family has given me in many ways. My brother Robert was first to introduce me to the trickster. Both he and my sister Dyan gave me the emotional support needed throughout this project. I thank my niece Dhyandra for the Ganesha statue that opened and closed each writing session. I also thank my daughter Ananda for putting some incredible books into my hands and her passionate interest in my work.

I want also to acknowledge Linda Pauer, my best friend, for reading and reviewing the manuscript. Her suggestions were excellent and her friendship provided much needed balance. Similarly, I appreciate Jungian analyst Valerie McIlroy not only for her comments and criticisms but also for her seminar on the *Mysterium Coniunctionis* in which I participated during this period. I also want to thank another friend without whom I would not have met Jeremy Tarcher. Although Diana Klimek has been a friend for many years I never thought that she would be the one to help make the necessary connection that led to the publication of my work.

I also extend my heartfelt appreciation to my dear friend and minister of Unity of Tustin, Dr. Marj Britt. Marj has been there for me in so many ways. She helped me connect the soul of psychology with the spirit of the divine. Along with her husband, Paul Tyman, alchemy comes alive.

Another blessing in my life is Jungian analyst Pan Coukoulis. The many wonderful conversations we have had over the years helped shaped my personal understanding of Jungian psychology and the living philosophy of Zorba. Pan is more than a friend and mentor, he is my spiritual father.

I am also deeply indebted to Jungian analyst Robert Johnson. He helped bring me into consciousness as a young man. His confidence in me over two decades provided the cornerstone on which this book rests.

One of the biggest blessings in my life is my wife, Cynthia. Not only did she read, review and edit the manuscript many times, she put up with me during some very trying moments. Her gentle soul and wisdom are woven into every page of this book. There are no words to express the loving gratitude I give to her.

I also acknowledge Jeremy Tarcher for seeing my vision, finding me and publishing this book. Many thanks also go to David Grof for initially editing the book and Putnam's director, Joel Fotinos. I am very grateful for Joel's overseeing the publication, his seminar at Unity of Tustin and his guidance. Finally, I owe a debt of gratitude to Mitch Horowitz, senior editor at Putnam and editor of this book. Working with Mitch has been something of an alchemical dance. Alchemy has a way of either expanding or contracting anyone who dares write about it. At every turn Mitch has been there to have me focus when the subject threatened to explode or have me expand when I was obsessing on unnecessary details. I am grateful for his humor, friendship and faith in my work.

I also want to acknowledge many of my patients from whom I have learned the healing value of divine suffering.

With all this loving support I hope my book deepens our insights into alchemical psychology and shows that dreams really do come true.

Index

About the Author

THOM F. CAVALLI, PH.D., is a practicing clinical psychologist who specializes in Jungian-oriented psychotherapy. He also provides seminars and workshops on a wide range of Jungian and Alchemical topics. To contact him, call (714) 731-3238, write to 161 Fashion Lane, Suite 101, Tustin, CA 92780, E-mail to illavac@hotmail.com or go to www.AlchemicalPsychology.com